PR!

PR!

A *Social* HISTORY *of*
SPIN

Stuart Ewen

BasicBooks
A Division of HarperCollins*Publishers*

FIRST EDITION

Designed by Laura Lindgren

Library of Congress Cataloging-in-Publication Data
Ewen, Stuart.
    PR! : a social history of spin / Stuart Ewen. — 1st ed.
      p. cm.
    Includes bibliographical references and index.
    ISBN 0-465-06168-0
    1. Public relations 2. Public relations—United States. I. Title.
HM263.E849   1996   .
659.2—dc20   96–2243

96 97 98 99 00 ❖/RRD 10 9 8 7 6 5 4 3 2 1

For Paul and Sam

La più divina delle poesie
è quella, amico,
che c'insegna amare!

—Rodolfo, in Giacomo Puccini, *La Bohème*
(Libretto by G. Giacosa & L. Illica)

CONTENTS

CREDITS

Over the course of a century—justly or not—the terms *PR* and *public relations* have become widely accepted shorthand for subterfuge and deception. Between the lines of any book about the rise of public relations, then, exist unavoidable issues of honesty.

This having been said, I feel compelled to testify that the presence of one individual's name on the title page of this book is—as is often the situation with books and other such creations—somewhat misleading. Creative work is invariably sustained by vital collaborations, and in the case of this book this has been especially true. With this in mind, and to correct any such misconceptions, I embrace the chance to acknowledge those people whose forbearance and friendship have allowed me to write the book you are about to read.

First among my collaborators is Elizabeth Ewen. For about thirty years, Liz has scrutinized nearly every word I have written for publication. She has helped me to understand when I am communicating effectively, when I am not. Her ideas and insights have informed mine. She has been my most discerning editor and audience. Her prodigious capacity to read—to reflect critically on what she is reading—have helped me to become a writer. To take a phrase from the novelist Richard Powers, this "book is the dance card of ideas we shared in the foyer of our joint life."

Unlike Liz, some of my collaborators are doubtless unaware of the contributions they have made to this book. Much of my research, for example, was done fairly anonymously at the New York Public Library; the Wexler Library of Hunter College; the libraries at Princeton and Columbia universities; the AT&T Corporate Archive at Warren, New Jersey; and at the NAM Archive at the Hagley Museum and Library in Wilmington, Delaware. In each case, these libraries and their staffs—by providing their customary services—helped me enormously.

In certain instances, however, librarians or archivists went beyond the call of duty, taking a special interest in this project. Ron Sexton—

currently librarian at the Carnegie Foundation—escorted me on many explorations through the stacks of the Watson business library at Columbia University. At the AT&T Archive, Sheldon Hocheiser was an invaluable tour guide. Pamela Wonsek, my friend and colleague at the Wexler Library at Hunter College, also took a special interest in my project. The National Association of Manufacturers' willingness to open its historical archives to me added a rich dimension to the history told in Part IV of this book.

In each research venue, I benefited also from the efforts of graduate research assistants. Steve Duncombe and Andy Mattson were, on many occasions, my travel companions on visits to libraries and archives. At times they scouted things out for me on their own. Their marvelous efforts and their sensitive noses for good historical evidence landed me a considerable cargo of material.

Other students at Hunter College and the City University of New York (CUNY) Graduate School made significant contributions to my research and my thinking. Among them, Michelle Matthews, Susan Dessel, Lee Greller, Danielle Schwartz, Micki McGee, and William Tally deserve special mention. So, too, does Mark Pennings, my visiting doctoral student from the University of Melbourne.

As the book moved toward production, Janet LeMoal and Nic Sands were welcome comrades and editorial assistants. Their outstanding efforts made space for me to turn my attention toward teaching and other school-related responsibilities, secure that my manuscript was in able and conscientious hands. Janet's contribution to the visual dimension of this book was additionally helpful.

I want to recognize the meaningful contribution of students who enrolled in my CULT[ure] of Publicity course, taught at Hunter College between 1993 and 1995. When I first began teaching the class, I was feeling a bit lost. I had not yet found my voice as far as the book's subject matter was concerned. The 120 or so students who took the class during that period—through their critical listening, their thoughtful interventions, and their humane patience—helped me to find my way.

Two members of the Hunter College administration—Laura Strumingher Schor and Carlos Hortas—have been, over a period of years, unsparing in their support of the inquiry that has led to this book. At a moment when many public higher education "leaders" subserviently pay tribute to a prevailing philosophy of money, their continued encouragement of intellectual investigation demands special recognition.

I also want to thank colleagues at Trent University in Ontario and at the Gottlieb Duttweiler Institut in Zurich, who provided me with pleasant opportunities to try out pieces of this book at early stages in their development.

Alongside such distinctly human support, my ability to conduct necessary research was also supported by a two-year PSC-CUNY funding grant from the PSC-CUNY. This money helped to underwrite a number of pivotal research trips. It also paid for the transcription of taped interviews.

A number of leading actors in public relations history provided me with extended face-to-face or telephone interviews. Some, as you will see, appear directly in the pages that follow. All those who spoke with me, however, augmented my understanding of the subject. Among the interviewees, Edward L. Bernays—the PR pioneer whose career dated back to the years preceding World War I—stands out. Though approaching 100 years of age when we got together, his sharp wit and indefatigable spirit animated me. The interest that he took in this project and his willingness to correspond with me about it were precious beyond words. Though Bernays and I saw the world very differently, I am unhappy that he did not live to see this book—and his role in it—in print.

Other interviewees also merit recognition as contributors to this work. My neighbor Richard Weiner was an essential guide from early on. His broad experience in the field of PR, as well as his associations with many in the profession, provided me with numerous important leads.

Leo Bogart's abiding goodwill—and firsthand knowledge of Standard Oil's PR activities during the late 1940s—supplied me with fertile directions for my inquiry. Conversations I've had with him over the past few years have helped me repeatedly. My dear friend, Julius C. C. Edelstein, provided personal recollections of Franklin D. Roosevelt's White House and of the important place of public relations within it. I cannot overstate my debt to him, and to Nancy Edelstein as well. Our regular dinners together provided good company and much food for thought.

In my visit to his home in Connecticut, W. Howard Chase was a charming host and informative chronicler of public relations history.

He offered a compelling example of the ways in which some in the field of public relations earnestly sought to make large corporations more accountable to the needs of ordinary Americans. Given many of my own penchants and predispositions, this was a dimension I needed to learn something about. Chester Burger was also a gracious host and informative guide. His insider's knowledge of the rise of media consultancy was enormously useful to me. Shelley and Barry Spector, two present-day professionals, provided me with important visual materials and sound advice. Interviews with Eugene Secunda and Philip Lesly were also useful.

I would love to have been able to acknowledge Leone Baxter here. Her furtive efforts to squelch federally insured health care legislation in the late 1940s, for example, deserve some explanation from her own point of view. Her refusal to grant an interview has left empty spaces in the history that follows.

Contact and discussions with many friends were powerful nourishment for mind and soul. Serafina Bathrick, Phineas Baxandall, Ros Baxandall, Paul Breines, Steve Brier, Phyllis Ewen, Ferdinando Fasce, Linda Gordon, Allen Hunter, Julie Kaye, Andrando del Mondo, Gail Pellett, Marc Perry, Roz Petchesky, Chuck Reich, Sheila Rowbotham, Anthony Saridakis, Herb Schiller, Harry and Elaine Scott, Stephan Van Dam, and Joel Zucker have all been there for me. My parents Scotty and Sol Ewen read and discussed pieces of this book with me, to my considerable benefit. At critical junctures, Rita Meed helped guide me through spells of confusion. The folks at the All State Café routinely provided Liz and me with an agreeable place to chill.

More than thirty years ago, my teacher and friend George Mosse introduced me to some ideas that have flowered within this book, particularly in Parts 2 and 3. Though we see each other only on rare occasions, ongoing connection to him and his ideas has been very important to me.

As ever, my soul mates at the Massachusetts Institute for a New History (MINH), in Truro, rate special recognition. For over twenty-five years they have provided me with an unbroken circle of friendship and advice.

I must also extend credit to my longtime associate Archie Bishop, who as creative director of Billboards of the Future has once again permitted me to include materials that will appear in the forthcoming *Encylopœdia Billboardica.* Bishop's other contributions to the graphic dynamics of this book also demand special recognition.

Though he departed from Basic Books just as this volume was heading into production, my old friend and editor Steve Fraser played a vital role in this book's realization. When Steve left Basic Books, Karen Klein—my project editor—assumed responsibility as caretaker for this book. As it proceeded through an often perilous production process, she has been its—and my—intrepid advocate.

Last, my sons Paul Scott Ewen and Sam Travis Ewen, to whom I dedicate this book, have taught me well over the years. Their deep love and understanding, along with their Promethean creativity, are inspiring to me.

It is of great consequence to disguise your inclination and to play the hypocrite well; and men are so simple in their temper and so submissive to their present necessity that he that is neat and cleanly in his collusions shall never want people to practice them upon.

—Nicolo Machiavelli, *The Prince*, c. 1512

Frankly, to manufacture thought
Is like a masterpiece by a weaver wrought.

—Goethe, *Faust*, 1832

Public sentiment is everything. With public sentiment nothing can fail; without it nothing can succeed. He who molds public sentiment goes deeper than he who enacts statutes or decisions possible or impossible to execute.

—Abraham Lincoln, 1860

[N]ewspapers have transformed . . . unified in space and diversified in time the conversations of individuals . . . even those who do not read papers but who, talking to those who do, are forced to follow the groove of their borrowed thoughts. One pen suffices to set off a million tongues.

—Gabriel Tarde, "On Opinion and Conversation," 1898

[We] must become a cult, write our philosophy of life in flaming headlines, and sell our cause in the market. No matter if we meanwhile surrender every value for which we stand, we must strive to cajole the majority into imagining itself on our side. . . . [O]nly with the majority with us, whoever we are, can we live.

It is numbers, not values that count—quantity not quality.

—Everett Dean Martin, *The Behavior of Crowds*, 1920

A leader or an interest that can make itself master of current symbols is the master of the current situation.

—Walter Lippmann, *Public Opinion*, 1922

With the development of modern mass communication there is increasing difficulty in distinguishing propaganda material from non-propaganda material. . . . The conscious selection by editors of "stacked news," as well as their unwitting publication of copy prepared in the interest of special groups, complicates, even for those readers who would distinguish, the discrimination between propaganda and other material. . . . The most innocent material, on the surface, may actually be quite other than it seems.

—Malcolm Willey, "Communication Agencies
and the Volume of Propaganda," 1935

When an industry has finished its financing, when it has mastered the problems of production, it no longer needs a board of directors where the bankers and production men and engineers dominate. Its major problem for the future will be public relations. . . . Part of the places vacated on the boards of directors when some of the bankers and lawyers and production men retire will be filled by public relations men—by men who have come up through the sales and advertising departments. . . . The age of public relations has only just begun.

—Bruce Barton, 1936

The engineering of consent is the very essence of the democratic process, the freedom to persuade and suggest.

—Edward L. Bernays,
"The Engineering of Consent," 1947

If business succeeds in establishing public confidence in its goals, then the public will follow the counsel of business leadership as the means for reaching those goals.

The public relations moral of all this is: Declare your end or goal in respect of public interest before you begin selling your means for reaching that goal.

—Claude Robinson, president,
Opinion Research, Inc., 1947

The day has clearly gone forever of societies small enough for their members to have personal acquaintance with one another, and to find their station through the appraisal of those who have any first-hand knowledge of them. . . .

Publicity is an evil substitute, and the art of publicity a black art. But it has come to stay. Every year adds to the potency and to the finality of its judgements.

—Justice Learned Hand, 1952

[P]ublic relations is the white hope of our restless times.

—Milton Fairman, director of
Borden dairy company, 1952

Remember! At General Electric, Progress is our most important product.
— Ronald Reagan, host of the *General Electric Theater*, 1955

O Lord and God. You are the original image maker. You created us in Your image and likeness, a "little less than the angels." May we have the courage to take You as a model.
— Rev. Ulmer Kuhn, "Prayer for Public Relations"
at Tri-State PR Seminar, Public Relations
Society of America, 1964

The communication that is most nearly real, that involves the person by making him almost a part of it, has the greatest power to sway him. . . . When a subject appears to be all around him, a person tends to accept it and take it for granted. It becomes part of the atmosphere in which he lives. He finds himself surrounded by it and absorbs the climate of the idea. . . . It must be most deftly developed to reach into the subconscious of the person and tune to his urges, interests and desires. Mere expression of the communicator's point of view will not succeed; it must be attuned to the mental and emotional bent of the audience.
— Philip Lesly, *The People Factor:
Managing the Human Climate*, 1974

In every poll I have seen in the past three years, nearly 70 percent of the American people say they get their news from television. The number alone is scary and ought to cause those who are still literate to sit down and think about the day when we will simply plug the TV cord right into our eye sockets.

As a so-called image maker, I am torn between thinking about how I can best take advantage of this trend, and where it is likely to lead us. It is not hard to picture a scenario not unlike *The Dating Game*, where three candidates give their qualifications, smile, and answer questions about how old they were when they were allowed to car-date, and the studio audience presses a button to indicate their favorite.
— Michael Deaver, public relations adviser
to Ronald Reagan, 1987

[W]e are spawning a generation of reporters and news directors who no longer place any value on the written word, the turn of the phrase, the uncut long, hard question. All we care about are the almighty pictures, the video, the story count—and that it moves like a bat out of hell.

We barely listen to what is said any more.
— Andrew Lack, president of NBC News,
December 1995

PART 1

Stagecraft and Truth in an Age of Public Relations

1
Visiting Edward Bernays

W HEN I BEGAN the research for this book—attempting to discover the social and historical roots that would explain the boundless role of public relations in our world—one of my first stops along the way was a sojourn with Edward L. Bernays, a man who, beginning in the 1910s, became one of the most influential pioneers of American public relations, a person whose biography, though not widely known, left a deep mark on the configuration of our world.

Born in Vienna in 1891, Bernays was the double nephew of Sigmund Freud. (His mother was Freud's sister; his father was Freud's wife's brother.) His family background impressed him with the enormous power of ideas and accustomed him to the privileges and creature comforts of bourgeois existence.

Bernays was also a farsighted architect of modern propaganda techniques who, dramatically, from the early 1920s onward, helped to consolidate a fateful marriage between theories of mass psychology and schemes of corporate and political persuasion.

During the First World War, Bernays served as a foot soldier for the U.S. Committee on Public Information (CPI)—the vast American propaganda apparatus mobilized in 1917 to package, advertise, and sell the war as one that would "Make the World Safe for Democracy." The CPI would become the mold in which marketing strategies for subsequent wars, to the present, would be shaped.

In the twenties, Bernays fathered the link between corporate sales campaigns and popular social causes, when—while working for the American Tobacco Company—he persuaded women's rights marchers in New York City to hold up Lucky Strike cigarettes as symbolic "Torches of Freedom." In October 1929, Bernays also originated the now familiar "global media event," when he dreamed up "Light's Golden Jubilee," a worldwide celebratory spectacle commemorating the fiftieth anniversary of the electric lightbulb, sponsored behind the scenes by the General Electric Corporation.

Though Bernays was by birth an Austrian Jew, his work and vivid writings served as an inspiration for Joseph Goebbels, the notorious Nazi propaganda minister—or so public relations folklore records.

Bernays's influence would continue to hold sway well into the post–World War II era. To put it simply, Bernays's career—more than that of any other individual—roughed out what have become the strategies and practices of public relations in the United States.

I had encountered Bernays before. In the early 1970s, while writing a book on the social history of advertising—*Captains of Consciousness*—I had happened upon some of his writings, mostly from the 1920s. In the pages of the book, he fittingly looms as an eloquent and influential ideologue of an American consumer culture in formation.[1]

Then, in the mid-1980s, while working on another book (*All Consuming Images*), I again ran into Bernays. This time it was primarily through his writings from the forties and fifties, when, as an enduring student of mass persuasion, he helped to educate political leaders on the uses of the mass media and on the particular advantages of visual symbols as instruments for what he christened the "engineering of consent." Once more, through the agency of his fertile and suggestive writings, Bernays had emerged as a leading character in one of my manuscripts.[2]

Both times my encounters with Bernays were like those that usually take place between historians and the "historical figures" they write about. They were exchanges between old documents and the inquiring mind of their reader and interpreter. As I commenced work on my social history of public relations early in 1990, I assumed, reasonably, that Bernays was long gone. Once more, the picturesque record that he had left behind was as close as I was likely to get to him.

•   •   •

Soon, however, I stumbled onto the fact that my reasonable assumption was incorrect. In a conversation with a neighbor of mine, Richard Weiner—who is a prominent member of the public relations fraternity—I learned that Bernays was, in fact, still alive, residing in Cambridge, Massachusetts.

Weiner instructed me: "If you're going to do this book, you've got to talk to Eddie Bernays." I was astonished and delighted to hear Bernays referred to in the present tense; I was also amused to hear him referred to as "Eddie." Behind the aura of a historical figure, stood a guy called Eddie. I obtained Bernays's telephone number and set out to arrange an interview. He was then on the brink of his ninety-ninth birthday, and I didn't know what to expect. Would he see me? Would he be enfeebled? He was very old.

An exploratory call to Bernays reached an answering machine. A woman's voice, official in tone, informed me that I had reached the offices of "Dr. Edward L. Bernays" and that "Dr. Bernays" was currently unavailable. I was instructed to leave a message. For a man of almost one hundred, Bernays was still communicating an air of business as usual.

I told the machine:

My name is Stuart Ewen. I am a historian, a writer. I'm currently working on a book on the social history of public relations. I would very much like to come to Cambridge, to visit with "Dr. Bernays" in order to conduct an oral history interview.

I left my phone number and indicated that should I not hear back from him shortly, I would call again. Two days later, I received a phone call at home from Bernays.

It felt weird, like a dream. Given my experience tracking his historical footprints, it was like talking—via Dixie cups and a string—with a piece of history. His voice was soft, a bit hoarse, the voice of an elderly man, to be sure, but he also sounded deft and businesslike.

He asked me about myself, my background, where I taught, the book I was writing. I told him that I was a cultural historian, with a particular interest in the ways that the mass media have crisscrossed with the experiences of twentieth-century American life. I told him that I knew a great deal about him, his life and contributions, and added that I had recently published a book exploring the influence of commercial imagery on the contours of American society.

Without missing a beat Bernays retorted, scrappily, "Of course, you know, we don't deal in images. . . . We deal in reality."

My fascinating encounter with Bernays had begun. I had already been offered a lesson from the master. Ideally, the job of public relations is not simply one of disseminating favorable images and impressions for a client. For Bernays and, as I would learn, for many others in the field, the goal was far more ambitious. Public relations was about fashioning and projecting credible renditions of *reality* itself.

Rather than pursue the interview by telephone—I wanted to meet him face to face—I arranged to visit Bernays at his home on Columbus Day 1990. In the weeks preceding our scheduled meeting, I refamiliarized myself with some of his writings: *Crystallizing Public Opinion* (1923); *Propaganda* (1928); "The Engineering of Consent" (1947); and his autobiography, *Biography of an Idea: Memoirs of Public Relations Counsel Edward L. Bernays* (1965). I also looked at a few writings I'd never read before: books, some short pamphlets, and speeches. Bernays, meanwhile, sought to put his own spin on the forthcoming interview. He sent me a photocopy of a biographical piece about him that had appeared recently in a special issue of *Life* magazine, listing the one hundred most influential Americans of the twentieth century.

■ ■ ■ ■ ■

On the chill, gray morning of October 12, 1990, I took the shuttle from LaGuardia to Logan Airport in Boston, leaving myself enough time to arrive at Bernays's home for our scheduled one o'clock interview. Crossing the Charles River into Cambridge, the cab took me toward a maze of old, tree-lined streets bordering Harvard Square and stopped by the large red number 7 that Bernays had informed me marked his house. The house itself was stately, a large, white woodframe, surrounded by some hedges, unpretentious. Walking up the path to the door, I did not know what to expect.

I rang the doorbell and waited for an answer. A minute or two passed, and there was none. Not a sound. Had he forgotten? Was the

apparent wit with which he had spoken to me on the phone only illusory? I rang again, and waited. Then, after another minute or so had
passed and I had begun to grow disconsolate, I heard soft footsteps
moving slowly toward the door. "Bernays?" I thought. Instead, a Chinese woman, of middle age, opened the door a crack and said, "Yes?"
I told her who I was; that I had, a couple of weeks before, scheduled
an interview for this afternoon with Mr. Bernays.

She looked at me quizzically, then muttered something about his
having been ill yesterday. Inviting me into the house and directing me
to wait in the first floor library, she disappeared to inquire whether he
was up to seeing me.

As I waited, I inspected the shelves of the spacious, high-
ceilinged room in which I stood. It was a remarkable collection of
books, thousands of them: about public opinion, individual and
social psychology, survey research, propaganda, psychological warfare, and so forth—a comprehensive library spanning matters of
human motivation and strategies of influence, scanning a period of
more than one hundred years. These were not the bookshelves of some
shallow huckster, but the arsenal of an intellectual. The cross-hairs
of nearly every volume were trained on the target of forging public
attitudes. Here—in a large white room in Cambridge, Massachusetts—was the constellation of ideas that had inspired and informed
a twentieth-century preoccupation: the systematic molding of public
opinion.

Captured in thought, I suddenly heard steps moving swiftly
toward the library door. Assuming it was the Chinese woman again,
to report on Bernays's condition, I braced myself for bad news. But
as the door swung open, there—standing before me in a comfy-
looking brown, three-piece suit and tie and transmitting a sparkle
through his wizened eyes—was a puckish little man with thin, shaggy
white hair. The swift steps I'd heard were those of Bernays, moving
toward the threshold of his one hundredth year. Despite years of pondering him as a shrewd and cynical manipulator of public consciousness, I was immediately entranced. His physical countenance
reminded me of pictures I had seen of an aged Albert Einstein.
Bernays moved toward me and, with smiles, we exchanged formal
introductions. "I want you to have this," I said, and handed him an
inscribed copy of my last book, *All Consuming Images,* which he

accepted with a nod. He then instructed me that we should go upstairs, to his office, for the interview.

He led me to the bottom of a tall staircase. On the left side there was a chair-elevator, the kind one associates with wealthy invalids in the movies. "You ever ride on one of these things?" he asked me.

"No, I've only seen them in pictures," I responded frankly.

"Get on!" he commanded me, like an elfin carny beside an amusement park ride.

I turned around and sat down, my feet resting on a metal platform at the base of the chair. "Move your feet." he ordered.

"What?"

"Move your feet back."

Without understanding, I drew my feet to the back of the platform, leaving a narrow ledge in front of them. Suddenly, he stepped onto the ledge, his small pear-shaped body hovering over mine. "Should I hold you?" I asked, concerned for his frail bones.

"No," he responded dismissively, as he pushed a button on the side of the chair; we glided up together and, turning a slight corner toward the end of the voyage, arrived on the second story. At the summit of the climb, Bernays hopped off onto the landing, and I—somewhat shakily—proceeded off behind him. "We don't deal with images," I thought, "we deal in reality."

He led me through a dark room off the landing. Its walls were covered with scores of framed black-and-white photographs, many of them inscribed. Wordlessly, yet eloquently, the pictures placed my ancient host close to the heartbeat of a century. Bernays on his way to the Paris Peace Conference, 1919. Bernays standing with Enrico Caruso. Bernays and Henry Ford. Bernays and Thomas Edison. Bernays and Dwight David Eisenhower. An inscribed photo portrait of his uncle, Freud, was also conspicuous. Bernays with the "great men," at the "great events" of the twentieth century. I looked . . . awestruck. He said nothing. In silence, I was fascinated, entranced by it all.

From the photo gallery, we stepped into his small office, a solarium, and took seats by a cluttered desk. We began to talk. He started by asking me questions: about myself, my background, and what had attracted me to his work in particular and—more generally—to the broader study of communications in twentieth-century America.

I opened with a rhetorical question. "How can you deal with twentieth-century culture without dealing with . . . ?"

". . . the basis of the exchange of ideas that makes the culture," he completed my thought.

Coming from different vantage points, from different epochs, we understood each other. He knew what I was looking for. Within my historical study of public relations, I sought to make sense of the peculiar processes of representation and perception—the "exchange of ideas," as he put it—that have come to distinguish cultural life in the era of mass communication.

■   ■   ■   ■   ■

The next four hours were vintage Bernays. Again and again, I heard word-for-word reiterations of themes, stories, even specific catch-phrases that I had encountered many times before in his writings.

Nonetheless, beyond the actual experience of meeting with Bernays, some parts of the interview were new to me, contributing to the scope and texture of the history that follows. I was particularly intrigued, for example, by Bernays's reflections on the connection between his thinking and that of Walter Lippmann, who published a book entitled *Public Opinion* in 1922, just one year before Bernays's first public relations manifesto, *Crystallizing Public Opinion,* appeared. (Bernays's book, *Propaganda,* 1928, would later follow Lippmann's sequel to *Public Opinion, The Phantom Public,* by one year.) There are, however, some aspects of the interview that are worth mentioning here, aspects that reflect on the history and meaning of public relations itself.

■   ■   ■   ■   ■

First, throughout the interview, Bernays expressed an unabashedly hierarchical view of society. Repeatedly, he maintained that although most people respond to their world instinctively, without thought, there exist an "intelligent few" who have been charged with the responsibility of contemplating and influencing the tide of history. Bernays perceived me as one of these "few," so he was willing to share his outlook with me in straightforward terms.

Though he had written extensively, over a lifetime, about democracy and the important role that public relations plays in a democratic society, Bernays, himself, was clearly no democrat. He expressed little respect for the average person's ability to think out, understand, or act upon the world in which he or she lives.

"There are strange things about the culture," he intoned. "The average IQ of the American public is 100, did you know that?"[3] Assuming I grasped what for him was obvious, Bernays then sketched a picture of the public relations expert as a member of the "intelligent few" who advises clients on how to "deal with the masses . . . just by applying psychology."

As a member of that intellectual elite who guides the destiny of society, the PR "professional," Bernays explained, aims his craft at a general public that is essentially, and unreflectively, reactive. Working behind the scenes, out of public view, the public relations expert is "an applied social scientist," educated to employ an understanding of "sociology, psychology, social psychology, and economics" to influence and direct public attitudes. Throughout our conversation, Bernays conveyed his hallucination of democracy: A highly educated class of opinion-molding tacticians is continuously at work, analyzing the social terrain and adjusting the mental scenery from which the public mind, with its limited intellect, derives its opinions.

Undoubtedly, this point of view offers a glimpse into Bernays. More important, it reflects a foundational conceit governing the field of public relations more broadly. While some have argued that public relations represents a "two-way street" through which institutions and the public carry on a democratic dialogue, the public's role within that alleged dialogue is, most often, one of having its blood pressure monitored, its temperature taken.[4]

■　■　■　■　■

It should be noted that Bernays, at the time of our conversation, thought that the field of "public relations" had failed to live up to his "professional" expectations. "Today," he related to me with some dismay, "any nitwit or dope or anybody can call himself or herself a public relations counsel. I had a young woman call up two months ago, and she said I hear you're nice to young people. Can I come in and see you? And I said, what do you do? She said, 'I'm in public relations.' So

I made a date with her, and when she came in—she was about twenty-seven years old, a young woman, apparently intelligent—

"I said, 'What do you do?'

"She said, 'I'm in public relations.'

"I said, 'I didn't ask you that. I asked you what you did.'

"She said, 'I give out circulars in Harvard Square.'

"She was in public relations! [The term *public relations*] hasn't only been misused, but people have used the name for press agents, flacks, publicity men or women, individuals who simply try to get pieces into the paper that are favorable to a client. Whereas, by my definition, a public relations person, who calls themselves [*sic*] that, is an applied social scientist who advises a client or employer on the social attitudes and actions to take to win the support of the publics upon whom his or her or its viability depends."

■　　■　　■　　■　　■

Another phase of the interview deserves special mention. I came to visit Bernays because he was both a participant in, and a witness to, the rise of public relations over a period of nearly three-quarters of a century. Anticipating the interview, I hoped that his recollections would provide me with some new and clear sense of the particular historical soil out of which public relations, as a phenomenon, grew. In this regard I was, for the most part, frustrated.

Bernays's take on public relations was remarkable in that it tended to ignore the particular processes or details of the periods that had given rise to it. Throughout the interview, he described public relations as a response to a transhistoric concern: the requirement, for those people in power, to shape the attitudes of the general population.

For Bernays, public relations reflected the refinement of techniques developed to serve ancient purposes. He appeared to have thought little about his life or his field as bearing the imprint of a specific historical era. As I prepared to depart from him, I felt a bit disappointed in this regard.

Then, as we began discussing the means by which I would get from his house back to the airport, a curious conversation unfolded. Amid a general complaint about the cost of taxicabs, and after counseling me to save my money and hop a trolley, Bernays indicated that he had never learned how to drive an automobile. I expressed surprise. He explained that he had simply never had to learn to drive; among his family's train of up to thirteen servants, there was always a chauffeur. Bernays then proceeded to tell me the story of one chauffeur in particular, a man he called "Dumb Jack."

Each day, he related to me, Dumb Jack would awaken at five o'clock in the morning and prepare to drive Bernays and his wife (and partner in public relations), Doris Fleishman, to the office. The trusty chauffeur would then return to the family home to carry their two daughters to school. From there, he would return to the office to chauffeur Bernays and his wife to business meetings throughout the day, taking time out to retrieve the daughters from their school. At the end of the day, according to Bernays, a subdued Dumb Jack would step into the kitchen and, as the cook prepared the evening meal, would sit at the kitchen table, lay his head in his hands, and take a nap. He would go to bed at nine, only to begin his routine again the next morning at five. Comparing this situation favorably to the cost of one cab ride to the airport today, Bernays ended his story by saying that for all this work, Dumb Jack received a salary of twenty-five dollars per week and got half a Thursday off every two weeks.

"Not a bad deal," Bernays confided, characterizing the benefits that his family had derived from Dumb Jack's years of compliant service. Then, with a lilt of nostalgia in his voice, he concluded his story: "But that's before people got a social conscience."

At that moment, in that nostalgic reverie over a bygone era, my quest for historical explanation—or at least a piece of it—was satisfied. In an incidental reference to "social conscience," Bernays had illuminated a historic shift in the social history of property, shedding inadvertent light on the conditions that gave birth to the practice of public relations. As the twentieth century progressed, people were no longer willing to accommodate themselves to outmoded standards of deference that history, for millennia, had demanded of them.

Bernays was the child of a bourgeois world that was, in many ways, still captivated by aristocratic styles of wealth, in which relations among the classes were marked, to a large extent, by deep-seated patterns of allegiance—of obedience and obligation—between masters and servants. Like Mr. Stevens (the Anthony Hopkins character) in *Remains of the Day*, Dumb Jack was also a child of these circumstances.

The "social conscience" to which Bernays had referred arrived at that moment when aristocratic paradigms of deference could no longer hold up in the face of modern, democratic, public ideals that were boiling up among the "lower strata" of society. At that juncture, strategies of social rule began to change, and the life and career of Bernays, I should add, serves as a testament to that change.

The explosive ideals of democracy challenged ancient customs that had long upheld social inequality. A public claiming the birthright of democratic citizenship and social justice increasingly called upon institutions and people of power to justify themselves and their privileges. In the crucible of these changes, aristocracy began to give way to technocracy as a strategy of rule. Bernays came to maturity in a society in which the exigencies of power were—by necessity—increasingly exercised from behind the pretext of the "common good." Bernays, the child of aristocratic pretense who fashioned himself into a technician of mass persuasion, was the product of a "social conscience" that had grasped the fact that a once submissive Dumb Jack, in the contemporary world, would no longer be willing to place his tired head quietly in his folded hands at the end of each day, only to awaken and serve again the next morning. Born into privilege, developing into a technocrat, Bernays illustrates the onus that the twentieth century has placed on social and economic elites; they have had to justify themselves continually to a public whose hearts and minds now bear the ideals of democracy.

As I pursued my research following my encounter with Bernays and repeatedly ran into the fear of an empowered public that ignited the thinking of early practitioners of public relations, the story of Dumb Jack—the man who was no more—came to mind again and again, reminding me of the human flesh that encircles the bones of broad institutional developments.

■   ■   ■   ■   ■

Another story bears repeating here. Toward the middle of our interview, hoping that I could gain insight into the way Bernays approached his practical work, I asked him to describe how he would plan and attend to a specific public relations assignment. First of all,

Bernays instructed, one must rid one's mind of the conventional "press agent" image. "We've [speaking of himself] had no direct contact with the mass media for about fifty years." Rather, he continued, the job of a public relations counsel is to instruct a client how to take actions that "just interrupt . . . the continuity of life in some way to bring about the [media] response."

"How would you do that?" I asked.

Bernays thought for a moment and then turned toward his desk, where he had earlier placed the copy of my book. He picked it up and began to fondle its cover between his small, pinkish-gray fingers, glancing down at the front of the book, reading, to himself, the descriptive material and blurbs that appeared on its back. Then, with a tone of momentousness in his voice, he turned to me:

> If you said to me, 'I would like more readers of this book' [tapping the cover] . . . I would immediately get in touch with the largest American consumer association. And I would say to the head of the consumer association, 'There are undoubtedly . . . I can't tell you the exact percentage, but X percentage of your members who are very definitely interested in the images that come from a finance capitalist society and who I think would enjoy hearing about that. Why don't you devote one of your twelve meetings a year to consumer images, the name of a new book, and I think it may be possible for me to get the author to talk to the New York meeting and you then make an arrangement with American Tel and Tel and have a videotape made of him beforehand and in thirty of the largest cities of the United States that have the American Consumer League, you listen to an in-depth concept of consumers and images. . . .'

Then Bernays turned to me and, with an abracadabra tone in his voice, summarized the imaginable result of his hypothetical phone call to the head of the country's largest consumer association:

> Every one of the consumer groups has contacts with the local paper, and in some cases the AP may pick it up, or Reuters, and you become an international star!

I must acknowledge that I was thoroughly charmed. Here I was, sitting with Edward Bernays—innovator and artiste of modern public relations—listening to him apply his costly wizardry to me and my book. I couldn't get over it and thought to myself, "What a flatterer. This guy really knows how to polish up the old apple." For weeks after the interview, I was tickled by the incident, retelling it to friends, students, whoever had the patience to listen. For me, the story captured Bernays's engaging personality, his ingenious thought process, his ability to garner a response.

Then, about three months after the interview—the incident having faded from my immediate memory—I received a most surprising telephone call. It was from Steven Brobeck, president of the Consumer Federation of America, one of the nation's largest and most influential consumer organizations. Brobeck wanted to know if I would be willing to serve as a keynote speaker at the upcoming Consumer Congress in Washington, D.C., a convention that would bring together more than a thousand members of consumer organizations from around the country. He wanted me to speak about American consumer culture and the ways that seductive commercial images are routinely employed to promote waste and disposability. C-Span, I was informed, would be taping my keynote speech and would then cablecast it across the country.

I still do not know whether Bernays's hand was behind this invitation or whether the phone call was merely a result of sly coincidence. When I inquired as to the origin of the invitation, nowhere was there any clear-cut, or even circumstantial, evidence of Bernays's intervention.

But then I recalled another point in our lengthy conversation, when Bernays sermonized on the invisibility with which public relations experts must, ideally, perform their handiwork.

When I mentioned to him that, even though *Life* magazine had included him in the list of the one hundred most influential Americans in the twentieth century, most Americans would probably not know who he was, he responded:

I'm sure of it. . . . To the average American your name has to be Walter Cronkite, or . . . [you have to be] the most beautiful girl . . . some movie actress they know. . . . In public rela-

Edward Bernays at ninety-nine: "If you said to me, 'I would like more readers of this book' (tapping the cover of my book) . . . I would immediately get in touch with the largest American consumer association. And I would say to the head of the consumers' association . . . 'Why don't you devote one of your twelve meetings a year to consumer images?'" PHOTO: 1991 © BARRY SPECTOR

tions, just as in law, you don't—nobody knows who the lawyer of most people is, and that lawyer may do more than the brain of the man who is theoretically doing it. . . . And I think it should be that way because nobody knows who my doctor is. I mean, except friends. And he may be the basis of my living.

And there I was; the mystery still unsolved. Yet the question remained, and remains, open. Things had uncannily come to pass much as Bernays had described in his hypothetical disquisition on the work of a PR practitioner, and I was left to ponder whether there is any reality anymore, save the reality of public relations. Magnified by my seductive encounter with Bernays, it is this question and its

Stuart Ewen
Hunter College
City University of New York

Bernays: "Every one of the consumer groups has contacts with the local paper, and in some cases the AP may pick it up, or Reuters, and (poof!) you become an international star!" ARCHIE BISHOP

implications for contemporary life that stand at the heart of this book.

■   ■   ■   ■   ■

One last point. I had gone to Cambridge to interview Bernays and gather hidden details about the history of the hidden—yet omnipresent—activity of public relations. In retrospect, I had greatly underestimated the individual with whom I would be talking. I had presupposed that this keenly aware shaper of public perception, this trader in realities, was at the same time open to being candidly cross-examined. Yet in the days following our meeting, it became clear to me that my entire visit had been orchestrated by a virtuoso.

He had even offered me the key by which the pageantry of our encounter might have been unlocked. During the extensive taped interview that I assumed I was conducting, Bernays had at one point turned to me and announced:

> News is any overt act which juts out of the routine of circum-
> stance. . . . A good public relations man advises his client . . .
> to carry out an overt act . . . interrupting the continuity of
> life in some way to bring about a response.

From the time I had approached the door of his house, waiting impatiently for an answer; to my ride on the staircase elevator; to my walk through the gallery of historical photographs; on to the time, five hours later, when we parted company, Bernays—who still claimed to charge $1,000 per hour consulting fees—was giving me, free of charge, an empirical object lesson in public relations. Above all else that I gathered from my journey to Cambridge, this was the prime benefit of my brush with Bernays: experiencing the man himself—still spry at one hundred—in action.[5]

2
Dealing in Reality: Protocols of Persuasion

FOR THOSE AMONG my readers who are also writers, you know too well that writing can be a lonely and painful task. No matter how effortlessly the words may appear to flow on a finally printed page, behind those words—unseen—lie countless hours, weeks, even years of quandary, confusion, and doubt. As with movies—in which the semblance of spontaneity and reality usually corresponds to the extent to which a film has been laboriously constructed, worked, and reworked—words that reside on a page usually require frustrating periods of tedious assembling, reassembling, and editing. Even in works of "dispassionate" scholarship, of which this book is not an example, stagecraft and truth inevitably collide.

For me, the burdens of creation have especially characterized work on this book. It has been more than ten years since I first got the bright idea to write a book about what, at first glance, appeared to be the most "natural" of topics: the role of public relations in twentieth-century American life. Unhappily, it was this sense of "the obvious" that made this project so difficult for me.

Living in a society in which nearly every moment of human attention is exposed to the game plans of spin doctors, image managers, pitchmen, communications consultants, public information officers, and public relations specialists, the boundaries of my inquiry appeared seamless, and the shape that my analysis should take, illusive. Surveying the American cultural habitat, I observed that nearly every arena of public communication—the windows through which we come to know our world—was touched by the deliberate activities of "compliance professionals."[1] As I proceeded, the necessary distance from my subject matter seemed impossible to achieve.

Delving into the historical record, searching for footprints of the people, ideas, and events that had propelled the growth of a "PR" culture, I discovered a similarly daunting terrain. The intersections between the rise of *public relations* and those broader historical turns that have altered the fabric of *public life* were also ineffable—or at least difficult to identify or describe. Repeatedly, just as I believed I was nearing a point of clarity, I would be overcome by the sinking feeling that my topic had, once again, slipped through my fingers. In this condition, I was becoming increasingly difficult to live with.

Along with these vexations, another phantom soon began to haunt my intellectual soul. Here I was, writing about a topic that was essentially public—whatever that term may mean—yet my research and writing activities were overwhelmingly private. Inspecting timeworn documents in the Wertheim Study at the New York Public Library or pouring through materials in the AT&T Archives in Warren, New Jersey, or trying to make sense of my interviews with Bernays and numerous other public relations pioneers and practitioners, I was tormented by a sense of isolation. Though I was discovering a fascinating history, unearthing some eloquent artifacts, I desperately craved a more social milieu in which to discuss and think about what I was encountering. (On occasion, I must insert, this sense of isolation was relieved by my research associates, Steve Duncombe and Andy Mattson. They accompanied me on a number of fruitful archival expeditions, furnishing aid, insight, and much-appreciated companionship.)

In the spring of 1993, I moved toward a decision that would, in time, prove indispensable to the completion of my project. I resolved to begin teaching a course—a plainly unfinished course—in which I would establish my opportunity to exchange ideas with others (students at Hunter College, City University of New York, where I teach), to air and test out my discoveries and thoughts on the social history of publicity and promotion in twentieth-century America. It felt risky—*What if I had nothing to say?*—but, to my confused and lonesome mind, imperative.

In the fall of that year, nearly three years after I had gone to visit Edward Bernays in Cambridge, Massachusetts, I started teaching my brand-new course to an assembly of upper-level undergraduate students at Hunter. Consistent with my subject matter, and following Bernays's injunction to create something that "juts out of the routine . . . to bring about a response," I furnished the course with a deliberately enigmatic and provocative title: The CULT(ure) of Publicity.

I began teaching the course with the expectation that my subject matter would cover the rise of public relations practices in the United States and would explore those ideas, events, and individuals that have had an impact on this development. I opened the course with the story you have just read: of my visit to Bernays, of the charming lesson he gave me on the practice of public relations, of the ways this visit prefigured the study that follows.

Though I expected that the course would be of interest to students—examining a prominent, if taken-for-granted, feature of their world—it did not occur to me that the class, itself, would provide the students and myself with a venue for testing out public relations techniques. Once again—as was the case with my earlier assumption that Bernays was no longer alive—I was wrong.

In mid-September I received a phone call from Maria Terrone, who runs the public relations office for Hunter College. She had just heard from Lynn Palazzi, a reporter for *New York Newsday,* one of the city's three tabloid dailies. Palazzi was interested in writing a story about "interesting courses being taught at colleges throughout the city" and wanted to talk to me about the CULT(ure) of Publicity. Terrone wanted to make sure I was willing to talk with Palazzi and that I would permit her to visit my classroom.

Within a few days, on Monday, September 20, I received a congenial telephone call from Palazzi herself. I responded to her request in a friendly, yet professorial, tone. "I would be glad to have you come," I told her, "but this is a serious course, and I don't want to have it turned into a circus." I told her that I must insist on two conditions.

First, I asked her not to bring a photographer to class or to take any pictures herself. Taking pictures, I explained, would unavoidably disrupt the class session, which I didn't want.

Second, I told her that I did not plan to inform the class that she would be coming, again to "avoid disruption." She should try to enter the classroom so as to blend in with the students. I was confident, I added, in her ability to achieve anonymity; it was still early in the semester, and students had not yet familiarized themselves with everyone else in the class.

She accepted the stipulations with good humor and even seemed to relish the knowledge of being in on a harmless deception. "I look very young," she informed me, injecting that she would be able to blend in quite effortlessly.

An unusual opportunity had dropped into my lap. On Wednesday afternoon, September 22—the session directly preceding Palazzi's upcoming visit—I met with my class and informed them that "next Monday a *Newsday* reporter will be coming to our class." I informed them of her purpose—to write an article on interesting courses being taught around the city; I also told them that she would be coming to class with the belief that none of the students would know she was there. I suggested to the class that this provided us with a perfect occasion to test out some of the techniques outlined by Bernays. I added that in 1947, in an essay entitled "The Engineering of Consent," Bernays had provided the following guidance for our good-natured mischief. "News is not an inanimate thing," he had instructed. "It is the overt act that makes news, and news in turn shapes the attitudes and actions of people."

A good criterion as to whether something is or is not news is whether the event juts out of the pattern of routine. The developing of events and circumstances that are not routine is one of the basic functions of the engineer of consent. Events so planned can be projected over the communication systems to infinitely more people than those actually participating, and such events vividly dramatize ideas for those who do not witness the events.

The imaginatively managed event can compete successfully with other events for attention. Newsworthy events, involving people, usually do not happen by accident. They are planned deliberately to accomplish a purpose, to influence our ideas and actions.[2]

What could we do to turn our class into "news"? Given the fact that a newspaper reporter was actually coming to our class—fully expecting that she'd be inconspicuously observing a routine class session in process—we began to discuss what we as a group might do clandestinely to shape the experience of the class for her, so as to influence the way she would write about the class. This, after all, was what public relations experts do all the time. With an infectious sense of amusement, we ventured into the intoxicating realm of PR strategizing.

Students excitedly offered suggestions about what might be done to put a "spin" on things. Some of the early suggestions verged on the comical. One student suggested that the entire class should address me as "Dad" during the class session. Another student proposed that each time I said something to the class, students would rise and recite an occult chant. Some responded angrily to these ideas, saying that they would only succeed in making the class look ridiculous. Others added that the reporter, unless she was comatose, would surely figure out that she was being put on. It was our job, some inserted, to do something noticeable that, at the same time, seemed like "reality."

This led into a discussion of what our goals were. Were we simply interested in jutting out, or did we want to jut out for a particular purpose? The purpose, most students quickly agreed, was to make the class "look good," "look interesting," meet the reporter's standard of "intriguing." Suggestions poured out from the students, and by the end of the class period, we had decided upon the following plan:

1: In terms of supplying provocative subject matter for the reporter, the class decided that we'd open up the class with students bringing in articles they'd clipped from local newspapers. *Newsday* articles would be prominent.

   Reading passages from their clippings, students would interpret how each article—though outwardly an objective news report— was shaped by the handiwork of public relations professionals.

2: Students were interested in communicating the impression that this was an exhilarating course and that they, as students, participated with enthusiasm. To achieve this aim, we decided that students, throughout the class period, would raise their hands to indicate an interest in participating in the discussion. They decided that they would do so prominently and regularly but with enough constraint to ensure an aura of realism. We arrived at a set of silent signals to keep the discussion moving: Those students who actually had something to say would raise their right hands; those with nothing to say, who were only adding to an imago of participation, would raise their left hands. That way, no one would be embarrassed.

3: Our last plan was, in retrospect, the most perilous. Someone in the class broached the idea that everybody should arrive in class on Monday dressed in black. Her feeling was that this visual touch would add a tone of mystery, a sense of import, a kind of bohemian intellectual tone to the proceedings. One man in the class objected, insisting that the color black would effect a funereal—accordingly negative—impression. Partial to wearing black myself, however, and ignoring the man's admonition, I unwarily endorsed this last suggestion.

Surrounding all these tactical decisions stood one overarching strategic commitment. Under no circumstances, we vowed, should anyone let on that he or she was aware of the stranger among us. The die was cast, the plan was laid, and the class was adjourned.

On Monday, September 27, Palazzi arrived at my office. She was right about looking "like a student." She appeared to be in her early twenties, and her casual dress (black jeans, a pink top, Doc Martens oxfords) was appropriately studentlike. My attire (black jeans and boots, a black shirt and vest) likewise seemed unexceptionable.

We began our interview without any indication of what would soon follow. She asked me about what motivated me to teach the class. We also discussed the course's scope and my pedagogical goals.

Then, in an instant, I realized that public relations thinking had already left an imprint on her visit. Specifically, she asked why I had "spelled" the course name as I had: CULT(ure) of Publicity, instead of Culture of Publicity. She indicated that my typographical (pre)TENSION was what had initially caught her eye about the course. I explained that that was "the idea": to incorporate the wizardry of my subject matter directly into the course title, to make it stand out from the usual course. I added that my emphasis on the word *CULT,* was also a reference to the ways that public relations people often define their job as one that requires mesmerizing, more than informing, the public mind.

As class time drew near, I asked her to enter the room on her own, like any student coming from a prior class. I was concerned, I told her, that if we entered the class together, the students might think she was a "special guest." She agreed and told me she would probably be giving me a call over the next week, to do some "follow-up." I said "Fine," and then we parted company.

At 4:15 PM—five minutes late, to let the visual impact of our plan sink in—I entered the class and walked to the front. I looked out at the class and was stunned. Nearly every student, about forty people, was in attendance. All but Palazzi (whose pink top stuck out at the far left of my vision) were arrayed in black—an unnerving sight. I was paralyzed, feeling, for an instant, that I had walked in on some demonic conclave and sensing a chilling moisture surfacing on my skin. Nothing had prepared me for the effect our visual stunt would have on *me.*

Then, in another instant as I focused past the black and discovered my students' expectant and empathic faces our good-natured, if positively weird, deception proceeded as planned. Aside from the eerie darkness of the gathering, our plan fared well. The students had brought in clippings and they participated energetically. An authentically stimulating discussion unfolded. After a while, I moved on to talk about the uses of publicity during the Progressive Era, with students using agreed-upon hand signals to ask questions, offer comments, or look interested along the way.

I must confess, however, that the visual shock of the tableau never left my consciousness. And when the class ended, and I noticed Palazzi bolt abruptly out of the room, I had the uneasy feeling that our scheme had backfired on us, that the sartorial gloom had spooked her.

•　　　•　　　•

A week after the exercise had taken place, I had still not heard from our reporter. I assumed my worst fears were right, that the scene had so alarmed her that she had decided to drop us from the list of courses she would be surveying. I almost blinked, and I thought of calling her, but decided that a phone call would only confirm that something had been up. Weeks and then months followed; I received no call from Palazzi and no word that the article had appeared. I and the students brushed aside our misbegotten stab at doing PR and went about our business.

As the course persisted into late November, and the episode dimmed from memory, I again received a call from Terrone. She was calling to let me know that she had just heard from Palazzi; the article was about to appear.

On December 1, I purchased *Newsday* and eagerly leafed through to find an article entitled "College Lite," a compendium of "intriguing and just plain wacky stuff falling from the ivory tower this fall." Though I was somewhat put off by the disdainful headline—which I assumed the reporter had nothing to do with—I looked down to the body of the piece and searched for the section dealing with my course. Here, in its entirety, is Lynn Palazzi's description of the course:

> Almost 50 blocks north of Druks' 21st Street classroom [a reference to another course described in the article], Jefferson's most famous writing—The Declaration of Independence—is being deconstructed and taught, not as a historical document, but as the ultimate piece of propaganda. Stuart Ewen, a media-studies professor at Hunter College has built a course titled "The CULT(ure)of Publicity" around the guiding principle that our society has evolved into a publicity-ridden place where "truth is largely defined as that which will sell to an audience."
>
> Ewen says his goal is to encourage his students—25 or so urban hipsters wearing varying shades of black—to cast a more critical eye upon the images and messages they're bombarded with every day. With current front-page fodder for discussion, the class often sounds less like a lecture and more like a coffee-house exchange of ideas. Ewen explains the

altered spelling of "culture" suggests "some kind of mes-
merism, a power other than reason."

"This is a society where people feel they're constant targets
of instrumental messages, and that often makes them feel
paranoid, as if others are pulling the strings," he says. "As a
result, I think they're very interested in getting a handle on it."

One way Ewen helps broaden students' understanding of
the power of PR is by giving them a backstage pass into the
world of corporate image-making. Because PR strategists are
unwilling to speak about campaigns currently in development,
Ewen compensates by going back to documents like the
selected letters of P. T. Barnum or proceedings from a 1928
AT&T conference and working forward to let students see
how the other half thinks.[3]

That afternoon, as the class convened for its regular Wednesday
session, we looked over the article with glee. All were dazzled by the
significance and success of our experiment. While the article's version
of the actual class substance was slipshod and, to some extent, inac-
curate, our blueprint for "impression management" had clearly
achieved its goals.

The eccentric typography of the course title had drawn comment
and explanation. The decision to use news items as a centerpiece for
spirited discussion had secured the reporter's attention. The combination of black clothing and free-flowing—if somewhat packaged—
participation had transformed us into a group of "urban hipsters,"
participating in "a coffee-house exchange of ideas." Palazzi's underes-
timation of the class's size only reflected the convincing semblance of
intimacy we had created. Gratified and amused, we congratulated
ourselves on having mastered the Way of Spin.

■ ■ ■ ■ ■

In truth, though, one need not have enrolled in The CULT(ure) of
Publicity to have pulled off our little coup. The ability to publicize—
self, product, concept, issue, or institution—is a basic survival skill in
contemporary life, and field-tested publicity techniques are everywhere to be found. Beyond the assistance our studies were providing,
the lessons that guided us in our strategic approach to a visiting

Newsday reporter are repeated, again and again, across the expanse of our cultural horizon. If our academic parlor game was, on the scale of things, innocuous and amusing, the use of public relations techniques—as routinely employed by institutions of social, economic, military, or political power—may lead to more serious consequences:

- Bernays, throughout his long career, insisted that public relations is the science of "creating circumstances," mounting events that are calculated to stand out as "newsworthy," yet, at the same time, which do not appear to be staged. The field of public relations continues to hold to this dictum, routinely mapping out pre-arranged occurrences that are projected to look and sound like impromptu truths. A potent specimen of this practice can be found in the months that preceded the U.S. entry into the Persian Gulf War in the winter of 1991.

  Some months before, during the fall of 1990, a particularly alarming story began to be circulated by American news agencies. Following the Iraqi invasion of Kuwait, the report affirmed, Iraqi soldiers entered hospitals in Kuwait City and removed hundreds of premature infants from incubators, leaving them to die on cold hospital floors. Appearing again and again in the American news media, the story attested to the profound cruelty of the invasionary force.

  The source of this story was an anonymous fifteen-year-old Kuwaiti girl, called Nayirah, who had testified to the horrific events before the Congressional Human Rights Caucus on October 10, 1990. According to her story, she was a "hospital volunteer" and a firsthand witness to the purported barbarism. To ensure her continued safety, the head of the caucus announced, the girl's true identity had to be kept secret.

  Only much later, after the Persian Gulf War was fading into the historical record, did it turn out that "Nayirah" was, in fact, Nayirah al-Sabah, daughter of the Kuwaiti ambassador to the United States. Her actual whereabouts, at the time the alleged cruelties had taken place, were questionable; she had been witness to no such events.

  Beyond the dubiousness of her tale, it also turned out that the meeting of the Congressional Human Rights Caucus itself had been the brainchild of Gary Hymel, a vice-president of Hill and Knowlton, one of the largest public relations firms in the world. Hymel had graciously provided the caucus with all the witnesses that it heard. Hymel and Hill and Knowlton were on the payroll of the Kuwaiti royal family in exile and had been given the assignment of manufacturing public support for this U.S. military intervention.[4]

Nayirah's shocking testimony was but one created circumstance in an involved plan to inflame American public outrage. Within a few months, tales such as hers had readied the public mind and had led the nation into war.

• The calculated simulation of enthusiasm—a significant aspect of our classroom encounter with the *Newsday* reporter—is also common within contemporary culture. In a variety of configurations, the "applause sign" has ascended as a social principle. Statistical poll results are continuously broadcast, emphasizing the popularity (or lack thereof) of politicians; policies; products; and, of course, wars. "Grassroots" expression is now being manufactured by firms specializing in the generation of "extemporaneous" public opposition or support. (In the PR industry, such orchestrated "grassroots" mobilizations are referred to as "Astro Turf Organizing.") A 1993 *New York Times* article delineated the activities of one such firm:

> Consider Bonner & Associates, which occupies an entire floor of one of Washington's pricier office buildings. . . . This company is among a new breed of Washington firms that has turned grass-roots organizing techniques to the advantage of its high-paying clients, generally trade associations and corporations. . . . [T]he new campaigns are sometimes intended to appear spontaneous. . . . [T]he rise of this industry has made it hard to tell the difference between manufactured public opinion and genuine explosions of popular sentiment.
>
> Bonner & Associates specializes in seizing on unformed public sentiment, marshalling local interest groups and raining faxes, phone calls and letters on Congress or the White House on a few days' notice.[5]

---

arti•FACT

In 1993-94, as the Clinton administration moved to establish federally guaranteed medical coverage for all Americans, the Medical-Industrial Complex (M-I-C) went into high gear in an effort to defeat the legislation and protect its highly profitable status quo. In a colossal public relations blitz, calculated to turn public opinion against universal health insurance, more than one hundred fifty million dollars was spent by an alliance of vested interests: the pharmaceutical industry, the insurance industry, the American Medical Association, and other elements of the illness establishment.

In order to smother public fervor for comprehensive health care legislation, however, the M-I-C had to present its case as if it were coming from ordinary Americans. To effect this charade, a number of purported citizens' organizations sprang up, expressing apparently homespun opposition to federally guaranteed health care.

One such group was the **Coalition for Health Insurance Choices** which proclaimed itself "A Coalition of thousands of Americans, from every walk of life and every corner of the country, who are concerned about health care reform," but was actually funded by the Health Insurance Association of America, a lobbying group for the insurance industry. In a series of television ads produced by this group, two ordinary Americans, "Harry and Louise," conveyed their personal fears about the prospect of guaranteed health care.

Another "third party" front group was **RxPartners**, which sought to manufacture a seemingly "grassroots" defense of unregulated pharmaceutical pricing policies, but was—in fact—established by a confederacy of large drug companies including Bristol-Myers Squibb, Eli Lilly, Hoffmann-LaRoche, Searle, Upjohn, and Warner Lambert. To construct the semblance of a public outcry against proposed drug price controls, **RxPartners** employed "Astro-turf organizing" techniques. As seen in an actual example [Figure 1, below], pre-written letters, with pre-addressed envelops, were sent to people throughout the United States, ready to be signed and mailed to an appropriate Senator or Congressman.

> The Honorable Daniel Moynihan
> United States Senate
> Washington, D.C. 20510
>
>
> Dear Senator Moynihan:
>
> I am opposed to price controls, particularly on an industry as innovative as pharmaceuticals. This industry is the world's leader in developing new wonder drugs that help millions of Americans every year.
>
> We cannot take the risk that price controls will adversely affect the research and development of new medicine for future generations, especially since price controls have never worked.
>
> Sincerely,
>
>
> Elizabeth Ewen
> ▬▬▬▬▬▬▬▬▬▬
> New York, NY ▬▬▬

Figure 1: An actual astro-turf organizing letter generated by RxPartners, a "third party" front organization which really spoke for huge pharmaceutical corporations.

ARCHIE BISHOP

- The use of unspoken visual techniques to create a mood—an approach that in our classroom ground plan was a risky but ultimately effective element—is also rampant throughout the society. Presidents deliver speeches before dramatic backdrops, carefully selected to bring about the desired responses. Corporations invest millions on logo designs, conceding that typography has a miraculous ability to convey a particular sensibility or feeling.

More and more, the microscopic details of public communication practice reveal the fingerprints of such thinking. A paradigmatic example of this arrived, unsolicited, in my mailbox at Hunter College some time back.

While at first glance its source and intent are ambiguous, *Life Is in the Balance* turned out to be a lavishly produced "educational" brochure from the Dow Chemical Corporation, posing an argument against the environmental regulation of the petrochemical industry.

> A key question is whether or not the government should have the final say in most risk reduction. Or should it be up to the individual person to decide when he wishes to purchase potentially risky substances . . .
>
> [R]isk-taking is part of the balance that makes life worth living. We can't deny our children that legacy of hope and challenge by deciding for them that life should be cushioned against all risk. They should have some choice in their own tomorrow—a choice to risk sorrow and learn from it, and above all, the right to risk failure for success and joy.[6]

In the booklet, escalating stockpiles of toxic waste or the serious environmental hazards associated with petrochemical industries go unmentioned. An emotional rhetoric of "individual" choice and the rights of "our children" provides a heavily laden disguise for the interests of corporate power.

Yet beyond the confines of conventional language, in a wordless attempt to resonate with the public's increasingly critical ecological consciousness, the booklet is clad in a forest green cover, is filled with burnt umber pencil sketches, and is printed in earth tones. Optical suggestion—a feeling tone of environmental responsibility—is used to varnish the stony argument that toxicity and the purported contamination of the biosphere are groundless anxieties. Implicit within all this is a public relations truism: It's not what you say, but how you say it, that matters.

- The extent to which the techniques of our classroom experiment were able to convey a persuasive intellectual tone for Palazzi's article, while the substance of the class discussion—as it appeared in her story—was misrepresented or neglected is likewise not unusual. This imbalance is an exemplary result of public relations strategies that are aimed at creating impressions while, in the process, bypassing or downplaying substantive content. Though in our planning session there was some emphasis placed on the kind of materials we'd be discussing in the following class, the greater part of our effort was spent talking about activities that would magnify and enhance the class's aura.

Such calculations may occur in the most incongruous circumstances. On May 4, 1992—as Los Angeles burned in the wake of rioting—*Advertising Age* (a trade journal of the allied advertising and public relations industries) published the following front-page panacea for handling the social upheaval:

> *The time to bring the power of advertising to bear on the urban rioting that broke out last week is now. . . . There are those who believe the issues involved have nothing to do with the advertising business, that poverty, despair and many forms of racism are at the root of the problem. . . . We don't agree. Certainly, economic conditions play a role, but so does a shared set of values that make community possible. Voices of restraint are urgently needed to counter the angry voices of those bent on violence and theft.*[7]

The article then suggested that running-shoe companies—given their widely acknowledged credibility in the ghetto—provided natural pipelines for the nullification of inner-city rage. While a torrent of such publicity followed the LA riots—under a catchy slogan, Rebuild the Dream—much of South Central LA still lies in rubble, and the gadgetry of image-management continues to be employed as an approach of first resort.

This kind of thinking—prizing message before substance—has become typical in our society. The downplaying of substantive social conditions and the familiar reliance on brand-names or celebrities to address social ills is a peculiar and, as social problems intensify, will be an increasingly problematic feature of our culture.

■   ■   ■   ■   ■

As should be apparent from these several case histories, the methods employed by our CULT(ure) of Publicity class, while bracing for a *Newsday* reporter's visit, embody techniques that are widespread within present-day American society. Yet these contemporary illustrations of PR practice reveal something more. Public relations cannot be understood simply as an array of value-free techniques employed for steering news coverage or influencing public opinion. The rise and consequence of public relations within our world must also be placed in relation to the motives, the assumptions, and the history of power.

Standing behind the story of Nayirah, for example, are petroleum interests in the Middle East, interests that have guided the history and fate of that region for more than a century. Without scrutinizing historical patterns of power in that area of the world, the story of Nayirah and the war it helped to instigate makes little sense.

Similarly, the existence of organizations like Bonner & Associates, which can muster a display of "grassroots" sentiment, on behalf of powerful clients at a moment's notice, can only be comprehended if placed within a historical context in which elites have been compelled, more and more, to recognize and respond to the weight of "public opinion."

The visual techniques employed by Dow Chemical Corporation, in *Life Is in the Balance*, must likewise be contextualized within the long—sometimes deadly—history in which American business, particularly the petrochemical industry, has habitually resisted governmental regulation and public accountability. It must also be seen in relation to over a century of public antagonism toward habitual corporate arrogance.

Last, *Advertising Age*'s suggestion that advertising should be employed to subdue popular outrage in South Central Los Angeles discloses a now entrenched reflex of American business: to employ ideological pabulum in lieu of addressing concrete social and economic inequities. Embedded within such schemes lies a nervous preoccupation with the perils of democracy that has chaperoned the growth of corporate public relations for nearly a century.

• • •

In a democratic society, the interests of power and the interests of the public are often at odds. The rise of public relations is testimony to the ways that institutions of vested power, over the course of the twentieth century, have been compelled to justify and package their interests in terms of the common good.

In the 1920s, for example, when Bernays published his pioneering handbooks, *Crystallizing Public Opinion* (1923) and *Propaganda* (1928), he described modern society as one in which "the masses" had become increasingly bold, increasingly threatening to the customary interests of order. There is, he wrote, an "increased readiness of the public, due to the spread of literacy and democratic forms of government, to feel that it is entitled to its voice in the conduct" of all aspects of society.[8] This sense of entitlement, he spelled out, was the inherent outcome of a historical process that had placed new and treacherous demands on the doorposts of "the higher strata of society."

> The steam engine, the multiple press, and the public school, that trio of the industrial revolution, have taken the power away from kings and given it to the people. . . . [A]nd the history of the industrial revolution shows that power passed from the king and the aristocracy to the bourgeoisie. Universal suffrage and universal schooling reënforced this tendency, and at last even the bourgeoisie stood in fear of the common people.[9]

In the face of such challenges from below, Bernays argued, the ability to shape and direct public opinion had become essential to the maintenance of order. In 1923, paraphrasing ideas that he borrowed from the German sociologist Ferdinand Tönnies, Bernays maintained that "the future of civilization" lay in the capacity of elites to guide public opinion efficiently.

> It is certain that the power of public opinion is constantly increasing and will keep on increasing. It is equally certain that it is more and more being influenced, changed, stirred by impulses from below. The danger which this development con-

tains for a progressive ennobling of human society and a progressive heightening of human culture is apparent. The duty of the higher strata of society—the cultivated, the learned, the expert, the intellectual—is therefore clear. They must inject moral and spiritual motives into public opinion.[10]

"Intelligent men," Bernays instructed five years later, "must realize that propaganda is the modern instrument by which they can fight for productive ends and help to bring order out of chaos."[11] More than the deployment of grand-scale parlor tricks, Bernays understood his work as a response to endemic social conflicts, as a strategy for combating or—better yet—managing democratic appetites.

The perpetual hazards of democracy and the need to meet and circumvent popular opposition continue to percolate in the public relations literature. Philip Lesly, a prominent figure in the American public relations fraternity going back to the 1940s, publishes a bimonthly newsletter, *Managing the Human Climate,* in which he discusses issues encompassing public relations and public affairs. Here again, in the cogitations of a PR pundit, we encounter a note of forewarning, a beleaguered sense that "the masses" are banging at the gate.

"Issues are increasing and activism is booming again," begins the September–October 1993 issue of *Managing the Human Climate.* Deploring those who protest about AIDS, global warming, abuse of the elderly, and civil rights, Lesly concludes that the "climate of our times is *focusing on those who claim to be victims*—of everything except their own failings." "Together," he argues, this "Victims Movement" constitutes a *"majority*—a formidable array of opposition to established organizations and institutions." To those in charge of such organizations and institutions, he warns, this requires a "sophisticated strategy to survive."

Lesly's rhetoric reverberates with a sense of social and historical emergency. Depicting opposition groups as a social contagion, he argues that the "ability to fend off such activism now calls for a 'vaccine' against unsound assaults, just as polio required the Salk and Sabin vaccines."[12] The March–April 1994 issue of *Managing the Human Climate* reiterates the disease analogy:

- No organization now can afford to let the climate of attitudes develop by accident or through outside forces. It must work to create its own climate.
- This calls for constant efforts to anticipate . . . to read trends that may create the climate to be coped with. It is now far more effective to "inoculate" the publics in advance rather than react when an attack comes.[13]

There are a number of tactical suggestions in the newsletter—how to shape the "public agenda," how to "funnel" information into the "opinion-forming process"; warnings not to "attack opponents' positions head-on. Don't debate"; "Couching things in the self-interest of the audience is now mandatory"; and so forth—but at the core of Lesly's recommendations lies a vision of a society in which the forces of order are threatened, at every juncture, by the forces of "self-inflicted chaos." He concludes, urgently:

The trend toward chaos is so pronounced that there now are instruction books on how to live with it. The real need is how to live without it: *If you want any control over your life and your loved ones', oppose decontrol and deconstruction wherever it pops up.*[14]

In the face of such hyperbole, it is easy to be dismissive. Yet as I've roamed around the historical record, looking for footprints that might illuminate the emergence of an Age of Public Relations, I've encountered such expressions of unease with democracy again and again. For nearly a century, the attempt to contain the forces of "chaos" has possessed the evolution of PR thinking and, more than anything else, it is the glue that holds the history of corporate public relations together. It is to that history and that persistent struggle with "chaos" that we now must turn.

PART 2

"The Crowd Is in the Saddle": Progressive Politics and the Rise of Public Relations

3

Truth Happens: An Age of Publicity Begins

IN 1907 THE EMINENT American philosopher, William James, published a book entitled *Pragmatism: A New Name for Old Ways of Thinking*. In its pages he summed up a lifetime of tortuous speculation on the foundations of human belief, on the volatile mental processes through which people come to know and comprehend their world.

Though sixty-five years of age and approaching the end of his life, James continued to propose ideas about truth that dismissed the notion that there are any such things as timeless verities. At an age when many find refuge in unbending conservatism, James held to the conviction that *there are no absolute truths;* there is no consummate gospel by which people—regardless of their circumstances—may live.

Truth, insisted James, exists in a perpetual state of flux. It is nothing more than a by-product of human history, an intrinsic outcome of people interacting with their world and elaborating—or disputing—shared assumptions about its terms. "The truth of an idea," James declared, "is not a stagnant property inherent in it. Truth *happens* to an idea. It *becomes true, is made true* by events."[1]

Then—appropriating a fitting analogy in a society in which a market economy and large-scale finance capital were increasingly shaping the terms of national life—James likened the substantiality of truth to that of paper money.

> Truth lives . . . for the most part on a credit system. Our
> thoughts and beliefs "pass," so long as nothing challenges
> them, just as bank-notes pass so long as nobody refuses them.

As long as people accept the value of each other's truths, he
explained, these truths assume the character of legal tender. They are
passed from person to person without thought or comment like dollar
bills. If, however, events or discoveries occur that weaken or challenge
a people's faith in these ideas, James contended, "the fabric of truth"
breaks down "like a financial system with no cash-basis whatever."[2]

In short, James's solution to the riddle of truth was that truth is
something that results from an ongoing—if generally unacknowledged—audit in the public mind. When that audit fails to substan-
tiate the validity of a truth or of a previously accepted body of truth,
an entire system of belief, a worldview, stands in jeopardy and will—
by stress of historical circumstances—turn to dust. In place of old,
discarded truths, James maintained, new ways of seeing will
inevitably arise, truths that are once again able to withstand the
scrutiny of public examination.

James's interpretation of truth as something profoundly
unstable—susceptible to the processes and judgments of ongoing
social verification—was not merely an eccentric example of American
philosophical speculation. When James wrote that "truth happens to
an idea," many contemporaries concurred. Such observations were
increasingly in the air.

Conforming to the logic of its own perspective, "pragmatism's
conception of truth" was itself a by-product of the history that it
occupied. James's impression of a world in which truth endures a
chronic state of critical appraisal and the outlines of reality are in a
constant state of flux spoke to an environment in which pitched battles over meaning were already taking place—battles to name *what
is*, to define the social, political, and economic contours of America's
future.

The period between the end of the Civil War and the first decade
of the twentieth century was, for many people in the United States, a
period of profound confusion and turmoil. From being a highly
regionalized, preindustrial nation in which a relatively disparate

middle class (comprised, for the most part, of Anglo-American merchants, professionals, artisans, and small landowners) set the social, economic, and cultural patterns of life in provincial towns and rural areas, America was now becoming a society driven—in unison—by an expanding industrial behemoth. Large-scale national economic consolidation was under way in a wide range of industries, and— more and more—a small number of powerful, disdainfully arrogant men were dictating the social circumstances and life rhythms of countless people throughout the United States.

This all-encompassing truth inescapably gave rise to others. For the customary, localized middle classes—small-businessmen and others who saw themselves being overshadowed and rendered obsolete—the disdainful misconduct of "robber barons" and the palpable encroachments of giant enterprises were particularly loathsome. A sense that their world was being torn asunder and that they were being rapidly propelled toward indigence began to fester among their ranks. In response to the transgressions of corporate monopoly and large-scale industrialization, the search to restore social and economic stability to their lives—*to bring order to the life of the nation*— emerged as a middle-class obsession.

Amid this "search for order," customary principles of liberalism were thrown into question.[3] The exponential growth of monopolistic fortunes and the accompanying spread of human misery were conditions that compelled middle-class people to rethink many of their customary assumptions. Most dramatically, the once-sacred principle of *free enterprise* was being reexamined by an increasingly critical public eye.

At the time of the American Revolution, the unfettered pursuit of private enterprise had been widely accepted as a keystone of democratic society. To middle-class soldiers of the Enlightenment—confronting a soaring mountain of bureaucratic encroachments by an absolutist, mercantile state—the rights of ordinary citizens to pursue their private interests and private economic activities without state interference represented the defense of individual freedom and the marrow of liberalism. Such ideas persevered until the mid-nineteenth century as the relatively inclusive population of white, Anglo-American men continued to enjoy conditions of prosperity and status within what was still a small-scale, highly localized way of life.[4]

By the late nineteenth century, however, the pursuit of profit and the character of private wealth had changed considerably. The dynamic ether of an unencumbered marketplace—once the touchstone of democratic faith—was now making "machines of men, robbing them of their humanity and turning them into cool calculators of personal advantage."[5]

Private industrial fortunes were being built, in large measure, through the crushing and absorbing of local small-scale enterprises. With this, many among the middle class saw their own fortunes diminishing, their prospects dim. Though most among them struggled to maintain the appearance of doing well and some held stubbornly to a gospel of wealth—looking to captains of industry as models for emulation—a widening circle of middle-class life was beset by chafing anxiety.

Ira Steward's 1873 description of the "native middle classes" of New England provides us with a poignant portrait of the forlorn hopes that were stalking the vicinity of middle-class existence.

> Very few among them are saving money. Many of them are in debt; and all they can earn for years, is, in many cases, mortgaged to pay such debt. . . . In the faces of thousands of well-dressed, intelligent, and well-appearing people, may be seen the unmistakable signs of their incessant anxiety and struggles to get on in life, and to obtain in addition to a mere subsistence, a standing in society. . . .
>
> The poverty of the great middle classes consists in the fact that they have only barely enough to cover up their poverty, and that they are within a very few days of want, if through sickness, or other misfortunes, employment suddenly stops.
>
> No one can describe the secret feeling of insecurity that constantly prevails among them concerning their living, and how it will be with them in the future; and while actual hunger and want may never be known, their poverty is felt, mentally and socially, through their sense of dependence and pride. They must work constantly, and with an angry sense of the limited opportunities for a career at their command.[6]

Exacerbating such conditions, predatory—virtually unaccountable—heads of corporations had taken control of economic life, taking on the traits of the despots that eighteenth-century democrats had fought so vigorously to overthrow. Characterizing the railroad and shipping magnate, "Commodore" Cornelius Vanderbilt, as a man who had built a "kingdom within the republic," the journalist Henry Demarest Lloyd gave voice to a perspective on private wealth that was beginning to gain popularity among a widening sector of besieged middle-class Americans.[7]

Shielded by once-sacrosanct safeguards of laissez-faire, an imperious monarchy, this one dominated by a parvenu clique of robber barons, had been reborn. Breaking from axioms of the past, which had preached the sanctity of free enterprise, a widening population of middle-class people began to look toward the state and toward the device of regulation as necessary instruments for controlling the rapacity of those who held unrestrained private wealth. The compass of middle-class liberalism was changing polarity. In the shadow of newly emerging realities, laissez-faire—once the linchpin in the middle class's notion of its rights—was coming into question. For many, it was beginning to be seen as a remnant of "outworn economic beliefs."[8]

Adding to widespread middle-class apprehensions of chaos, the human complexion of America itself was changing, becoming increasingly alien. Massing at the borders of American life, a fearsome Babel of "otherness" overshadowed middle-class sensibilities. Successive waves of immigrants, arriving in the United States to provide cheap labor for expanding industries, were perceived as embodying a social emergency that, unless contained, would inundate and swallow besieged middle-class American truths.[9] "The typical immigrant," warned Josiah Strong in 1885, "is a European peasant, whose horizon has been narrow, whose moral and religious training has been meager or false, and whose ideas of life are low. Not a few belong to the pauper and criminal classes."[10]

Amid the threat of deluge, answers to anxious questions—What is an American? What is the American way of life? What is America's future?—were increasingly unclear. Social and cultural unease, colored by Anglo-Saxon supremacism, began to escalate among the native middle classes just as new immigrants to American cities were materially altering the choreographies and meanings of American life. In countless immigrant neighborhoods, in the urban slums of a once and future promised land, it should be added, the newcomers were likewise struggling to maintain or discover their own understandings of the truth.

Amid the limbo of the modern, pragmatism's volatile conception of truth was being impelled by forces of history, enacted in the orbits of everyday life. The United States was becoming a bubbling laboratory in which warring versions of reality and truth were being proposed, experimented with, and developed. As the nineteenth century drew to a close and the sense of imminent social fragmentation accelerated, one of the most compelling and resonant of these new truths began to emerge from within the ranks of the embattled middle class itself.

From the 1870s onward, in response to the social pandemonium of industrialization, a growing assembly of middle-class Americans sought to provoke a new national dialogue. At the center of this assembly, a number of influential journalists took on the role of "Progressive publicists," drummers on behalf of social reform. The excesses of big business, the aggregate explosion of social misery, and the sense of impending social catastrophe provided abundant raw materials for their incensed jeremiads.

It was the increasingly distraught and doubtful middle class that provided the audience for these Progressive agitators, men like Edward Bellamy, Henry George, and Henry Demarest Lloyd. Amid a world being swamped by the forces of chaos, the rational projections of these men seemed to propose the possibility of order.

Bellamy was a journalist who wrote for the *Springfield Union* in Massachusetts. In 1888, he strayed from newspaper jargon to publish a novel entitled *Looking Backward.* The book, which combined a harsh critique of the present day with a sanguinely utopian picture of the future, would have a profound impact on American thinking for decades to come. Written toward the close of a century marked by enormous industrial growth and torn by an abyss of human suffering, the novel embodied an insistent call for fundamental social change.

Bellamy's novel was narrated by a man named Julian West, a well-to-do New Englander of the late nineteenth century who, following an astonishing hundred-year episode of suspended animation, awakens into a new and radically changed world. Forecasting life at the end of the twentieth century—our own time—*Looking Backward* provided a receptive reading public with a vivid and fervently logical conception of a future society, still predicated on industrial production, yet now guided by humane reason.

Against the industrial exploitation, pauperism, and widespread urban squalor that ruled the second half of the nineteenth century, Bellamy envisioned a future that would be governed by clearheaded intellect, by a machinery of production and distribution that was organized, not for the pursuit of profit, but according to the guideline of human need. In Bellamy's utopia, the common good of humanity had finally prevailed over an age-old ethic of greed.

In place of parasitic robber barons and socially irresponsible corporations, Bellamy predicted that "the people" would—by the close of the twentieth century—finally take "control of their own business." If the fabric of late-nineteenth-century life was riddled with "demagoguery and corruption," Bellamy proposed the emergence of a new and just society, where the "conditions of human life" and the "motives of human action" had changed. One of Bellamy's twentieth-century characters summarizes the chasm separating the two Americas in the following terms:

> In place of the dreary hopelessness of the 19th century . . . its profound pessimism as to the future of humanity, the animating idea of the [new twentieth-century world] . . . is an enthusiastic conception of the opportunities of our earthly existence . . . the unbounded possibilities of human nature. The betterment of mankind from generation to generation, physically, mentally, morally . . . [is now] recognized as the one great object supremely worthy of effort and sacrifice.[11]

Reading such words, even today, one can appreciate the degree to which Bellamy's indictment of industrial existence, as well as his belief in the urgency of social change, represented a profound assault on the chaotic conditions of late-nineteenth-century capitalism. In ways that echoed another nineteenth-century publicist, Karl Marx, Bellamy favored foundational changes in the social relations that controlled the machinery of production and the fabric of the human condition. Yet unlike Marx, Bellamy's vision of transformation was not founded on the premise of violent upheaval or inevitable class conflict.

The "good society," proposed in *Looking Backward,* would be the outcome of a rational process of social evaluation. It would be the result of newly arrived at truths and the collective handiwork of something called "public opinion."

> The change had been long foreseen. Public opinion had become fully ripe for it, and the whole mass of the people was behind it. There was no more possibility of opposing it by force than by argument.[12]

According to Bellamy's prophecy, it would be the force of public opinion—opinion bolstered by the instrument of reason—that would perform the task of remaking the world for the benefit of all humanity. Deliberating upon the social facts and considering the requirements of humankind, an informed and intelligent "public" would be the agency through which a new historical epoch would be initiated. As a telling example of Progressive publicity, *Looking Backward* was intended to provide the middle-class public with some of the rational arguments necessary to arrive at such a conclusion.

For those of us who have been schooled by an age of hype—in which image managers, spin doctors, and legions of ideological cosmeticians routinely package truth for public consumption—expectations such as Bellamy's sound remarkably naive. Yet notions like his, forecasting an orderly future forged by the hand of public reason, were at home in the minds of many middle-class Americans in the twilight years of the nineteenth century. Among journalists of the period, Bellamy was hardly alone. Parallel thoughts—the belief that literary petitions and candid facts, presented before the "court of public opinion," might activate a movement of social enlightenment— were simultaneously occurring to a growing number of influential writers.

In 1879, for example—the same year that John D. Rockefeller consolidated his notorious Standard Oil Trust—another newspaperman, Henry George of the *San Francisco Evening Post,* published a pivotal treatise entitled *Progress and Poverty.* As Rockefeller proceeded to seize 90 percent of the American petroleum industry, George's best-seller condemned "the vice and misery that spring from the unequal distribution of wealth and privilege." As the oil baron proclaimed that "it is my duty to make money and still more money," George appealed to those reasonable souls who would repudiate this kind of thinking, those who sought to achieve "a higher social state."[13]

The social facts underlying industrial progress, George argued, represented a profound betrayal of hope. At its inception, George sought to remind his readers, the industrial age had seemed bountiful with promise. Steam-powered machinery would lighten working people's toil, and an unparalleled capacity to produce goods would render poverty a thing of the past. In popular fantasy, George recounted, "the golden age of which mankind have always dreamed," seemed on the horizon.[14] Now, however, engulfed by economic depression and an epidemic of social desolation, the vision that some day even "the man with the muck-rake" might drink in "the glory of the stars" was fading from the mind's eye.

Cold reality had set in. "We are coming into a collision with facts which there can be no mistaking," wrote George. "From all parts of the civilized world come complaints of industrial depression." Amid the pandemonium of progress and in spite of a "prodigious increase in wealth-producing power," there lay a growing mass of human decay.

> This association of poverty with progress is the great enigma of our times. It is the central fact from which spring industrial, social, and political difficulties that perplex the world, and with which statesmanship and philanthropy and education grapple in vain. . . . So long as all the increased wealth which modern progress brings goes but to build up great fortunes, to increase luxury and make sharper the contrast between the House of Have and the House of Want, progress is not real and cannot be permanent.

These conditions, George maintained, were pushing industrial society toward the edge of a dangerous precipice. "The tower leans from its foundations," he warned, "and every new story but hastens the final catastrophe."[15]

George's intent, however, reached beyond the goal of mere description. The material conditions being described, he believed, provided the public and the future with an ineluctable agenda. George held to the belief that by publicizing the agonies of industrial life and by mandating his prescribed mandate for a "single tax" on land, the hopes embedded in the industrial revolution might finally be realized. "The reaction must come now," he implored his readers, supposing that publicity and the summoning of middle-class public opinion could provide the necessary emollient for change.

In 1881, when Henry Demarest Lloyd—an editor at the *Chicago Tribune*—published an article in the *Atlantic Monthly* entitled "The Story of a Great Monopoly," he was driven by a similar conviction.[16] A detailed elaboration of the human wreckage that lay in the wake of the Standard Oil Trust, this article was also more than a simple chronicle of events. Like George's *Progress and Poverty* or Bellamy's soon-to-be-published novel, Lloyd's saga of Standard Oil was motivated by a belief in the power of public opinion to forge social change. In a corrupt world, Lloyd proclaimed, "Publicity is the great moral disinfectant."[17]

To these three men, and to a generation of Progressive journalists who followed in their footsteps, the term *publicity* had not yet assumed today's connotation of mendacious cunning. If anything, it was understood as a crystalline light by which an unraveling society and its toxic contradictions might be illuminated and brought to order. It was the salve that would help to eradicate a social plague, a righteous weapon that would rouse the middle-class public to resist the tide of social crime that had seized control of industrial America. Implicit within these beliefs was the Jamesian intuition that the process by which truth happens could—with the tool of publicity—be willfully engineered.

By the turn of the twentieth century, the circle of writers and journalists speaking to—and for—the anxiety-ridden middle class had widened, and a number of mass-circulation magazines— America's premier national mass media—began to blossom from the soil of their estrangement. Dubbed "muckraking" by Teddy Roosevelt in 1906, a swelling torrent of critical, questioning, reform-minded publicity, largely assuming the form of investigative journalism, began to reshape the discourse of public life.[18]

Driven by an escalating concern over corporate and governmental corruption, muckraking was a moral indictment of big business, an assault against the "barbarians . . . from above" who were reigning over American social and economic life. Running through the publicists' writings was a gnawing concern for the increasingly "limited opportunities" of the traditional middle class and the declining status of their citizenship in a society where economic centralization and the buying and selling of political influence were becoming the rule. As Upton Sinclair summarized it in 1908:

> See, we are just like Rome. Our legislatures are corrupt; our politicians are unprincipled; our rich men are ambitious and unscrupulous. Our newspapers have been purchased and gagged; our colleges have been bribed; our churches have been cowed. Our masses are sinking into degradation and misery; our ruling classes are becoming wanton and cynical.[19]

A critique of excessive corporate power, rampant political corruption, and a bitter sense of middle-class injury constituted the fundamental ingredients of "muckrake" journalism. A mercenary business system and its political henchmen were seen as jeopardizing the "common good" in every corner of American life. "[P]olitics is business," wrote Lincoln Steffens in 1904. "That's what's the matter with it. That's what's the matter with everything—art, literature, religion, journalism, law, medicine—they're all business. . . . The commercial spirit is the spirit of profit not patriotism; of trade and dickering, not principle."[20]

At the heart of this argument lay a venerable conception of the public and a desire "to apply the standards of public life" to the distended behemoth of big business.[21]

This idea of the public was, to a great extent, rooted in eighteenth-century Enlightenment thought. Born amid the vitality of the marketplace, this decidedly middle-class public came to the fore by waging a social, intellectual, and political offensive against the outmoded truths of the ancien regime—truths buttressed by blind faith and brute force. Assuming reason to be the common birthright of humanity and the critical examination of knowable facts to be the natural instrument of truth, this public, as described by the philosopher Jürgen Habermas, was premised on the paradigm of informed, literate men, engaged with one another in an ongoing process of "critical-rational" debate.[22]

•   •   •

Such a vision was eloquently expressed by Thomas Jefferson in his second inaugural address, when he declared that the "diffusion of information and the arraignment of all abuses at the bar of public reason, should be the creed of our political faith—the text of civil instruction." Intrinsic, here, was the assumption that democracy depended on the existence of a literate middle-class public, apprised of current events, continually engaged in discussion.

In many ways the Progressive faith in publicity was heir to this conception of a conversant democratic public. Following the teachings of the Enlightenment, many publicists understood factual disclosure to be a technique for revealing new and urgent realities. Through the laying out of material facts and the publishing of information, the public would become activated. The truth of rife corruption, the facts of economic brutality, the recital of noxious living conditions—in and of themselves—would animate the public and ignite a movement for social reform.

Progressive journalism, at its core, was committed to breaking the willful secrecy of power by providing fact-filled exposés of institutional corruption and greed. "From whatever point of view the trust problem is considered," wrote Progressive economist Henry C. Adams in 1902, "publicity stands as the first step to its solution."[23] Over the first decade of the twentieth century, this liberal and materialist faith in the publicity of facts gave rise to an unprecedented blizzard of social documentation. Progressive intellectuals, social scientists, settlement-house workers, and others produced surveys, one after another, to record those social facts that, they believed, embodied a tangible argument for reform. Hull House "Maps and Papers"; W. E. B. DuBois's pioneering study, *The Philadelphia Negro;* Paul Kellogg's *Pittsburgh Survey;* and numerous other studies of the period were each motivated by a conviction that publicized facts were instruments of social transformation, energizing food for the public mind.

"There is only one sure basis of social reform and that is Truth," declared DuBois and Granville Dill in *The Negro Artisan;* a "careful detailed knowledge of the essential facts of each social problem," they reasoned, will provide a "logical starting place for reform and uplift." Ray Stannard Baker, another leading publicist of the period, recalled some years later that "facts piled up to the point of dry certitude, was what the American people then needed and wanted."[24] For many in this generation of reformers, the instrument of the fact was tantamount to the discovery of light. "There is something majestic about a fact," waxed Mary Simkhovitch of the Greenwich House settlement in New York City. "Contact with facts, forcibly perceived, made a never forgotten dent on our plastic minds."[25] Through surveys and writings, these people sought to activate a public outcry on behalf of social order and reform, though it must be added that "reform," in large measure, was but a shorthand for accountability to the concerns of middle-class Americans, particularly their worries about "urban problems—labor and social welfare, municipal reform, the interests of the consumer."[26]

■   ■   ■   ■   ■

Wedged against this Enlightenment belief in the natural power of facts, in the inherent ability of facts to promote and quicken public debate, however, Progressive publicity was touched, at the same time, by different conceptions of who the public was and what made it tick. This distinctly more modern vision of the public was being forged at the juncture of social developments that were dramatically reshaping the terrain of American culture in the years surrounding the fin de siècle.

First, the middle-class public that provided an audience for the muckrakers was significantly different from the eighteenth-century public that had made the American revolution. If the middle-class public of the late eighteenth century had actualized itself—economically and politically—amid the democratic energies of the marketplace, the public of the late nineteenth century was marked by its near-religious commitment to privacy.

Assailed by feelings of economic and social insecurity and fearful of the alien and "dangerous" elements that seemed to govern life in city streets, this middle class had retreated from its formerly activist role and had retired to a more insular style of existence, living in staid neighborhoods, protected from the fearsome energies of the street. From the privileged haven of their firesides, thoughts that wandered toward the poorer sections of town "called up a vague and alarming picture . . . something strange and alien: a vast crowded area, a foreign city within our own."[27]

Against these fears, "the home" was solemnized as a necessary "refuge from the world," a "defense against" the "hostile powers" of society at large. This ardent embrace of seclusion is richly expressed in a tribute to "The Home" that appeared in *Godey's Ladies Book* in February 1894.

> [T]here is an instinctive feeling in the heart of man that society is not friendly to the development of those impulses and emotions upon which his happiness as an individual depends. He is perpetually called upon to spend his energies, no suggestion is made that he should conserve them. And so, looking about for some place in which to recuperate his exhausted forces, he conceived the idea of erecting a little bulwark against the outside world, in which those matters personal to himself should be carried on privately and in quiet.[28]

Though a hundred years earlier, the public had defined "the pursuit of happiness" as something activated in the social realm, the *Godey's* article revealed a quest for happiness that had migrated anxiously to the private sphere. "Home," the article announced, is nothing less than "the ability to shut out what is inimical to us and to shut in all the influences that are harmonious and agreeable to ourselves."

Whereas social optimism, civic engagement, and a pristine faith in reason had been the birthmarks of the late-eighteenth-century public, individual anxiety, a sense of impending chaos, and guarded habits of insularity enveloped middle-class life a hundred years later. The geographic segregation of classes had reformulated the topography of the urban map, and the parlor had replaced the square as the locus of middle-class life. This was an increasingly privatized public, one that was experiencing "public life" from afar—as spectators.

If the physical environs of middle-class existence were becoming more detached, however, mental connections to the world at large were, simultaneously, breeding. Nourishing a trend toward middle-class spectatorship, a new and increasingly disembodied public sphere was being spawned by the dramatic growth of mass-circulation media between the early 1880s and the First World War.

It began with newspapers. As was the case in other pivotal industries, financial consolidation and technological innovation combined to alter the character and scale of big-city and small-town journalism. Newspapers, like nearly everything else, were becoming embroiled in giant enterprise.

> In circulations, in the number of pages per issue, and in volume of advertising, the great newspapers grew to sizes scarcely dreamed of before, while figures representing investments, costs, and revenues reached astonishing totals.[29]

The distributions of individual newspapers multiplied, and with the flowering of large newspaper chains—led by E. W. Scripps—people in a wide diversity of locales were being provided, on a daily basis, with congruous constructions of reality. Powerful commercial locomotives, newspapers and news chains—linked further by the expanding information network of the wire services—transported standardized news, information, and editorial perspectives through what was fast becoming a national media culture. Counterbalancing their growing material seclusion, middle-class readers were discovering incorporeal companionship as members of a more and more boundless newspaper audience. From the refuge of their middle-class homes, they were becoming part of a virtual reading public, more sweeping and synoptic than anything that had preceded it.

Shortly, middle-class magazines began to contribute to this trend. Prior to their modern metamorphosis, middle-class magazines had been relatively expensive (thirty-five cents) and their circulations small. A cloistered tone and genteel subject matter mirrored the insularity of their readers' lives. "Magazines of the old school," wrote Fredrick Lewis Allen, were "highly respectable publications which ladies and gentlemen liked to display on their library tables." These magazines served to reinforce the "interests of culture—a culture daintily remote from the crass concerns of everyday life."[30] The encomium to "The Home" (in *Godey's Ladies Book*) is but one vivid example of this tendency.

By the early 1890s, however, trends that had overhauled newspapers began to transfigure magazines as well. Changes in "the art of printing—glazed paper made from wood pulp, much cheaper than rag-paper, and an advance in photography followed by improvements in the art of printing photographs," permitted the inexpensive production of opulent magazines. Meanwhile modern corporate organizations, including, to some extent, capitalization by newspaper chains, propelled mass, national magazine circulation.[31]

Starting with *McClure's* and *Munsey's Magazine*—then *Hampton's, Everybody's, Colliers, Cosmopolitan, Scribner's,* and *The American Magazine*—a new generation of magazines began to emerge. With cover prices of ten to fifteen cents, circulations grew exponentially. If 50,000 people was considered an enormous readership prior to 1890, between 1900 and 1912, some magazine circulations soared to 1 million.[32]

Yet the ability to assemble huge audiences was not merely an outcome of financial or technical innovation. The capacity to draw a crowd was also grounded in a new journalistic idiom that was breezy, worldly, and—following yellow journalism's lead—sensationalistic. These were flamboyant journals, recalled Mark Sullivan; they were designed to entertain a home-centered audience with titillating stories and pictures of the world at large. Photographs were employed with "liberal extravagance," and features provided gossip about "actresses or queens, or persons deemed socially important."[33] Another important piece of the new magazines' entertainment formula was "muckrake" journalism.

With huge middle-class readerships, the magazines provided a far-reaching platform for the dissemination of progressive publicity, yet the stylistic ambience of these media and the besieged, anxious sensibilities of their readership began to alter the assumptions of that publicity. Here, in mass magazines and newspapers, an Enlightenment faith in the "diffusion of information" before the "bar of public reason" was being shadowed closely by another, more modern, media genre: sensational exposés: tawdry tales of corporate greed, municipal depravity, and moral decay. A significant turn had been taken. For those of us who have been flooded by a cascade of "tabloid television," a now familiar media milieu was in the process of being born.

This journalistic shift can be witnessed on a number of fronts. By the early 1890s, New York City police reporter Jacob Riis was making expressive contributions to a journalism that was simultaneously reformist and sensationalist. His livid reports on ghetto street gangs in New York, for example, traversed a shaky tightrope between fact-based social probe and unabashed emotional appeal.

> The gang is the ripe fruit of tenement-house growth. . . . The tenement received and nursed the seed. The intensity of the American temper stood sponsor to the murderer. . . . New York's tough represents the essence of reaction against the old and the new oppression, nursed in the rank soil of its slums. Its gangs are made up of the American-born sons of English, Irish, and German parents. They reflect exactly the conditions of the tenements from which they sprang. Murder is as congenital to Cherry Street or Battle Row, as quiet and order to Murray Hill. The "assimilation" of Europe's oppressed hordes, upon which our Fourth of July orators are fond of dwelling, is perfect. The product is our own.
>
> Such is the genesis of New York's gangs. Their history is not so easily written. It would embrace the largest share of our city's criminal history for two generations back, every page of it dyed red with blood.[34]

Edwin Markham's poem, "The Man with a Hoe," provides another eloquent case in point. Published in the *San Francisco Examiner,* initially in 1899, it was printed and reprinted, cutting "eastward across the continent like a contagion."[35] A grim meditation on the human price of industrialization, Markham's poem pondered the "slow but awful degradation" of the working class; it was a powerful petition to the conscience of the nation. In contrast to social surveys that sought to provide a middle-class public with the "essential facts of each social problem," "The Man with a Hoe" was a Gothic dirge, posing visions of neglectful "masters, lords and rulers in all lands" against the "dread shape" of a human being "bowed by the weight of centuries." Evoking the teachings of Genesis and searching for God's image in this "monstrous thing," Markham found, instead, the unmistakable footprints of devastation and evil, a man cut off from "the light . . . the music . . . and the dream."

Who made him dead to rapture and despair,
A thing that grieves not and that never hopes,
Stolid and stunned, a brother to the ox?
Who loosened and let down this brutal jaw?
Whose was the hand that slanted back this brow?
Whose breath blew out the light within this brain?

Like Mary Shelley's hideous creature in *Frankenstein*—though clearly less intelligent—the "Hoe-man" was a misbegotten and dehumanized brute, propelled toward monstrosity by the heedlessness of his creators.

O masters, lords and rulers in all lands,
Is this the handiwork you give to God,
This monstrous thing distorted and soul-quencht?
How will you ever straighten up this shape;
Touch it again with immortality;
Give back the upward looking and the light;
Rebuild in it the music and the dream;
Make right the immemorial infamies,
Perfidious wrongs, immedicable woes?

O masters, lords and rulers in all lands,
How will the future reckon with this Man?
How answer his brute question in that hour
When whirlwinds of rebellion shake all shores?
How will it be with kingdoms and with kings—
With those who shaped him to the thing he is—
When this dumb Terror shall rise to judge the world,
After the silence of the centuries?[36]

A "dumb Terror" rising "to judge the world," Markham's human beast of burden was at once a wretched victim and a hideous "prophecy." More than a paradigmatic case study or an unambiguous social fact, he was an unveiled expression of the profound psychological ambivalence toward the urban poor that haunted the minds of his middle-class readers.

Elsewhere in the mass magazines, lurid and moralistic tones carried readers' imaginations into smoke-filled backrooms of politics,

Mass magazines in the first decades of the twentieth century reflected the contra-dictions of the Progressive reform movement. In its racist characterization of African Americans, Irish, Jews, and Italians, this cover of a 1913 "Pro-Suffrage Number" of *Life* magazine combined liberal reform-mindedness with middle-class foreboding about an urban, largely foreign, population that possessed the rights of democratic citizenship. COURTESY ANDREW MATTSON

sequestered board rooms of corporations, and perilous alleyways of urban slums. Gruesome tales of "white slavery" added a pornographic twist to the growing practice of muckrake sensationalism. Novels and book-length exposés also rolled off the presses, their writing style and ominous-sounding titles (*The Octopus, The Jungle, The Shame of the Cities*) further testifying to the growing fascination with melodramatic narrative.

Intrinsic to nearly all such exposés lay the notion of a violated middle-class public, overwhelmed by greed, decent but dispirited, desperately in need of deliverance. Listen:

> The politicians were struggling for nothing, apparently, but the offices and the graft to which they hoped to be elected. The corporations, over them all, were apparently using them all to keep themselves above the laws by owning the sources and the agents of the law. And the people? the "dear people"? In not one of the private conversations or secret caucuses of the politicians, do I remember hearing the people mentioned except in the way that the directors of a "wildcat" mining company might speak of the prospective shareholders whom they had yet to induce to buy stock.[37]

Shortly into the new century, the river of muckrake publicity had become torrential. The exposure of social ills was, itself, evolving into a profitable industry. "Exposure," observed George W. Alger in the *Atlantic Monthly* in 1907, had become "the typical current literature of our daily life."

> They expose in countless pages the sordid and depressing rottenness of our politics; the hopeless apathy of our good citizens; the remorseless corruption of our great financiers and business men, who are bribing our legislatures, swindling the public with fraudulent stock schemes, adulterating our food, speculating with trust funds, combining in the great monopolies to oppress and destroy small competitors. They show us our social sore spots, like the three cheerful friends of Job. They show us the growth of business "graft," the gangrene of personal dishonesty among an honorable people, the

oppressing increase in the number of bribe-takers and bribe-givers. They tell us of the riotous extravagance of the rich, and the growth of poverty. . . . The achievement of the constructive elements of society has been neglected to give space to these spicy stories of graft and greed.[38]

At the end of the first decade of this century, the success of progressive publicity was considerable, but it was also double-edged. On the one hand, the enormous growth of reform-minded journalism and of its readership revealed the unprecedented power of the mass media as a tool for assembling the public nationally around a variety of social concerns. It was this public that brought a generation of Progressive politicians into office, locally and nationally, in the years between 1900 and 1914. It was this public that was stirring some businessmen to question customary policies of secrecy.

On the other hand, the phenomenal flowering of Progressive publicity revealed something else, something that—in the long run—would pose hard questions concerning the limitations of democracy in twentieth-century America. Behind the sensationalization of Progressive publicity lay signs that the public had changed in consequential ways. If the public had once been active in shaping the political life and social intercourse of the nation, the new public was defined increasingly by its vulnerable condition of isolation and spectatorship. Readers of mass-circulation newspapers and magazines were witnesses to society, no longer within the public square, but from the sanctuary of their parlors.

Unable to imagine any longer the existence of a powerful and socially engaged public, Progressive writers began to wander from a faith in the lucid powers of fact and public reason. In the absence of a participatory public sphere, morality plays, pitting good against evil, stories imbued with what Lincoln Steffens would describe as a tone of "astonishment, shame, and patriotic indignation," appeared to touch a spectator-audience more effectively than mere factual recitations of social conditions. Here, at the fateful crossroads joining mass-circulation journalism with the atomized and anxious middle-class readership, a conception of truth predicated on rational public discourse encountered another manner of truth, one confirmed—more and more—by graphic overtures to private emotion. Pledges of facticity continued, but the practices of "civil instruction" were beginning to be altered.

4

Controlling Chaos

BY 1914, PROGRESSIVISM STOOD at a fateful juncture. The movement for reform was now in its third decade, and what had begun as agitation by outsiders had left an indelible mark on mainstream American political life. Journalists, literati, politicians, clergymen, professionals, even some whose allegiances lay conspicuously on the side of business, were convinced that private enterprises needed to become more responsive to public concerns.

While this vast and varied assembly continued to call for business reform, however, another worry was coming to dominate their distinctly middle-class imaginations. Amid a burgeoning of militant working-class politics at home and abroad, fears of revolt from below began to overshadow the problem of corporate greed. "Whirlwinds of rebellion," prophesied fifteen years earlier in "The Man with the Hoe," seemed dangerously near at hand.

These feelings of disquiet left their imprint on a wide range of American biographies. At first glance, Walter Lippmann, a prominent Progressive intellectual, and Ivy Lee, a journalist who became one of America's premier corporate public relations men, might appear to have had little in common. Yet the lives of both were shaped by the anxieties of this defining historical moment.

Lippmann's life, in a number of its details, illustrates one important trajectory of this period. Before 1910, while a student at Harvard, he had engaged in stirring exchanges with William James and was inspired by the philosopher's impious approach to the problem of truth. As a student, Lippmann was also rallied by urgent social problems of the day, questions like those posed by Lincoln Steffens in his 1903 *McClure's* exposé of moral decay in St. Louis. *"Will the people rule? Is democracy possible?"* Steffens had asked. Lippmann would spend a considerable portion of his life addressing the implications of these questions.

Graduating from college in 1910, Lippmann joined the ranks of Progressive publicists as a writer of muckraking pieces for *Everybody's* magazine under the tutelage of Steffens himself. Shortly thereafter, he joined the Socialist Party, a "rational" choice pursued by numerous reform-minded intellectuals of the day.

By 1914, however, Lippmann had abandoned his flirtation with socialist convictions. The rift was evident when, during that year, he published the widely hailed *Drift and Mastery*—a book that provoked Theodore Roosevelt to dub Lippmann "the most brilliant man of his age."[1] Within the pages of this book, the precocious twenty-five-year-old—already a confidant of President Wilson—reflected on a nation in peril.

While Lippmann continued to grapple with persistent patterns of corporate excess, visions of impending social chaos and upheaval—a revolt of the masses—had begun to modulate these concerns. Images of *the people ruling* were, for Lippmann, assuming an air of menace. Ongoing middle-class hostility toward big business—once understood as a constructive catalyst for social reform—had now become, to Lippmann's increasingly conservative mind, an inadvertent stimulus of social disintegration. As attacks on the practices of big business mounted and an increasingly militant working-class movement challenged the very concept of privately held wealth, Lippmann became more and more alarmed.[2]

Whatever corporate leaders did, he observed distressfully, their intentions and activities were being chased by a relentless chorus of suspicion. The pursuit of profit itself was colored by a taint of malevolence. In a country once "notorious for its worship of success," Lippmann wrote, public disfavor was being heaped "savagely upon those who had achieved it."[3]

In the pages of *Drift and Mastery,* Lippmann held the muckraking press—which had built circulations by plumbing the depths of middle-class estrangement—largely responsible for this hazardous turn of events. The impact of the "popular press of America," he wrote, "is enormous, and for years it has been filled with 'probes' and 'amazing revelations.'" Though he admitted the need for business and government to embrace "new standards" of behavior, he thought that a lurid mass culture of inquest and exposé had turned reckless. With one eye on reform and the other aimed at the escalating perils in the street, Lippmann concluded that the popular media of "exposure" and their countless tales of "wrongdoing" were contributing to an unwholesome atmosphere of social unrest that threatened to spin out of control.

"There is in America today," he remarked uneasily, "a distinct prejudice in favor of those who make the accusations." While Lippmann acknowledged that corporate improprieties persisted, he saw the growing whirl of accusation as a collective psychological malady, a dangerous condition of paranoia, that, unless checked, posed a greater danger to society than the excesses of wealth.

In urban slums and industrial precincts, Lippmann observed, the aliens were growing restless. Society, loosened from a foundation of trust, was adrift.

> The sense of conspiracy and secret scheming which transpire is almost uncanny. "Big Business," and its ruthless tentacles, have become the material for the feverish fantasy of illiterate thousands thrown out of kilter by the rack and strain of modern life. It is possible to work yourself into a state where the world seems a conspiracy and your daily going is beset with an alert and tingling sense of labyrinthine evil. Everything askew—all the frictions of life are readily ascribed to a deliberate evil intelligence, and men like Morgan and Rockefeller take on attributes of omnipotence, that ten minutes of cold sanity would reduce to a barbarous myth.[4]

Lippmann's concerns mirrored those that had been aired by eminent Progressive politicians for some years. President Theodore Roosevelt, for example, saw the public fury engendered by unregulated corporations as carrying America toward the brink of chaos. "Corporation cunning," the president lamented in an interview with the *New Haven Register* in 1909, "has developed faster than the laws of nation and State. Corporations have found ways to steal long before we have found that they were susceptible of punishment for theft. Sooner or later, unless there is a readjustment, there will come a riotous wicked, murderous day of atonement. If it is not by sword and powder and blood, it must come by peaceful compromise. These fools in Wall Street think they can go on forever! They can't!"

If blind arrogance among corporate leaders needed to be thwarted, Roosevelt's platform for averting social disorder reached beyond the simple regulation of business. "Muckraking" (as he contemptuously christened the new investigative journalism in 1906) and a public culture of exposé were also contributing to a climate of disorder, feeding the flames of insurrection. They, too, were in need of restraint.

Here the president drew critical distinctions. Moralistic publicity that highlighted struggles of good versus evil was, to Roosevelt, more than acceptable. Spotlighting anomalous cases of misconduct, he believed, was a valid and responsible enterprise. Journalism that challenged the equity of the business system itself, however, was toying with the forces of revolt.

> So far as this movement of agitation throughout the country takes the form of a fierce discontent with evil, of a determination to punish the authors of evil, whether in industry or politics, the feeling is to be heartily welcomed as a sign of healthy life.
>
> If, on the other hand, it turns into a mere crusade of appetite against appetite, of a contest between the brutal greed of the "have-nots" and the brutal greed of the "haves," then it has no significance for good, but only for evil. If it seeks to establish a line of cleavage, not along the line which divides good men from bad, but along that other line . . . which divides those who are well off from those who are less well off, then it will be fraught with immeasurable harm to the body politic.[5]

By 1914, the dread of social chaos had restructured the priorities of mainstream progressivism. A conservative "search for order," as historian Robert Wiebe has defined it, was eclipsing once-revered ideals of popular democracy. Fearful of the "illiterate thousands thrown out of kilter by the rack and strain of modern life" and unnerved by the extent to which a publicity of exposure was engendering an atmosphere of social drift, Progressives looked for new strategies that might be employed to contain this impending social crisis. In this quest, a growing number turned toward the new ideas and techniques of the social sciences, hoping to discover foolproof instruments for diagnosing social problems and achieving social stability.

For the first generation of twentieth-century reformers, the scientific gathering of empirical data—social surveys—had been seen as a mighty instrument of social improvement. Social surveys, they had believed, would provide the public with a social agenda for the future. To Lippmann and a growing number of others, however, the social sciences appealed less in their ability to create an informed public and more in their promise to help establish social control.

As Lippmann explained in *Drift and Mastery,* in a society plagued by a mounting ethos of disarray, order required the application of the "discipline of science" to democracy. Social engineers, social scientists, armed with their emerging expertise, would provide the modern state with a foundation upon which a new stability might be realized.[6] Social improvement, Lippmann concluded, would be the fruit of applied social science more than of mobilized public outrage. Against mythical phantasms of an approaching apocalypse, novel strategies of social management and the conviction that a technical elite might be able to engineer social order were becoming increasingly attractive. The issue of group dynamics and the attempt to identify the objective underpinnings of subjective life were shaping the discourse of social analysis.

To some extent, this instrumental association between social science and social management had been brewing since the late nineteenth century. Accompanying a democratic current of social analysis that sought to educate the public at large, another—more cabalistic—tradition of social-scientific thought was emerging, one that saw the study of society as a tool by which a technocratic elite could help serve the interests of vested power.

A pivotal figure in this tendency was the French social psychologist Gustave Le Bon. Le Bon's 1895 book, *The Crowd: A Study of the Popular Mind,* soon became a Bible to a growing body of people who were worried by a climate of popular unrest. Translated into English in 1896 and quickly appearing in a number of other languages, *The Crowd* had a resounding impact on an entire generation of social thought.

Though Le Bon was a "scientist," said his biographer Robert Nye, his "reading public probably rivalled that of many contemporary novelists."[7] His writing style was clear and compelling, and his tone of social emergency engaged the multiplying anxieties of the middle classes through much of the industrialized world. Among his early readers was Theodore Roosevelt, who was deeply affected by Le Bon's writings. Throughout his presidency—Roosevelt would acknowledge when the two finally met (at Roosevelt's insistence) in June 1914— he had kept the Frenchman's writings always near at hand.

Le Bon's book spoke to the deep fears of a world in which the liberal ideal of natural rights had moved beyond its roots in middle-class life and had given rise to more inclusive conceptions of popular democracy. The Paris Commune of 1870 and the spread of socialist ideas among the Parisian working class were terrifying examples of this ominous historic current.

Successfully suppressed throughout much of history, Le Bon maintained, "the opinion of the masses" was now overtaking the historical stage. "To-day," he lamented, "the voice of the masses has

Gustave Le Bon, seated at a table: "The crowd is always intellectually inferior to the isolated individual." THE BETTMANN ARCHIVE

become preponderant. . . . The destinies of nations are elaborated at present in the heart of the masses, and no longer in the councils of princes." Not an anomaly, the revolt from below was characteristic of a "transitional" period in which old hierarchical structures of power had been eroded by Enlightenment principles of democracy, while modern techniques of scientific knowledge had not yet uncovered ways to establish social order.

"The entry of the popular classes into political life," Le Bon wrote, "is one of the most striking characteristics of our epoch of transition."

> The masses are founding syndicates before which the authorities capitulate one after the other; they are also founding labour unions, which in spite of all economic laws tend to regulate the conditions of labour and wages.
>
> To-day the claims of the masses are becoming more and more sharply defined, and amount to nothing less than a determination to destroy utterly society as it now exists, with a view to making it hark back to that primitive communism which was the normal condition of all human groups before the dawn of civilization.
>
> The divine right of the masses is about to replace the divine right of kings.

Framing Le Bon's dread of the masses lay his belief that—unlike the revolutionary middle-class "public" that had come to the fore in the eighteenth century—the crowd was "little adapted to reasoning." Le Bon argued that individuals of the middle class were still defined by rational powers of "conscious personality," but the masses—who reveal their identity only within the tinderbox of the crowd—were propelled solely by their passions. If middle-class individuals were capable of reflection, Le Bon ventured, the crowd was only able to react.

> It is only by obtaining some sort of insight into the psychology of crowds that it can be understood how slight is the action upon them of laws and institutions, how powerless they are to hold any opinions other than those which are imposed

upon them, and that it is not with rules based on theories of pure equity that they are to be led, but by seeking what produces an impression on them, and what seduces them.[8]

Years later, such ideas about the "psychology of crowds" would have a profound influence on evolving strategies of publicity. Initially, Le Bon's book served to bear out—under the banner of science—middle-class fears of imminent popular insurrection. *The Crowd,* in validating the need for social control, also provided a theoretical justification for American concerns as encountered in the thought of Roosevelt and Lippmann.

How to achieve social control, however, was a complicated issue. The dramatic spread of Progressive publicity and the growth of a mass audience that was consuming its revelations pointed simultaneously in two different directions.

On the level of its content, this publicity had alerted an enormous number of people to the excesses of wealth, the corruptions of politics, and the desolation of the urban poor. It had, to the detriment of business interests, consolidated a public around the banner of reform and had contributed to the atmosphere of instability that so worried Roosevelt and Lippmann.

Yet on another—perhaps more important—level, the spread and influence of muckraking had also harbored suggestions about how public opinion might be more effectively managed. With the emergence of the mass media as a connective tissue of modern life, things were happening to the texture and dissemination of information that were in the process of altering the physics of perception, changing the ways that people saw, experienced, and understood the material world and their place within it.

While Le Bon's social psychology furnished a scientistic justification for middle-class daydreams of social mastery, it was another Frenchman—a close friend of Le Bon named Gabriel Tarde—who provided powerful suggestions as to how social mastery might indeed be accomplished. Le Bon's treatise concentrated, for the most part, on the gnawing problem of the crowd. In response, Tarde—whose writings are barely known today, but who was, at the time, one of the world's preeminent social scientists—focused on *"the public."*

If some were terrified by the exposés of the muckraking press, Tarde's analysis reached beneath the surface to grasp the significance of the growth of a national and international media apparatus, new kinds of newspapers and magazines, and a different order of audience. Rejecting Le Bon's notion that "the voice of the masses has become preponderant," Tarde proclaimed in 1901 that the crowd, in fact, was a "social group of the past." It is *the public*—an entity that functions according to a different set of laws than the crowd—that constitutes "the social group of the future."

Elaborating on this idea, Tarde constructed a prophetic argument, the implications of which would be of enormous consequence to the field of public relations as it arose and expanded across the terrain of twentieth-century life. Unlike the public of the eighteenth century, which actualized itself in face-to-face conversation and inhabited the material locale of the marketplace, the *modern public* was, Tarde asserted, an essentially "spiritual collectivity, a dispersion of individuals who are physically separated and whose cohesion is entirely mental."[9]

Writing at a moment when the growth of modern media industries—wedded, internationally, by transoceanic telegraph wires—was quickening, Tarde's work delineated a world in which the material foundations of human perception were changing in consequential ways. People's opinions and conversations, he reported, were no longer grounded in the immediacy of their lives. If the public and its conversations had once emanated from a distinct material environment—the marketplace, for example—the new public that Tarde spied at the fin de siècle had become considerably more abstract, disembodied.

The market was less and less a particular place, but had become an increasingly boundless phenomenon, coextensive with society itself, held together by modern webs of transportation and communication. Within this far-reaching market, the public no longer gathered in a physical sense. Its connections to society were essentially metaphysical, more and more individualized.

Occupying a "purely spiritual" milieu of mental cohesion, Tarde explained, the public was now being assembled as a scattered, yet connected, collection of newspaper readers. "The invention of printing," he noted, "has caused a very different public to appear, one which never ceases to grow and whose indefinite extension is one of the most clearly marked traits of our period." If conversations once emanated from the public outward, Tarde observed, today public conversation is shaped by the expanding media apparatus.

> The press unifies and invigorates conversations. . . . Every morning the papers give their publics the conversations of the day. . . . This increasing similarity of simultaneous conversations in an ever more vast geographic domain is one of the most important characteristics of our time.[10]

In their ability to accomplish a "mutual penetration of hearts and minds," Tarde argued, modern newspapers embodied a far-reaching network by which human thought and perception were in the process of becoming standardized.

> [N]ewspapers have transformed . . . unified in space and diversified in time the conversations of individuals," he wrote, adding that "even those who do not read papers but who, talking to those who do, are forced to follow the groove of their borrowed thoughts. One pen suffices to set off a million tongues.[11]

Along these intangible yet dynamic grooves of thought, Tarde beheld compelling hints of a more governable future. The emerging mass media, their universal presence, their ability to transport "thought across distance," provided channels—if properly employed—through which consciousness might be managed, a chaotic world brought to order.

Modern journalism—and the new, incorporeal public it was assembling—represented, in Tarde's view, the culmination of an evolutionary process that was guiding society toward greater and greater cohesion. Assuming a Darwinian inflection, Tarde portrayed the newspaper as the centerpiece of a higher order of communication, one that would, in time, erase the conflicts that had marked human interaction throughout history. "The newspaper," Tarde concluded, was completing "the age-old work that conversation began, that correspondence extended, but that always remained in a state of sparse and scattered outline—the fusion of personal opinions into local opinions, and this into national and world opinion, the grandiose unification of the public mind."[12]

If Le Bon saw the mischievous and destructive "crowd" as the propelling force of contemporary life, Tarde was considerably more sanguine regarding the possibility of social order. Tarde was convinced that the vast, spiritual unity of an intrinsically malleable public would, in the end, supersede the crowd as the determining force of modern history.

Tarde saw the crowd as the "social group of the past" because "[w]hatever its form . . . it is incapable of extension beyond a limited area." The public, on the other hand, "can extend indefinitely, and since its particular life becomes more intense as it extends, one cannot deny that it is the social group of the future."[13]

Tarde was not alone in this perception; his outlook on press and public reflected the spirit and condition of modernity. A decade earlier, in his paradigmatic study of *Gemeinschaft und Gesellschaft (Community and Society)*, the German sociologist Ferdinand Tönnies had offered a similar rendering of his rapidly changing world. Within that world, Tönnies concluded, the newspaper had become an unprecedented machinery for the manufacture and marketing of public opinion, a channel through which a particular faction could "present its own will as the rational general will."

"In this form of communication," he wrote "judgments and opinion are wrapped up like grocers' goods and offered for consumption in their objective reality." "Objective reality" had assumed the quality of merchandise, it was being "prepared and offered to our generation in the most perfect manner by the newspapers, which make possible the quickest production, multiplication, and distribution of facts and thoughts, just as the hotel kitchen provides food and drink in every conceivable form and quantity."

As did Tarde, Tönnies apprehended some of the ways that newspapers had significantly changed as implements of power. While eighteenth-century newspapers and pamphlets had been revolutionary extensions of public discourse, the modern press had become an instrument of social order: " 'making' and 'working upon' public opinion, . . . determining and . . . changing it." Mindfully employed,

Tönnies contended, the press could shape and control public discourse in ways that surpassed even the coercive powers of the state.

> [T]he press is the real instrument ("organ") of public opinion, weapon and tool in the hands of those who know how to use it and have to use it. . . . It is comparable and, in some respects, superior to the material power which the states possess through their armies, their treasuries, and their bureaucratic civil service. Unlike those, the press is not confined within natural borders, but, in its tendencies and potentialities, it is definitely international, thus comparable to the power of a permanent or temporary alliance of states.

Closing his discussion of modern public opinion, Tönnies added that it was in the United States—"the most modern and Gesellschaft-like state"—that this evolution could be found in its most perfected form.[14]

As the new century unfolded, many other social scientists embraced this view of the modern public and its inherent susceptibility to mental regimentation. More than mere instruments of communication, the media were being seen as cognitive connecting points joining an extensive highway of perception. American social psychologist Edward A. Ross, for example, described the unfolding mass media as the basis of a prodigious "space-annihilating" apparatus, remarkably suited to placing the public mind in uniform.

> Presence is not essential to mass suggestion. Mental touch is no longer bound up with physical proximity. With the telegraph to collect and transmit the expressions and signs of the ruling mood, and the fast mail to hurry to the eager clutch of waiting thousands the still damp sheets of the morning daily, remote people are brought, as it were, into one another's presence. Through its organs the excited public is able to assail the individual with a mass of suggestion almost as vivid as if he actually stood in the midst of an immense crowd.
>
> . . . [O]ur space-annihilating devices make a shock well-nigh simultaneous. A vast public shares the same rage,

alarm, enthusiasm, or horror. Then, as each part of the mass becomes acquainted with the sentiment of the rest, the feeling is generalized and intensified. In the end the public swallows up the individuality of its members.[15]

British political theorist Graham Wallas—one of Lippmann's most influential teachers at Harvard—seconded Ross's lyricism regarding the possibility of managing the attitudes of a modern public. With the invention of the printing press in the mid-fifteenth century, Wallas asserted, it became "possible for intercommunication of Thought to take place without bodily presence." Now, in the twentieth century, "owing to the enormous distribution of printed and written matter," he declared, "Organized Thought has become typical."[16]

Even among those who didn't share an ardor for social engineering, this sense of a disembodied, increasingly malleable public was gaining prominence. Writing in the *Atlantic Monthly* in 1914, antimodern playwright and essayist Oswald W. Firkins fretted over the ways that new systems of communication had transformed "the world into a vast amphitheater," undermining conventional patterns of time, space, and public life. Human attention on a global scale, observed Firkins, was "now meshed in the coils of journalism and telegraphy, at practically the same moment." People were being drawn together as parts of a vast, transnational audience while encountering their world in increasingly individualized and abstract terms. Among a "vast body of spectators," people were processing common cultural experiences, while public life was becoming more and more fragmented.

The same effect that is visibly manifest in the audience at a play or concert, the packing of humanity in solid and uniform rows for the enjoyment of a common experience, is brought about in a less pictorial and obvious form by the simultaneous perusal of the newspaper and the magazine. We sit in a crowd by our own firesides.[17]

This revamped vision of the public—a pliant and "spiritual collectivity" bound together by the agency of newspapers—provided a suggestive counterpoint to the horrifying phantasm of the crowd. While antibusiness muckraking had clearly demonstrated that even a "spiritual collectivity" might prove menacing to the status quo, the notion of a media-made public proposed other possibilities as well.

If *the crowd* was marked by its physical presence and a congenital resistance to reason, a mass-mediated *public* might—if strategically approached—be reasoned with.

If *the crowd* was an assembly of people that threatened to take over the street at any moment, *the public* was something more hypothetical, made up of people who were separated from one another.

If *the crowd* defined itself through social action, the modern *public* was shaped by the more passive consumption of published information, of facts or things that sounded like facts.

If *the crowd* was perceived as dangerous, driven by irrational appetites, *the public*—as an audience of readers—seemed more receptive to ideas, to rationalization, to the allure of factual proof. Comprised of spectators, it was also seen as infinitely safer and more controllable. What the public saw, heard, and knew were all, according to this analysis, subject to the influences of editorial control. "The crowd may be stampeded into folly or crime by accidental leaders," Ross argued in 1908, but the "public can receive suggestions only through the columns of its journal, the editor of which is like the chairman of a mass-meeting, for no one can be heard without his recognition."[18]

■　　■　　■　　■　　■

Over the decade leading up to the First World War, nervous meditations on the public and the crowd left an appreciable mark on the direction of Progressive thought and discussion. Yet liberal reformers were not the only people touched by such reveries. Individuals loyal to the interests of business also began to react to the mounting climate of recrimination.

The degree to which such concerns filtered into the upper echelons of American big business during this period is, with few exceptions, questionable. A quick survey of the industrial strife that occurred during these years indicates that many corporate leaders continued to address their world with an attitude of hardened arrogance. Industrialists and financiers fought to bypass regulation, and even when antitrust legislation was enacted, corporate behavior remained, for the most part, unaffected. Rather than attempt to offset the indignation of society, corporate policy often appeared calculated to provoke it.

As assaults against big business persisted however, and the mass culture of exposé evolved, modern meditations on the public began to stoke the imaginations of people who wished to come to the defense of business. A new generation of middle-class conservatives—offspring of the Gilded Age who continued to espouse the gospel of wealth— also saw corporate postures of arrogance and secrecy as leading toward a dreadful and inevitable social conflagration.

One of these people was Ivy Lee, a still-green newspaper man who, in 1903, embarked on a career as one of America's first and most prominent, practitioners of corporate public relations. As it evolved, Lee's career integrated the urgency of Le Bon's apprehensions with Tarde's sense of imminent possibility.

The devoted son of a conservative Georgia minister, Lee was torn between a strong admiration for audacious captains of industry and a concern over the mounting social disturbances of early-twentieth-century life. Arriving in New York City, having graduated from Princeton in 1898, Lee immediately gravitated toward "persons who did things in a big way." He was fascinated by the daredevil action of Wall Street and spellbound by the intoxicating "clash of business personalities" that he witnessed there.[19]

At the same time, Lee was haunted by the historical nightmare that had been outlined by Le Bon. As Lee (along with a small cluster of other pioneers) inaugurated the field of public relations, it was this collision of sentiments—the divinity of private wealth and the danger of the crowd—that motivated him. When he approached businessmen with the offer of his services, the explosiveness of the social climate stood at the forefront of his sales pitch.

"There was a time," Lee cautioned a gathering of railroad executives in 1916, "when you thought that you were running a private business." In the face of widespread antibusiness sentiment and calls for regulation, he continued, such assumptions were obsolete.

[Y]ou suddenly find you are not running a private business, but running a business of which the public itself is taking complete supervision. The crowd is in the saddle, the people are on the job, and we must take consideration of that fact, whether we like it or not.

Using words filched (though unattributed) from Le Bon, Lee concluded that "The people now rule. We have substituted for the divine right of kings, the divine right of the multitude."[20] Given these circumstances, Lee argued that it was imperative for men of business to manufacture a commonality of interests between them and an often censorious public to establish a critical line of defense against the crowd. The successes of muckrake journalism and emerging intu-

Ivy L. Lee waiting to be called before the Federal Industrial Relations Commission to testify about his work for the Rockefellers following the Ludlow Massacre.
THE BETTMANN ARCHIVE

itions regarding the journalistic grooves of borrowed thought suggested to Lee and others a route by which that goal might hopefully be achieved.

Given that the public was increasingly being seen in terms of their status as readers of newspapers, it is not surprising that Lee—like most of the first generation of PR men—began his career as a newspaperman, a reporter for the *New York Journal,* the *New York Times,* and the *New York World.* He was familiar with the "inky avenues" through which the message of progressivism had traveled and he believed that the same roadways might be employed to promote the outlook of big business.

It is also remarkable the extent to which the first generation of PR men described their work using the Progressive idiom of their time. As many Progressives were gravitating toward techno-rational models of "expertise" and "engineering" in the quest to manage the chaos of industrial life, early public relations men also assumed a technocratic visage. Rev. Gerald Stanley Lee—a second cousin of Ivy Lee, whose thinking had a profound impact on the PR pioneer—defined the job of the public relations expert as that of a "news engineer."[21] The news engineer, he maintained, was a student of those techniques that "get news through to the public." Ivy Lee adopted an ex cathedra intonation as well, terming himself simply "a physician for corporate bodies."

Like the Progressive publicists, early public relations people surrounded themselves with a rhetoric of facticity. Public relations practitioners presented themselves primarily as dispensers of facts that would provide the public with the means to understand better the soundness of a corporation's policy or perspective.

This notion of a PR man as a candid dispenser of facts was assiduously cultivated by Lee. A demeanor of openness was constructed to counterbalance customary concerns over corporate secrecy. When he opened an office with his first partner, George Parker, they adopted the motto Accuracy, Authenticity, Interest and promised to "present only topics of real interest, phrased so as to attract the attention of both editors and readers—never sensational, never libelous, always accurate, always trustworthy, always readable." In an announcement distributed to city editors, they proclaimed:

This is not a secret press bureau. All our work is done in the open. We aim to supply news. This is not an advertising agency. . . . Our matter is accurate. Further details on any subject treated will be supplied promptly, and any editor will be assisted most cheerfully in verifying directly any statement of fact. . . . In brief, our plan is, frankly and openly, on behalf of business concerns and public institutions, to supply the press and the public of the United States prompt and accurate information concerning subjects which it is of value and interest to the public to know about.[22]

This decision to disseminate facts, however, did not yet reflect a fundamental change in business practice. Public relations had not yet arrived as an essential element of the management structure, and secrecy—in most contexts—continued to be the corporate norm.

When Lee's or others' services were obtained, it tended to be in response to an immediate and particularly troublesome crisis. At the beginning, public relations experts were generally called in to perform what today is called, "damage control." When Lee went to work for the Anthracite Coal Operators' Committee of Seven in the spring of 1906, for example, it was only in response to the bad press they had received four years earlier during a strike in the coal industry in Pennsylvania. In 1902, while coal operators held to a code of silence, union leaders had cultivated friendly relations with reporters. Within a favorable press climate, the miners had achieved many of their goals.

In 1906, as another strike threatened, the operators engaged Lee to befriend the press. At Lee's suggestion, the coal operators proclaimed an unaccustomed policy of full cooperation with the press:

The anthracite coal operators, realizing the general public interest in conditions in the mining regions, have arranged to supply the press with all possible information. Statements from the operators will be given to the newspapers through Ivy L. Lee. He will also answer inquiries on this subject and supply the press with all matter that it is possible to give out.[23]

These efforts bore positive results. Newspaper editors were flattered by this unusual display of openness, and the coal operators received better treatment in the press.

Lee's well-known work on behalf of the Rockefeller family, which commenced in 1914, was also initiated for damage control. In the early decades of the century, the Rockefeller name was widely despised in the United States. Historical experience, publicized in journalistic exposés by Henry Demerast Lloyd and Ida Tarbell, had befouled the public reputation of John D. Rockefeller and Standard Oil. None of this seemed to faze the old man, until the Ludlow Massacre of 1914, in which fourteen striking miners, miners' wives, and children were viciously slaughtered on behalf of Rockefeller mine interests in Colorado—the Colorado Iron and Fuel Company.

In the aftermath of the massacre, a firestorm of public outrage erupted and then, two weeks later, the U.S. Commission on Industrial Relations instituted the first in a series of hearings to inquire into the slaughter at Ludlow and to uncover the circumstances that had led to the grisly event. The Rockefeller family denied any involvement in the decision to send in militiamen, but as countervailing evidence began to surface, proving their complicity in the massacre, John D. Rockefeller, Jr., was convinced that something had to be done. Ivy Lee was hired by the Rockefeller family to "secure publicity for their views."[24]

Here, as elsewhere in the formative years of his career, Lee clad his activities in a camouflage of facticity. In a society in which "the fact," though often sensationalized, still held sway as the lingua franca for public communication, Lee's work following Ludlow consisted of producing a series of circulars entitled "Facts Concerning the Strike in Colorado for Industrial Freedom." Between June and September 1914, these nationally distributed broadsides came out every four to seven days. In an attempt to cultivate middle-class allies, the bulletins were sent to opinion leaders throughout the country: "public officials, editors, ministers, teachers, and prominent professional and business men." Though filled with calculated inaccuracies—Lee's dispatches, for example, routinely exaggerated the salaries received by union organizers—the bulletins were designed to simulate objective evidence, proving that the pillage at Ludlow was the work not of the mine operators and their armies, but of "well-paid agitators sent out by the union."[25]

One bulletin presented distorted documentation purporting to demonstrate that editorial sentiment in Colorado's newspapers was overwhelmingly against the strikers. Disregarded in this report was the fact that those editors who were surveyed all worked for papers run by the coal companies.[26]

Another bulletin offered an authentically couched report from Helen Grenfell, identified simply as the "Vice-president of the Law and Order League of Colorado." Her apparently firsthand account certified that the battle at Ludlow was initiated by the strikers and that fires that engulfed the miners' tent colony were the accidental result of an "overturned stove or an explosion." Unmentioned in the report were the facts that Grenfell was not, in fact, an eyewitness to events at Ludlow and that she was the wife of a railroad official whose company profited from carrying Colorado coal.

Never one to shy away from juicy denunciations, another of Lee's bulletins claimed that "Mother" Jones, an eighty-two-year-old union organizer, was "a prostitute and the keeper of a house of prostitution."[27]

Close beneath the surface of these "facts," Lee's public relations work reflected a newly emerging variation on the theme that "truth happens to an idea." Repeated and dispersed along the grooves of borrowed thought, something asserted might become a fact, regardless of its connection to actual events.

Lee's working definition of truth and its inherent subterfuge came to light in January 1915, when he was called to testify before the U.S. Commission on Industrial Relations that was conducting hearings on the carnage at Ludlow. Questioned directly by the commission's chairman, Frank P. Walsh, Lee's remarkably frank responses provide a lucid picture of early corporate public relations activities and the characteristic cynicism with which they were most regularly pursued.

Q: Mr. Rockefeller had told you to be sure and get the truth?

A: Yes.

Q: How did you go about it?

A: By the truth, Mr. Chairman, I mean the truth about the operators' case. What I was to do was to advise and get their case into proper shape for them.

Q: You got your information entirely from them, then?

A: Yes.

Q: When they gave you newspaper clippings purporting to tell certain facts, did you ask them whether they knew they were true?

A: I did not.

Q: Did you ask them from what newspapers they were taken?

A: I really can't remember. I believe so, Mr. Chairman.

Q: Did you know that their attorney owned one of the newspapers . . . ?

A: No . . .

Q: You were out there to give the facts, the truth about the strike, the fullest publicity?

A: Yes, the truth as the operators saw it. I was there to help them state their case. I was to help them get these facts before the greatest number of people likely to read them.

Q: What personal effort did you ever make to ascertain that the facts given you by the operators were correct?

A: None whatever. I had no responsibility for the facts and no duty beyond compiling them and getting them into the best form for publicity work. I took the facts that Mr. Welborn gave me on his word. I have no reason to believe that word was not given in perfectly good faith.[28]

Implicit within Lee's testimony—striking in its tone of ethical detachment—were a set of what, today, have become commonplace presuppositions of public relations practice. If suitable facts could be assembled and then projected into the vast "amphitheater" of public consciousness, he reasoned, they could *become truth.*

Harnessed to the idea that *the truth is something that can be merchandised to the public* was an approach to the standards of factual evidence that represented a prophetic break from their Enlightenment roots. If Enlightenment faith had held that facts were instruments of knowledge by which informed citizens would rule their own destiny, now the "fact" was being marshaled, from both sides of the aisle, as a dramatic device, a conscious play to the balcony. The presumed connection between "the fact" and objective measures of evaluation was vanishing. The *fact* had surfaced as the *factoid.*

The contempt for truth that permeated his use of facts was something that Lee evidently could live with. The "divine right of the multitude" and the mounting dangers it posed required it. In 1916, speaking to the same group of railway executives to whom he had earlier invoked Le Bon's phantasm of the crowd, Lee confided:

> It is not the facts alone that strike the popular mind, but the way in which they take place and in which they are published that kindle the imagination. . . . Besides, What is a fact? The effort to state an absolute fact is simply an attempt to . . . give you my interpretation of the facts.[29]

In these words and in his career Lee demonstrated that the ambitious dream of Tarde, to engineer "the grandiose unification of the public mind," was in the process of finding a practical facilitator.

5

"Educate the Public!"

IF IVY LEE SUPPOSED that "the facts" he propagated would induce the public to see things through the Rockefellers' eyes, the response his press work received cast a dark shadow over this assumption. Lee's efforts did little to cleanse the reputation of the Rockefellers—or of Standard Oil—in the public mind. Even thirty years after the Rockefellers first hired Lee—in 1945—a high-level executive of Standard Oil of New Jersey (still a Rockefeller company) was forced to concede that the "history of Standard Oil in its relations with the public has not been too fortunate."

> Back in the days after the turn of the century, in the "trust busting" days of Teddy Roosevelt, Standard Oil was regarded as the prime example of a powerful, grasping, iniquitous business organization. . . . In the 30 years or more that followed, very little was done to offset this idea.[1]

On occasion Lee was able to convince John D. Rockefeller to partake in some minimal public relations schemes. In some of these instances, news coverage improved. An arranged golf match between the old man and a reporter for the *New York World,* for example, yielded a series of cheerful puff pieces presenting "the human side of the Rockefellers."[2] Such publicity stunts, however, misrepresent the normal cast of Lee's work—or of Rockefeller's public posture—during their long association. Standard Oil's policies toward the public changed little, and Lee was left, for the most part, with the formidable task of interpreting the Rockefeller family's oil and energy interests to an often critical press and public.

Lee's work for the Rockefellers embodied the limits faced by most of the journalists who crossed the line into corporate public relations work during the early years of the century. Unremitting corporate arrogance made their work extremely difficult. At best, their efforts bore mixed results. While some pliant publications provided an open forum for their pronouncements, countless others continued to portray corporations and their press agents in extremely negative terms.

Following the Ludlow Massacre, for example, despite the fact that Lee's press releases were intended to curry favorable news coverage for Rockefeller interests, the bulletins were widely dismissed as roguish prevarications.

"During the Colorado coal miners' strike," the *San Francisco Star* reported, "the Rockefellers hired Ivy L. Lee to present their side of the controversy to the public in a series of bulletins masquerading as 'Facts Concerning the Strike in Colorado for Industrial Freedom.' . . . The chief trouble with Ivy Lee," the article concluded, "is his disposition to wander from the fireside of truth. Testimony given before the Federal Commission on Industrial Relations—even that given by some of the mine owners—shows that Lee twisted facts, and invented some that he couldn't find outside of his imagination."[3]

The *Toledo Blade* reported that "throughout the Colorado troubles, pamphlets, circulars and letters fairly rained down upon the newspapers. It was a flood, a deluge. If it converted or influenced anyone, we have not heard of it. A broad reading of the American press indicated that the stuff went into the waste baskets throughout the country just as it did here. It swelled the postal receipts and added to the tonnage of houses that buy waste paper. But as for education, there was no result at all."[4]

Poet Carl Sandburg, writing in the *New York Call,* dismissed Lee as a "hired slanderer" and a "paid liar."[5] Meanwhile, in a two-part *Harper's Magazine* exposé presenting an itemized rebuttal of Lee's strike bulletins, the progressive journalist George Creel discredited the "entirely false view of the situation" presented in the pamphlets and accused Lee of being a would-be "poisoner of public opinion."[6] The sobriquet "Poison Ivy" would hound Lee for years.

Yet there was another—less apparent—facet of Lee that merits some consideration here. It emerged briefly during his testimony before the U.S. Commission on Industrial Relations. At one point in his long deposition, Lee made a suggestive excursion from an otherwise unscrupulous discourse on "the facts" concerning Ludlow. Responding to a question about his personal affiliation with the Rockefeller family, Lee began to speculate on the proper relationship that ought to exist between a public relations specialist and his corporate client.

"My idea," he started off, "is that the principal himself should be his own publicity agent; that the function for a person like myself . . . should be to advise with the man who is to take responsibility for the act itself as to what he should do and what he should say, and that he should do the same."[7] Commandeering the technocratic patois of his day, Lee explained that his paradigm of public relations was something that reached beyond the standard conventions—and mostly cosmetic habits—of press agentry.

> Publicity is not a game; it is a science. The difference
> between the two is as wide as the discrepancy between a press
> agent and a doctor of publicity. The function of a press agent
> is to put things across. The problem of a doctor of publicity is
> to induce his patient to behave in such a way as to commend
> himself unto the approval of a good city editor.[8]

In this conjecture, Lee's idealized vision of corporate public relations was hitching its wagon to Progressive ideas. Business leaders themselves, he speculated, must finally see the light and assume hands-on responsibility for making the institutions that they run more authentically responsive to the common good.

> Publicity in its ultimate sense means the actual relationship
> of a company to the people, and that relationship involves far
> more than saying—it involves doing. An elementary requisite
> of any sound publicity must be, therefore, the giving of the
> best possible service.[9]

A "doctor of publicity" would operate as an unfailing behind-the-scenes adviser—an invisible counsel—offering perpetual guidance on what to say, how best to behave, and even how to restructure a corporation for the purpose of securing public confidence. Intrinsic to this view was the insight that press releases alone could not generate a sympathetic climate of public opinion. The public must witness changed behavior—an altered deportment—on the part of a company and its leaders. Lee christened such unaccustomed intercourse between public interest and corporation policy a "two-way street," a self-congratulatory phrase that has persevered in canonical folktales of the public relations industry ever since.[10]

Lee's own career never came close to achieving the goal of a two-way street. Indeed, during the early years of the century, there were few captains of industry who yet felt obliged to move in this direction.

There was, however, one notable exception to this general rule: a man named Theodore Newton Vail, who, starting in 1907, was president of the American Telephone and Telegraph Company (AT&T). More than any other corporate chieftain of his era, Vail approximated the vision of business leadership that Lee conjured up in his testimony before the U.S. Commission on Industrial Relations in 1915.

To some extent, the link between AT&T and public relations strategy predated Vail's presidency. From the beginning of the century—while most corporations paid little attention to the temperature of public opinion—unique exigencies impelled the Bell System, as it was called, to look upon "public relations" as a vital element of its corporate policy.

By the turn of the century, the AT&T leadership was already committed to establishing a privately owned, nationwide monopoly over an important new public service, the telephone.[11] This objective was set in the midst of a society in which anticorporate, antimonopoly sentiments—calls for governmental regulation and governmental ownership of public utilities—were approaching their zenith. To reach the objective of a Bell System monopoly over all wire communication in the United States, company leaders reasoned, the public had to be diverted—at least in respect to AT&T—from its general distrust of big business. With this, the wheels of an innovative public relations apparatus—one that continues to operate at full speed—began to turn.

•   •   •

The establishment of a Bell System monopoly faced acute challenges from two general directions. From one side, there were widespread calls for governmental ownership of telephone service, an approach that was taking hold in Europe and elsewhere. Many argued that phone service—drawing an analogy from the U.S. Post Office's jurisdiction over written and printed communications—should be "postalized," government run.

AT&T also faced headstrong competition from numerous localized independent phone companies. In a society in which huge national corporations were commonly despised and relatively few individuals yet required frequent access to long-distance phone services, a number of local telephone companies possessed "sentimental" advantages over AT&T and enjoyed a great deal of public support.

Confronted by these threats, AT&T, in 1903, engaged the services of a recently founded enterprise known as the Publicity Bureau, located in Boston. The Publicity Bureau, a partnership of experienced former newspaper men, was already achieving a reputation for being able to place prepackaged news items in papers around the country, and Frederick P. Fish, president of AT&T, believed that this know-how might be serviceable in the defense of the Bell System's corporate game plan.[12]

James T. Ellsworth, a seasoned journalist with the Bureau, was given the job of steering the AT&T account. One of the first things to happen under Ellsworth's guidance was the decision to jettison all corporate use of the expression "Bell System." "It seemed injudicious to use the term Bell System," he would later explain, because this phraseology "suggested a trust." With this, a new public identity was ushered in—"the Bell Companies"—a designation more in tune with the anticorporate spirit of the time, one that suggested a loose federation of localized businesses.[13]

Beyond this early example of corporate image management, Ellsworth methodically generated public relations pieces—crafted to read like impartial feature articles—for syndication to newspapers around the country. He also assumed the task of promoting friendly relationships with editors and publishers around the country, particularly in those territories where competition from "the independents" or antitrust sentiments posed particular problems for AT&T interests.

In 1903, for example, regional phone companies posed a problem for AT&T in Kansas City, which had recently granted a franchise to an independent, and in Milwaukee, which seemed to be on the brink of doing so. "These two cities being considered in a critical condition at the time the publicity work started," Ellsworth later recalled, he "was sent to survey the ground."

What he found was daunting. AT&T interests were under fire, and the corporation had few opportunities to defend itself. "At Kansas City," Ellsworth remembered, "the newspaper situation was so antagonistic that the local Bell Company—the Missouri and Kansas Telephone Company—had no means of presenting its facts to the public." Adding to this problem, there was little practical PR wisdom for him to fall back on during those early years; "organized publicity was little more than a theory and practically no one knew how to practice it."

Developing a strategy out of his firsthand journalistic experience, Ellsworth took a first step, which was based on his understanding of newspaper economics. By 1900, advertising—not circulation—was already the prime source of income for most newspapers, and Ellsworth fully comprehended the unspoken power that advertisers could exert over editorial policy and content. AT&T's publicity work in Kansas City, therefore, began by directing significant advertising revenues toward a number of local newspapers.

These economic seedlings soon bore fruit. With the lubricant of advertising dollars, Ellsworth was soon providing suddenly compliant editors with a diverse range of packaged articles, already typeset and ready to be placed. Ad revenues, Ellsworth recounted, "broke the ice" with these newspapers, and the Missouri and Kansas Bell company was "given access to the news columns of the several papers in Kansas City and had an opportunity to make itself better understood."[14]

In a 1904 memorandum to AT&T executives, the Publicity Bureau was already boasting that it had "disabused the public mind" of the "Twenty Million Dollar Trust Myth" that had surrounded the Missouri and Kansas Bell company. Milwaukee, the Bureau reported, would soon be theirs.

Internally, AT&T was pleased with the Bureau's work. Walter S. Allen, AT&T's corporate liaison with the Publicity Bureau, reported to President Fish that it should become increasingly easy to get pro-AT&T articles published. In a memo that reflected the increasingly sophisticated sensitivity of the newspaper as a communications environment, Allen asserted that the key to maintaining friendly relations with newspapers was to continue paying for advertising. Publicity articles, he cautioned, must appear to remain on the "news" side of the stylistic border that separates journalism from overt salesmanship. Though articles might be promotions for AT&T, they should not appear to be so. "Each new story presented," Allen explained, "can be made more and more frankly a Bell advertisement, but it can not be allowed to degenerate into material which will be considered by the editors of such a nature as to justify them in charging for it as paid reading matter at the standard rate of one dollar per line." To maintain this fine distinction, he continued, AT&T must ensure that publicity articles would be written only by experienced "newspaper writers."[15]

In time, Allen believed, these crack news writers would be skillful enough to translate the long-range intention of AT&T—to establish unchallenged control of all telephone communications in the United States—into a journalistic idiom that would be acceptable to a public that was generally hostile to monopoly. In a July 1904 letter to Fish, Allen elaborated:

> The objective point of the policy of this company, as I understand it, is . . . to secure as complete a system throughout the country as is possible, and to that end everything which educates the public in the use of the telephone is of ultimate advantage to this company. The work of this Bureau seems to me well adapted to interest the public, and as the foothold becomes more secure in newspaper circles it will in all probability be possible to lead many of them to the point we desire to reach, namely, the education of the public to the belief that the telephone system is necessarily national in character.[16]

While these documents reveal that AT&T's corporate leadership was, early on, paying exceptional attention to public relations concerns, the particular PR strategy being described was not that exceptional. Though on a grander and more credible scale than that employed by other companies, it was still predominantly press agentry. Farmed out to an independent contractor, public relations was not yet a part of the corporate fabric.

Initial enthusiasm for the Publicity Bureau's work soon proved premature. Despite the agency's earlier proclamations of triumph, by 1906 "the state of public opinion concerning large corporations" had deteriorated considerably, as had AT&T's public reputation in relation to independent regional phone companies. Writing again to Fish, in October of 1906, Allen complained that "much talk of the independents as to the Bell methods and the Bell theories passes muster with the mass of people . . . as being true."

In an ambience of escalating crisis, AT&T's leaders began to entertain the need for "radical change" in their effort to generate more amicable public relations. "It seems to me essential," wrote Allen to Fish, "that if this company is to secure the co-operation of the public, a more aggressive position as regards the presentation of its claims to the consideration of the public must be taken."[17]

It was at this decisive moment, that AT&T moved toward Lee's fantasy of proper public relations. In 1907, AT&T took its public relations activities out of the hands of the Publicity Bureau and placed them under the direct supervision of a new chief executive, Theodore Newton Vail, a man who had been employed by the Bell System in years past. To assist him, Vail hired Ellsworth away from the Publicity Bureau and placed him at the head of the newly created AT&T Information Department.[18]

Vail was, for his era, an unusual kind of corporate chief. Unlike most business leaders of the time—who kept a deliberate distance from public view—Vail saw public relations as a key ingredient of corporate leadership in the twentieth century. In this sense, his elevation to the presidency of AT&T constituted a dramatic rejoinder to the philosophy of men like John D. Rockefeller and others who rated the appellation robber baron. Vail was a quintessential "corporate liberal."[19] In his desire to curry favorable public opinion and in his multilevel campaign to project and nurture an altruistic corporate identity, he embodied a business-oriented variant of the Progressive impulse.

As president of a privately held public utility, Vail was in a unique position to appreciate the delicate balance between the interests of a large corporation and a middle-class public that was expected to purchase its services or invest in its stock. From this vantage point, Vail demonstrated a business class consciousness that was rare among his peers. Within an often bitter anticorporate milieu, he cultivated a conciliatory style of leadership, predicated on the belief that conventional business practices—unless modified—posed a threat not only to the interests of privately owned utilities, but to the viability of corporate capitalism in general.

There was "danger, grave danger," Vail forecast, if business continued to choose the incentive of short-term profit over the more strategic question of long-term survival.[20]

> Our personal rights will not amount to much if they come in conflict with public greed or selfishness, or with public prejudice. For this reason and these reasons, and for the preservation of society such as we can live under, it is necessary that we subordinate our personal and selfish desires to what is best for all, and keep alive in the minds of the public the necessity of this subordination.[21]

In its sense of imminent peril, Vail's worldview was remarkably close to that of Walter Lippmann in *Drift and Mastery.* Like Lippmann, Vail believed that the flammable alliance of corporate arrogance from above and radical forces from below was propelling society toward chaos. Echoing familiar middle-class anxieties, Vail was troubled by a vast population of impoverished immigrants who, as they transfigured American society, presented a mounting threat to the social order.

> Millions of immigrants . . . with no realization of any difference between liberty and license, were cut loose from the restraint imposed upon them by custom and tradition, and without education or ideas of public obligations were put on a political equality in every respect with those who by experience and generations of education were prepared for all the rights of higher citizenship.

These "discontented forces," Vail continued, were being incited by agitators who were forging them into "an influence in the politics of this country that must be reckoned with."[22] Decrying a distending tide of democracy, Vail asserted that social progress could not be achieved at the expense of social distinction.

> No matter what may be the future of "uplift" or development some conditions will never change. . . . [S]ome must bear the physical burden, some the mental, and some the financial. There must be mutual concession and subordination of the individual to the comfort of all. There must be leaders and followers, for without organization there can only be chaos.[23]

Like Lippmann, Vail also believed that the middle-class public was being misguided by "utopian" theorists and the general ambience of recrimination they were fomenting. Persisting habits of corporate greed, he allowed, contributed a kernel of truth to the accusations.

> The public have been educated entirely by those whose entire capital is in exciting class prejudice and class feeling. Mismanagement and unprincipled promotion and combination have furnished the agitators with some material, which freely coupled with misstatements, misinformation and misinterpretation of rightful things . . . have produced deplorable results.

Against these false prophets and their teachings, Vail contended, corporations must furnish an alternative truth. "The only thing to bring about a millennium, is to be as active in giving correct information, and in upsetting of heresies and delusions, as others have been in cultivating them."[24] As the "private rights" of corporations are dependent on "public acquiescence," the public must be "educated" toward a greater understanding of these rights.[25]

Vail's commitment to "educating" the public was a critical piece within a sophisticated political outlook. Consistent with the thinking of the Progressives, his notion of "the public" was emphatically middle class; Vail's commitment to the practice of corporate public relations was rooted in the conviction that if educated to be more sympathetic toward business, this public might serve as a buffer against the greater threats that lurked below.

Against the danger of chaos from below and to nullify public "delusions," Vail formulated a far-ranging public relations strategy aimed at convincing the middle class that their interests and the interests of the Bell Companies were congenial. More than press agentry, Vail's PR policy was planned to provide middle-class phone subscribers with tangible proof that AT&T's corporate policies were responsive to the needs of an anxious public.

Phone rates were established to project this priority. At a time when long-distance service was used, for the most part, by businesses, AT&T regional companies inflated long-distance telephone costs to subsidize their local phone rates. With the Bell Companies offering the only comprehensive national telephone service, businesses engaged in interstate commerce had little choice but to go with AT&T. Meanwhile, the surcharge levied on business users permitted AT&T to provide local service at a price that was affordable to most middle-class subscribers, people who only rarely relied on long-distance lines.

Other policies were more semiotic in nature. Though AT&T was controlled exclusively by a male hierarchy, a conscious decision was made to give the direct link between the public and the corporation—the telephone operator—a woman's voice. The employment of female operators, who would begin each phone transaction with a courteous "Number please?" established AT&T as a prescient innovator of the "user-friendly interface."

At a time when there was widespread middle-class unease over exploitative working conditions, AT&T advertised internal labor policies designed to encourage "esprit de corps . . . morale" among employees. For AT&T's primarily Anglo-Saxon workforce, Vail promised wages scaled to match "the very highest that are paid for any similar class of work" and an unprecedented employee health program to provide "benefits for sickness and disability."

Ultimately, AT&T's success rested on its ability to project a sympathetic corporate personality. Vail insisted that this required a sure understanding of the public mind; the "whole question of public relations" was increasingly conceived in terms of the company's ability to present itself "through the eyes of the public." This objective demanded new ways of thinking. As never before, company executives were encouraged to become students of public attitudes and opinions, to familiarize themselves with the public's point of view on a range of relevant issues. Though this idea is a cliché of public relations today, at the time it constituted a dramatic break from the disdainful short-sightedness of the past, a move toward a more socially conscious style of corporate behavior.

"Get the public's view point," said E. K. Hall, Vail's vice president, to a meeting of his New England managers; "see if you can work out the problem from that basis."

> Don't bristle at the man who makes a complaint, but make him feel that he is doing you a favor. Most people are reasonable, and if you take this point of view you can make him not only reform his opinion of your company, but respect you as an individual.[26]

All these strategies—cut-rate local phone bills, the friendly greetings of Ma Bell, employee esprit de corps programs, presenting things through the public's eyes—were essentials in Vail's innovative effort to defend AT&T against a "curse of bigness." Yet it was his effort to place an altruistic spin on the idea of an AT&T telephone monopoly that occupied the core of his PR endeavors. This was the company's underlying corporate objective, and a contentious political climate required that it be adroitly pursued.

Vail's campaign to ennoble the concept of an AT&T telephone monopoly confronted difficult obstacles. In a nation in which the fear of "bigness" was widespread and most people still lived a more or less localized existence, provincialism had buttressed public loyalty to regional phone companies. In the face of this hurdle, AT&T's Information Department worked to advance the oracle of a different America, an America to come, in which people's lives—following the lead of the modern business system—would take on an increasingly national and cosmopolitan character. Within such a world, the limits of regional phone service would become clear.

It was the nervous public that provided Vail with the basic ingredient of his PR strategy. In a world where rapid change and a sense of drift were often dismaying facts of life, Vail's public relations was calculated to provide Americans with a consoling picture of the people they were in the process of becoming. Remarkably attuned to the nationalization of social and economic life that was rapidly taking place, his platform was founded on the majestic promise of "universal service."

People would be more dispersed yet more connected. Beyond claims of high-quality phone service, Bell public relations continually portrayed the ordinary phone subscriber as a person requiring contact with a wider world. "When you lift the Bell receiver," the company repeatedly announced, "you are in contact with the world."[27]

As president, Vail dramatically increased corporate funding for publicity matters and launched—for the first time in the company's history—an illustrated institutional advertising campaign, touting the "Bell System" as a service benefiting "all the people all the time." Vail personally approved "every piece of copy and made many suggestions."[28]

Proclaiming that "every Bell Telephone is the Center of the System," these ads encouraged telephone users to view the company not as a dark monopolistic leviathan, but as a beneficent mother figure who would make each and every one of them the center of her attentions. At the bottom of each ad stood AT&T's oath of infinite and equitable access: "One System, One Policy, Universal Service." The deftness of this strategy was its unprecedented openness. Rather than hide from AT&T's conspicuous size or its monopolistic ambitions, Vail energetically transformed these often maligned characteristics into pure and simple virtues.

Building on preexisting patterns of publicity, AT&T, under Vail's leadership, also expanded the bulk of materials produced and sent out to news services and newspapers. Beyond articles responding directly or implicitly to those hostile to an AT&T monopoly, many of these pieces were of a human-interest variety, designed to portray the telephone in general, and AT&T in particular, as the glue that holds a modern society together.

Vail personally prepared "a syllabus on the life history of the telephone" for publication in magazines, and other articles featured telephone etiquette; "girl" switchboard operators; and the role of the telephone in suburban life, in church life, in the wilderness, in the law,

Telephone service, a public trust

An Advertisement of the
American Telephone and Telegraph Company

THE widespread ownership of the Bell Telephone System places an obligation on its management to guard the savings of its hundreds of thousands of stockholders.

Its responsibility for so large a part of the country's telephone service imposes an obligation that the service shall always be adequate, dependable and satisfactory to the user.

The only sound policy that will meet these obligations is to continue to furnish the best possible service at the lowest cost consistent with financial safety. There is then in the Bell System no incentive to earn speculative or large profits. Earnings must be sufficient to assure the best possible service and the financial integrity of the business. Anything in excess of these requirements goes toward extending the service or keeping down the rates.

This is fundamental in the policy of the company.

The Bell System's ideal is the same as that of the public it serves—the most telephone service and the best, at the least cost to the user. It accepts its responsibility for a nation-wide telephone service as a public trust.

Engineering the Telephone

THE great Bell System, with its telephone highways connecting the farthest points of the country, is primarily a brain creation.

The telephone engineer is the genius of communication. Like the general of an army, he plans, projects and directs his campaigns far ahead. He deals with the seemingly impossible—transforming ideas and ideals into concrete facts.

His problems may involve doubling the capacity of a city's underground telephone system, or the building of a transcontinental line, or a serious war-shortage of supplies needed in telephone work.

Whatever the difficulties, they must be overcome so that the progress of the telephone shall continue equal to the ever-growing needs of the people.

It is not enough to provide only for the present—the future must be anticipated and discounted.

In the Bell System, more than two thousand highly efficient engineers and scientists are constantly working on the complex problems of the telephone business.

As a result, the service keeps step with present requirements and the assurance is given to every subscriber that the Bell System is prepared for whatever the future develops.

AMERICAN TELEPHONE AND TELEGRAPH COMPANY
AND ASSOCIATED COMPANIES
One Policy　　　One System　　　Universal Service

·LIFE·　　291

In The Public Service

The President of the United States works for 80,000,000 people all the time.

He needs rest and change to keep him fit for his work, and yet he cannot neglect his official duties, he must always be within reach.

When Washington was president he rode his horse as far as Mount Vernon and kept in touch by messenger with the affairs of state. The President to-day has a wider range and can seek the cooling breezes of the New England coast.

The long distance telephone keeps him in constant communication with the capitol and the nation.

The railroad will carry him back to Washington in a day, but usually he need not make even this brief journey. The Bell telephone enables him to send his voice instead, *not only to Washington but to any other point.*

The Bell system performs this service *not only for the President, but for the whole public.*

This system has been built up so gradually and extended so quietly that busy men hardly realize its magnitude or appreciate its full value.

Forty thousand cities, towns and villages are connected by the Bell system, which serves *all the people all the time.*

The Bell telephone has become the implement of a nation. It increases the sum total of human efficiency, and makes every hour of the day more valuable to busy men and women.

The highest type of public service can be achieved *only by one policy, one system, universal service.*

The American Telephone and Telegraph Company
And Associated Companies
Every Bell Telephone is The Center of the System. 1909

The advertisements in Everybody's Magazine are indexed. Turn to page s.

EVERYBODY'S MAGAZINE　143

Three print advertisements for AT&T: 1909, 1916, 1928. All follow Vail's public relations lead, emphasizing the idea of AT&T's public service. AUTHOR'S COLLECTION

in the army, and so forth. In each story the telephone was the star; the Bell System supplied the mis-en-scène that made the drama possible.

While magazine and newspaper publishers criticized many companies for attempts to secure "free publicity" in their pages, AT&T's self-conscious mix of paid advertising and packaged news items gained publishers' approval and often their active collaboration with AT&T's corporate goals.

This collaboration is apparent in a 1909 letter from H. W. Pool, advertising manager of *Moody's Magazine,* to Ellsworth. Pool was writing to offer the company advertising space on "the outside back cover" of an upcoming issue of the magazine for a fee of seventy-five dollars. "This issue," Pool continued, "will contain an exhaustive article of your company written by Mr. John Moody which is highly complimentary to your company." The exchange between favorable editorial coverage and advertising revenues was unabashedly affirmed as Pool inserted: "We believe that support from you from an advertising standpoint would prove mutually advantageous."[29]

The amalgam of syndicated public relations articles and paid institutional advertising—a mix that was cementing relations with editors even before Vail took over—continued to reap benefits for AT&T. In confidential meetings, regional directors of Bell Companies would swap detailed stories of how they had secured desirable press connections.

At a June 1914 meeting of the Bell Companies, Mr. Fortier, of Bell of Canada, reported to his corporate associates that "the relations of our Local Manager with the newspapers are such I think that any news story that is deserving of insertion, they will find no difficulty having it published in the papers. There are papers that we are on such exceptional terms with," Fortier continued, "that they will print practically anything within reason."

On the same occasion Mr. Sullivan, of Southwestern Bell, painted a graphic picture of friendships being cultivated to serve corporate interests. He explained:

We have in each General Manager's division a publicity agent. . . . [I]t is his business to know personally and intimately every newspaper reporter, newspaper man, and newspaper owner personally. One man in particular has succeeded in being intimately acquainted and being a friend of 98% of the editors and owners in his State. That friendship is played up in different ways; by calling on them once, twice, three or four times a year, by meeting with them at their conventions, and by assisting to entertain them. . . .[30]

These activities, however, do not fully reveal the nature of AT&T's Information Department (or, as it was later renamed, the Public Relations Bureau). More than simply producing and disseminating materials for publication, Vail's public relations operation also engaged in a continuous and detailed analysis of public opinion insofar as it related to AT&T's far-flung interests. Proceeding along terrain mapped—at least theoretically—by Gabriel Tarde, Vail intuited that the grooves of borrowed thought embraced complex networks of human interaction.

Beyond the authority of journalistic materials, there was a diverse range of other opinion shapers that influenced attitudes, that shaped conversations, in America. To be fully informed about relevant currents of popular thought, Vail surmised, it was essential to keep a corporate ear close to the ground. Toward this purpose, the Information Department, and later the Public Relations Bureau, deployed an intricate intelligence-gathering-and-surveillance apparatus, designed to provide the corporation with an ongoing profile of its adversaries.

AT&T's reconnaissance chores included the methodical collecting and clipping of newspapers, magazines, books, and "ephemeral pamphlets" from around the country on anything that appertained to the Bell System's corporate situation. Proposed legislation, as well, and even the spoken utterances of college professors, students, "radical politicians and progressive editors" were painstakingly monitored, to pinpoint potential sources of opposition and to provide an up-to-the-minute picture of "the general trend of public sentiment."[31]

Assembled from the findings of field operatives, weekly intelligence summaries were distributed to all AT&T executive officers and to executives and attorneys in the field. The purpose behind these exhaustive activities was simple: to permit AT&T to prepare for and "meet actual situations as they arise in advance of general public clamor."[32] Transcending the ex post facto strategies of "damage con-

trol" that marked most corporate PR of the period, AT&T's operations were designed to forecast and defuse problems before they
arose.

At times this meant shadowing people whose public statements
were felt to endanger company interests. In 1913, for example, David
J. Lewis, a Democratic congressman from Maryland, was barn-
storming local organizations, calling for a government takeover of
telephone service. To AT&T's Public Relations Bureau, Lewis's
"speeches before economic, civic and business societies throughout
the country, and particularly before the Granges . . . constituted an
appreciable form of publicity," one that demanded a corporate
response.[33]

Ellsworth, speaking at a confidential public relations meeting in
1914, addressed the Lewis problem directly. "We have had the occasion to sort of keep tab on him and follow him around," he reported.
This gumshoe behavior, he explained, was enacted to undermine
Lewis before he could arrive to deliver a speech.

> It has been our idea that it was a good thing to find out where
> he was going, and if possible to secure a list of the people or
> members of the Grange or Association or Society he was
> going to speak before, and circularize them before he got
> there. In some instances we found this was impossible
> because they would smell a rat and would not let us have the
> list of names till after he came around, but in every instance
> we have found we could get to people either before or after.[34]

To offset the impact of men like Lewis, the company also
arranged public debates on the question of governmental ownership
or other thorny issues. Pro-AT&T speakers—drawn ideally from the
community—were furnished with debating kits, indexes of relevant
issues, and other ammunition with which to mount an effective
response.[35] As never before, local forums of public discussion were
being infused with scripted lines.

Guiding these activities was Vail, a new breed of businessman
who—more than any corporate leader of the period—appreciated the
importance that public relations would assume in twentieth-century

American life. Along the way, Vail catapulted the telephone giant toward the forefront of modern public relations thinking and toward achieving the monopoly it so forcibly pursued.

At the center of Vail's managerial vision was his commitment to the idea of "education," his obsessional quest to convince Americans that the AT&T catechism of "One System, One Policy, Universal Service" would provide them with an interconnected future and a quality and efficiency of service that no other system could match.

Amid the often intense pandemonium of antimonopoly sentiment, Vail—an unflinching proponent of corporate progressivism—was convinced that proving AT&T's case was simply a matter of appealing to people's common sense through the presentation of facts, assisted by the agency of public reason. "Educate the public," he exhorted his executive corps in 1913. Their job, he continued was to present the public with those facts and arguments necessary for them to see AT&T's ambitions as conforming to their sense of their own best interests.

> It is you who must do it. . . . If you can impress upon . . . the public, the fact that we can give them better service than could be obtained under government ownership, and that a monopoly does not necessarily mean public disadvantage, the time will come. Before we can accomplish our plan for a universal . . . system, the public mind must be thoroughly imbued with its economies and advantages.[36]

Responding to an onrush of social agitation in 1909, Theodore Roosevelt had cautioned that "unless there is a readjustment" in the conduct of business in the United States, "there will come a riotous wicked, murderous day of atonement." The survival of capitalism, he believed, demanded a more comprehensive social vision on the part of businessmen. While most corporate leaders ignored this admonition, Vail was articulating a new vision of publicly engaged corporate management. The hidebound secrecy that had escorted earlier industrial development was now being challenged by a public relations-oriented conception of enlightened self-interest—an approach to corporate leadership that, in years to come, would gain a widening circle of disciples.

The distinction between a man like Vail and a man like Rocke-feller cannot be understood simply in the terms provided by muck-rakers' morality plays, dramas pitting the forces of good against the forces of evil. Neither can the differences between the two men be reduced to a matter of different temperaments. Whatever personal genius stood behind Vail's innovations, they were also framed by the particular exigencies of the industry over which he presided: tele-phone service.

Rockefeller had been part of a generation of industrialists and financiers who had assembled America's industrial base. Barons of finance, transportation, capital-goods production, coal, and petro-leum, these men controlled large-scale industries in which direct con-tact with the public or the need for public approval had seemed relatively minimal. Their activities were, for the most part, shielded from the middle-class public by a vast layer of local middlemen who had little power to influence the policies of large-scale industry and finance. Only on rare occasions, usually at moments of crisis, had these early captains of industry felt obliged to explain themselves.

Vail, on the other hand, oversaw a corporation that dealt directly with middle-class Americans. Its product—person-to-person tele-phone communication—was a fundamental component in the evolu-tion and assembling of a modern public of consumers. This historical proximity to the emerging consumer culture demanded that Vail's vision move beyond that of preceding industrial barons. The public and its problems stood unavoidably at the center of AT&T's long-term ability to achieve its corporate goals.[37]

There is another factor that may have contributed to Vail's apti-tude for public relations. It emanates from the changing choreog-raphy of public life itself and from Vail's particular vantage point on those changes.

In 1898 Tarde had depicted his contemporary "public" as "one which never ceases to grow and whose indefinite extension is one of the most clearly marked traits of our period." Just as newspapers had abetted a mode of public life that could "extend indefinitely," tele-phones were also inseminating that indefinite extension into the realm of people's private existence. Complimenting the development of newspapers and other mass media as the connective tissue of public life in the modern age, AT&T—in its vision of One System, One Policy, Universal Service—was engaged in the development of a pervasive network that would help connect private existence to that increasingly vaporous public realm.

When Edward A. Ross wrote of newspapers that "mental touch is no longer bound up with physical proximity" and that in the modern era "remote people are brought, as it were, into one another's presence," he might just as well have been describing the telephone. Both the newspaper and the telephone were engaged in reshaping the terms of public interaction.

Vail's insights into the architecture of a modern public and the importance of public relations echoed the perception of contemporary social thinkers, journalists, and others who were in positions that permitted them to witness a new consumerist way of life unfolding. All had an understanding that a "different public," as Tarde had described it, was in the process of being formed. This public consisted of individual consumers bound together not by the tendrils of kinship and community, but by modern instruments of communication. Vail's recognition of this new public's existence and the pathways by which it was informed also suggested the means by which those outlooks might be influenced. While many businessmen continued to disregard the terms of their world, public relations was an idea whose time had come.

6
House of Truth

EIGHT O'CLOCK in the evening, September 27, 1918. A brief interval between shows at a local movie house in Portland, Maine. As the house lights came on, Virgil Williams, a local bank manager known to many in the audience, rose determinedly from his aisle seat and strode toward the front of the theater. Then, in a voice that resonated beyond the last row of the auditorium, he began to address the 150 of his neighbors who had gathered that night to take in a couple of movies.

His words were fired by the Great War in Europe, a war that, for the past year and a half, had embroiled the lives of American servicemen. "While we sit here tonight, enjoying a picture show," he began deliberately, "are you aware that thousands and thousands of people in Europe—people not unlike ourselves—are languishing in slavery under Prussian masters?" Assuming an inflection of gravity, Williams continued.

> If we are not vigilant, their fate could be ours.
>
> Now, then, do you folks here in Portland want to take the slightest chance of meeting Prussianism here in America?
>
> If not, then you'll have to participate in summoning all the resources of this country for the giant struggle. In addition to buying Thrift Stamps, and War-Savings-Stamps to support our boys overseas, we must also hold fast the lines here at home.
>
> To do this, we must remain alert. We must listen carefully to the questions that our neighbors are asking, and we must ask ourselves whether these questions could be subverting the security of our young men in uniform.

You have heard the questions:

Is this a capitalists' war?

Was America deliberately pushed into the war by our captains of industry, for money-making purposes?

Are the rich coining blood into gold while the poor are taking on the greater burdens?

Take heed. These questions are not innocent. They can not be ignored.

These are questions constantly whispered by German sympathizers, openly asked by many others who simply do not understand.

Our response to these questions is plain. Our democratic system of income tax insures that the rates paid by those who are most well-off are greater than those rates paid by Americans who are less well-off. Tell those who ask such questions, that *all Americans* are sacrificing to defeat Prussianism, *to make the world safe for democracy.*

When you hear such questions, take heed. Do not wait until you catch someone putting a bomb under a factory.

Report the man who spreads pessimistic stories, or who asks misleading questions, or who belittles our efforts to win the war. Send the names of such persons—even if they are in uniform—to the Department of Justice in Washington. Give all the details you can, with names of witnesses if possible. Show the Hun that we can beat him at his own game. For those of you who are concerned for your own, or your family's safety, I can assure you that the fact that you made a report will never become public. *Make the world safe for democracy! Hold fast the lines at home!*

As Williams concluded his brief but urgent speech, he turned to sit down. Members of the audience offered him a small round of applause and, within moments, lights dimmed and the picture show resumed.

At first glance, Williams's oration may appear to have been a fairly impulsive occurrence, a battle-charged sample of a town-meeting heritage native to New England. This, however, was not the case.

Williams's visit to the movies was part of a carefully synchronized national mission; as he spoke to residents of Portland that evening, thousands of other people in theaters across the United States were being issued similar messages of alarm. Williams, along with 75,000 others, was a lieutenant in a nationwide brotherhood known as the "Four-Minute Men," a group of local opinion leaders—mostly small-businessmen, lawyers, and other professionals—who had been rallied to maintain home-front support for U.S. military involvement in the First World War. Nearly 150,000 times each week, men like Williams would rise before their communities to preach the holiness of the American war effort, to condemn the heresy of antiwar opinion.[1]

Despite its magnitude, the Four-Minute Men was but the tip of an even larger iceberg, only one aspect of an unparalleled publicity campaign being conducted by the U.S. Committee on Public Information (CPI), a vast propaganda ministry established by President Woodrow Wilson in April 1917, just one week after the United States had joined the European Alliance and had declared war on Germany.[2]

The unprecedented creation of the CPI—a comprehensive propaganda bureau intended to mobilize and channel popular enthusiasm—reflected a general awareness of "public opinion" among business and political elites in the United States during this disquieting period. It also revealed a heightened sensitivity to a number of specific problems that American political leaders faced as they moved toward a declaration of war in 1917. Government officials presumed that the majority of Americans would accept the decision to go to war, but there were significant pockets of antiwar sentiment and potential resistance that were causing them serious concern.

First of all, as he stood for reelection in 1916, President Wilson had run on the slogan, "He kept us out of war." Only a few months later, in the spring of 1917, a large number of native-born, middle-class Americans continued to hold Wilson to this oath. Particularly in western states, where many people embraced isolationist attitudes, there was a belief that events in Europe were not America's concern.[3]

Reflecting familiar patterns of xenophobia, there were also concerns about the loyalty of America's huge immigrant population. Beyond specific questions of German immigrants (Would their devotions lie with "the Hun"?) or of Irish Americans—who, on the whole, despised America's ally, the British—the dreadful reality of many immigrants' lives in America could not help but throw the allegiances of the foreign-born into question.

Millions from Eastern Europe and the "southern tier" of Italy, who had come to the United States "with the hope that they were coming to a land of promise," had been summarily "dumped into the Ghettos of the big cities."[4] In spite of expansive oratory about America as the great and democratic "melting pot," there was the sobering recognition among officials—as the American war effort commenced—that for many immigrants, "the melting pot had failed to melt"; the "Land of Opportunity" had not delivered on its promises.[5] The social strains and chronic industrial unrest that had marked the preceding decades only punctuated this potentially perilous fact.

"We let sharks prey on them, we let poverty swamp them, we did not teach them English," lamented George Creel, the Progressive journalist who would become the civilian director of the CPI. He, along with other watchful Washington insiders, believed that without a direct campaign to promote loyalty in immigrant communities, the foreign-born could not be counted on to embrace the American war effort.[6]

Compounding these fears, there was an overt and articulate political opposition to the war, even before U.S. involvement. Working-class and radical organizations, pacifists, anarchists and many socialists, maintained that this was nothing but a "rich man's war." Ralph Chaplin—a prominent member of the Industrial Workers of the World (IWW)—typified this perspective when, in a 1914 poem, he dubbed the European war a "Red Feast," a gruesome blood purge in which the flesh of workers was being devoured by rats, maggots, and capitalist "Lords of War."

"Go fight you fools!" Chaplin taunted those who would serve up their lives to the grim European banquet that was now under way.

> *Tear up the earth with strife*
> *And give unto a war that is not yours;*
> *Serve unto death the men you served in life*
> *So that their wide dominions may not yield.*
> *Stand by the flag—the lie that still allures;*

Lay down your lives for land you do not own,
And spill each other's guts upon the field;
Your gory tithe of mangled flesh and bone.
But whether in the fray to fall or kill
You must not pause to question why nor where.
You see the tiny crosses on that hill?
It took all those to make one millionaire.[7]

By 1917, lessons such as Chaplin's had left a deep imprint on the thinking of many. Instructed by compelling visions of a "Red Feast," many workers found it easy to interpret U.S. entry into the war as little more than a thinly veiled attempt to recover endangered Wall Street loans.[8]

International events only encouraged governmental anxieties about organized working-class resistance. In Great Britain, attempts to rally popular support for the war were seen as deficient; large sectors of the English working class felt little harmony with the cause. "That the working classes have to a certain extent failed to develop a sense of national unity is obvious enough," observed Wilfred Trotter, an eminent British social psychologist, in 1916. Socialistic, egalitarian aspirations were multiplying, Trotter noted, and Britain was now "faced with the possibility of having to make profound changes in the social system to convince the working-man . . . that his interests and ours in this war are one."[9]

Even more alarming, an earthshaking social revolution was in the process of unfolding in Russia. Working people were marching in the streets. The czar's army refused to fight for the allied cause and had then refused orders to shoot down protesting workers in Moscow and St. Petersburg. After February 1917, a weak interim government was succumbing to the weight of its own indecision, and a "proletarian" Bolshevik regime stood at the threshold of power. Such world historic contingencies only underscored the dread of social disorder and chaos that encircled the American decision to enter the war.

Sensing that middle-class public opinion was volatile and that a revolt of the masses was possible, a number of noteworthy social analysts began to lobby President Wilson, calling for the establishment of an ideological apparatus that would systematically promote the cause of war. One of these analysts was Arthur Bullard, a leading Progressive, who had been a student of Wilson when the president had been a history professor at Princeton.

Early in 1917, Bullard sent a copy of his recently published book, *Mobilising America,* to Wilson, hoping that the volume would influence the president's blueprints for war. Attuned to his era's belief in publicity as a "moral disinfectant" and its deep mistrust of secrecy, Bullard warned that installing conventional systems of governmental press control would be a mistake. Given perceptions of this as a "businessman's war," any overt policy of censorship would simply encourage deep-seated public suspicion.

Developing his plan from the lessons of Progressive journalism, Bullard argued that a flood of publicity would be key in rallying America to war. "Timid advisors will urge secrecy," he advised, "but the Government needs publicity. Nothing will do more to hearten us, to stimulate the mobilisation of Public Opinion, than knowledge of what is being done."[10] The wisest road to pursue when war is declared, he recommended, was to dispatch a steady flow of information to the public at large.

> First, last and all the time, the effectiveness of our warfare will depend on the amount of ardor we throw into it. . . . [T]he prime duty of our government, the first step in any mobilisation, must be the awakening of our interest. . . . [a] Call to Arms, which will electrify public opinion.

To accomplish this goal, Bullard proposed that the government should "organise a publicity bureau, which would constantly keep before the public the importance of supporting the men at the front. It would requisition space on the front page of every newspaper; it would call for a 'draft' of trained writers to feed 'Army stories' to the public; it would create a Corps of Press Agents. . . . In order to make a democracy fight wholeheartedly," he resolved, "it is necessary to make them understand the situation." America must, Bullard concluded, organize "propaganda campaigns to make the struggle comprehensible and popular."[11]

Bullard was fervent in this conviction:

> By every means at its disposal our Government must strive to get us thinking together. For unless that is accomplished

there is nothing but endless muddle before us, a welter of blunders, inefficiency and disgrace. We—the people of the United States—are the force back of the Government. Unless our Will to Win is passionate and determined, our Army and Navy will accomplish little.[12]

On March 11, in a private letter to the president, Walter Lippmann seconded Bullard's recommendation. With U.S. involvement less than a month away, he exhorted Wilson to create an official government news bureau, an agency that would advertise the war as one "to make a world that is safe for democracy." In wartime, Lippmann added cryptically, it is necessary to nurture "a healthy public opinion."[13]

On April 6, 1917, when the United States formally declared war, the issue of propaganda moved to the top of the president's agenda. On April 12, responding to an assignment from the president, Lippmann submitted a ground plan to Wilson, laying out specifics for a wartime "publicity bureau," a "clearinghouse for information on government activities" that would mobilize the propagandistic skills of artists, intellectuals, journalists, and other media professionals from around the country. Moving beyond a paradigm of publicity that was grounded in journalism, Lippmann's plan spoke of the need to rally a wide range of communications specialists, including people working in the "motion picture industry." Beyond propagating information, Lippmann suggested, the bureau should also direct a variety of relevant intelligence functions, "a monitoring of the foreign press . . . and the tracking down of 'rumors and lies'" that would undermine American morale.[14]

Heeding these admonitions, on April 14, 1917, Wilson took action to "hold fast the inner lines," issuing Executive Order No. 2594, which decreed the establishment of the CPI. From within the government, the committee's membership included the secretary of state, the secretary of war, and the secretary of the navy. To head the CPI, Wilson appointed Creel, a well-connected Progressive journalist, as its civilian chairman.

In light of Wilson's unease about possible liberal opposition to the war, the appointment of Creel was ingenious and adroit. Beginning in Kansas, in the mid-1890s, Creel had been part of the founding gener-

George Creel, civilian director of the CPI. NATIONAL ARCHIVES

ation of Progressive publicists, writers who built careers aiming their pens at governmental corruption and corporate excess. By 1910, he had acquired a national reputation as a top investigative journalist. Beyond his Progressive pedigree, Creel had also been an early champion of Wilson's run for the presidency in 1912; since then he had gained the president's notice and confidence.

Given the exigencies of the moment, Creel was precisely the kind of man Wilson needed to head a wartime publicity bureau. From a lifetime of experience, he understood "the importance of public opinion" in modern political life.[15] Creel was also acquainted with an extensive community of Progressive journalists around the country; Wilson believed that Creel could bring these potential "opinion leaders" into the fold, to establish a visible link between liberal ideals and pursuit of the war. On the whole, Wilson's assumption was justified. When war was declared, an impassioned generation of Progressive publicists fell into line, surrounding the war effort with a veil of much-needed liberal-democratic rhetoric.

Most important, Creel had been a conspicuous critic of big business—and of pro-business propaganda—in the years directly preceding the war. (It was Creel, after all, who, in *Harper's* magazine, had written a scathing critique of the Rockefeller interests and of Ivy Lee's role as the Rockefeller family's mouthpiece following the Ludlow Massacre.) In a political milieu in which skepticism about a "capitalists' war" was rife, who better to place at the helm of a propaganda ministry than a man whose anti–big business credentials were immaculate.

In a number of ways the active collaboration between progressivism and the war effort made historical sense. By 1917, the aims of progressivism and the agenda of the CPI were not that far apart.

For some time, Progressives had articulated a vision of the future in which intellectuals and social technicians would come to lead a new and rational world order. In 1917, with one of their own—Woodrow Wilson—at the helm of government, many saw the war as an opportunity for America and American liberal values to frame the world's future.

Moreover, fears of revolt from below had haunted the Progressive imagination for some years. The desire to govern and guide public perception—in order to effect the social order—was hardly alien to the philosophy of progressivism. When the moment to lead the public mind into war arrived, the disorder threatened by antiwar sentiments—particularly among the lower classes—was seen as an occasion that demanded what Lippmann would call the "manufacture of consent."

Last, there was a bridge between the domestic objectives of progressivism and an aggressive approach to world affairs that had roots going back to the late nineteenth century. From the period leading up to the Spanish-American War, there were many politicians, businessmen, and Progressives who discerned a relationship between the United States' ability to assume the world stage as a political and economic power and its ability to generate an improved standard of living for the masses of people at home.[16] As a generation of Progressives united around the war effort in 1917, many believed that the war—and its triumphal aftermath—would place the United States in an incomparable position to deliver on its timeworn pledge of prosperity for the many.

•   •   •

As director of the CPI, Creel brought an understanding of publicity to his post that had been nurtured by his experience as a Progressive publicist. Like many of his contemporaries, Creel had a finely
honed awareness of the paths along which ideas were carried, and he
applied this awareness expansively. The "House of Truth," as Creel
called the CPI, was extraordinarily sophisticated and far reaching,
providing an unequaled laboratory for pursuing local, national, and
international publicity work.[17] With the assistance of advisers, Creel
erected a publicity apparatus that, in scope and conception, transcended anything that had previously existed.

To some extent, the CPI built upon publicity strategies that had
been evolving in the United States since the late nineteenth century,
strategies that had come to the fore during the Progressive Era. In the
Domestic Section of the CPI, for example, the Division of News channeled thousands of "official war news" press releases through the mails
and along telegraph lines on a twenty-four-hours-a-day basis. Concurrently, the Foreign Section of the CPI, which maintained offices in over
thirty countries, used naval radio transmitters to "pour a steady
stream of American information into international channels of communication."[18] Syndicated "human-interest" features were also distributed, aimed at those readers who skipped over the news columns.

In a move that extended beyond existing public relations practices, a direct effort was made to influence media aimed at immigrant
populations. Developing contacts with six hundred foreign language
papers—published in nineteen languages—the CPI made special
appeals to a heterogeneous population whose loyalty was of special
concern.[19]

To "guide the mind of the masses" more directly, the CPI also
began publishing its own newspaper, the *Official Bulletin,* in May
1917.[20] Designed to set off a mental chain reaction, the *Official Bulletin*—with a circulation reaching 115,000—was targeted at public
officials, other newspapers, and any other "agencies of a public or
semi-public character equipped to disseminate the official information
it will contain."[21]

If the CPI elaborated on and extended the accumulated knowledge of public relations specialists, however, Creel was convinced that

newspapers alone could not do the job at hand. To achieve the ideological mobilization of an entire nation and to sell America's vision of the war globally, an extensive fabric of persuasion would have to be knit.

This undertaking required an expansion of both the tools and occasions for publicity. To that time, print journalism had been seen, for the most part, as the primary medium for shaping public opinion. The power of the printed word had stood at the core of the publicist's faith. The CPI went beyond this premise; in its publicly subsidized laboratories, it experimented quantitatively and qualitatively with other forms of media.

Transcending the confines of traditional press agentry, the CPI constituted a more audacious approach to publicity than had previously existed. To sell the war to Americans, Creel believed, an all-encompassing fabric of perception—every moment of human attention—had to be mobilized. "How could the national emergency be met without national unity?" he inquired rhetorically. "The printed word, the spoken word, motion pictures, the telegraph, the wireless, posters, signboards, and every possible media should be used to drive home the justice of America's cause."[22]

Though Creel was a journalist, his instincts for publicity were more familiar among people employed in the advertising industry. By 1917, advertising men were boastfully extolling the deftness with which they were able to induce resistant customers to purchase a growing variety of factory-produced consumer goods. Many in the industry also maintained that advertising techniques could also be used to sell social and political ideas and even to combat social discontent.[23]

Given the evolution of American advertising by 1917, this conceit made some degree of sense. By this time, advertising was more than a simple description—truthful or not—of goods. In a seductive mix of words and images, advertising had begun to associate goods with the emotional lives—the needs, cravings, aspirations, and fears—of the consumers to whom it spoke.

Acknowledging the already considerable power of advertising in American society, by 1917 Creel was approaching the conclusion that "people do not live by bread alone; they live mostly by catch phrases."[24] If advertising techniques could sell soap or face cream or biscuits, he reasoned, why not a war? "The work of the Committee was so distinctly in the nature of an advertising campaign," he explained some years later, "that we turned almost instinctively to the advertising profession for advice and assistance."[25]

Following this intuition, the CPI conscripted the advertising forces of the country on behalf of the war effort. "By . . . one stroke of President Wilson's pen," Creel explained, "every advertising man in the United States was enrolled in America's second line, and from the very moment of their enrollment we could feel a quickening of effort, the intensification of endeavor."[26] Under the leadership of William H. Johns, president of the American Association of Advertising Agencies and head of the George Batten advertising agency, the Advertising Division of the CPI generated hundreds of advertisements and billboards, at the same time pressuring newspapers around the country to donate free advertising space for the CPI.

If fact-oriented journalism had provided the model by which publicists sought to promote corporate interests and political intentions prior to the war, the CPI elevated the importance of advertising techniques and emotional appeals to a national political level. Coming out of a tradition of publicity that relied most heavily on the vehicle of words, the CPI ventured into constructing a language of images.

To supply illustrations for advertisements and for designing posters, the CPI deployed a Division of Pictorial Publicity, a brigade of volunteer artists, headed by Charles Dana Gibson—creator of the Gibson Girl and America's foremost commercial artist.[27] In conjunction with this division, the Bureau of Cartoons published the *Weekly Bulletin for Cartoonists,* a newsletter sent to 750 newspaper cartoonists around the country, that contained "ideas and captions" that cartoonists were expected to provide drawings for.[28]

Creel took particular pride in his ability to mobilize the graphic arts. Observing that "artists, from time immemorial" have often been seen as "an irresponsible lot," Creel declared that under the leadership of the CPI, "painters, sculptors, designers, illustrators, and cartoonists rallied to the colors with instancy and enthusiasm."[29]

Perhaps most prophetically, and following Lippmann's initial recommendations on wartime publicity, the nascent movie industry of Hollywood was also drafted into the CPI's publicity apparatus under the Division of Films. In a number of significant ways this innovation made sense.

Movies were an extraordinarily charismatic and universal form of communication. Unlike printed matter, literacy was not a precondition of movies' ability to speak to an audience. In the era of silent films, in which a wordless language of gesture was used to tell a story, knowledge of English was similarly unnecessary. This was an especially serviceable feature in a society that housed such an enormous population of immigrants.

A visual rhetoric of filmmaking was also developing that extended film's potential as a medium of persuasion. Techniques of cinematography (camera movement, the conscious use of close-ups, medium- and wide shots, the expressive play of shadow and light) and editing (crosscutting, montage, and the use of dissolves) each provided captivating vehicles for leading the eye and mind toward specific ways of seeing a story unfold.

In 1917, as official plans for wartime propaganda were being laid, the bewitching eloquence of film—its peculiar capacity to induce an altered state of consciousness among audiences drawn from all classes—was widely recognized as one of the medium's most salient properties.

A sea change in the capacity to touch the inner life of an audience, to transfigure the physics of perception, is palpable in the following description of cinema that appeared in a popular encyclopedia of modern technological wonders, published in 1915.

> Here, at last, is the magic of childhood—appearances, apparitions, objects possessed of power of movement and of intelligence. . . .
>
> For the motion picture does for us what no other thing can do save a drug. . . . It eliminates the time between happenings and brings two events separated actually by hours of time and makes them seem to us as following each other with no interval between them. Unconscious of this sixth sense of time, because it is so much a factor of our daily lives, ignorant of the fact that it is this and not our eyes alone which have been tricked, we leave the darkened theater with wonder in our hearts and admiration on our lips.[30]

Now, adding to the ability to capture a semblance of "reality" on film and to present social arguments through pictorial narratives, film was developing its own, unparalleled idiom of persuasion—a language that touched the recesses of inner life and spoke the uncanny vocabulary of dreams, permitting storytellers to enchant an audience silently with deep, psychologically charged ways of seeing.

Nowhere was the propagandistic potential of film more evident than in D. W. Griffith's *Birth of a Nation,* which had appeared in 1914. With enormous power, the film—which had war as its central theme—incited audiences into a frenzy of identification with racist Southern myths and contributed to the resurgence of the Ku Klux Klan. The film's ability to rally people to a cause provided a model for World War I propaganda.

To this point, the practices of publicity had been founded on the ability to communicate a semblance of news, of facticity. Now, from the intoxicating realm of entertainment, the medium of film had revealed a new, uncanny ability to transcend facticity for the purposes of persuasion, to reach a public on another, more emotional level.

Employing this powerful new tool—with all its suggestive implications—the CPI's Division of Films launched an unprecedented effort to deploy movies as implements of war. Under the division's direction, a number of feature films were produced for worldwide theatrical distribution: *Pershing's Crusaders, America's Answer, Under Four Flags,* and others, shown alongside more conventional Hollywood productions.

These propaganda films, however, were not directly produced by the CPI. Instead, the Division of Films maintained a "scenario department," which simply drafted general story outlines. These "scenarios" were then passed on to seasoned commercial film producers, whose job it was to introduce the magic of Hollywood, to ensure audience appeal.[31]

Distribution also drew on Hollywood know-how. As films were completed, their distribution was overseen by George Bowles, "an experienced theatrical and motion-picture manager," who had "made a name for himself" distributing and promoting *The Birth of a Nation.*[32]

On an international level, Hollywood's already considerable global allure was exploited as a wedge. To ensure the exhibition of CPI propaganda films around the world, movie producers were expected to attach a quid pro quo to their immensely popular feature films as they were exhibited around the world. As Creel explained it:

> Hollywood producers had to agree that no American enter-
> tainment films would be sold to any foreign exhibitor who
> refused to show the Committee's war pictures, and that none
> would be sold to houses where any sort of German film was
> being used. As exhibitors simply had to have our comedies
> and dramas . . . we soon had sole possession of the field.
> Much as they may have disliked our propaganda features,
> Douglass Fairbanks, Mary Pickford, and the Keystone Cops
> were a necessity.[33]

Beyond news, advertising, posters, political cartoons, and feature films, the CPI exploited countless other avenues of publicity as well. Academics from around the country were enlisted to write "authoritative" pamphlets on behalf of the war. Exhibitions at state fairs and other expositions were also mounted. Over 200,000 slides, stereopticon images, and photographs were likewise produced for exhibition in schools, churches, and other community centers.

Overall, in terms of the evolution of twentieth-century publicity, the CPI was built around a conception of the mass media that had never before been applied. Looming over each individual division was a conception of the mass media that saw them as parts of an interwoven perceptual environment. It was the espoused goal of the CPI to impregnate the entire fabric of perception with the message of the war.

Along with its sweeping use of media, the CPI broke ground in another critical way. In 1898, Gabriel Tarde had speculated on a hookup that existed between an evolving mass media system and patterns of personal conversation. Under the stewardship of Creel, such speculations guided concrete policy. In its attempt to manufacture a comprehensive universe of discourse, the CPI implemented pragmatic strategies that were overtly calculated to shape and direct the private conversations of everyday people.

This idea stood behind the creation of the Four-Minute Men. More than just a circle of men established to deliver rousing speeches throughout the country, the CPI's Division of Four-Minute Men was the centerpiece in a strategy designed to shape attitudes within the frame of people's daily lives. Four-Minute Men were chosen from among people assumed to be local community leaders, primarily business and professional men. Speakers were chosen not because of their support of the war—this would be a given—but because of the accustomed influence they had exerted over their neighbors' points of view in other contexts. Bellwethers of local thinking, these men were enrolled, according to Creel, to provide guidance for conversation throughout the country, "to bring some order out of oratorical chaos."[34]

If it was assumed that people in America's communities followed the viewpoints of their local leaders, local leaders, were simultaneously expected to echo the viewpoints of regional leaders (even more prominent business and professional men), and these men, in turn, were expected to follow leaders of the national organization. In short, the Division of Four-Minute Men was predicated on a hierarchical sociology of influence, a judgment that informal patterns of human interaction might be identified and exploited on behalf of the war.

On a weekly basis, this oratorical chain of command was administered through the *Four-Minute Man Bulletin,* an instructional newsletter that contained a "Budget of Materials," detailed guidelines for the speeches members would be expected to deliver in a given week. Issues of the bulletin introduced the general topic to be addressed each week: "Why We Are Fighting," "Unmasking German Propaganda," "Maintaining Morals and Morale," "The Danger to Democracy," and so forth. This theme was then divided into a five- to seven-part outline for the speech that was to be delivered. Specific information or ideas to be conveyed were also supplied. Samples of "typical speeches" were included as well. Speakers were encouraged to muster enthusiasm, and their performances were routinely monitored by local chairmen, who judged the competence of their delivery and offered suggestions for improvement. Those judged to be boring speakers were expeditiously removed from the Four-Minute Men speakers' circuit.

Together, these exercises ensured that in any given week, influential men throughout the country were addressing their neighbors with standardized speeches, covering identical topics, in a manner calculated to suggest spontaneity and evoke enthusiasm. Beyond simply dispensing a governmental line, Four-Minute Men were expected to get movie audiences to carry ideas and topics back into the community at large, to create what one bulletin characterized as "an endless chain of verbal messages."

If speeches were planned to instigate discussion, there was also concern that this discussion should remain governable. CPI leaders were wary about nourishing an atmosphere of impromptu "curbstone oratory." "It was imperative," reflected Creel, "to guard against the dangers of unrestraint."[35]

As such, Four-Minute Men cautioned audiences to discuss weekly topics within proscribed limits of conversation, to avoid those contexts that might inadvertently further a climate of unrest. "Only where men meet naturally to talk and to listen, at the table, at social gatherings, at noon in the workshop, at night at home, is discussion in place," advised a weekly bulletin.[36]

Augmenting the regular program for adults, which concentrated its efforts in movie theaters, the Division of Four-Minute Men also operated a youth group, the Junior Four-Minute Men, which focused on elementary and secondary schools. Speaking competitions for children were held, to be administered by teachers and principles whose loyalty was judged by their willingness to cooperate. The junior division also published the *National School Service Bulletin,* which provided teachers with topics for regular classroom discussion. Beyond putting America's educational system in uniform, these activities gave children topics that—it was expected—they would carry back into their homes.

Speakers also participated in an ideological policing function. Audiences were encouraged to identify, interrogate, and even report people in their communities who expressed antiwar sentiment.

To deal with potentially fractious communities, special brigades of speakers were deputized. African Americans—many of whom found it difficult to swallow the liberal rhetoric of the CPI while they were burdened by entrenched patterns of racism—were identified specifically as a troublesome group, in need of special attention. For example, in Brunswick, Georgia—where Jim Crow laws routinely subverted African Americans' rights—Alfred Wood, chairman of the "Regular Four-Minute Men," expressed worries that "colored people . . . seem particularly susceptible" to antiwar propaganda. Responding to this perceived problem, Wood drafted William A. Perry, a "responsible and patriotic colored man," to serve as chairman of a new organization, the "Colored Four-Minute Men of Brunswick."[37]

Within the purview of the CPI, every moment of human interaction became a suitable venue for publicity. Heated by the fires of war, the concept of public relations was moving beyond the borders of journalistic press agentry, attempting to encompass the ether of human relations itself. "Never before in history," wrote Charles and Mary Beard, "had such a campaign of education been organized; never before had American citizens realized how thoroughly, how irresistibly a modern government could impose its ideas upon the whole nation."[38]

The dual role of the Four-Minute Men—as a localized propaganda agency and a nationwide organization for extinguishing opposition to the war—offers a microcosm of what was, in fact, a much larger truth encompassing the activities of the CPI: the wholesale smothering of ideas and outlooks that ran against the grain of the official story. Part and parcel of the committee's success in mobilizing America's intellectual and creative resources for war was the simultaneous establishment of an ambience of censorship, calculated to discourage or punish impure thought.

Writing in 1935, Harold Lasswell—one of America's leading students of propaganda—observed that "the high importance of coordinating propaganda with all other means of social control cannot be too insistently repeated."[39] In the context of the First World War, while the CPI blanketed every nook and cranny of American life with liberal-sounding rhetoric, this formula was followed to the letter. A severe climate of suppression was being instituted throughout the United States.

In his public declarations Creel repudiated censorship and the squelching of opposition. "The work that is being carried on by the Committee on Public Information is not a censorship and never has been a censorship. It is a medium of expression," he maintained in 1918.[40] Yet underneath this pledge of openness, an atmosphere of suppression was taking hold.

The legal framework for this suppression was provided by the Espionage Act—passed on June 15, 1917—which upheld the censor-

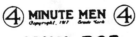

(TOP LEFT) Sample slide for projection on theater screens announcing a Four-Minute Man talk. (TOP RIGHT) CPI bulletin for teachers providing a list of available pamphlets and suggestions for the proper teaching of history. (BOTTOM LEFT) CPI magazine advertisement printed in the *Saturday Evening Post*. (BOTTOM RIGHT) A World War I poster warning soldiers to keep their lips buttoned, produced by the propaganda wing of the War Department, headed by Walter Lippmann. REPRINTED FROM MOCK AND LARSEN, *WORDS THAT WON THE WAR*.

ship of ideas considered injurious to the war effort. As widespread prosecutions took place, the carrot of "voluntary censorship" was continually toughened first, by the stick of the Espionage Act and then by the Sedition Act of 1918, "a statute which in effect made any criticism of the Wilson administration illegal."[41]

"Under the general terms of the Espionage and Sedition acts," wrote the Beards, "newspapers were continually silenced by orders and prosecutions. Individual critics of the war and the Wilson program were rounded up by the government, often without warrants of arrest, hustled to jail, held incommunicado without bail, tried in courts where the atmosphere was heavily charged with passion, lectured by irate judges, and sent to prison for long terms—in one case an adolescent girl for twenty years."[42]

To a large extent, the general climate of thought control was sustained by much of the ongoing work of the CPI: its repeated warnings that people must be "vigilant"; scrutinize their neighbors; listen in on others' conversations; and, if necessary, embrace the role of government informer.

More than a huge publicity apparatus, the CPI was the intrinsic outcome of new ways of thinking that had been percolating during the preceding decades. "The tossing about of symbols," noted one important analyst, became an increasingly serviceable "substitute for intellectual transaction." Amid the CPI, a decisive shift in the ways that publicists thought about the public and about shaping public opinion was revealed.

Whatever contradictions their actual practices may have contained, Progressive publicists—in the years preceding the war—had embraced Enlightenment notions about the work they were doing. They were seekers of "truth," exposers of "fact," exercisers of "reason." Proponents of corporate public relations, as has been seen in Ivy Lee and Theodore Vail, also couched their activities within an argot of facticity.

In public utterances about the CPI, it must be added, Creel—a dyed-in-the-wool Progressive—continued to do the same. "I do not believe that public opinion has its rise in the emotions," he wrote in 1918. "I feel that public opinion has its source in the minds of people, that it has its base in reason, and that it expresses slow-formed con-

CPI posters appealing to public emotion. NEW YORK PUBLIC LIBRARY, AUTHOR'S COLLECTION

victions rather than any temporary excitement or any passion of the moment."[43]

Yet despite his ongoing protestations that "We have never made any appeal to the emotions," the record of the CPI points toward a considerably different conclusion.

Under the direction of Gibson, for example, the pictorial work of the CPI was routinely aimed at the heart, not the head. "One cannot create enthusiasm for the war on the basis of practical appeal," Gibson maintained. "The spirit that will lead a man to put away the things of his accustomed life and go forth to all the hardships of war is not kindled by showing him the facts." Artwork produced for the CPI, he concluded, must "appeal to the heart."

Posters and other CPI-sponsored imagery complied with Gibson's instruction. In a Red Cross poster produced for the CPI, a photomontage juxtaposed a giant, close-up image of a protective nurse/mother over a wide camera shot of a body-strewn battlefield. In a striking, avant-garde composition, the war's harvest of death was powerfully transformed into a metaphor for nurturing security.

In another Red Cross poster, a Pieta-like image of a nurse/ Blessed Virgin was rendered, eyes raised to God, arms cradling a wounded, infant-Jesus-sized soldier in her arms. Beneath her the caption read: "The Greatest Mother in the World."

In yet another poster, a painterly portrait of a drowning mother and child, perishing as they sink beneath the surface of a dark green ocean, provided an emotive justification for the one-word mandate: "Enlist!"

Reinforcing such sentimental monuments to the American war effort, images of the enemy were built on a bedrock of fear, invoking an ineluctable climate of xenophobic paranoia. Many images portrayed an inscrutable enemy, lurking around every corner, threatening even the most apparently innocent circumstances. One CPI magazine ad, for example, displayed a picture of two women engaging in private conversation. Nearby, apparently combing through a newspaper, a man's eyes reveal that he is, in fact, eavesdropping on their conversation. Below the image was the caption "Spies and Lies" and a text that warned, "German agents are everywhere. . . . Do not become a tool of the Hun by passing on the malicious, disheartening rumors which he so eagerly sows. . . . You are in contact with the enemy today, just as truly as if you faced him across No Man's Land. In your hands are two powerful weapons with which to meet him— discretion and vigilance. Use them."

Another image depicted the enemy as a menacing spider wearing a German helmet, waiting to ensnare loose-lipped people in his web. "SPIES are LISTENING" announced the poster in resounding typography.

Still another image displayed a map of the United States, its geography renamed to offer a chilling picture of postwar America should the enemy be victorious. Now called "New Prussia," the familiar outline of the United States is studded with alien, Hun-inspired names: Heineapolis, Denverburg, Cape U Boat, the Gulf of Hate, and the like.

Reinforcing such terrifying visions of America's future, one macabre CPI poster displayed the Statue of Liberty "crumbling under German fire, with the burning ruins of New York City silhouetted against the background."[44]

This approach became routine within the CPI. In the Budgets of Materials they received, for example, Four-Minute Men were continually schooled in the particular serviceability of emotional appeals. In Bulletin No. 39, William Ingersoll (director of the division) told speakers that beyond presenting "facts and details" to "satisfy the reasoning faculties of our audiences," Four-Minute Men must also "appeal to the feelings, in which we stir the sentiment and emotion and arouse the desire to DO something" on the part of an audience.[45]

Elsewhere, in instructions for a speech on Liberty Bonds, the bulletin summarized the essence of an effective presentation, which was lifted directly from the nascent wisdom of advertising psychologists. "One idea—simple language—talk in pictures, not in statistics— touch their minds, hearts, spirits—make them want to win with every fiber of their beings—translate that desire into terms of bonds—and they will buy."[46]

• • •

In spite of Creel's insistent denials, the "House of Truth" was perched not on a foundation of facts, but upon a swamp of emotions. As a vast laboratory experiment in the molding of public opinion, the CPI moved away from earlier, rationalistic models that had been defined primarily by journalism toward communications strategies that aimed ineffably for the gut. This shift was summarized ten years later, when Harold Lasswell summarized the lesson of World War I.

[A] new and subtler instrument must weld thousands and even millions of human beings into one amalgamated mass of hate and will and hope. A new flame must burn out the canker of dissent and temper the steel of bellicose enthusiasm. The name of this new hammer and anvil of social solidarity is propaganda. Talk must take the place of drill; print must supply the dance. War dances live in literature and at the fringes of the modern earth; war propaganda breathes and fumes in the capitals and provinces of the world.[47]

As many among a generation of Progressive intellectuals flocked to serve as ideological emissaries for the CPI or lent their talents to other facets of the war mobilization, there were some who disapproved, seeing intellectual war service as a fickle betrayal of principles. Among them, it was Randolph Bourne, in a 1917 jeremiad entitled "War and the Intellectuals," who presented one of the most outspoken accounts of this metamorphosis.

Published barely two months after the United States had entered the war, Bourne's bleak epitaph for the abandoned social ideals of progressivism mourned that "it has been a bitter experience to see the unanimity with which the American intellectuals have thrown their support to the use of war technique." Progressives, who had once believed in the fertile powers of human reason, were now, according to Bourne, dealing with the American people as if they were "sluggish masses, too remote from the world-conflict to be stirred, too lacking in intellect to perceive their danger." From this vantage point, he continued, an intellectual legion of "socialists, college professors, publicists, new-republicans, [and] practitioners of literature, had assumed the iniquitous task of "riveting the war mind on a hundred million more of the world's people."

With bitter irony, Bourne mocked the conceit of these fallen ideal-ists, men who had opened "the sluices" in order to "flood us with the sewage of the war spirit."[48]

"War and the Intellectuals" was Bourne's funeral oration for the questioning social consciousness that had, in his estimation, marked prewar progressivism. Now, in the crucible of war, contem-plative humanistic ideals were giving way to a fateful brand of cyni-cism. People who had once believed in the ability to use "creative intelligence" to bring about a more humane social order were becoming dutiful technicians of mass persuasion, craven manipula-tors of consent.

In many ways, Bourne's obituary for the critical spirit of progres-sivism was prophetic. Bourne's vision of liberal intellectuals becoming "servants of power" not only spoke to their role during the war, but, to a large extent, described what would become of them over the decade that followed.

Progressive intellectuals had customarily been critics of big busi-ness, of its greed, exploitativeness, and inherent corruption. During the war, however, as corporations buttressed and profited from the war effort, critiques of big business subsided, giving way to a more receptive view of corporate America. After the war, this view would persist for the most part. At the same time, a preoccupation with the need to adjust public attitudes and the search for techniques by which this adjustment might be achieved were also carried into the postwar period. This mix of sensibilities—a greater friendliness toward big business and increased attention to the importance of molding public opinion—animated the lives of a growing class of American intellec-tuals as they moved from war service back into civilian life.

While there continued to be intellectual dissidents during the twenties, those who complied with a new way of seeing would prove to be far more consequential to the future development of public rela-tions thinking. Central to their perspective was a new understanding of who the public was and what were the most effective ways of influ-encing that public.

Before the war Progressive intellectuals had espoused the Enlightenment dictum that people—at least middle-class people—

were essentially rational, capable of evaluating information and then of making intelligent decisions. In the context of the CPI, "public opinion" became something to be mobilized and managed; the "public mind" was now seen as an entity to be manufactured, not reasoned with.

The war had also elevated the function of unreason, of the "night mind," for people engaged in the business of shaping public opinion. Reflected within this shift was a transformed conception of human nature itself. In their discussions of the public—of people in general—Brahmins of public opinion, educated by the war, were becoming increasingly conversant with psychological aspects of human perception. In the citadels of the Enlightened West, a naive faith in reason was beginning to fade from view. Publicists were beginning to look for unconscious or instinctive triggers that might be pulled to activate public passions.

Aligned with this search, publicists also began to broaden their understanding of the rhetorics of persuasion. If prior notions of publicity had been built on carefully constructed armatures of "fact," the CPI had unearthed the venerable power of symbols to inspire and sway the public's imagination.

Last, if preceding approaches to persuasion had focused on newspapers and periodicals as the primary arenas for forging public attitudes, the war had dramatized the existence of complex, interlocking networks of perception. In the context of the CPI, public relations moved beyond its myopic fixation on the printed page toward an increasingly sophisticated appreciation of the media environment overall and of the webs of influence that touch people in their everyday lives.

Within twenty-four hours of the Armistice, the CPI was summarily dismantled. In the aftermath of the war, it must be added, the reputations of Creel in particular and of Progressivism more generally suffered a decline, partly because of their roles in the promotion of the war. Yet the experiences gained in the CPI and its general lessons about the terrain of the public mind would inform the concerns of public relations specialists and affect the contours of American cultural life for decades to come.

PART 3

Changing Rhetorics
of Persuasion

7

Social Psychology and the Quest for the Public Mind

IN THE AFTERMATH of the First World War, American business leaders were buoyed by a renewed sense of confidence. As a colossal experiment in mass persuasion, the Committee on Public Information (CPI) had fostered a belief that public opinion might be managed, that a social climate, more friendly to business interests, could indeed be achieved. "The war taught us the power of propaganda," declared Roger Babson, the influential business analyst, in 1921. "Now when we have anything to sell the American people, we know how to sell it."[1]

At the center of this newfound assurance stood the wartime revelation that appeals directed at the public's emotions provided levers of influence that mere facts could never match. The postwar pronouncements of Ivy Lee—still one of the nation's preeminent practitioners of corporate public relations—provide rich evidence of this changed sensibility.

From the time Lee opened his practice in 1906 through the period just preceding U.S. entry into the war, he—like most of the first generation of corporate PR men—had dutifully employed the Progressive Era's idiom of *factual argument* and *rational persuasion* in describing his work. After the war, however, Lee's statements on the subject of public relations revealed a significant shift in emphasis.

Speaking with an interviewer from the *New York Evening Post* in the spring of 1921, for example, Lee wandered from a fairly familiar description of the press agent's calling to announce his growing attraction to psychoanalysis. "I have found" he confessed, "the Freudian theories concerning the psychology of the subconscious mind of great interest." Then, Lee added, "Publicity is essentially a matter of mass psychology. We must remember that people are guided more by sentiment than by mind."[2]

Some months later, while delivering a lecture on the vocation of public relations to a gathering at Columbia University's School of Journalism, Lee invited his audience to visit him at his offices, to "come down and let us show you our library, see the extraordinary collection of books on psychology, all the elements that go into the making of crowd psychology, mass psychology." He counseled the gathering:

> You must study human emotions and all the factors that move people, that persuade men in any line of human activity. Psychology, mob psychology, is one of the important factors that underlay this whole business.[3]

Lee, who had once characterized his publicity work as providing "the press and the public of the United States" with "prompt and accurate information," was assuming the mien of a necromancer. Public relations, he declared in 1923, was nothing less than the *"art of steering heads inside . . . the secret art of all the other arts, the secret religion of all religions."* This art, he proclaimed apocalyptically, held "the secret" by which "a civilization" might be preserved and "a successful and permanent business" built.[4]

This shift in Lee's thinking epitomized a broader change that was taking place in the way public relations specialists thought about their work. If, prior to the war, the idea of publicity was still grounded in a premise of rational argumentation—in the appeal to conscious reason—postwar conceptions of publicity were increasingly being premised on tactics of psychological manipulation, on seductive appeals to the subconscious recesses of mental life.

Without doubt, the war and the CPI had, for a generation of American intellectuals, accentuated the importance of the psychological factors of persuasion. Yet Lee's fascination with mass psychology and with the emotions of the crowd also reflected a vector of thinking that had begun to reveal itself before the war. From the turn of the century—even as most publicists continued to pay tribute the majesty of facts—another current of intellectual thought was emerging, one that argued that the entity known as "the public mind" was innately more susceptible to emotional entreaties than it was to rational appeals.

No individual contributed more to this perspective than Gustave Le Bon, whose widely acclaimed writings—particularly *The Crowd: A Study of the Popular Mind*—put the nascent field of social psychology on the map.[5] As discussed earlier, Le Bon's ghastly anatomy of the "crowd mind" spoke to the anxieties of the fin de siècle middle class, troubled by the spread of popular unrest.[6]

Yet beneath Le Bon's lurid treatise on the "entry of the popular classes into political life," *The Crowd* contained another—more fundamental—layer of analysis, one that threw into question his own repeated assertion that the middle-class public was still capable of rational thought.

"From the intellectual point of view an abyss may exist between a great mathematician and his bootmaker," Le Bon noted, "but from the point of view of character the difference is most often slight or non-existent." This argument, which addressed the issue of human nature itself, betrayed Le Bon's underlying conviction that among human beings in general, "the part played by the unconscious in all our acts is immense," while "that played by reason is very small."[7]

> The conscious life of the mind is of small importance in comparison with its unconscious life. The most subtle analyst, the most acute observer, is scarcely successful in discovering more than a very small number of the unconscious motives that determine his conduct. Our conscious acts are the outcome of an unconscious substratum created in the mind in the main by hereditary influences.[8]

Prior to the modern age, according to Le Bon's account, this intrinsic irrationality had been subdued by the civilizing process, guided by the conscious intelligence of a few superior individuals, and secured by the rigorous social order they created. Though instinctual traits continued to govern the behavior of inferior beings, he maintained, the rise of civilization and its hierarchical structures had—for centuries—kept their unholy tendencies in check.[9]

With the rise of mass democratic politics, however, and with the breakdown of religious and social hierarchies, inborn character was again emerging as the dominant force of history. An "unconscious substratum" that had lurked, all along, beneath the intellectual surface of civilization was again gaining "the upper hand." For Le Bon, the rise of the crowd mind embodied no less than the *return of the repressed,* the demise of a long-cultivated "conscious personality" in favor of the "unconscious activities" of the "spinal cord."[10]

The revolt of the masses and, with it, the elevation of mass politics, mass aesthetics, and mass destructiveness, meant that the conditions of the crowd were in the process of becoming universal, hegemonic. No one—not even those middle-class individuals who privately upheld the values of civilization—would be spared.

> Civilisation is now without stability, and at the mercy of every chance. The populace is sovereign, and the tide of barbarism mounts. The civilisation may still seem brilliant because it possesses an outward front, the work of a long past, but is in reality an edifice crumbling to ruin, which nothing supports, and destined to fall in at the first storm.[11]

To a number of intellectuals in the early years of the century, Le Bon's vision of a society dominated by unconscious forces was extraordinarily persuasive. It explained the chaos of industrial life. It mirrored the anxieties of people whose sense of order and meaning was unraveling. Amid Le Bon's reveries on the psychology of crowds, the customary dichotomization of the public and the crowd was beginning to collapse. An increasing number of other thinkers began to pursue a similar path of argument.

One of these thinkers was Robert Ezra Park, whose 1904 doctoral dissertation, "The Crowd and the Public," offers an articulate example of how some American Progressives were reading Le Bon.[12] Park—who would become one of the country's most influential sociological thinkers—presented his thesis as a preliminary survey of the emerging study of "crowd psychology," which he hailed as "a new arrival among the sciences." Le Bon's thinking left a conspicuous mark on Park's presentation.

In large measure—and true to his Progressive lineage—Park's treatise embraced Le Bon's surface argument that "the crowd" and "the public" constituted two distinct social forms: one marked by its brutish, impulsive, and "simple emotional state," the other by its intrinsic ability to engage in critical, rational debate.[13]

> Characteristically the crowd always functions at the perception stage of awareness-development, while the behavior of the public, which is expressed in public opinion, results from the discussion among individuals who assume opposing positions. This discussion is based upon the presentation of facts.[14]

Like Le Bon—who, on the surface, maintained that middle-class individuals were still capable of reason—Park intonated the idea that the "crowd mind" embodied the triumph of unreasoned instinct, whereas "public opinion" was the sum of "individual critical attitudes."[15]

With its concentration on the primacy of the individual and its fetishization of factual evidence, Park's "public" appeared to be both a monument to American middle-class values and a testimonial to the conviction that public deliberation provided a viable alternative to the collective hypnosis of the crowd. Beneath Park's neat separation of the "public" from the "crowd," however, lay a murkier reading of the present moment. Even as Park recited his characteristic Progressive cant, posing a reasonable public against an irrational crowd, his dissertation disclosed a gnawing sense of uncertainty about the actual soundness of "public opinion" in twentieth-century American life.

While Park did not venture toward an exegesis of hereditary human nature, he, like Le Bon, was deeply pessimistic regarding the fate of reason. Ideal types aside, gazing out at his contemporary world, Park was arriving at the judgment that "public opinion" was becoming less and less distinguishable from the "crowd mind." Citing the influence of the media in modern society, Park concluded that "so-called public opinion is generally nothing more than a naive collective impulse which can be manipulated by catchwords."

Modern journalism, which is supposed to instruct and direct public opinion by reporting and discussing events, usually turns out to be simply a mechanism for controlling collective attention. The "opinion" formed in this manner shows a form that is logically similar to the judgment derived from unreflective perception: the opinion is formed directly and simultaneously as information is received."[16]

Another important intellectual to follow in Le Bon's wake was the British political analyst, Graham Wallas. In what would become his classic study, *Human Nature in Politics* (1908), Wallas announced a dramatic break from the rationalist paradigm that had, to that time, dominated political theories.

The "intellectualist fallacy," as he described it, only obscured the actual forces at play in politics. Regardless of social class, Wallas contended, the powers of reason are far less than previously imagined.

Whoever sets himself to base his political thinking on a re-examination of the working of human nature, must begin by trying to overcome his own tendency to exaggerate the intellectuality of mankind. . . .

We are apt to assume that every human action is the result of an intellectual process, by which a man first thinks of some end he desires, and then calculates the means by which that end can be attained.[17]

In the face of these deductions, Wallas—whose thinking would have a substantial impact on the ideas of Walter Lippmann—concluded that "the empirical art of politics" was not founded on fact-based appeals to reason. Instead, he asserted, it "consists largely in the creation of opinion, by the deliberate exploitation of subconscious, non-rational inference."[18]

Wilfred Trotter's 1916 book, *The Instincts of the Herd in Peace and War,* only added to the growing conviction that human beings were more sensitive to unconscious, instinctual drives than they were to the powers of critical reason. Trotter—whose work, along with that of Le Bon and Wallas, would deeply influence a postwar generation of public relations experts—argued that without a fuller understanding of mankind's mental inheritance, any attempt to guide human affairs was futile. "No understanding of the causes of stability and instability in human society," he wrote, was "possible until the undiminished vigour of instinct in man is fully recognized."[19] Of particular interest to Trotter was the overwhelming impact of the "herd instinct," the unceasing need to gain the approval and camaraderie of the social group.

Terrified by existential isolation, Trotter contended, people are inescapably drawn toward "intimate dependence on the herd." This need to belong, he argued, "is traceable not merely in matters physical and intellectual, but also betrays itself in the deepest recesses of the personality as a sense of incompleteness which compels the individual to reach out towards some larger existence than his own, some encompassing being in whom his perplexities may find a solution and his longings peace."[20]

Given this hereditary need to find meaning in something larger than oneself, Trotter continued, the human being "is more sensitive to the voice of the herd than to any other influence."

It can inhibit or stimulate his thought and conduct. It is the source of his moral codes, of the sanctions of his ethics and philosophy. It can endow him with energy, courage, and endurance, and can as easily take these away.[21]

Simply put, Trotter theorized that the herd compensates for the innate solitude and anxiety that reside in the backrooms of individual life.

This aspect of Trotter's argument represented a significant shift from Le Bon's understanding of social psychology. Despite his utterances on human nature, Le Bon repeatedly maintained that in the crowd there was an eradication of a "conscious personality," but that this personality continued to define the mental life of individuals. In the crowd, he asserted, individuals were put "in possession of a sort of collective mind which makes them feel, think, and act in a manner quite different from that in which each individual of them would feel, think, and act . . . in a state of isolation." Le Bon's reiterated assertion that there was a critical distinction between group psychology and individual psychology was something that had substantially faded in Trotter.

To Trotter, the unconscious, instinctual inclinations of people in groups were inextricably linked to the unconscious and instinctual forces that prevailed over people as individuals. As the delirium of war engulfed Europe and the shock of modernity disrupted a customary sense of order, a trust in the persuasive powers of reason—even at the level of the middle-class individual—was vanishing. Human nature and motivation—in their essence—were being scrutinized, more and more, in relation to the siren song of the unconscious and the primal legacy of instinctual life.

Three years later, as the Great War reached its conclusion, this perspective on human behavior—the coupling of group and individual psychology—remained unshaken. "Recent social psychology," trumpeted Everett Dean Martin in his influential 1919 book, *The Behavior of Crowds: A Psychological Study,* "has abandoned the theory that social behavior is primarily governed by reason or by consideration." Borrowing words from a contemporary, psychologist William McDougall, Martin explained that "instinctive impulses determine the ends of all activities and supply the driving-power by which all mental activities are maintained. These impulses are the mental forces that maintain and shape all the life of individuals and societies, and in them we are confronted with the central mystery of life and mind and will."[22]

This shifting discourse, explaining group behavior in terms of the individual psyche, was evidenced most dramatically by the growing influence of Sigmund Freud and of psychoanalytic thinking more generally. In 1922, Freud entered into the evaluation of the "crowd mind" directly, when his slender study, *Group Psychology and the Analysis of the Ego* appeared. Fifteen years the Frenchman's junior, Freud's book approached Le Bon's work and subsequent social psychology with considerable respect.

Though Freud thought that Le Bon had presented a "brilliantly executed picture of the group mind," he took issue with Le Bon's basic assumption that the psyches of the group and of the individual were distinct and dissimilar entities.

The contrast between individual psychology and social or group psychology, which at first may seem to be full of significance, loses a great deal of its sharpness when it is examined more closely. . . . In the individual's mental life someone else is invariably involved, as a model, as an object, as a helper, as an opponent; and so from the very first, individual psychology . . . is at the same time social psychology as well.[23]

Le Bon believed "that the particular acquirements of individuals become obliterated in a group." To this, Freud posed the question: What is the "unity" that binds the individual to the group? "Something," he proclaimed, must "unite them."

Building on Trotter's argument, Freud retorted that groups had the ability to exercise "a decisive influence over the mental life of the individual" because the group provided the individual with a context in which to "throw off the repressions of his unconscious instinctual impulses," impulses that are "contained as a predisposition" within all individuals.[24]

Again and again, Freud responded to Le Bon's description of the "crowd mind" with parallels drawn from his studies of individual psychology. To Le Bon's description of the crowd as occupying a "hypnotic" state, Freud replied that the metaphor of hypnosis itself was drawn from the realm of the individual psyche.

To Le Bon's argument that "in groups the most contradictory ideas can exist side by side and tolerate each other, without any conflict arising from the logical contradictions between them," Freud responded that this "is also true in the unconscious mental life of individuals."

To Le Bon's declaration that groups "have never thirsted after truth," that they "demand illusions," Freud answered:

We have pointed out that this predominance of the life of phantasy and of the illusion born of an unfulfilled wish is the ruling factor in the psychology of neurosis. . . . Neurotics are guided not by ordinary objective reality but psychological reality.

To Le Bon's argument that groups think not in ideas, but "in images," Freud observed that this was also true "with individuals in states of free imagination."

Likewise, Freud maintained that groups' susceptibility to the power of "suggestion . . . is actually an irreducible, primitive phenomenon, a fundamental fact in the mental life of man," viscerally linked to his sexual existence.[25]

Though Le Bon had described the crowd, Freud concluded, he had not yet explained it. Following Trotter's lead, Freud's intervention suggested that the underlying forces that drive the psychology of the group are found in the psychodynamics of the individual. With *Group Psychology and the Analysis of the Ego,* a substantial intellectual change had been canonized. If initial speculations on the "group mind" had focused on the untamed, destructive urges of the urban masses, now, by the early twenties, the role of "unconscious, instinctual impulses" in human behavior overall had overtaken what had begun as a class-oriented analysis.

■   ■   ■   ■   ■

Le Bon's estimation of the modern age was, in many ways, profoundly pessimistic. While he allowed that it was not "easy to say as yet what will one day be evolved from this . . . chaotic period," much of *The Crowd* bewails the decline and death of "the civilised state." A similar sense of despondency agonized Wallas in *Human Nature in Politics* and Trotter in his 1916 meditation on the *Instinct of the Herd.* For any reader of *Civilization and its Discontents,* Freud's susceptibility to social despair is likewise unmistakable.

Yet if the trajectory of social psychology, from Le Bon onward, revealed a disheartened break with Enlightenment optimism, it simultaneously gave flight to less harrowing, more utilitarian, ideas. These ideas suggested that there was still the potential for social control—for the efficient exercise of power—in a world dominated by the forces of unreason. For the field of public relations, along with other modern professions, the influence of these speculations would be profound.

Throughout the pages of *The Crowd,* Le Bon wandered from his doleful funeral oration for civilization to propose ways that the conscious and instrumental use of science might, in fact, play a decisive role in the fate of the modern age. The key to this possibility lay in Le Bon's vivid discourse on the anatomy of "the popular mind," in which he itemized the mechanisms by which the unconscious energies of the crowd were commonly galvanized by irresponsible (socialistic) leaders. Within his catalog of demagogic technique, Le Bon began to provide a preliminary handbook for people who were interested in "managing the human climate."

Embarking on the subject timidly at first, Le Bon cautioned that "[a] knowledge of the psychology of crowds is today the last resource of the statesman who wishes not to govern them—*that is becoming a very difficult matter*—but at any rate not to be too much governed by them."[26] This knowledge rested, in essence, on a scientific understanding of the popular mind as something "perpetually hovering on the borderland of unconsciousness, readily yielding to all suggestions."[27]

If the "conscious personality" that Le Bon ascribed to the middle classes was still open to a language of reason, the perpetually unconscious crowd—in which reason gives way to the "feminine" traits of "impulsiveness, irritability, incapacity to reason," and the "absence of judgement and of the critical spirit"—was exploitable by an altogether different rhetoric of persuasion.[28] Propelled by its instincts, not its mind, Le Bon declared, the "crowd thinks in images," not words. "The image itself immediately calls up a series of other images, having no logical connection with the first." Turning to his apparently "rational" readers, Le Bon explained:

> [O]ur reason shows us the incoherence there is in these images, but a crowd is almost blind to this truth, and confuses with the real event what the deforming action of its imagination has superimposed thereon. A crowd scarcely distinguishes between the subjective and the objective. It accepts as real the images evoked in its mind, though they most often have only a very distant relation with the observed fact.[29]

Within this analysis of the crowd's thirst for "illusions" lay prescriptions for the modern exercise of power. Throughout history, Le Bon professed, civilization had always been "created and directed by a small intellectual aristocracy, never by crowds."[30] Now, in an era in which the "voice of the masses" was "preponderant," this aristocracy (social scientists) must explore the crowd mind to develop techniques by which mass hypnosis might be employed.

"Whatever be the ideas suggested to crowds," Le Bon instructed, "they can only exercise effective influence on condition that they assume a very absolute, uncompromising, and simple shape. They present themselves then in the guise of images, and are only accessible to the masses under this form. These image-like ideas are not connected by any logical bond . . . and may take each other's place like the slides of a magic-lantern . . . "[31]

"The imagination of crowds" is most effectively awakened when these images are presented dramatically, he added. "Crowds being only capable of thinking in images are only to be impressed by images. It is only images that terrify or attract them and become motives of action." "For this reason," he offered, "theatrical representations, in which the image is shown in its most clearly visible shape, always have an enormous influence on crowds."[32]

If "the imagination of crowds" is to be swayed, Le Bon advised, "the feat is never to be achieved by attempting to work upon the intelligence or reasoning faculty."[33]

> Crowds have always undergone the influence of illusions. Whoever can supply them with illusions is easily their master; whoever attempts to destroy their illusions is always their victim.[34]

Against approaches to publicity predicated on a rational audience and on the authority of journalistic facts, Le Bon was inclining toward strategies of persuasion grounded in the principles of drama, exploiting the mysterious power of the image as their primary idiom.

At the inner core of Le Bon's book, then, stood a fundamental challenge to the assumptions that had guided the Progressive publicists and had informed the schemes of early corporate public relations tacticians. "It is not . . . the facts in themselves that strike the popular imagination," Le Bon decreed, "but the way in which they take place and are brought to notice.

> It is necessary that by their condensation, if I must thus express myself, they should produce a startling image which fills and besets the mind. To know the art of impressing the imagination of crowds is to know at the same time the art of governing them.[35]

In his important 1974 study, *The Fall of Public Man,* Richard Sennett wrote of the past hundred years as an era marked by the rise of a "collective personality . . . generated by a common fantasy."[36] In the writings of Le Bon, one encounters the onset of a train of thought that supposed that whoever could compellingly produce and circulate "common fantasies" would be in a position to define the direction of that "collective personality."

As social psychology embraced the idea that instinctive, unconscious motivations were the decisive underpinning of social existence, Le Bon's proposals for governing the "crowd mind" began to be applied to the ways that social scientists approached the "public mind" as well. Old distinctions between the *public* and the *crowd* were giving way to ideas of an all-inclusive mass audience, driven, for the most part, by its sentiments. Among social psychologists, the ability of leaders to understand and engineer the unconscious, instinctual lives of the public was increasingly seen as a passport for accomplishing social stability. The dexterity with which a new class of experts could learn to manipulate symbols appeared to be the fortress that would protect the forces of order from the mounting tide of chaos.

If the "instinct of the herd" contributed to the rise of mass politics and social "instability," Trotter suggested in 1916, at the same time—if properly understood—it made people "remarkably susceptible to leadership." Leaders, he counseled, must master the manipulation of this instinct.

> [T]he only way in which society can be made safe from disruption or decay is by the intervention of the conscious and instructed intellect as a factor among the forces ruling its [the herd instinct's] development.[37]

Throughout history, Le Bon had theorized, social stability had always been the handiwork of "a small intellectual aristocracy." With Trotter's call for a rule by "conscious and instructed intellect," he was proposing not only the restoration of an elite coterie of thinkers, but of an "aristocracy" that was particularly versed in the science of social psychology and thus qualified to shepherd the unconscious lives of the public.

Martin—whose work would have a conspicuous influence on the thinking of Edward Bernays—enlarged on Trotter's view. Given the "controlling" influence that instincts exert on the dynamics of contemporary life and the "serious menace to civilization" that they pose, social and intellectual elites, he instructed, must learn to master and manipulate those instincts in order to safeguard the present social order. Like priests and necromancers of old, today's leaders must learn to mobilize the obscure inner lives of their flock.

"Crowd-behavior" is on the rise, he warned, rehearsing a theme that had become increasingly routine among middle-class intelligentsia since Le Bon had launched the phrase. "Events are making it more and more clear," he wrote, "that pressing as are certain economic questions, the forces which threaten society are really psychological." With a tone of emergency he chalked out the modern alchemy of rule:

> *We must become a cult, write our philosophy of life in flaming headlines, and sell our cause in the market.* No matter if we meanwhile surrender every value for which we stand, *we must strive to cajole the majority into imagining itself on our side. . . .* [O]nly with the majority with us, whoever we are, can we live. *It is numbers, not values that count—quantity not quality.*[38]

During the 1920s, such ideas—fortified and substantiated by the war experience—would inform the outlooks of a widening circle of American intellectuals, people who sought to employ social science as a tool for guiding the inherent irrationality of the public mind. Embedded within this development lay two momentous shifts.

First, at the turn of the century, people engaged in publicity work were inclined to draw a distinction between a state of irrationality, which they attributed to the working classes, and an innate ability to exercise critical reason, which they ascribed to the middle-class public, of which they were a part. This assumption of critical reason had informed most of their public relations activities. For publicists of the 1920s, however, irrationality had become the habitual filter through which human nature, in its most general terms, was understood. Within this schema, reason had become the lone province of experts—scientific thinkers such as themselves—whose designated role was to employ that reason to save society from its inherently unreasonable nature.

Second, and equally significant, conjectures regarding the appropriate rhetoric for persuasion had undergone a decisive change. If democratic Enlightenment ideals had nourished the assumption that an informed populace was best maintained by the publication and distribution of factual information and reasoned opinion, the specter of an instinctively driven public pointed toward a theater of stirring symbols as the primary tool of persuasion. As the 1920s proceeded and in decades that followed, these shifts would leave a deep imprint not only on public relations thinking, but on the cultural fabric of American life itself.

8

Unseen Engineers: Biography of an Idea

B Y THE EARLY 1920s, the pragmatic lessons of the war, coupled with the prevailing wisdom of social psychology, had moved a growing sector of the American intelligentsia to two conclusions. First was the belief that a modern, large-scale society, such as the United States, required the services of a corps of experts, people who specialized in the analysis and management of public opinion. Second was the conviction that these "unseen engineers"—as Harold Lasswell called them—were dealing with a fundamentally illogical public and therefore must learn to identify and master those techniques of communication that would have the most compelling effect on public attitudes and thinking.

Nowhere did these concerns merge more eloquently than in the thinking of two men whom we have already encountered. One was Walter Lippmann who was, by the 1920s, America's most esteemed theorist and advocate of public-opinion management. The other was Edward L. Bernays, a former theatrical press agent and evangelist for the Committee on Public Information (CPI), who—from the twenties onward—built upon many of Lippmann's insights and applied them in general practice. Together, the impact of these men on the shape of twentieth-century American society would be colossal.

Though only in his early thirties, Lippmann had been influencing American social and political thought for more than a decade. Over those years he had gravitated from an earlier commitment to the ideal of popular sovereignty toward a more cynical and utilitarian outlook, one that historian Robert B. Westbrook characterized as "democratic realism."

"The democratic realists of the twenties," Westbrook wrote, "focused their criticism of democracy on two of its essential beliefs:

> the belief in the capacity of all men for rational political action and the belief in the practicality and desirability of maximizing the participation of all citizens in public life. Finding ordinary men and women irrational and participatory democracy impossible and unwise under modern conditions, they argued that it was best to strictly limit government by the people and to redefine democracy as, by and large, government for the people by enlightened and responsible elites.[1]

At the heart of this perspective was the problem of how to mediate between the democratic aspirations of *ordinary men and women* and the conviction that elites must be able to govern without the impediment of an active or participatory public. For Lippmann, the ability to "manufacture consent," to employ techniques that could assemble mass support behind executive action, was the key to solving this modern puzzle.[2] In two important books—the widely hailed *Public Opinion,* published in 1922, and a lesser-known book, *The Phantom Public,* which appeared five years later—Lippmann laid out his ideas on how this formidable objective might be accomplished.

Lippmann's analysis rested on a set of assumptions regarding the ways he thought ordinary people experienced the world. Though he accepted the existence of an objective reality and believed that scientific intelligence was, through careful study, capable of comprehending it, Lippmann argued that the average person was incapable of seeing that world clearly, much less understanding it. Recalling Plato's well-known parable of the cave, Lippmann maintained that it was humanity's fate to engage with the world not in immediate proximity to its events, but primarily through "pictures in our heads."

The gulf between perception and reality, Lippmann believed, was an ancient one, yet it had widened significantly with the rise of "The Great Society": a modern world in which geographic distance; the complexities of social, political, and economic life; and the hypnotic pull of the mass

Walter Lippmann
NIKOLAS MURAY

media spawned conditions in which the authority of such "pictures" was becoming more and more prevalent.[3] In this increasingly cosmopolitan society, he maintained, new technologies and new networks for disseminating words, sounds, and images had irrevocably transformed the wellsprings of common knowledge. As the world grew larger and more complex, people's ability to make sense of their universe was becoming less and less grounded in the terrain of immediate experience. Against the tangible immediacy of people's lives, he recounted, worldviews were being educated by words and pictures carried from afar. Formulating a quintessentially twentieth-century vocabulary, Lippmann argued that mass-mediated words and pictures commingled in people's minds, constituting a credible—though often fallacious—"pseudo-environment," a virtual reality informing ordinary thought and behavior.[4] In the process, an increasingly precarious architecture of truth was taking hold.

For Lippmann, the propensity to live according to "the medium of fictions" was fortified from two directions. First—inspired by the political insights of his mentor, Graham Wallas, and underscored by Freud's analysis of the unconscious—Lippmann asserted that innate human psychology was little inclined toward logic. "We do not know for certain how to act according to the dictates of reason," he wrote. "The number of human problems on which reason is prepared to dictate is small."[5] Public opinion, therefore, was an essentially "irrational force."[6]

Second—reflecting an amalgam of Pavlovian psychology and anthropological thinking—Lippmann believed that "man's reflexes are . . . conditioned."[7] People's ways of seeing and experiencing their world were nothing more than an extension of their cultural milieu, of a commonly held way of seeing and experiencing reality—common fictions or, as Lippmann put it, "the habits of our eyes."

Not only events that occur beyond the physical orbit of people's lives, but even immediate experiences were invariably filtered through a set of previously existing cultural outlooks and expectations. These habitual ways of seeing, he continued, were organized around a battery of "stereotypes," mutually shared mental templates that—in advance—gave shape and meaning to the experiences that people had and the ways that they visualized them.

In contrast to conscientious scientific analysis—which strives to sustain an objective relationship with the subject matter being studied—run-of-the-mill patterns of thought were, to Lippmann, trapped within self-fulfilling systems of categorization. For most people, then, objective understanding was unattainable.

> For the most part we do not first see, and then define. We define first and then see. In the great blooming, buzzing confusion of the outer world we pick out what our culture has already defined for us, and we tend to perceive that which we have picked out in the form stereotyped for us by our culture.[8]

He elaborated on this process further:

> We imagine most things before we experience them. And these preconceptions, unless education has made us acutely aware, govern deeply the whole process of perception. . . . They are aroused by small signs. . . . Aroused, they flood fresh vision with older images and project into the world what has been resurrected in memory.[9]

Lippmann asserted that this was the way that cultures invariably operate. "[H]ighly charged with the feelings that are attached to them," a given culture's repertoire of stereotypes is the glue that binds people to one another within a group, providing them with the underpinnings of their "universe," establishing the invisible "fortress" by which they maintain their "tradition(s)."[10]

Lippmann's discourse on the foundations of human knowledge led him in two directions at once. First, consistent with his democratic realism, it buttressed his repudiation of the "original dogma of democracy," an Enlightenment ideal that assumed people's ability to comprehend rationally and act on their world. If people cannot accurately know their world, he inquired, how can they be expected to act wisely on it?[11]

Second, Lippmann's stark contrast between customary thinking and scientific analysis suggested that while an average person was beguiled by a "medium of fictions," a scientifically trained "social analyst" was in a position to identify and manipulate the ways these fictions would operate. If patterns of perception can be unearthed, if scientists can uncover the "habits" of people's eyes, they may also learn to engineer "pseudo-environments" that could persuade people to see their "larger political environment . . . more successfully."[12] As Ronald Steele, Lippmann's biographer, explained, Lippmann's epistemology "showed why reason alone could not explain human behavior," yet "at the same time suggested how emotions could be channeled by reason."[13] "Though it is itself an irrational force," Lippmann explained, dredging up Gustave Le Bon's vision of the dreaded crowd, "the power of public opinion might be placed at the disposal of those who stood for workable law as against brute assertion."[14]

This capacity to harness public opinion demanded a working knowledge of the modern social and psychological sciences to monitor and chart the unconscious forces at work behind the facade of public opinion. "The new psychology . . . the study of dreams, fantasy and rationalization," he indicated, "has thrown light on how the pseudo-environment is put together." The would-be director of public opinion must also be conversant with customary patterns of influence, the psychodynamics of leadership within the population he wishes to influence, and the ways that leaders have historically been able to sow ideas in other people's minds.[15]

With this model of cognitive engineering in mind, Lippmann's most practical contribution to public relations thinking was his sys-

arti•FACT

Figure 1: Matthew Brady portrait of candidate Lincoln.

Figure 1: Engraving based on Brady portrait.

Today it is difficult to imagine a successful political candidate whose face is not known to the public-at-large. This has not always been true. The visual packaging of politicians only dates back to the mid-nineteenth century, when photography began to allow physical appearances to circulate as never before. The first presidential candidate to benefit from this development was Abraham Lincoln. Lincoln's election prospects were enhanced by an 1860 campaign photo portrait of him, made by the prominent New York studio photographer Matthew Brady. [See Figure 1]

In life Lincoln is said to have been a homely looking man, with a protruding adam's apple and a deeply furrowed face. In present-day parlance, he was not photogenic. Given this liability, Brady used photographic license to transform Lincoln into a more physically attractive candidate.

Photographic historian Susan Kismaric describes the process: "In preparing his subject for the 'shoot,' Brady modified Lincoln's gangling appearnace by pulling up the candidate's collar to make his neck look shorter; he also retouched the photograph to remove the harsh lines in Lincoln's face."*

Thus embellished, Lincoln's face was ready for public dissemination. The portrait "was reproduced as a line engraving in *Frank Leslie's Illustrated Weekly* [See Figure 2] and *Harper's Weekly*....It was also used on campaign posters and buttons...." Lincoln, according to Kismeric, credited Brady's portrait—in large part—for his election to the presidency.

* Susan Kismeric, *American Politicians: Photographs from 1845 to 1993* (New York, 1994), pp. 14-15.

ARCHIE BISHOP

tematic approach to how media might be understood and exploited. It was not enough, for example, to see the press as the shaper of public opinion. Modern leadership required specialists who would formulate how the press itself would cover a given issue. "[P]ublic opinions must be organized *for the press* if they are to be sound, not *by the press* as is the case today." Political science was, for Lippmann, the science that would frame public opinions for the press.[16] Its primary aim would be perception management.

Developing ideas that would become twentieth-century public relations catechism, Lippmann cautioned that to govern the way that the press will cover an event, access to that event must be consciously restricted. "A group of men who can prevent independent access to the event" are in a position to "arrange news of it to suit their purposes." He continued:

> Without some form of censorship, propaganda in the strict sense of the word is impossible. In order to conduct a propaganda there must be some barrier between the public and the event. Access to the real environment must be limited, before anyone can create a pseudo-environment that he thinks is wise or desirable.[17]

Central to Lippmann's vision of successful propaganda were his insights regarding the unparalleled powers of persuasion being uncovered by modern technologies of mass communication, particularly the cinema. Social psychologists, from Le Bon onward, had repeatedly declared the power of symbols to galvanize the crowd mind, but such pronouncements rarely moved beyond a cryptic, somewhat cabalistic, plane of analysis. Lippmann was among the first to take such metaphysical assertions and ground them in a practical analysis of the modern media system. He delineated the specific ways that images and narrative conventions worked on an audience and how they might be used.

Key to his exegesis was the belief that "pictures," "visualization" generally, provided the most effective passageways into inner life. "Pictures," he postulated, "have always been the surest way of conveying an idea, and next in order, words that call up pictures in memory."[18]

Modern life, Lippmann was convinced, had spawned technical conditions that allowed this capacity to be exploited as never before. If previous modes of mass communication—the printed word in particular—required an educated process of decoding to be understood, new media had made the process of interpretation "effortless." With cinema, a way of seeing reached an audience predigested. Mesmerizing likenesses of reality itself, movies provided a powerful model that could instruct the propagandist on how he might efficaciously construct "pseudo-environments."

In the whole experience of the race there has been no aid to visualization comparable to the cinema. . . .

Photographs have a kind of authority over the imagination to-day, which the printed word had yesterday, and the spoken word before that. They seem utterly real. They come, we imagine, directly to us without human meddling, and they are the most effortless food for the mind conceivable. Any description in words, or even any inert picture, requires an effort of memory before a picture exists in the mind. But on the screen the whole process of observing, describing, reporting, and then imagining, has been accomplished for you. Without more trouble than is needed to stay awake the result which your imagination is always aiming at is reeled off on the screen. The shadowy idea becomes vivid.[19]

For Lippmann, however, the ability to enlist the public eye was not simply a result of new visual technologies. Strategies of mass impression were also being revealed by the ways that these new technologies were being used. A still youthful film industry was in the midst of developing narrative formulas—approaches to storytelling—that presented the propagandist with powerful inklings of how the emotions of the public might be effectively rallied. Inspired by the example of Hollywood, Lippmann began to envision game plans for persuasion that, though novel within his world, are today standard practices.

"In order not to sit inertly in the presence of the picture," Lippmann noted, "the audience must be exercised by the image." (This conclusion mirrored Freud's theory of "object cathexis," the process by which a person's innermost desires or ideals are projected onto an external object or another human being.) Hollywood, Lippmann observed, routinely achieved this state of being by providing visual "handles for identification," signals by which an audience might immediately and unconsciously learn "who the hero is," and so on.

Applying psychoanalytic insights to the task of propaganda, Lippmann emphasized the importance of *identification* in the psychic life of an audience as a device for capturing an audience's affections.

> In order . . . that the distant situation shall not be a gray
> flicker on the edge of attention, it should be capable of trans-
> lation into pictures in which the opportunity for identification
> is recognizable. Unless that happens it will interest only a few
> for a little while. It will belong to the sights seen but not felt,
> to the sensations that beat on our sense organs, and are not
> acknowledged. *We have to take sides. We have to be able to take
> sides. In the recesses of our being we must step out of the audi-
> ence on to the stage, and wrestle as the hero for the victory of
> good over evil. We must breathe into the allegory the breath of
> life.*[20]

Simply put, the distance between an audience's unconscious desires
and the drama they are watching must be strategically dissolved.
"The formula works," Lippmann explained, "when the public fiction
enmeshes itself with a private urgency."

To promulgate such opportunities for identification, Lippmann
instructed, propagandists must also learn from popular tastes in
movies. Projected pseudo-environments must successfully negotiate
between the public's *fantasy life* and their sense of *what is possible.*
"Our popular taste," he calculated, "is to have the drama originate in
a setting realistic enough to make identification plausible and to have
it terminate in a setting romantic enough to be desirable, but not so
romantic as to be inconceivable."[21]

Raised in a world that looked toward fact-based journalism as the
most efficient lubricant of persuasion, Lippmann turned toward Hollywood, America's "dream factory," for inspiration. Never before had
an American thinker articulated in such detail the ways that images
could be used to sway public consciousness. Appeals to reason were
not merely being discarded as futile, they were being consciously
undermined to serve the interests of power. It is here, at the turning
point where Lippmann unqualifiedly abandoned the idea of meaningful public dialogue, that the dark side of his ruminations on the
power of the image was most dramatically revealed.

Throughout the pages of *Public Opinion,* Lippmann had asserted
that human beings were, for the most part, inherently incapable of
responding rationally to their world. Yet as he analyzed and hashed
over the ways that images might be employed as tools of leadership,

another aspect of Lippmann's thinking rose to the surface. For Lippmann, it was not so much people's incapacity to deliberate on issues rationally that was the problem; it was that the time necessary to pursue rational deliberations would only interfere with the smooth exercise of executive power. For Lippmann, the appeal of symbols was that they provided a device for short-circuiting the inconvenience posed by critical reason and public discussion.

To Lippmann, symbols were powerful instruments for forging mental agreement among people who—if engaged in critical dialogue—would probably disagree. "When political parties or newspapers declare for Americanism, Progressivism, Law and Order, Justice, Humanity," he explained, they expect to merge "conflicting factions which would surely divide if, instead of these symbols, they were invited to discuss a specific program."[22]

Five years later, in *The Phantom Public,* Lippmann added that serious public discussion of issues would only yield a "vague and confusing medley," a discord that would make executive decision making difficult. "[A]ction cannot be taken until these opinions have been factored down, canalized, compressed and made uniform."[23]

No technique was more effective for unifying public thinking and derailing independent thought, Lippmann argued, than the informed employment of symbols as instruments of persuasion. The symbol, he wrote, is "like a strategic railroad center where many roads converge regardless of their ultimate origin or their ultimate destination." Because of this, "when a coalition around the symbol has been

arti•FACT

By the 1920s, a growing number of politicians and political strategists were embracing the idea that calculatingly constructed images could be used as tools for galvanizing popular passions.

A telling example if this assumption occurred in 1927, when a soon-to-be-famous politician visited a photographer's studio to have a series of portraits made. This was not a conventional sitting, however. These photos were taken as the politician stood boldly before the camera, rehearsing grandly dramatic gestures as he lip-synched to a recording of one of his own speeches. Later, he would study the pictures with great care, seeking to perfect the visual impact of his oratorical presence.

To see the results of this extraordinary photo session, turn to the next page.

ARCHIE BISHOP

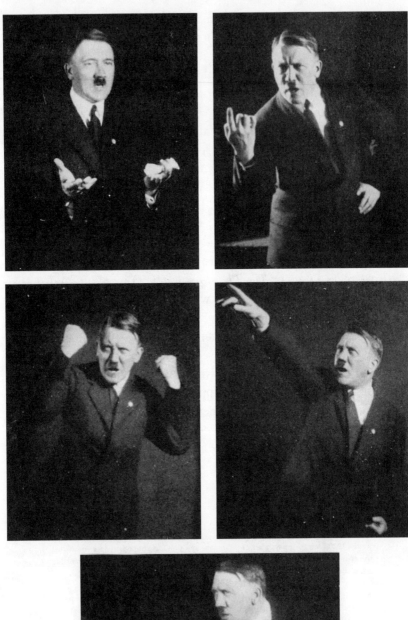

effected, feeling flows toward conformity under the symbol rather than toward critical scrutiny of the measures under consideration.

In its adamant argument that human beings are essentially irrational, social psychology had provided Lippmann—and many others—with a handy rationale for a small, intellectual elite to rule over society. Yet a close reading of Lippmann's argument suggests that he was concerned less with the irrational core of human behavior than he was with the problem of making rule by elites, *in a democratic age,* less difficult.

Educated by the lessons of the image culture taking shape around him, Lippmann saw the strategic employment of media images as the secret to modern power, the means by which leaders and special interests might cloak themselves in the "fiction" that they stand as delegates of the common good. The most compelling attribute of symbols, he asserted, was the capacity to magnify emotion while undermining critical thought, to emphasize sensations while subverting ideas. "In the symbol," he rhapsodized, *"emotion is discharged at a common target and the idiosyncrasy of real ideas is blotted out."*[24]

This general understanding infused Lippmann's formula for leadership:

> The making of one general will out of a multitude of general wishes is not an Hegelian mystery . . . but an art well known to leaders, politicians and steering committees. It consists essentially in the use of *symbols which assemble emotions after they have been detached from their ideas.* Because feelings are much less specific than ideas, and yet more poignant, the leader is able to make a homogeneous will out of a heterogeneous mass of desires. The process, therefore, by which general opinions are brought to cooperation consists of *an intensification of feeling and a degradation of significance.* Before a mass of general opinions can eventuate in executive

(OPPOSITE) A 1927 series of studio portraits taken by Heinrich Hoffmann, Hitler's personal photographer. Later published in *Hitler: Eine Biografie in 134 Bildern* (Berlin, Verlag Tradition Wilhelm Kolk, 1931). PHOTOS COURTESY OF RAY R. COWDERY

action, the choice is narrowed down to a few alternatives. The victorious alternative is executed not by a mass but by individuals in control of its energy.[25]

The conscious maneuvering of symbols, in short, was the mediation between popular aspirations and the exigencies of elite power that he and a generation of democratic realists had been looking for.

> He who captures the symbols by which public feeling is for the moment contained, controls by that much the approaches of public policy. . . . A leader or an interest that can make itself master of current symbols is the master of the current situation.[26]

Intrinsic to this outlook was Lippmann's firm belief that most people are inescapably oblivious to their world and cannot not "be expected to deal" intelligently "with the merits of a controversy." The most one can hope for is that the public can be guided to respond to "easily recognizable" symbols "which they can follow." The immediate task of leadership, he judged, is to uncover and project those signs that can most efficiently guide the public mind.

> The signs must be of such a character that they can be recognized without any substantial insight into the substance of a problem. . . . They must be signs which will tell the members of a public where they can best align themselves so as to promote the solution. In short, they must be guides to reasonable action for the use of uninformed people.[27]

From the vantage point of the 1990s, one cannot avoid being struck by Lippmann's clairvoyance; the extent to which his analysis of symbols—how they may be employed to sway the public—sounds uncomfortably familiar. The use of media images to stir emotions and circumvent thought is, today, a near universal feature of public discourse. During the twenties, however, these ideas were less prophetic than prescriptive; they provided a powerful way of seeing that many— particularly the growing battery of people involved in publicity work and opinion management—were looking for and prepared to embrace.

■   ■   ■   ■   ■

One of these people was Bernays. By 1922, Bernays's outlook—like Lippmann's—had already been stamped by the presumptions of social psychology. Early encounters with the writings of Gabriel Tarde, Gustave Le Bon, Graham Wallas, and Wilfred Trotter had deeply affected his worldview. Also, as Freud's double nephew, psychoanalytic thinking had come to him with his mother's milk.

When he read *Public Opinion,* Bernays was impressed by the scope of Lippmann's hypotheses—the suggestive connections between social psychology, the modern media system, and the ability to achieve the "manufacture of consent"—yet he found Lippmann's work too academic.

> Lippmann treated public opinion on a purely theoretical basis. He never got down to matters of changing it. He talked of it as if he were a sociologist discussing a social caste system . . . abstractly. And I was surprised. Here he was, a working newspaper man. [28]

This frustration with Lippmann was rooted in Bernays's pragmatic background, first as a journalist, then as a press agent. Upon graduating from Cornell in 1913 at the age of twenty-two, Bernays embarked on a brief career as a journalist, editing two medical magazines: the *Medical Review of Reviews* and the *Dietetic and Hygienic Gazette.* Even then, his uncanny aptitude for "press agentry" was evident.

An early look at this flair for unseen engineering can be found in the work Bernays did—while still editing medical magazines—to foster the success of a controversial play entitled *Damaged Goods.* Written by the French playwright Eugene Brieux, the drama presented the tale of a syphilitic young man who, against the advice of his physician, marries and subsequently sires a syphilitic child. Beyond its melodramatic content, the play is a brief on behalf of public health education, taking aim at Victorian customs that kept subject matter such as syphilis strictly under wraps.

The play first caught Bernays's attention when, as editor of the *Medical Review of Reviews,* he published an article by a doctor commending *Damaged Goods* as a welcome antidote for the conspiracy of silence that enveloped the issue of syphilis. A few months later, when Bernays learned that the play was about to be produced in New York City, his knack for publicity kicked into gear.

Writing to Richard Bennett, the play's producer, Bernays offered the backing of his journal. "The editors of the *Medical Review of Reviews*," he wrote, "support your praiseworthy intention to fight sex-pruriency in the United States by producing Brieux's play. . . . You can count on our help," he added. Bennett and the twenty-two-year-old Bernays soon met to discuss the play and to determine how Bernays might assist with its production.

> Bennett leaned forward and said, "I have been interested in *Damaged Goods* for several years. A play so frank, so sincere can accomplish enormous good. . . . Sex diseases should no longer be concealed. I hope to interest legislators in the seriousness of the social disease the play discusses and force them to pass reform laws."
>
> "Yes, yes of course," I murmured, enthralled.

Despite their shared enthusiasm for the play, formidable road-blocks stood in the way of its production. The prevailing moral climate in New York was hardly conducive to the open exploration of such an explicit topic. Anthony Comstock, who headed the New York Society for the Suppression of Vice, had already "closed other shows he thought too daring." The Police Department and the mayor's office had supported these closings.[29]

As Bernays encountered these difficulties, he underwent a fruitful transformation from green medical editor to innovative publicist. While most publicists of the day understood their job as merely handing press releases to reporters or staging ritualized press conferences, Bernays's instinct was to operate more clandestinely, behind the scenes, invisibly staging events or "circumstances" that the press would—out of habit—consider newsworthy.

From his anonymous perch as "editor" of the *Medical Review of Reviews*, Bernays announced the establishment of a new organization, a disinterested third party that he named the *Medical Review of Reviews's* Sociological Fund Committee. Its professed objective was to advance public instruction about venereal diseases. References to *Damaged Goods* were nowhere to be found.

Bernays then proceeded to ask people from among New York's upper crust to lend their support to the educational campaign by joining the committee and making donations. "I was careful to invite men and women whose good faith was beyond question and would be responsive to our cause," Bernays later explained. He recruited individuals—both liberal and conservative—whose names carried implicit authority. "Dr. Simon Flexner of the Rockefeller Institute for Medical Research . . . Rev. John Haynes Holmes of New York's Unitarian church . . . John D. Rockefeller, Jr. . . . Mrs. Rose Paster Stokes, a social worker . . . Mrs. William K. Vanderbilt . . ." and others.

Not coincidentally, the inaugural project of the Sociological Fund Committee was to back the production of *Damaged Goods*. Bernays figured that the committee's endorsement would serve two purposes simultaneously. First, it would erect an impervious fortress against the assaults of Comstock or other guardians of public morality. Second, in light of its carriage-trade membership, it would spawn a network of well-heeled individuals, interested in bracketing themselves among New York's high society and, therefore, willing to support *Damaged Goods* in the name of a "worthy cause."

Bernays's plan worked like a charm. Instead of negative publicity, the play received enthusiastic coverage in the press. In testimonials, Rockefeller heralded the play as "breaking down the harmful reserve which stands in the way of popular enlightenment," while Edward Bok, editor of the *Ladies Home Journal,* proclaimed the production "a very hopeful and significant event." A special performance for President Woodrow Wilson and other political dignitaries in Washington generated national press for the play. Road companies soon toured; a film was made.[30]

During a period when *Damaged Goods* might easily have suffered the wrath of the morals squad, the blessing of an official-sounding front group and a furtive if conscious mobilization of private networks of influence transformed the play into a virtuous tool of "enlightenment." Working clandestinely, exploiting the prestige of individuals whose ability to lead the opinions of others was already well established, Bernays displayed an uncommon genius for social engineering that would define his career and would sharpen the focus of public relations thinking.

By way of the *Damaged Goods* episode, Bernays tumbled upon his true aptitude. Abandoning journalism, he became a full-time publicist. Functioning initially as a theatrical press agent, Bernays enjoyed a good deal of early success, representing the interests of Diaghilev's Ballet Russe, Nijinsky, Enrico Caruso, and other major attractions of the day.

During the war years, Bernays joined the army of publicists rallied under the banner of the CPI and concentrated on propaganda efforts aimed at Latin American business interests. Within this vast campaign of "psychological warfare," as he described it, Bernays—

A 1917 photograph of Edward L. Bernays *(extreme right)* during his career as a theatrical press agent. Here he is supervising the arrival of one of his most illustrious early clients, Enrico Caruso (emerging from automobile). Later that year, Bernays would take a position with the CPI, a pivotal step in his metamorphosis into Edward L. Bernays, counsel on public relations. COURTESY SPECTOR & ASSOCIATES, INC.

like others of his generation—began to develop an expanded sense of publicity and its practical uses.[31]

Bernays now envisaged public relations as a potent social instrument that, in the hands of disciplined specialists, might be employed for significant purposes. The "astounding success of propaganda during the war opened the eyes of the intelligent few in all departments of life to the possibilities of regimenting the public mind."[32] Publicity, he was persuaded, could be used to "organize chaos," to bring order out of confusion and social disarray.[33]

From the early twenties onward, Bernays's vision of himself and of his mission began to assume an air of historical consequence. Standing at a "divide between what I had done—my press agentry, publicity, publicity direction—and what I now attempted to do," he discarded the bespattered term *press agent* and substituted for it a more exalted title. Applying a bit of press agentry to his own vocation, he would henceforth refer to himself as "counsel on public relations." Eliciting a deliberate association with the legal profession, which advised clients on how to maneuver their ways through the complexities of law, Bernays described a counsel on public relations as one who would prescribe for a client the most effective ways to navigate an increasingly complicated, often hostile, social environment.[34] "I just took it [the term *counsel*] from law. And instead of saying 'Counsel on Legal Relations,' I said 'Counsel on Public Relations.'" At the heart of this newfound "profession" stood Bernays's belief that it was essential for public relations to be conversant with and make use of the modern social and psychological sciences in their work.

This conviction was only fed by Lippmann's widely read conjectures on public opinion and by the dialogue in influential circles that they provoked. Bernays decided to enter the fray. More than simply a public relations practitioner, he would soon situate himself as the most important theorist of American public relations. In contrast to Lippmann, however, Bernays believed that his firsthand experience in the field of publicity would facilitate the development of a more practical approach to mobilizing public opinion.

In 1923, just a year after Lippmann published his tome, *Public Opinion,* Bernays answered with his own book, *Crystallizing Public Opinion.* Five years later—again just a year after Lippmann's *The*

Phantom Public appeared—Bernays published a second book on public relations, *Propaganda*.

If Lippmann's prose was intended to sway the thinking of socially cognizant leaders and intellectuals, Bernays's writing style was meant for practitioners in the trenches; his primary interest was to frame the job of public relations counsel in ways that would allow practitioners to take advantage of the insights of modern social and psychological thought. Lippmann's books were filled with intricate ruminations on the processes of human epistemology and theoretical speculations on how these processes might pertain to the project of molding public opinion. Bernays's books were punctuated throughout by vivid narratives—stories of Bernays's earliest campaigns, other public relations feats, and commonplace sales situations—each presented to demonstrate how social psychology, and the social scientific approach more generally, might be employed in the everyday work of a publicist.

In *Crystallizing Public Opinion,* for example, Bernays recalled the work he had done for *Damaged Goods* to demonstrate the usefulness of Trotter's discussion of the herd instinct: the ineluctable pull exercised by groups and their leaders on the unconscious lives of individuals. The herd instinct, Bernays explained, provided a back door through which the play was sold to the public.

> "Damaged Goods," before its presentation to America in 1913, was analyzed by the public relations counsel, who helped to produce the play. He recognized that unless that part of the public sentiment which believed in education and truth could be lifted from that part of public opinion which condemned the mentioning of sex matters, "Damaged Goods" would fail. The producers, therefore, did not try to educate the public by presenting this play as such, but allowed group leaders and groups interested in education to come to the support of Brieux's drama and, in a sense, to sponsor the production.[35]

"Trotter and Le Bon," Bernays instructed readers of his 1928 book, *Propaganda,* "concluded that the group mind does not think in the strict sense of the word. In place of thoughts it has impulses, habits and emotions. In making up its mind," he continued, "its first impulse is usually to follow the example of a trusted leader. This is one of the most firmly established principles of mass psychology."

For the public relations counsel, Bernays advised, the tacit authority of existing groups or of trusted group leaders could be applied to a wide diversity of situations. "It operates in establishing the rising or diminishing prestige of a summer resort, in causing a run on a bank, or a panic on the stock exchange, in creating a best seller, or a box-office success."

To illustrate this wide applicability, Bernays cited publicity work done for a meat packer, to enhance the sale of bacon. Old-style publicity, he explained, would have relied on "full-page advertisements" encouraging consumers to "eat more bacon." "Eat bacon because it is cheap, because it is good, because it gives you reserve energy." The consequence of such a campaign, rooted in the product's own attributes, would, according to Bernays, be minimal. A more successful approach, he recommended, would be to appeal to the attributes of available consumers, to root the campaign in an analysis of "the group structure of society and the principles of mass psychology."

The publicist would ask himself, *"Who is it that influences the eating habits of the public?* The answer, obviously, is: *'The physicians.'"* The modern publicist, then, must attempt to persuade "physicians to say publicly that it is wholesome to eat bacon." The publicist, he explained, "knows as a mathematical certainty, that large numbers of persons will follow the advice of their doctors, because he understands the psychological relation of dependence of men upon their physicians."[36] The ability to employ the credibility of trusted authorities was the key to getting people to eat more bacon.

To Bernays, recent scientific ideas concerning the mental processes of individuals and groups provided the public relations specialist with powerful expedients for both apprehending and influencing the public mind. Offering the prosaic case of a man on the verge of purchasing an automobile as an example, Bernays explained to readers that the car's mechanical properties had little to do with his decision.

Men are rarely aware of the real reasons which motivate their action. A man may believe that he buys a motor car because, after careful study of the technical features of all the makes on the market, he has concluded that this is the best. He is almost certainly fooling himself. He bought it, perhaps, because a friend whose financial acumen he respects bought one last week; or because his neighbors believed he was not able to afford a car of that class; or because its colors are those of his college fraternity. . . .

[M]any of man's thoughts and actions are compensatory substitutes for desires which he has been obliged to suppress. A thing may be desired not for its intrinsic worth or usefulness, but because he has unconsciously come to see in it a symbol of something else, the desire for which he is ashamed to admit to himself. . . . A man buying a car may think he wants it for purposes of locomotion. . . . He may really want it because it is a symbol of social position, as evidence of his success in business, or a means of pleasing his wife.[37]

While Bernays believed that the social sciences presented individual practitioners with an indispensable assortment of techniques for mounting effective publicity efforts, he also possessed a more ambitious social vision, one that apprehended the unfolding role of public relations within the modern architecture of power. "In our present social organization approval of the public is essential to any large undertaking," he observed. For Bernays, the growth of public relations was a necessary response to this pesky historical condition.[38] It is in this dimension of his thinking that Bernays joined the tradition of social thought that had been initiated by Tarde and Le Bon. In this aspect of his work, Bernays and Lippmann were nearly indistinguishable.

Subscribing to Lippmann's vision of modern society and its conditions, Bernays saw the public relations counsel not simply as a person who applied modern scientific know-how to his work, but also as one of the "intelligent few" who must, within democratic society, "continuously and systematically" perform the task of "regimenting the public mind." These "invisible wire pullers," as Bernays tagged public relations experts, would provide the skills necessary to bring about a successful negotiation between the chaos of popular aspirations and exigencies of elite power.[39]

Broaching a theme that he would repeat—to the embarrassment of many in the public relations profession—for decades to come, Bernays announced that "the conscious and intelligent manipulation of the organized habits and opinions of the masses" had become an indispensable feature of "democratic society."[40] With the masses pounding at the doors of "the higher strata of society," he noted, ruling elites were turning to propaganda as the scientifically informed tool through which public submission might be achieved.

> The minority has discovered a powerful help in influencing majorities. It has been possible so to mold the mind of the masses that they will throw their newly gained strength in the desired direction. Propaganda is the executive arm of the invisible government.[41]

Beyond serving the narrow requirements of individual clients, public relations experts were those who specialized in pulling "the wires which control the public mind" and creating that propaganda.[42] Reaching beyond the modest pretensions that had surrounded the work of traditional press agents, Bernays described the public relations counsel as one who was a master at creating pseudo-environments—"creating pictures in the minds of millions" by staging seemingly spontaneous events—that would quietly induce the public to comprehend the world in a desired way.[43] In describing this idea, Bernays's rhetoric was, as was his habit, monumental:

> When Napoleon said, "Circumstance? I make circumstance,"
> he expressed very nearly the spirit of the public relations
> counsel's work.[44]

Within this grandiosity, however, Bernays was beginning to delineate a pragmatic outline for how a public relations specialist might be trained to "become the creator of circumstance." First, the public relations specialist must be a careful student of the media and of the organized networks of communication through which the majority of people gain their "picture" of the world-at-large: "advertising, motion pictures, circular letters, booklets, handbills, speeches, meetings, parades, news articles, magazine articles and whatever other mediums there are through which public attention is reached and influenced."[45] Most people, he added "accept the facts which come to them through existing channels. They like to hear new things in accustomed ways."[46]

Despite the public's reliance on familiar sources of information, however, the PR expert's study of communication must—at the same time—be timely and dynamic, continually in touch with "the relative value of the various instruments" and the changes that affect the masses' responsiveness to particular media forms. "If he [the PR counsel] is to get full reach for his message he must take advantage of these shifts of value the instant they occur."[47] In this proposal, Bernays prophesied the development of the entire field of media consultancy, certainly an outstanding feature of present-day society.

Second, those interested in fashioning public opinion must be sociologically and anthropologically informed; they must be meticulous students of the social structure and of the cultural routines through which opinions take hold on an interpersonal level. They must consider the imprint of sex, race, economics, and geography on public attitudes.[48] It was also important to understand existing networks of influence—family, community, education, and religion—for example, as well as the undeclared patterns of leadership that operate within each of them. "If you can influence the leaders," Bernays instructed, "you automatically influence the group which they sway."[49] Such knowledge was not only serviceable for approaching people in groups, but also functioned when addressing individuals. "[E]ven when he is alone," Bernays intoned, a person's mind "retains the patterns which have been stamped on it by the group influences."[50]

Just as the public is used to receiving information through accustomed channels, Bernays added, a social group's outlook is bounded by certain accepted "structures . . . prejudices . . . and whims." These, too, must be factored into the calculations of the publicist. "The public has its own standards and demands and habits," he explained. "You may modify them, but you dare not run counter to them." An organization that would use modern propaganda techniques "must explain itself, its aims, its objectives, to the public in terms which the public can understand and is willing to accept."[51] Therefore, an ongoing "scientific" study of the public, a "survey of public desires and demands," is an essential device for a public relations strategist.[52] Though social surveys, focus groups, and related forms of instrumental demographics are unexceptional today, Bernays's suggestion that molders of opinion must be ongoing monitors of social attitudes was, during the 1920s, innovative; Bernays saw the unfolding apparatus of mass impression with an oracular gaze.

Third—confirming the adage that an acorn never falls too far from the tree—Bernays contended that, above all, the public relations counsel must be a watchful student of the public psyche. "If we understand the mechanism and motives of the group mind," he asked rhetorically, "is it not possible to control and regiment the masses according to our will without their knowing it?" "The recent practice of propaganda," he answered, "has proved that it is possible . . . within certain limits."[53]

Those limits, as Bernays understood them, were bounded only by a propagandist's ability to understand the mechanisms of individual and mass psychology. "Mass psychology is as yet far from being an exact science," he allowed, "and the mysteries of human motivation are by no means all revealed." Nevertheless, he believed,

> theory and practice have combined with sufficient success to permit us to know that in certain cases we can effect some change in public opinion with a fair degree of accuracy by operating a certain mechanism, just as the motorist can regulate the speed of his car by manipulating the flow of gasoline.[54]

The implications of this statement were, for Bernays, obvious. Just as an advertising man must comprehend the product-buying habits of prospective consumers, the public relations counsel must be conversant with the ingrained "thought-buying habits" through which public opinion operates.[55] Simply put, a publicist must comprehend "the mental processes" of the public and "adjust" his propaganda "to the mentality of the masses."[56]

In describing this "mentality," Bernays assembled a hodgepodge built from various modern psychological theories. Reprising the now familiar motif of public irrationality, Bernays argued that people hold on to their ideas within "what one psychologist [referring to Trotter] has called 'logic-proof compartment[s] of dogmatic adherence.' " For the publicist to pursue his trade effectively, it was necessary for him to understand these perceptual cubbyholes, these proclivities toward "*a priori* judgement" and create circumstances deliberately planned to engage with these peculiar "psychological habits."[57]

Amplifying this point, Bernays borrowed heavily from Lippmann. Lifting language directly from *Public Opinion* and then adding his own practical spin, Bernays explained that the "stereotype" provided the public relations specialist with a particularly useful tool.

> The public relations counsel sometimes uses the current stereotypes, sometimes combats them and sometimes creates new ones. In using them he very often brings to the public . . . a stereotype they already know, to which he adds new ideas, thus he fortifies his own and gives a greater carrying power.[58]

Elsewhere, Bernays's approach to the public mind blended Freudianism with Trotter's instinct theory. "[T]he individual and the group are swayed by only a very small number of fundamental desires and emotions and instincts," he declared. "Sex, gregariousness, the desire to lead, the maternal and paternal instincts, are all dominating desires of the group." These desires, he offered, are "sound mechanisms" upon which a public relations expert "can base his 'selling arguments.' "[59] "The public relations counsel," he wrote in another context, "can try to bring about . . . identification by utilizing the appeals to desires and instincts."

At still other times, Bernays's psychological thinking was simplistically Pavlovian. When "millions are exposed to the same stimuli," he informed readers of *Propaganda,* "all receive identical imprints."

Regardless of its sources and its customary bombast, however, Bernays's geography of the public mind was focused on one objective: the systematic forging of public opinion. To execute this task, he advised, the propagandist must abandon all attempts at reasoning with the public. In order for it to respond appropriately, Bernays maintained, the public must have reality predigested for it.

> Abstract discussions and heavy facts . . . cannot be given to the public until they are simplified and dramatized. The

refinements of reason and shading of emotion cannot reach a considerable public.[60]

Bernays designated this streamlined version of reality "news." When reality is distilled down to its most "simplified and dramatized" form and is able to make an "appeal to the instincts" of the public mind, he explained, "it can aptly be termed news." The creation of "news," then, was for Bernays the essential job of the public relations counsel.

In order to appeal to the instincts and fundamental emotions of the public . . . the public relations counsel must create news around his ideas. . . . He must isolate ideas and develop them into events so that they can be more readily understood and so they may claim attention as news.[61]

Within this elitist strategy—which embellished on Lippmann's notion that it was imperative for leaders to anticipate and forestall the public's "critical scrutiny" of issues—a profound metamorphosis in the way that society defined *information* was being normalized. If, at the turn of the century, "news" had been understood as a faithful extension of an *objective* world, Bernays approached "news" as an essentially *subjective* category, something that took place—and could be generated—in the pliant minds of the audience at whom a parcel of information was being directed. If news had once been understood as something out there, waiting to be covered, now it was seen as product to be manufactured, something designed and transmitted to bring about a visceral public response.

Bernays's conception of what constituted "news" was, at the same time, intimately tied to a transformed rhetoric of persuasion. Like others who had journeyed along the pathways of social psychology, Bernays saw *the symbol* as the most powerful psychological megaphone for reaching and persuading the public.[62] Ultimately, then, the public relations counsel must be an expert in the meaning and serviceability of symbols, of those "reflex images" that will provide him with mesmerizing "short-cuts" for realizing an acceptable public reaction.[63] "[T]he public as a group does not see in shaded hues," he explained.

> The very need of reaching large numbers of people at one time and in the shortest possible time tends toward the utilizations of symbols which stand in the minds of the public for the abstract idea the technician wishes to convey. . . . Such a use of appeals must, it goes without saying, be studied by the expert.[64]

A PR specialist's capacity to mobilize the public's instincts, he explained with equanimity, rests on his "ability to create those symbols to which the public is ready to respond; his ability to know and to analyze those reactions which the public is ready to give; his ability to find those stereotypes, individual and community, which will bring favorable responses; his ability to speak in the language of his audience and to receive from it a favorable reception are his contributions. The appeal to the instincts and the universal desires is the basic method through which he produces his results."[65]

Foreshadowing an escalating population of "compliance professionals" who would follow in his footsteps, Bernays's intellectual aptitude was focused, almost exclusively, on maneuvering symbols to effect a desired, often unconscious, social response. In the wake of this development, the tide and texture of American public life would never be the same.

For Bernays, an increased reliance on the eloquence of symbols and the idea of a public driven primarily by instinct went hand-in-hand. This perspective would fire his career from the 1920s onward.

But if Bernays was the most systematic proponent of public relations, he was also a man of his times. In the mid-1930s, reflecting on a world in which public relations and related propagandistic activities had become omnipresent, Lasswell portrayed the intellectual classes as made up of those people "who live by manipulating contentious symbols."[66] Granting this definition, Bernays—dexterous "imagineer" of the public mind—had, by the mid-1920s, come to the fore as an archetypal twentieth-century American intellectual.[67]

Into the early years of the twentieth century, as long as American society continued to uphold the principle of reason, the printed word had, with few exceptions, been the favored instrument in the tool kit of publicists. Now, in a world conceived as being ruled by unconscious and irrational forces, publicists in general were turning away from *the word* and, more and more, looking toward *the image* as their preferred tool of public address.

Around the turn of the century, the anxious reveries of men like Gustave Le Bon, Edward A. Ross, and Wilfred Trotter had inspired dreams of a new intellectual aristocracy, people who—through the conscientious application of social scientific methods—would be able to bring order to a dangerously chaotic world. In the years following the end of the First World War, Lippmann and Bernays—exemplifying an emerging class of propaganda specialists—had taken these skittish fantasies and transformed them into a widely accepted strategy of social engineering. A world in which public relations experts, advertising strategists, image managers, and architects of calculated spectacles would increasingly manufacture the terms of public discourse was in the process of taking root.

9

Modern Pipelines of Persuasion

D URING THE 1920s and 1930s, a period that embraced titanic economic expansion and, subsequently, ravaging economic collapse, the practices of public relations in particular, and of planned propaganda campaigns more generally, grew exponentially. From a variety of vantage points and roused by a range of concerns, observers noted foundational changes in the American social fabric.

One of these observers was Harold Lasswell, a political scientist who would emerge—by the mid-thirties—as the United States' foremost student and bibliographer of propaganda activities.[1] In 1927, while still a young professor at the University of Chicago, Lasswell summarized the growth of organized propaganda that had taken place over the preceding decade.[2] "Propaganda," he wrote of the period since World War I, had arisen as "one of the most powerful instrumentalities in the modern world." The attempt to control opinion through the conscious manipulation of "significant symbols, or . . . by stories, rumours, reports, pictures and other forms of social communication," had become routine.

The social and political implications of this development were profound. Widespread "discussion about the ways and means of controlling public opinion," he concluded, "testifies to the collapse of the traditional species of democratic romanticism and to the rise of a dictatorial habit of mind."[3]

In the face of troublesome democratic ambitions that had been mounting for more than a century, corporate and governmental leaders looked to an increasingly sophisticated opinion-molding apparatus as their tool of first resort. "Propaganda," Lasswell wrote with incisive candor, "is a concession to the wilfulness of the age."

> The bonds of personal loyalty and affection which bound a man to his chief have long since dissolved. Monarchy and class privilege have gone the way of all flesh, and the idolatry of the individual passes for the official religion of democracy. It is an atomized world, in which individual whims have wider play than ever before, and it requires more strenuous exertions to co-ordinate and unify than formerly. The new antidote to wilfulness is propaganda. If the mass will be free of chains of iron, it must accept its chains of silver. If it will not love, honour and obey, it must not expect to escape seduction.[4]

Progressive educator John Dewey—one of twentieth-century America's most adamant public champions of participatory democracy—observed this same development with dismay. In a 1930 book, *Individualism Old and New,* he described the society around him as one in which popular consciousness was in the process of being engulfed by a dreadful and ubiquitous apparatus of mass persuasion. The critical edge of an informed and independent-minded public— the vital linchpin of democracy—was daily being blunted by a perpetual flow of psychological trickery. "We live exposed to the greatest flood of mass suggestion that any people has yet experienced," he lamented.

> The need for united action, and the supposed need for integrated opinion and sentiment, are met by organized propaganda and advertising. The publicity agent is perhaps the most significant symbol of our present social life. There are individuals who resist; but, for a time at least, sentiment can be manufactured by mass methods for almost any person or cause.[5]

For Dewey this historical outgrowth—unless somehow checked— represented "the eclipse of the public" as an articulate force in American life, an end to the eloquent promises of democracy. In the face of "artificially accelerated" public responses, he concluded, "independent personal judgement" was becoming impossible.[6]

Though intellectuals played—and continue to play—a pivotal role in assembling and serving a modern publicity culture, the dramatic spread of organized propaganda activities cannot be understood simply as a product of intellectual deliberations. The routinization of propaganda in the United States was inescapably connected to fundamental shifts that were under way in society more generally, shifts that were transfiguring the definitions of "public life" during the 1920s and 1930s.

One of the most powerful of these changes was in American media institutions: their structure, their reach, their variety, and their ownership. Consonant with changes taking place in American business more generally, the period between the late nineteenth century and the 1920s saw a momentous expansion and consolidation of media industries.

In newspapers, conventionally seen as the prime arena for public relations, the metamorphosis was multifaceted. While powerful newspaper chains had begun to propagate in the years preceding the turn of the century, by the twenties these chains had gained a virtual stranglehold on newspaper publishing. Fueled by the growth of the modern consumer culture and by the advertising revenues it was generating, the grooves of borrowed thought were becoming more and more far reaching while their content was being shaped by a declining number of news sources and by uniform, nationally disbursed, editorial perspectives.[7]

The impact of this standardization was considerable. Through the flux of newspaper chains and other sources of national enlightenment, a society once defined by its remarkable variety of cultural backgrounds and by its distinct regionalism was being melded into generic ways of seeing, shaped by the priorities of modern commercial enterprise. In 1929, Roy Howard, head of the huge Scripps-Howard newspaper chain, expressed his approval of this development, clearly aware of its intrinsic capacity to manage the attentions of a once unruly public mind.

> [T]his tremendous advance in the development of the small
> dailies of the country, which is a direct result of syndication

and chain operation, has, by a system of setting in action identical thought processes in all communities of the nation at almost identically the same time, annihilated provincialism in the United States and contributed to the development of a true American hegemony that is the marvel of the rest of the world.[8]

Though Howard's hyperbole belies the fact that the American mind was not yet marching fully in lockstep, the implications of what he was describing were not lost on Ivy Lee and other public relations practitioners of the period. Whatever its limits may have been, the "trend toward consolidation" in newspapers, as Lee characterized it in 1929, meant that reliable, national channels for disseminating a message existed as never before.

Earlier in the century, press agents were required to approach local newspapers, editor by editor, to situate PR materials in a range of locales. Now, local editors were more likely to be compliant employees of a national news apparatus. Single entry points existed through which a publicist could reach publics in a variety of regions all at once.

This phenomenon, and its particular utility to the publicist, was the centerpiece of Lee's 1929 publication, *The Press Today: How the News Reaches the Public*. In his discussion of the contemporary newspaper system and his detailed road map of the modern highway system of persuasion, Lee provided an illuminating picture of the ways that public relations experts were becoming students of the media system and of the ways that Tarde's turn-of-the-century theoretical insights were maturing into the basis of a concrete, carefully considered, strategy.

In spite of new, printless forms of mass media that were emerging, Lee argued, the newspaper remained an essential arena for publicity work. "Since 1922 newspaper circulation in the United States has increased 38 per cent. This growth is relatively four times as great as the increase in population during the same period," he observed. While newspaper readership widened, however, Lee noted that these readers were being informed by a narrower assortment of papers and news sources. "In spite of the expansion [in readership]," he wrote, "the actual number of newspapers had declined and the basis of organization has shifted from the independent unit to the combine."

> There are at present over fifty groups of chain operated news-papers in the United States, ranging from two or three papers in a single town to the Gannett and Copley organizations in the East and West respectively, and the two nationwide com-bines of Hearst and Scripps-Howard. The four groups above mentioned include 87 of the nation's leading papers.[9]

Shunting aside criticisms that consolidation meant that the local "editor of the chain newspaper does not serve the community on whom his revenue depends, but serves the head of his organization who has probably no personal interest or acquaintance with the com-munity," Lee articulated the perspective of the chains' owners.

> "Chain newspaper development does not mean journalistic monopoly," as one prominent group owner [unnamed] observes. "It means elimination of economic weaklings; fewer but more virile ownerships."
>
> Moreover, while the editorials of the independent daily may reflect only the opinions of its single editor, the editorials of a chain paper are likely to reflect the opinions of a group of leading and recognized writers. Because of its wide scope the direction of the editorial page of a chain newspaper has a broader viewpoint.

Enhancing the reach of this "broader viewpoint," Lee added, news-paper chains were "establishing journals in some rural communities which might otherwise be without adequate sources of news."[10] Within such rationalizations lay Lee's recognition that these "virile owner-ships" were permitting modern principles of mass production and of national market standardization to be applied to the practices of public relations.

Beyond these shifts in print journalism, other developments in the American media system were providing fertile soil for the growth and ingenuity of public relations practices. One of the most portentous of these developments was the birth of commercially based broadcast radio, beginning in Pittsburgh in 1921. Started as a local merchandising experiment to boost the sale of Westinghouse radio receivers, by the mid-twenties broadcast radio had rapidly expanded into a pervasive national medium, dominated by two RCA-owned, sponsor-supported commercial networks.[11]

Centered in New York City, also the base of operations for the flowering public relations industry, these portals into America's radio system were particularly close at hand. As was the case with newspaper chains, the broadcast network system made the single entry-point dissemination of publicity relatively effortless. Also following the lead of chain-owned newspapers—which, from the twenties onward, were increasingly subsidized via a nationally based advertising industry and by promotions for the brand-name products of national corporations—radio broadcasting in the 1920s and 1930s was underwritten, in large part, by national commercial enterprises.

Mirroring trends that had shaped the distribution of gas and electricity throughout much of the United States, radio was also developing, for the most part, as a privately owned utility, pumping information and entertainment directly into people's homes. Requiring no significant degree of literacy on the part of its audience and providing people with a captivating link to the outside world, radio gave interested corporations, or politicians, unprecedented access to the inner sanctums of the public mind.

The evolution of chain newspapers tended to delete independent perspectives and homogenize newspaper journalism. Similarly, big business's control of radio meant that broadcasting would also begin to weed out localized—or otherwise aberrant—sensibilities, proffering, instead, a growing repertoire of national, commercially guided, cultural stereotypes. Here, motion pictures were instructive. Hollywood was already busy delineating these stereotypes for a national audience.

There was a significant—if, today, largely unknown—"popular opposition" that challenged the domination of broadcasting by giant radio corporations, seeking to establish American radio as a medium open to a more extended range of "nonprofit and noncommercial" voices. But federal policies and regulations of the twenties and thirties (most notably the Radio Act of 1927 and the Communications

Act of 1934), for the most part, provided public assistance to privately owned, profit based, commercial radio.[12]

In a society joined by modern networks of mass communication, the *public sphere* itself was becoming the property of corporate gatekeepers. The long-term impact of this trend in *who has a say* in America continues to be a real issue. From the vantage point of corporate public relations specialists, however, this general tendency and the system of sponsorship that financed it meant that both print and broadcast media were becoming more and more congenial to a *business point of view.*

Radio's potential as a vehicle for political propaganda was also becoming evident by the mid-twenties. In 1926 the Philadelphia *Public Ledger,* noted an important shift in the tactical thinking of politicians. While prior to the 1924 elections the "political gentry paid . . . little attention to radio and broadcasting," the paper noted, radio was now perceived as "a new political weapon of infinite possibilities." Assuming an inflection recalling the windy axioms of Gustave Le Bon and Walter Lippmann, the paper added:

> These possibilities are far better understood now. . . . *The man, the group or the organization able to "control the air" would own a tremendous political advantage.*[13]

By the mid-thirties radio had grown as an institution, and people were spending more and more time listening to their sets. In light of this development, some imagined radio as something which could become a powerful tool for public education and enlightenment.[14] Others expressed concern that radio was interfering with the customary "interests and activities" of the home. "Family conversation," along with other traditional aspects of home-life, wrote one critic," is the greatest sufferer."[15]

For others, however, radio's propagandistic potential was its most salient feature. Writing in the *Annals of the American Academy of Political and Social Science* in 1935, for example, William Hard explained that "radio can have any one of several relationships to public opinion." He elaborated, exhibiting a remarkably subtle comprehension of radio's particular utility as an attitude shaping instrument.

In the first place, it can be used for the direct and unabashed "manufacture" of public opinion. It is especially suited to that sort of social deviltry. It enters the home as an amusing guest. It brings with it primarily that most charming of all offerings—music. It adds to music the thrill of the dramatic sketch and the laugh of the comic sketch. Throughout these enticements it is addressing its hosts at their hearthside, not with the impersonal appeal of printed characters but with the living voices of individual performers who seem in time to become intimate friends. It then, having established itself as entertainment, can pass smoothly and almost imperceptibly into propaganda, and, by means of carefully edited "news" and carefully contrived "talks" can do more than any other known agency to convey palatable doses of truth—or of untruth—to the public.[16]

Complementing the growth of a modern media apparatus, other developments were unfolding that also promoted the conceit that public opinion might be efficiently engineered by trained technicians. In his early writings, Edward L. Bernays had repeatedly decreed that an effective public relations counsel must be a tireless student of the sociological terrain: of public propensities, opinions, and behavior. As he made this pronouncement, innovations were already afoot that would assist in the actualization of this prescription.

During the 1920s and 1930s, a trend toward public-opinion measurement—the use of instrumental surveys to study and guide public attitudes—was becoming manifest. As never before, the public and its sentiments were routinely being monitored as the objects of "scientific" study.

The use of social surveys, of course, was not new. Early in the century, Progressive social analysts and reformers had done pathbreaking statistically based studies—such as Paul Kellogg's *Pittsburgh Survey* or W. E. B. DuBois's study of *The Philadelphia Negro*—but these, for the most part, were launched for the purpose of documenting persistent social inequities and for corroborating an agenda of reform.[17]

Even before the First World War, things began to change. Business analysts began to see survey research as a commercially useful tool. The advertising industry, given its intimate involvement with the problem of consumer response, was an early advocate of market research. At the same time, some business-school professors and social scientists began to advance market research as an academic concern. One of these professors was Paul Cherington, who taught at the Harvard School of Business between 1908 and 1919. The originator and teacher of one of the United States' first university courses in the field of "marketing," by 1911 Cherington was beginning to focus his energies on the problem of "consumer research." Under Cherington's leadership, noted historian Jean M. Converse, "Harvard became an influential force for intellectual organization of the field in sampling and analysis."[18]

By the early twenties, Cherington moved from the ivory tower directly into the business world, using an income-based framework for the analysis of market attitudes as director of research for the J. Walter Thompson advertising agency. From the early twenties, a growing number of people followed Cherington's lead. Daniel Starch commenced his practice in market research in the twenties, and his 1923 book, *Principles of Advertising,* was one of the first by a psychologist to discuss the significance of psychographic research as an element of marketing.[19] Elmo Roper also began his long career in survey research in the mid-twenties.

By the end of the decade, the study of public attitudes was moving beyond the concerns of advertising and marketing per se, to inform a more comprehensive approach to corporate thinking. It is not surprising that American Telephone and Telegraph (AT&T) was one of the first major American corporations to recognize the need for ongoing survey research as a component of corporate public relations work. Speaking at a 1929 meeting, company president Arthur Page told his public relations staff that survey research must increasingly become a part of their arsenal. The Bell System, he asserted, must learn to be a watchful student of public sentiments, to understand the present business milieu, and to anticipate problems the company might face in the future.

Citing a number of concrete situations in which public feeling might encroach upon corporate interests—aesthetic concerns about AT&T plants built along American highways, worries that holding companies and financial speculation might lead to an economic crash, and mounting hostility to the growth of chain stores—Page suggested that such issues, unless proficiently addressed, could cloud the future of business in general, and AT&T in particular. "[T]he prognostication of public moods and public trends may seem a little intangible," he conceded, but it was critical for the company to attempt to do so.

> [T]here are a great many kinds of different streams of public emotion which it is important for us to know about, not only their present nature but what they are likely to be in the future, and what we have spent this session upon has been an effort to give enough examples in a rough way to convince you that we ought to organize the study of such things and . . . organize them so that the executive officers of this business will not have to make decisions relating to the political hazards of the business . . . without any staff work but merely out of their own judgements.[20]

Responding, in large part, to the social, political, and economic conditions of the Great Depression (see Part 4), the growth of market surveys and public opinion research accelerated during the 1930s. An important contributor to this trend was an organization known as the Psychological Corporation, a consortium of academic psychologists, that had been established in 1923. Under the direction of Henry C. Link (a Yale-trained psychologist) the corporation's objective was to apply the methods of behavioral psychology to the needs of American business.[21]

Henry Link did not quarrel with the overarching theoretical assumption of social psychology: the idea of an irrational public. By the early thirties, this perspective was fairly common in business and social scientific circles. On the other hand, Link questioned the extent to which the tradition of social psychology provided businesses or other institutions, with a clear basis for practical action and a sound instrument for analyzing an irrational public. In this regard, he argued, social psychology was more confusing than explanatory; it did not offer a sensible instrument for analyzing or influencing the attitudes and behavior of the public.

The psychological theory of instincts (or fundamental drives) stated, in effect, that the operations of the mind were based on a number of inherited emotional mechanisms. There was the sex instinct, the parental instinct, the fighting instinct, the herd instinct, etc., etc. . . . This was very plausible, but when psychologists began to enumerate all the instincts and to describe the actions and feelings to which they gave rise, difficulties immediately arose. . . . Different psychologists enumerated from one to forty instincts and were never able to arrive at an agreement as to just how many there were, what they were, or what actions they led to.[22]

"Psychology, as it is popularly understood, consists of many speculative theories drawn from the infancy of the subject and now obsolete," he proclaimed. The approach of the Psychological Corporation would be different, more practical. It would move toward "the study of people's behavior as a clue to their present and future wants."[23] "This change may be summed up crudely as follows," he wrote.

The old psychology was a study of how the mind thinks; the new psychology is a study of how the mind acts. The old psychology of advertising, for example, concerned itself with discovering . . . which had the strongest appeal, the most effective copy, the greatest interest value, the best attention value, etc. The new psychology is concerned with discovering what advertisements are most effective at getting people to buy. Not what people think or think they think, but what they actually do about certain advertisements is the important question.[24]

During the depression, such thinking answered the needs of an increasingly desperate business environment. "STORES NEED FACTS ON BUYING HABITS . . . KNOWLEDGE COUNTED VITAL, BUT LITTLE PROGRESS HAS BEEN ACHIEVED SO FAR," blazoned the *New York Times* on April 5, 1931.

Probably at no time in the last decade has actual knowledge of consumer buying habits been as vital to successful and profitable retailing as it is today. There is quite general agreement among executives in the field that retailers would be in a far better position to meet the disconcerting complications of current economic conditions if the result of painstaking surveys into this problem were available. Yet, surprisingly enough, comparatively little progress of a well-defined nature has been achieved.[25]

Using undergraduate and graduate students at universities around the country to conduct survey research, the Psychological Corporation—under Link's direction—established a quarterly Psychological Sales Barometer, the first ongoing examination of consumer attitudes and behavior: the brand-names people purchased, the advertising slogans they remembered, and so forth.[26] Link also advocated the use of recently developed accounting equipment to codify survey results, anticipating the role that computers would eventually play in the monitoring of public attitudes.

The most highly developed technique for measuring buying behavior is that made possible by the electric sorting and tabulating machines. These ingenious devices have made it feasible to record and classify the behavior of the buying public as well as the behavior of those who serve that public on a scale heretofore impracticable. . . . [T]he deduction from these records of important summaries and significant facts has been made relatively easy. The technique developed by various merchants, with the use of these devices, exemplifies the behavioristic psychological method in almost its ideal form. It is the quantitative study of analysis of human behavior in the nth degree.[27]

Psychological Corporation surveys began by examining attitudes and behavior that were expressly relevant to marketing. Within a few years, however, the scope of the Psychological Sales Barometers broadened to include the study of opinions about current events, politics, and the corporate system overall.

By the mid-thirties, *Fortune* magazine launched its own poll, conducted by a partnership of Cherington and Roper. George Gallup and his American Institute of Public Opinion followed soon thereafter.[28] Shortly, Claude Robinson would establish Opinion Research, Inc., in

Princeton, New Jersey. As never before, the public was becoming an object of minute statistical analysis, continuously scrutinized and pigeonholed for instrumental purposes. An Age of Polling, in which the temperature of the public would be taken on an ongoing basis, had commenced.

For compliance professionals in the twenties and thirties, the flowering of survey research was of immediate and practical utility. Early in the 1920s, public relations specialists described their profession as a "two-way street." Their job, they maintained, was to present the habitually misinterpreted interests of large institutions to the public while interpreting the habitually ignored interests of the public to the organizations that served it. Within the "two-way street" analogy, public relations presented itself unequivocally as the lubricant of democratic reciprocity.

In the simultaneous unfolding of a national media system and of a modern machinery for measuring public opinion, a social infrastructure for this so-called two-way exchange of interests was being built. The mass media, dominated by commercial interests, would provide subservient channels through which a broad public might be schooled to a corporate point of view. The polling system and a burgeoning market research establishment would provide the channels through which the public would be known and then responded to. Pollsters would henceforth be the messengers through whom the public interest would be ostensibly articulated. Abstract, statistical renditions of democracy and of the public itself were appearing; ideals or memories of a participatory public were being annulled.

Self-promotions from within a nascent polling establishment only bolstered this trend. The unambiguous equation of polling with democracy was promulgated by Cherington, who described opinion polls as nothing less than the "*Vox Populi*, speaking wisdom through 'chi-squares,' 'medians' and 'cumulative means,' 'standard deviations,' and other strange statistical gadgets." Polling, he maintained, "gives new meaning to a whole list of such common terms as 'free speech,' 'democracy,' 'social reform,' 'labor movements,' 'consumer demand,' and even 'public opinion' itself." Statistical research would be the method through which democracy would finally be brought to a large-scale society in which the common good was too often ignored. He narrated a history in the making.

> Democracy, on a small scale, is able to express itself swiftly and with certainty. . . . [T]he New England town meetings . . . and similar instances could be cited if evidence were needed. But for nearly 100 years beginning about 1835, with the growth of our cities, states and the country as a whole, the people have become less and less able to say what they thought concerning many vital matters. . . .
>
> Within the past five years a significant change has come about. The principles of statistical sampling, already worked out in other fields . . . have been applied to this job of giving voice to public opinion. . . .
>
> If democracy is 'government by the people,' and if it depends for its very life on free expresssion of unstampeded common sense, then by this newly applied technique of giving it a voice, we see the importance of the true and representative cross-section. . . . The prime requisite of an effective democracy is that it must get at some satisfactory balance between all kinds of people.[29]

The implications of public-opinion measurement for democracy, however, are considerably more problematic than any such fairy tales allow. Dewey's description of America as a society in which public sentiment was being systematically manufactured became, in many ways, only more pertinent in the age of polling. Beyond measuring public opinion, polls were also powerful tools for misrepresenting, even forging, public opinion.

One aspect of polling that threw Cherington's ideology into question was the method by which samples were gathered and organized. Public opinion measurement, in its quest for useful demographic categories, also served to reproduce and fortify nondemocratic tendencies that persisted in the society at large. This contradiction is apparent in Roper's account of how population samples were routinely categorized for the *Fortune* magazine surveys. "[O]urs is a sliding scale." The population was analyzed, he explained, according to "economic status." Roper then went on to itemize the breakdown.

"At the top are the 'A's' who might also be called the 'prosperous.'"
Following these, he described the B's, the upper middle class; the C's,
the lower middles, and the D's, "or the poor."

Revealingly, Roper reported that this scale was applied only to
surveys of the white population. "Depending on the nature of the
study being conducted," he wrote, "we sometimes have a fifth group,
'N,' composed of Negroes." In a society torn by institutional racism,
in which many African Americans did not enjoy the rights of citizenship, the classifications used in the Roper poll only fortified this tendency. Though differences among whites were distinguished by a
hierarchy of economic status, African Americans were analyzed only
in terms of race. In an eloquent instance of the ability of polling to
validate injustice and of its limited utility as a democratizing device,
the American population was seen simply as A, B, C, D, and N.

Another problem with public-opinion measurement as an instrument of democracy was its inability to gather data without, at the
same time, influencing the ways that the data would turn out. Early
in his career, Link acknowledged that the way questions were posed
would have a decisive impact on the answers that a pollster received.
"[T]he form of a question," he wrote, has much "to do with the
answers obtained. . . . [H]ow precarious is this matter of measuring
public opinion," he conceded.[30] Implicit within Link's admission was
the suggestion that carefully worded questions could be crafted in
order to elicit any desired response. Polls could be used as evidence of
public support—or outrage—by which any private concern might
justify itself as acting in the public interest. With large corporations
serving as the most profitable clients of the survey-research
industry—as has continued to be the case since the twenties—the
imprimatur of "public opinion" polls has been routinely exploited to
support a wide variety of business agendas.

This issue of who controls the polling apparatus disturbed a
number of contemporaneous observers. Psychologist Leonard Doob,
for example, rejected polling as "almost worthless as a contribution to
a systematic science," insofar as it was primarily employed by private
industry to exploit public desires for commercial gain.[31] Robert Lynd,
a prominent American sociologist, wrote that a "major barrier to . . .
a socially constructive use of public opinion polls is that these polls
are in private hands for private profit."[32] If this was the public, it was

primarily the public as filtered through the interests and imperatives of business enterprises.

Lynd also voiced concern about the way polls themselves had attained the status of news. Reported on in newspapers or cited on the radio, public opinion polls were becoming statistical applause tracks, "useful manipulative devices on the level of propaganda," for encouraging those on the fence to join the crowd. "[P]ublic opinion polls," Lynd wrote, were an example of democracy "working in reverse." Rather than serving to communicate and empower public opinion, opinion polls were being used to manufacture and package public opinion.

> They operate actually to confirm the citizen's false sense of security in totalling up "what the majority think." . . . [T]he false sense of the public's being "boss" that they encourage operates to narcotize public awareness of the seriousness of problems and of the drastic social changes many contemporary situations require.[33]

Writing in the *Annals of the American Academy of Political and Social Science* in 1935, Malcolm M. Willey voiced similar anxieties over the ways that the findings of polls were coming to constitute a subtle and uniquely effective form of modern propaganda.

> An individual may be moved to action through repetition, as, for example, in advertising; but *his action is made more certain if he is made to realize that thousands, even millions, of others are thinking and feeling as he himself does.* Herein lies the importance of the contemporary communication network; it not only carries its symbols to the individual, *it also impresses upon him a sense of numbers.*[34]

Polls produced coldly mathematical information that, at the same time, exerted a profoundly emotional influence. Insofar as Wilfred Trotter's "herd instinct" continued to serve as a significant rudiment of human behavior, polls offered a numerical herd with which one might identify, a subliminal mental magnet for deciding what to think and how to behave.

•   •   •

The concerns voiced earlier regarding the manipulative potential of survey research continue to resonate. Whether the public opinion apparatus enhances or diminishes the meaning of democracy is still an inescapable question. For a mounting legion of public relations and propaganda specialists during the 1920s and 1930s, however, an invaluable instrument had been devised, one that served them in two distinct ways.

First, the obsessive mining and measuring of public attitudes—opinion polling and marketing surveys—were transforming the idea of public opinion into a valuable resource for systematic commercial and political exploitation. The public was becoming a commodity; its opinions were being packaged and sold to the highest bidder. Coincidentally, as exemplified in Roper's discourse on sampling methods, those sectors of the population whose race or amount of disposable income was not seen as socially, commercially, or politically desirable were only further marginalized or rendered incommunicado in the polls.

Second, for a brotherhood of propagandists continually on the lookout for new channels of influence, polls themselves were becoming an expressive, yet enigmatic, medium of persuasion. With numerical eloquence, they provided an often confused population with silent civic lessons. In the results of polls, a modern public came face-to-face with itself—or a numerical facsimile thereof—and was offered wordless counsel on what or how to think. The measurement of public opinion and its manufacture were becoming less and less distinguishable.

In a 1984 article, Marvin Olasky, a historian of public relations, astutely characterized Bernays as "one of the first" of his profession "to realize fully that American 20th Century liberalism would be increasingly based on social control posing as democracy, and would be desperate to learn all the opportunities for social control that it could."[35] During the twenties and thirties, the expansion of a commercial media system and the statistical pageantry of opinion polling helped to transform Bernays's prophetic intuition into a generic feature of contemporary American life. Opportunities for "democratic" social control were only ripening.

10

Optical Illusions

AT THE CLOSE OF the 1920s, Georges Duhamel, an eminent French writer, made a sojourn to the United States. Like Alexis de Toqueville a century before, Duhamel wished to survey the state of American society, imagining that in the United States Europeans might discover "scenes from the life of the future" that awaited them.

Published in 1931—under the title *America the Menace*—Duhamel's narration of his visit portrayed modern America as a "devouring civilization," motored by a torrential apparatus of publicity. Wherever one turns, he told his readers, publicity beckons with "the serene persistence of machines," seeking to ensnare "the bewildered gaze of the passer-by."[1]

American "civilization," as Duhamel described it, was overwhelmingly visual. Having forsaken all fidelity to truth, the publicity machine was generating a ceaseless riot of optical stimulants, "flashes, repetitions, and explosions," that were "conceived to excite the reflexes of a sedentary mollusk." Aimed at titillating the nervous system, more than educating the mind, here was a culture that "presents to the people only images that are elementary, powerful, and seductive." For Duhamel, American publicity was "a triumph of disharmony and disorder," a "*charivari* of light," a provocation intended to induce what he termed "a kind of masturbation of the eye."[2]

Overwhelmed by these seductions, Duhamel felt his sense of reality, his liminal sense of his own existence, slipping away.

> Everything was false. The world was false. I myself was perhaps no longer anything but a simulacrum of a man, an imitation Duhamel. . . . My thoughts were no longer under my

control. . . . [M]oving pictures usurped the place of my own ideas.[3]

Duhamel's hyperbole is remarkable, yet his description percep-tively discerned developments that had, by the late twenties, left an unambiguous mark on the terrain of American life. The "masturba-tion of the eye," as Duhamel so pregnantly put it, was becoming a diagnostic attribute of twentieth-century American culture and a self-conscious strategy employed by the compliance professions. Traces of these developments haunt the archives of persuasion.

On June 11, 1923, for example, William P. Banning, director of public relations for the American Telephone and Telegraph Company (AT&T), rose to address a Bell System Publicity Conference being convened in New York City.[4] His presentation echoed a concern that had persistently guided the thinking of the corporation's leadership for nearly twenty years: the importance of maintaining ongoing public support for AT&T's monopolistic control of telephone and tele-graph services in the United States.

Yet if Banning's topic was familiar, the tilt of his thinking was not. His speech encompassed an altered view of how AT&T's corpo-rate idée fixe might best be guarded. Banning's words signaled a tan-gible break with the creed of Theodore Vail.

Between 1907 and 1917—the years of Vail's presidency—AT&T had been an innovative advocate of corporate public relations, at a time when few big businesses had seen the necessity. In an anti-big business, antimonopoly political milieu, Vail had instructed, AT&T's ability to achieve and preserve its long-term corporate objectives demanded a heedful quest for public support. Throughout Vail's tenure, this meant an unremitting campaign to "educate" the public, to provide middle-class Americans with *reasoned, fact-based explana-tions* as to why an AT&T monopoly was in their own—and America's—best interests. At the core of this strategy lay the Progres-sive doctrine that the public was a body that might be reasoned with.

As Banning stood before his staff in 1923, however, this founda-tional assumption was palpably absent. History, the First World War, and the genesis of modern psychological thinking had all left their marks on AT&T's corporate state of mind, and Banning's speech represented a clear repudiation of Vail's resolute faith in a rational public. Addressing the subject of institutional advertising—advertising designed to promote a corporation overall, rather than a particular product or service—Banning counseled his troops to disabuse themselves of the notion that the public was educable through reason.

It was hard for "telephone men" to think about the public in this new way, he acknowledged. As modern professionals, committed to the enhancement of life through scientific and technological progress—he flattered his audience—the instincts of telephone company employees were propelled by rational modes of thinking. Like other highly educated offspring of the modern age, they were used to applying reason to the tasks before them. Because of its logical disposition, Banning generalized, "[i]t is natural for a telephone company to assume that facts should be the basis of its advertising appeals."

> The telephone business is an engineered business and that betokens accuracy in everything. It tends to make telephone men literal men. It is a business involving infinite detail for proper functioning. It needs public considerateness, and intelligent use of telephone facilities, as a help toward its successfulness. That leads to a wish to teach the public, so as to increase the public's knowledge and considerateness.

If the logic of company men was unimpeachable, however, the same could not be said about the public. The public's inherent nature was simply not responsive to logical entreaties. Though you might wish it to be otherwise, Banning told his staff, the public is not "composed of electrical engineers." Characterizing the public mind for them, Banning submitted the analogy of an impassioned sports crowd. "Go to a big ball game," he suggestively derisively, "and you'll see your public."

Reasoned argument and factual evidence would simply not appeal "to the individual typifying the composite public, who is a bromidic though good-natured person, with too many troubles of his own to bother with those of a monopoly, who would rather be amused than instructed." The AT&T publicist, therefore, must endure "the public as it is, not as he would like it to be."

Recalling Edward L. Bernays's dictum that organizations must employ only those appeals "to which the public is ready to respond" and must be capable of foreseeing "those reactions which the public is ready to give," Banning extended the following general guideline for the making of an effective publicist:

> If he keeps the homely saying in mind that molasses is better than vinegar, if he will remember that *an appeal to the heart, to the sentiments, is more resultful than one based on logic,* he has the beginnings of a good technique. [Emphasis added.]

This having been said, Banning reprimanded his staff, indicating that too little of their work was inspired by an accurate understanding of the public. It "looks as though it might have been written by an engineer. . . . You have talked about facts and figures . . . as though you expected every newspaper reader who saw one of your advertisements to jump at it and gain its valuable information for his very own." Such an approach to public relations, he asserted, was misguided. Whether Banning was conversant with Freud's notion of object cathexis—with the proposition that love induces a "humble subjection . . . toward the loved object" comparable to the relationship that develops between a hypnotized subject and a hypnotist—is not known. In Banning's thinking, however, the gist of Freud's perspective was implicit.

> The job of the Publicity Directors of the Bell System is to make the people understand and *love the company.* Not merely be consciously dependent upon it—*not merely regard it as a necessity—not merely take it for granted, but to love it—to hold real affection for it—make it an honored personal member of their business force, an admired intimate member of the family.* [Emphasis added.]

In a variety of ways, Banning's remarks mirrored the "wisdom" of his time. Nestled in the folds of his presentation were the footprints of Gustave Le Bon and his progeny; the pragmatic lessons of the First World War and the Committee on Public Information; and Bernays's prescription that a successful public relations specialist will be a devoted student of the human psyche.

For AT&T and for corporate America more generally, however, the implications of Banning's speech were revelatory. They marked the emergence of a new, emotionally directed vernacular by which corporations would be increasingly addressing and seeking to influence their publics.

As AT&T's rendering of the public gravitated from one empowered by reason to one propelled by emotion the oratorical techniques of corporate publicity shifted as well. If, when Vail ran the company, AT&T publicity was dominated by a reliance on the medium of printed word— and for deliberately reasoned proofs—now the corporation began to lean toward a more pictorial and impressionistic notion of persuasion. Banning's 1923 speech would provide eloquent evidence of this change.

Instead of seeing an institutional advertisement as a logical argument, buttressed by information, Banning encouraged his staff to think of each ad as an arousing visual experience, designed to evoke an essentially psychological response.

> Think of your whole advertisement as a picture, and I believe you will find the problem of securing an attractive result will be simplified. Consider the border of your advertisement as its frame, consider the illustration as the cottage, or the group of trees, or the lovers, or the other human or animal centers of interest which appear on most canvases.

Written text was still present, but it was becoming increasingly subservient to the image—the newly rediscovered, vital centerpiece of a message being delivered.

> [C]onsider your type matter as the foreground of the picture, which gives the proper setting to the illustration. . . . The picture and the caption together must entice the reader into the text or he will never get there; and the text must carry him through to the signature [the corporate logo] if you want him to get the whole story. Though the value of an advertisement is by no means lost if the picture and the headline are of sufficient attractive value to stop the reader for a moment, for while the text may be slighted, each person who hesitates

> through interest generated by illustration and heading will at
> least want to know their source and will glance at the signa-
> ture. *You don't care if the text is neglected if the rest of the*
> *advertisement gave the right impression.* [Emphasis added.]

Where text was employed, it too must be guided by the paradigm of
the image; it should be written to trigger feelings above thought.

> Be humorous without being cheap. Be friendly without being
> fresh. Remember that a laugh will accomplish more than much
> logic; that entertainment is far more appreciated than instruc-
> tion; that the average human animal will only receive logic or
> instruction when it is clothed in entertainment. . . . That is
> what makes the motion picture so invaluable.

In a dramatic break from AT&T's public relations past, Vail's
principle of public education was being sacrificed to the premeditated
management of impressions. Banning's paradigm was a calculated
optical seduction. Gustave Le Bon's contention that the crowd
"thirsts for illusions," "thinks in images," and is most effectively
mastered by "a startling image which fills and besets the mind" was
in the process of being transformed into a step-by-step approach to
corporate communications.

In addressing an unreasoning public, Banning concluded, *the
image* is a more dependable instrument of persuasion than *the word*.
Walter Lippmann's notion that symbols are dynamic tools for assembling "emotions after they have been detached from their ideas," that
they are "strategic railroad centers" that magnify "feeling" while
downgrading "significance," had moved beyond the speculative realm
and was working its way into the highest levels of business thinking.

By the twenties, Banning's awareness of the image as a tool of
public relations was not unusual. Comparable ideas were percolating
elsewhere in the business world, particularly among those companies
that were engaged in the manufacture of consumer goods, companies
for whom the cultivation of public loyalties was essential. While many
businesses continued to disregard public concerns, propaganda specialists in some of America's largest corporations turned to visual
strategies to propagate altruistic, service-oriented corporate images.[5]

Corresponding to this development, as a postwar generation of would-be opinion molders absorbed the tricks of their trade, the utility of symbols was becoming a standard element in their training. Beginning in New York City—the nerve center of the nation's communications industry—universities began to offer formal courses in public relations techniques in which the study of the image as an instrument of persuasion occupied a prominent place in the curriculum.

Teaching one of the first of these courses, at NYU in 1923, Bernays brought his own particular slant to the subject of PR, forsaking journalistic paradigms that had framed public relations theory up to that point, emphasizing the importance of symbols and their capacity—when systematically applied—to set off unconscious chains of mental association.[6]

Simultaneously, at the New School for Social Research, Harry Overstreet—a prominent social psychologist—launched a lecture course, Influencing Human Behavior, in which he, too, accentuated the centrality of nonrational mental life and the ways that images might be employed to gain access to that life.

"[G]iving people the facts" as a strategy of influence, he told his students, has been a failure; the appeal to reason has been "an enterprise fraught with a surprising amount of disappointment."[7] Persuasion, he argued, cannot be achieved through the dissemination of factual information, but requires the capacity to strike the inner lives of the public, "to arouse the more important but slumbering wants into action."[8]

Because most people are "visual minded," he added, the most assured way of reaching this goal is to translate a message "into visual form" and thus to "increase its power."[9] He elaborated on this:

> [W]ords and pictures are tools. They are tools for communicating ideas, stimulating interests, arousing feelings and emotions. The sole question we have to ask about these tools is, which of them does the tool-work most effectively?
>
> When we state the issue in this way there can be no doubt about the answer. "A picture, with a few words of explanation, will make it possible to get over an idea in one minute that would require two minutes without the picture."[10]

Like Banning, Overstreet asserted that even words must be thought about and employed imagistically. "If we can cast aside the colorless, abstract words of ordinary currency, and substitute words which suggest images; if we can create what people shall see . . . we add not only to the clarity of our thought, but also to the power of our influence over human behavior."[11]

To learn how to guide thought and behavior, Overstreet continued, students must explore the little understood realm of visual language. "[W]e must learn what pictures have to say," "learn to speak the language of pictures."[12] Those interested in influencing human behavior "must make some deliberate effort to train . . . [themselves] in the power to create and transmit visual images.[13]

Modern intellectual life, he added, had done little to enhance this understanding. "[I]ntelligent people" are little equipped to use the "clearest and simplest means for transmitting ideas." If anything, intellectuals are afflicted with visual agnosia, the incapacity to appreciate or make sense of visual experience and communication.[14] Schooled by the print-biased values of the Enlightenment, they dismiss images as appendages of primitive life, remnants of totemic culture, earmarks of "lowbrow" existence.[15] Overstreet's course—which provided the basis for a widely read book, *Influencing Public Behavior*, published in 1925—was designed to help correct this regrettable deficiency.

In his lectures, Overstreet outlined two distinct categories of imagery with which students must become conversant. The first of these was the grouping he termed "imitative pictures." The second, and more important, was the category of "selective pictures." "Imitative pictures" were those that replicated—or sought to replicate—*reality* as seen by the eye. Photography was the paradigmatic expression of this genre, and Overstreet discussed a photograph's ability to convey a sense of *objective truth* where written text would fail:

A photograph, or photographic drawing, of a dress, or gun, or bicycle, or building is . . . far more effective than a verbal description . . . The eye grasps instantly a hundred details, gets the "wholeness" of a thing in picture form, where it would crawl along slowly from word to word of a description and in the end have no clear image.[16]

If "imitative pictures" could be persuasive, Overstreet saw "selective pictures" as even more potent tools of influence. Focusing a viewer's attention on a particular aspect of reality—omitting what might interfere—a "selective picture" was capable of prompting a particular mental experience. Moving beyond the eye, such pictures addressed the "eye of the mind" and pointed speechlessly toward a distinct way of seeing. If the "imitative picture" simulated the *objective* world, the sway of the "selective picture" was more intimately linked to the *subjective* life of a viewer.

If the reference point for the "imitative picture" was documentary photography, the "selective picture" drew its strength from the "power of all art." It performed its magic through "the power of selective emphasis." If the "imitative picture" was informative, "selective imagery" was hypnotic; it could be applied to trigger a "suggestion."

One might, he instructed, employ a "selective picture" to "induce an imagined experience" in the mind of a viewer, a serviceable mental occurrence that will guide a person, unconsciously, toward certain desired conclusions or actions. In the face of the narcotic "power of suggestion," Overstreet added, the spectator will be unaware that he is even in the process of being persuaded. He explained:

> The secret of all true persuasion is to induce the person to persuade himself. The chief task of the persuader, therefore, is to induce the experience. The rest will take care of itself.
>
> The secret of it all . . . is that a person is led to do what he overwhelmingly feels. Practice in getting people to feel themselves in situations is therefore the surest road to persuasiveness.[17]

Overstreet's remarkably visual vocabulary—like Banning's—reflected a way of seeing that was becoming increasingly routine in American society during the twenties. Yet the revolution toward a ceaseless "masturbation of the eye" was not simply an offspring of the twenties; it was also propelled by profound technological and aesthetic developments that had been touching the vistas of visual life for decades.

Overstreet's designation of *photography* and *art* as the dual touchstones by which modern approaches to persuasion should be guided reflected an implicit understanding of ways that both these deeply interwoven realms had been knocking at the doors of perception for some time and had—before the twenties—already left deep marks on the idiom and trajectory of twentieth-century thought.

■   ■   ■   ■   ■

From the 1830s onward, no innovation was a greater catalyst for modern, visual ways of thinking than photography. More than an invention, photography soon became a towering social metaphor, a Promethean index of truth, announcing the power of images to grip—and direct—the public's imagination, as the printed word had done during the previous century.[18]

The rise of photography altered the physics of perception; it seemed to initiate a seamless collaboration between the eye of a person *taking* a picture and the physical world from which the picture was being *taken*.[19] The very idea of "taking a picture" suggested that a photograph was not something created as a deliberate artistic act, but was simply lifted—still true to itself—from the objective world. An ancient wall dividing subjectivity and objectivity had apparently been scaled; the shadows on the wall of the cave, it seemed, were no longer shadows; *they were real.*

Many experimented with photography as an art form, but the photograph's most prepossessing quality was its magnetic claim to facticity. Even when transported from the time and circumstance in which a picture was taken, even when removed from the context of lived experience, the photograph continued to enjoy the status of tangible evidence. Photographs not only verged on truth, they quickly became a currency of truth: in newspapers and magazines, where wood engravings were certified with a caption reading "based on a photograph"; in police investigations and courts of law, where photographs bore witness to wrongdoings; in the documentation of historic events (Gettysburg, the hanging of the Lincoln conspirators); in providing an exciting opportunity to see distant places as if one were there; and in ordinary family albums, where photos recorded private histories or authenticated personal identities.[20]

Photography's ability to publicize convincingly a way of seeing as if it were truth was exploited early on to serve a range of social agendas. During the latter half of the nineteenth century, for example, photography was routinely employed in the United States and England as a tool for "scientifically" validating a panoply of Anglo-Saxon prejudices regarding race, class, gender, and general standards of normalcy. Using the medium of photography, phrenologists (nineteenth-century students of criminal typology) and other "authorities" organized visual catalogs of human stereotypes in which the physiognomies of good and evil, of madness and criminality, and of refinement and brutishness were afforded an ostensibly objective existence. Reformatories and workhouses for children published photographic before-and-after evidence, visually verifying how hard work and stern discipline combined to transform shiftless street urchins into diligent little citizens. An inventory of apparent facts was being itemized, and with it, palpable benchmarks against which social truth might be measured were being established.

Given their iron faith in the "majesty of facts" and the camera's ability to transmit a countenance of truth, it is little wonder that some innovative Progressives seized upon photography as a weapon in the struggle for social reform. Against images that fortified the status quo, a number of Progressive photographers, from the 1890s onward, began to amass a body of countervailing visual facts, facts suggesting that something was fundamentally amiss in Anglo-Saxon America, proclaiming the urgency of "social uplift."

First among these photographers was Jacob Riis, a New York journalist who—along with a team of photographic assistants—initiated the practice of urban-reform photography in the United States.[21] Riis's stark photographic portraits of the filth and chaos of New York's slums constituted a silent, yet extraordinarily persuasive appeal to a generation of middle-class Americans agonized by a search for order. Historian Peter Hales explained that "Riis meant his photographs to be seen with a particular mindset."

> They were to be deliberate, shocking antitheses to the cultural demands of his age—the demands for order, cleanliness, light, uniformity, spaciousness, and all the other accoutrements of the Victorian mindset . . . By linking the lack of these reified qualities to the urban condition itself, Riis hoped to embolden his audience to action.[22]

Implicit in Riis's effort was the recognition that no matter how "objective" a picture may appear, photographs are never neutral. Each expresses a particular point of view. While Overstreet drew a theoretical line between the "imitative" imagery of photography, which was ostensibly *objective,* and "selective" images, which presented a *subjective* way of seeing, the social development of photography suggests that this division was specious. While some images may make a claim to objectivity, all are "selective," all harbor and express a point of view.

With this thought in mind, Riis and the circle of photographers who worked for him employed photography to spotlight the squalor, degradation, and moral disintegration that took place in the slums. Their images were intended to horrify.

Other Progressive photographers, particularly Lewis Hine, used photography to emphasize the inherent dignity of working people, hoping to elicit an admiration for the subjects of his photographs in the minds of middle-class Americans who encountered them in Progressive publications. In either case, photography revealed itself as a double-edged medium through which seemingly incontestable renditions of reality might, at the same time, serve to further a particular social outlook.

The link between photography's apparent facticity and its extraordinary ability to persuade was evident to Hine. Speaking to a gathering of social workers in 1909, Hine noted that businessmen had "long ago settled" that advertising pays. It was now time for social workers to follow the same dictum. "Servants of the Common Good" must learn to "educate and direct public opinion." Toward this goal, he continued, photography—particularly pictures reinforced by "social pen pictures," his own visual-minded term for captions—provided a peerless instrument of publicity.

Hine offered a photograph of a young spinner, a girl working in a Carolina cotton mill, as an example. Simply by itself, he observed, the picture "makes an appeal." With a compelling caption, the appeal takes on an accelerated urgency. He then suggested a caption that might be used in conjunction with the picture:

> *The idea of oppression was realized by this dismal servitude.*
> *When they find themselves in such condition at the dawn of*
> *existence—so young, so feeble, struggling among men—what*

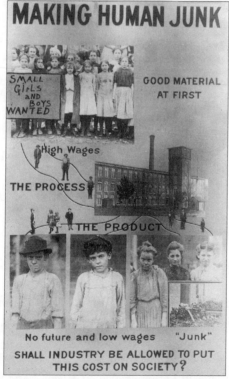

Two Lewis Hine creations: one, the portrait of a young girl working in a cotton mill and the other, a flowchart collage presenting an argument against child labor.

*passes in these souls fresh from God? But while they are chil-
dren they escape because they are little. The smallest hole saves
them. When they are men, the millstone of our social system
comes in contact with them and grinds them.*

"With the picture thus sympathetically interpreted," Hine exclaimed,
"what a lever we have for social uplift."

Yet alongside his praise of photography as an unparalleled instrument for the "revelation of truth," Hine had another, considerably
more uneasy, awareness of the pull that images—all images—exert
on viewers. The mysterious attraction of images, Hine allowed, is in
their capacity to touch something primitive in the mental life of
humankind. Images, he asserted, speak "a language learned early in
the race and the individual." The apparent objectivity of photography,
Hine believed, only enlarges the image's magnetism and its perils.

"The average person," he noted with ambivalence, "believes
implicitly that the photograph cannot falsify." Precisely because of
this realism, photographs can be used as instruments for the abridg-
ment—even the falsification—of reality. "[W]hile photographs may
not lie," he observed knowingly, "liars may photograph." In this
inherent tension, lay photography's potential for both good and evil.
Hine advised photographers who wished to serve the cause of social
uplift to adopt unimpeachable ethical standards in their work. We
must "see to it," he told them, "that the camera we depend upon con-
tracts no bad habits."[23]

■　　■　　■　　■　　■

Beyond the ways that photographs could be used to document and
publicize social facts objectively, there were other aspects of photography that spoke to the power of images to move people on more
unconscious and irrational planes of perception. If the rise of photography suggested ways by which instrumental—if phantom—objectiv-
ities might be conveyed, it simultaneously magnified a relationship
existing between images and mental life, between pictures and the
ineffable structures of memory itself.

There is a scene in Orson Welles's *Citizen Kane* in which, in an
attempt to explain the meaning of "Rosebud," Kane's former business
manager Bernstein—now an old man—ruminates on the texture of

human remembrance, recalling his own youth. "A fellow will remember a lot of things you wouldn't think he'd remember," he began, "You take me."

One day back in 1896 I was crossing over to Jersey on the ferry, and as we pulled out there was another ferry pulling in. And on it there was a girl waiting to get off. A white dress she had on, and she was carrying a white parasol. And I only saw her for one second. She didn't see me at all. But I'll bet a month hasn't gone by since, that I haven't thought of that girl.

In capsule form, Bernstein's haunting tale speaks to the psychodynamics of the mind, the power of the incidental to inscribe itself upon a life, to gain a subjective significance that far outweighs the objective magnitude of the moment from which it was drawn. This is also a power of photography.

When first introduced in the late 1830s, photography captivated the "wondering gaze" of humanity. Oliver Wendell Holmes, Sr., an avid amateur photographer, wrote of photography as a "mirror with a memory." With it, he observed, one could fix "the most fleeting of our illusions, that which the apostle and the philosopher and the poet have alike used as the type of instability and unreality." Alongside their claim to "scientific objectivity," photographs also spoke the vernacular of illusion and fantasy.

In their ability to entrap the evanescent moment—defying the passage of time itself—photography also eluded customary notions of mortality. Photographs had the capacity to grab transient gestures, to enshrine the commonplace, the incidental, to hold onto things that previously survived only as faint, if potent, glimmers of recollection.

Sigmund Freud wrote extensively of the powers that such ephemeral impressions exerted in the economy of the psyche. Forgotten, apparently incidental moments of life, he maintained, stood at the heart of character development, providing elemental keys to our desires and discontents. Within each of us, these mementos lie concealed, asserting their influence, awaiting rediscovery. More than the question of pseudo-objectivity, the insights of psychoanalysis may stand at the center of photography's allure; its ability to replicate the immeasurable power of the moment in the frame of human experi-

The Power of Images

The spellbinding POWER OF IMAGES is not new. The ornamentation of life is an indelible element of human history; it has been practiced time immemorial. Indeed, some have argued that it is precisely this propensity for fashioning representations of themselves and their world which distinguishes humans from other forms of animal life.

Figure 1: Image from the Caves at Lascaux

Prehistoric artifacts suggest that images occupied a venerated place in the lives of the earliest humans. Nearly thirty thousand years ago, for example, in a place that is today called France, a gallant primordial artist journeyed deep into the dangerous bowels of the earth in order to paint a portrait of a bison on the wall of a cave. [See Figure 1] Footprints on the cave floor indicate that few others trekked down to look at this picture or the others that were painted nearby. For people who lived by the hunt, this picture may have been a cult offering to an earth whose gifts determined whether or not they would be able to survive.

Millennia later, as a Mayan statue of Tlazotoetl—the Moon Goddess—gave birth to herself [See Figure 2], yet another image commemorated the natural underpinnings of human existence. For the farmers who revered Tlazotoetl, the analogy between the moon and the female miracle of birth made consummate sense. As the recurrent cycles of the moon marked the seasons, they also recorded the reproductive cycles by which crops were planted, cultivated and harvested. The visual affinity between the moon and human reproduction makes

Figure 2: Moon Goddess gives birth to herself

further sense if one recalls that a woman's menstrual cycle normally corresponds to the lunar month.

Within "pagan" images such as these, one senses a cultural outlook that was—at once—both supernatural and extraordinarily grounded; magical, yet powerfully aware of nature and of the perennial processes which sustain human life.

Today this has changed in consequential ways. If images once spoke on behalf of eternal meanings, today they have no half-life. As images partake in a perpetually changing field of vision, they contribute to an escalating sense of meaninglessness. If images, even of deities, were once embedded in the processes of nature, today's spectacle is detached from the natural world. Disembodied—occupying no time or place—it is, above all else, ungrounded.

Already by the mid-19th century, disembodied images had altered the physics of perception, changing people's sense of reality, as well as their understanding of the relationship between images and the physical world. Commenting on the recent arrival of photo-

ence. The photograph, as nothing before it, could preserve the girl in the white dress and arrest the impassioned eyes of a young man standing on a ferry boat. In its pregnant stillness, photography could stoke the depths of longing. In light of such considerations, Duhamel's pornographic characterization of American modernity— its incessant *masturbation of the eye*—assumes an oracular wisdom.

Figure 3: 1991 photo of a bus stop poster, New York City, taken during first week of the Persian Gulf War. Is this public enlightenment or visual demagoguery?

Looking around our world today, one cannot help but be struck by Holmes' clairvoyance. In art and economics, insubstantial representations supply the currency of everyday life. Mechanically reproduced images are lifted from any source, applied to any surface, to transmit any idea or to sell any product. The origin of the image is far less significant than the use to which it is put. In the process, meanings are constantly being renegotiated. Amid the spectacle, the notion that there may be enduring actualities, or that there should be a dialog between human consciousness and the material world, seem hopelessly antiquated, inappropriate to our times. The implications of this development are both contradictory and complex.

In the hands of cynical product advertisers and calculating political manipulators, the escalating fluidity of images has advanced the ability to provoke specious or misleading mental associations [See Figure 3: Gannett Poster Promoting Gulf War] in order to stimulate a serviceable public response.

Conversely, in the hands of a critical and reflective public, the ability to juxtapose and disseminate images may permit people to draw illuminating connections between seemingly separate issues, to communicate ideas which allow them to comprehend their world more clearly. [See Figure 4] For this to happen, universal access to both the tools and the channels of public communication is essential.

graphic technology in *The Atlantic Monthly*, in 1859, Oliver Wendall Holmes, Sr. described the camera as having severed people's customary connection to the material world:

Form is henceforth divorced from matter [he wrote]. *In fact, matter...is of no great use any longer except as the mould on which form is shaped. ...Every conceivable object of Nature and Art will soon scale off its surface for us. Men* [he predicted] *will hunt all curious, beautiful grand objects, as they hunt the cattle in South America, for their skins, and leave the carcasses as of little worth.*

"Proposal for a New Flag" © Archie Bishop 1981

Figure 4: This image, combining the motif of the American Flag with the Universal Product Code, comments on a society where consumption has replaced citizenship, where business interests have undermined democratic values.

Links between image and inner life were quickened by the development of cinema from the early twentieth century onward. Applying new forms of visual storytelling, innovative filmmakers began to employ optical subjectivity consciously as the foundational language of film. The cinematographer's lens and the editor's juxtaposition of shots and scenes became surrogates for what Overstreet would later call the "eye of the mind," or what Rosalind Kraus—borrowing from Walter Benjamin—has termed "the optical unconscious."[24]

Focusing on small, itinerant details, the camera could move in, infusing the commonplace with uncommon significance, and linger expectantly on things that, in conscious life, might command little attention. Through calculated plays of shadow and light, moods could be silently imprinted upon occurrences, providing a subjective rendering of objective events. In montage, crosscutting, and other techniques of editing, subliminal processes of mental association provided a grammar of filmic storytelling that further fused—or confused—the relationship between forms of visual expression and the contours of psychological life.

In darkened theaters, movies were serving to transform the dynamics of inner life into a mass entertainment. "The film," Benjamin wrote in 1936, "has enriched our field of perception with methods which can be illustrated by those of Freudian theory." The language of cinema, he argued, impersonated the language of unconscious psychological life. He enlarged on this theme:

> By close-ups of things around us, by focusing on hidden details of familiar objects, by exploring commonplace milieus under the ingenious guidance of the camera, the film, on the one hand, extends our comprehension of the necessities which rule our lives; on the other hand, it manages to assure us of an immense and unexpected field of action. . . . With the close-up, space expands; with slow motion, movement is extended. . . . Evidently a different nature opens itself to the camera than opens to the naked eye—if only because an unconsciously penetrated space is substituted for a space consciously explored by man. . . . The act of reaching for a lighter or a spoon is familiar routine, yet we hardly know what really goes on between hand and metal, not to mention how this fluctuates with our moods. Here the camera intervenes with the resources of its lowerings and liftings, its interruptions and isolations, its extensions and accelerations, its enlargements and reductions. The camera introduces us to unconscious optics as does psychoanalysis to unconscious impulses.[25]

By the 1920s, photographs and movies had deeply affected the visual experience of everyday life, altering the ways that people saw and understood their world. The association between image and inner life, however, the dawning of an "unconscious optics," as Benjamin put it, was happening far beyond the boundaries of photography or film. In a wide range of artistic and intellectual arenas, the full-tilt pandemonium of modernity was spawning new, increasingly psychological ways of seeing.

Pondering the peculiar mental fabric of the modern metropolis in 1903, Georg Simmel, the esteemed German sociologist, delineated a world in which the visual commotion of urban existence was destabilizing the senses.

> The psychological basis of the metropolitan type of individuality consists in the intensification of nervous stimulation which results from the swift and uninterrupted change of outer and inner stimuli. . . . With each crossing of the street, with the tempo and multiplicity of economic, occupational and social life the city sets up a deep contrast with small town and rural life with reference to the sensory foundations of psychic life.[26]

Against the slow rhythms of customary social existence and its relatively narrow vistas, Simmel saw the perpetual motion of the modern city as furnishing the basis for new ways of experiencing life. In its crowded thoroughfares, its mechanized modes of production and conveyance, its money-driven fixations, and its endless array of optical stimulants, the city provided a potent context for reimagining and reconfiguring the world. The notion of life as a spectacle was becoming pervasive; a condition of unceasing nervous distraction was increasingly the norm.

This state of nervous distraction was beginning to inundate the arts in general. In Europe, artists were less and less content with the task of duplicating the mien of an "objective" world and more and more interested in probing the mental, sensual, and experiential filters through which individuals encountered and sensed that world. Drawing upon the energies and dilemmas of industrial existence, "modern art" was becoming a spirited, if anxious, visual theater in which artists struggled to address the ascendancy and tumult of the machine age, the optimism and dissonance of contemporary life.

In painting, sculpture, architecture, and theater, the "shock of the new" and the exploration of subjective existence were becoming fixations of artistic expression. In a procession of modern movements—cubism, dada, and surrealism, among others—artists sought to usher audiences into the unsettling environs of a "second world," an optical realm in which the idea of objective reality itself was thrown into question.[27] If realism or naturalism had celebrated the enterprise of imitating a consciously perceived world, modern art was entering and attempting to map out the unconscious terrain of the psyche.

Modernism highlighted the ways that images can convey a particular way of seeing; it accentuated the ways that symbols and subjectivity are unavoidably intertwined. By the time Marcel Duchamps's jarringly abstract nude descended a staircase in New York's Seventh Regiment Armory in 1913, these explosive ways of seeing proposed by European modernists had made their way to America, and—in combination with photography, cinema, and other visual permutations—were likewise kindling American imaginations.

For those concerned with guiding human perception and behavior, modernism affirmed changes in visual culture that had been unfolding for some time. "The new art," wrote the American merchandising prodigy Earnest Elmo Calkins, "was imaginative rather than realistic. *It attempted to suggest rather than to show.*"[28] For Calkins and others, modern art was providing a functional vocabulary for "selective picturizing," a way of understanding the relation between images and the powers of suggestion.

Reading the pronouncements of persuasion professionals and surveying American material culture from World War I onward, one finds that the spin toward an eloquence of images is unambiguous. As historian Roland Marchand discussed, advertisers of the twenties and thirties embraced a belief that images were the most efficient tools for bypassing the critical thought processes of consumers. Motivational psychologists speculated that if words stimulated thought and provoked unwelcome "conflict and competition," pictures were capable of unleashing "a ready-made and predictable response."[29] At the same

THE ENCYCLOPÆDIA BILLBOARDICA   1313

Visual Eloquence

In the years preceding the First World War, most people desiring to influence public opinion still looked toward the printed word as the most effective instrument at their disposal. This propensity paid tribute to the likes of Paine and Jefferson, Madison and Hamilton, Enlightenment men who raised their pens to shape the thinking of a nation in its infancy. More than a century later, as muckraking journalists and corporate public relations specialists competed for public sentiments, both continued to embrace this faith in the word.

During the First World War

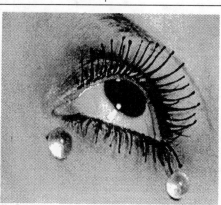

Man Ray, 1933

and on into the 1920s, however, this outlook began to shift. Where once the published word had been accepted as the primary tool of persuasion, now *the image* seemed to provide the most foolproof door to the public mind. From that time forward, VISUAL ELOQUENCE has increasingly been employed as a favored instrument of public address.

Despite this historic shift, however, little about our education prepares us to comprehend this magnetic allure. In an age of images, the power exerted by "visuals" over the public imagination remains only cursorily understood.

A partial corrective for this is suggested in "To See, And Not See," a 1993 case study by the neurologist Oliver Sacks. [See NOTE at end of article.] Sacks' study describes a man called "Virgil" who, though "blind since early childhood," has his eyesight surgically restored at the age of fifty. The article focuses on the formidable difficulties Virgil encounters with the onset of sightedness; his inability to process the visual data provided by his eyes.

While Virgil's "retina and optic nerve were active," and were "transmitting impulses" to his brain, Sacks reports, his mind "could make no sense of them."

Virgil's incapacity *to see,* was rooted in the perceptual habits that he had developed during his formative and extended years of blindness. Unable to see with his eyes, Virgil—like others without sight—had become used to building his conception of the world out of "sequences of impressions (tactile, auditory, olfactory)." For the blind, Sacks explains, *reality* is the product of an incremental and deliberative mode of perception. It is something that must be gathered over time.

Seeing with one's eyes, Sacks argues, is qualitatively different. Once learned, sight allows for "simultaneous visual perception, the making of an instantaneous visual scene." If people *without sight* must carefully construct their sense of the objective world, common patterns of *seeing* encourage the perception of objectivity in an instant, with little con-

time, industrial designers and graphic artists were increasingly sensitive to the ways that the *look* of a product or the design of its packaging could be employed to stimulate a positive "emotional reaction in the beholder."[30]

The field of public relations was no exception. If PR was, as Bernays argued, the art of "creating circumstances," the period stretching from the war into the thirties witnessed a decided move

---

1314   THE ENCYCLOPÆDIA BILLBOARDICA

scious deliberation. Virgil's troubles derived from the fact that he was thoroughly unprepared for this strange way of seeing.

The story of Virgil and his troubles highlights the ways that, while people may inhabit the same physical universe, their outlooks on that universe may be very, very different. In suggestive ways, Sacks' discussion of Virgil may also shed light on the shift that took place from strategies of persuasion predicated on the printed word, to strategies built on a foundation of images.

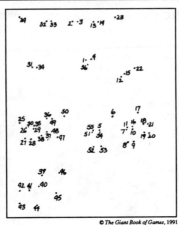

© *The Giant Book of Games*, 1991

Both images and printed words rely on our sense of sight, but understanding words on a page is different from the "reading" of an image. Phenomenologically, the reading of words is closer to the mode of perception that Sacks associates with blindness. For most people, reading is a slow and consciously interpretive process. Unlike images—which employ a vernacular of the eye, and can transmit a cosmology in an instant—printed words must be deciphered, one after another, and combined sequen-

tially in order for their *reality* to be ascertained. (You are undoubtedly aware of this at the moment.) Like a child's follow-the-dots puzzle, reading provides a step-by-step way of seeing that is not immediately legible, which only becomes apparent through a process of heedful assembly.

It is precisely this process of deliberation which may help us to understand why public relations specialists and other propagandists turned away from the published word and embraced, more and more, a rhetoric of images. To these modern pioneers of persuasion, independent public deliberation was something to be avoided at all costs. In its apparent capacity to advance a worldview in a bedazzling moment, and to stun the public mind into submission, *the image* was conceived to be an effective antidote to critical thought.

NOTE: For a fuller discussion of Virgil's plight, see Oliver Sacks, "A Neurologist's Notebook: To See and Not See." *The New Yorker*, May 10, 1993, pp 59-73.

© BILLBOARDS OF THE FUTURE

toward the creation of circumstances that were mounted explicitly for visual coverage. Conventional press releases continued to be produced and doled out to accommodating journalists, but an enlarged appreciation of the eloquence of images foreshadowed an American century in which the silver tongue of visual oratory would define, more and more, the terms and limitations of public address.

PART 4

Battles for the "American Way"

11
Silver Chains and Friendly Giants

B Y THE LATTER HALF of the 1920s, there was a growing confidence that business had shaken off the shackles of public distrust, that a gospel of unfettered commercial enterprise—condemned throughout the Progressive period—had reclaimed the faith of the American public. "Public opinion is no longer inclined to be unfavorable to the large business merger," announced Edward L. Bernays in 1928, a year in which corporate combinations were escalating. "In the opinion of millions," Bernays related, "mergers and trusts" were now understood as "friendly giants and not ogres." This welcome turn of events, he explained deterministically, could be directly attributed to the maturation of public relations techniques, "to the deliberate use of propaganda in its broadest sense."[1]

To some extent Bernays's reading of the situation was valid. Throughout the twenties, a growing array of large businesses were disseminating "canned" news and editorial columns to thousands of newspapers across the United States. To E. Hofer, who ran the country's largest distributor of such materials, these items were calculated to uphold the canon of laissez-faire capitalism, to reduce "the volume of legislation that interferes with business and industry . . . to minimize and counteract political regulation of business . . . to discourage radicalism by labor organizations," to argue for "reasonable taxation" of business income, and to "campaign against all socialistic propaganda of whatever nature."[2] Correspondingly throughout the twenties, many large corporations methodically infiltrated national and local organizations—Chambers of Commerce, farmers' groups, fraternal orders, civic organizations, church groups, and so forth—for the purpose of shepherding the public mind toward pro-business attitudes and opinions.[3]

The image of the corporation as a "friendly giant" stood at the center of many companies' public relations activities. "Successful business is business plus personality," instructed S. M. Kennedy, a marketing expert. "The more a business is crowded with personality, the faster it will grow and prosper."[4] Others echoed the imperative of "humanizing business" and labored to purge the image of the "soulless corporation" from the public mind.[5]

For a number of companies, endeavors to broadcast an altruistic portrayal of business were comprehensive and far reaching. Through a vast publication bureau—which pumped out an endless flood of photographs, posters, calendars, glass projection slides, and other visual materials—the General Electric Corporation (GE) carefully painted a picture of itself as a company preoccupied by the task of ushering the American public into the promised land of modern electrical living.[6] The American Telephone and Telegraph Company established a motion picture bureau that "distributed films free of charge to schools, civic groups, church organizations, and even commercial theaters as a part of regular entertainment programs." Citing Bell System estimates, historian Alan R. Raucher reported that by the end of the twenties, these films were seen by a yearly audience of more than 50 million Americans.[7] A mythology of capitalism was blossoming in which business enterprise and public vision were being carefully orchestrated in a spectacular pas de deux, and the "silver chains" of public relations—as Harold Lasswell had dubbed them—were playing a conspicuous part.

Nowhere was this evolution more evident than in "Light's Golden Jubilee," a worldwide media celebration, held on October 21, 1929, to observe the fiftieth anniversary of Thomas Edison's invention of the electric lightbulb. Meticulously staged to look like a spontaneous tribute, a global outpouring on behalf of an entrepreneurial legend and his Promethean invention, the event was largely the handiwork of Bernays, serving behind the scenes as a paid impresario for GE and for the National Electric Light Association (NELA), a secret holding company through which GE had gained substantial control over electrical manufacturing in the United States.[8] Bernays's efforts were, at once, brilliant and invisible; as events unfolded, it was as if history was simply running its course.

For months beforehand, all kinds of activities were extemporaneously mounted to galvanize public anticipation. A U.S. commemorative postage stamp, in honor of the Jubilee, went on sale in Menlo Park on June 5. The *Saturday Evening Post, Scientific American,* and other magazines carried features and pictorials heralding the Edison celebration. Souvenir editions of the *New York Herald,* dated October 21, 1879, were distributed, announcing the birth of an invention that "burned without gas or flame," that would be "cheaper than oil." George M. Cohan wrote a song, "Edison—Miracle Man," and sheet music was distributed around the world. "[T]he country's press was moving," delving into "every angle of the celebration," Bernays boasted more than thirty years later.

> Mayors and Governors issued proclamations to celebrate Light's Golden Jubilee. Universities offered lectures on Edison and the implications of his discovery. Educational groups conducted essay contests. Librarians displayed books about Edison. Museum heads arranged exhibits that would illustrate the history of light.

Then, on October 21, it happened. The centerpiece for the event was in Dearborn, Michigan, where an ancient Thomas Edison—standing in a reproduction of Independence Hall that had been erected by his admirer, Henry Ford—switched on a replica of his first incandescent lightbulb. At that signal, Edison's act was repeated in nations around the world, where people had been mobilized to turn on their lights in a spectacle of planetary togetherness. Arriving in Dearborn on a facsimile of a railroad train that Edison had worked on, President Herbert Hoover—along with captains of finance and industry (J. P. Morgan, Jr.; John D. Rockefeller, Jr.; Charles M. Schwab; Owen D. Young; and Adolph Ochs), famous inventors (Madame Curie and Orville Wright), and other notables—looked on in admiration.[9]

Yet despite the glare of such pyrotechnics, it would be myopic to assume that public relations exercises alone could have been responsible for the intensification of pro-business sentiments during the

Two of Edward L. Bernays's personal mementos from "Light's Golden Jubilee," his globally promoted media event that was staged in Dearborn, Michigan, in 1929. (ABOVE) A medallion struck to commemorate the fiftieth anniversary of Edison's electric light. (BELOW) A front page of a special edition of the *Detroit Times* that covered the occasion. COURTESY SPECTOR & ASSOCIATES, INC.

twenties. A number of other, more substantial, factors contributed to this tendency. Most conspicuously, the years between 1921 and 1929 marked a period of widely acclaimed economic prosperity not just for businessmen, but for many among the general population as well.

This is not to say that there wasn't still a great deal of social hardship. Much of the nation's farm population was plagued by a decade of persistent agricultural depression. Millions of industrial workers wrestled with low wages, insecure job conditions, and recurrent periods of unemployment. In either setting, illness or accident could be economically catastrophic.[10]

Beyond these economic deprivations, an extended period of anti-radical political repression—launched in the early twenties by Attorney General A. Mitchell Palmer and enforced by federal and local police agencies—forged a psychological climate in which people were less and less willing to question authority openly. In the wake of this repression, the labor movement and unions lost organizational strength and the rights of many industrial workers were weakened.

Yet beside these conditions, other more promising developments were taking hold. The enormous growth of new consumer-goods industries and the breakneck expansion of consumerism as a way of life were creating a situation in which corporate America and a large sector of the population seemed to be joined in a relationship of apparent mutual interest. "The rapid evolution during the twenties of the mass-production-consumption society," argued historians George Mowry and Blaine Brownell, forged a reciprocal bond between "the consuming crowd" and the "corporate boardroom" that was unprecedented. In a consumer economy, "the health of one" was inherently linked to "the health of the other."[11]

In its expansive rhetoric, Mowry and Brownell's proclamation is far too all-encompassing—millions were excluded from the barbecue—but their argument mirrors the perceptual climate of the times. Wesley C. Mitchell, head of the National Bureau of Economic Research, reporting to President Hoover in 1929, described a large-scale consumer economy in which an entire way of life was changing.

Scarcely less characteristic of our period than unit-cost reductions is the rapid expansion in the production and sale of products little used or wholly unknown a generation or even a decade ago. Among consumers' goods, the conspicuous instances are automobiles, radios and rayon. But the list includes also oil-burning furnaces, gas stoves, household electrical appliances in great variety, automobile accessories, antifreezing mixtures, cigarette lighters, propeller pencils, wristwatches, airplanes and what not.[12]

Alongside automobiles, appliances, and assorted other goods, a modern entertainment industry was invigorating "the growing interdependence of the large corporations and the masses," Mowry and Brownell contended. "Without the film and radio industries, it is doubtful that the mass-production-consumption culture could have fastened itself on the country as rapidly as it did." They elaborated:

By 1922, 40 million cinema tickets were being sold weekly, and radio was carrying news and advertising into 3 million homes. By the end of the twenties, the weekly movie audience had more than doubled, and few people in the country were long out of earshot of a radio receiver. In 1929, $852 million worth of receiving sets were sold, the profits from which, when added to the millions the broadcasting industry received in advertising revenues, bulked significantly in the total corporate income of the country.

Implicitly, Mowry and Brownell continued, the content of Hollywood films affirmed the spirit of consumption:

The typical heroine wore expensive clothes, furs, and elegant jewels, and either lived in a mansion or flitted between the deluxe hotels of the world; the hero, usually without visible means of support, was as splendidly accoutered, drove the fanciest automobile, and pursued the most attractive young women. . . . The movie credo was of sustained consumption, not production. And continually reiterating this theme, the industry became midwife to the birth of the leisure-seeking, pleasure-demanding, materialistic consumer society of modern America.[13]

Through the lens of such media, in the ubiquitous narratives of advertising, in the apparently boundless inventories of a perpetual marketplace, corporate America—at least for those who were able to enjoy its booty—seemed to be furnishing the merchandise for the good life.

Amid the commotion, Sinclair Lewis's character, George Babbitt, became a symbol of the middle class's split from Progressivism and its infatuation with a new religion. He was a man, Lewis narrated, "whose god was Modern Appliances." Each morning he awoke to "the best of nationally advertised and quantitatively produced alarm-clocks, with all modern attachments, including cathedral chime, intermittent alarm, and a phosphorescent dial." Upon awakening, Babbitt "never put on B.V.D.'s without thanking the God of Progress that he didn't wear tight, long, old fashioned undergarments."[14]

The new religion, however, was not simply built on a foundation of faith. Economic practices that took hold in the twenties made conversion increasingly possible for a wide number of people. For many who had been schooled by fears of decline or by timeworn lessons of scarcity, the effervescent economy of the twenties seemed to offer a road map toward Easy Street. The middle class appeared to be experiencing a happy resurgence, and a growing, if still quite limited, number of wage earners were offered the promise of becoming "middle class." While farm communities throughout the country endured a steep economic decline and a great number of working-class Americans experienced low wages and "technological unemployment" in volatile industries, for others, circumstances looked brighter.

In a 1925 study of "real wages," University of Minnesota economist Alvin Hansen reported that there had been a "phenomenal" per capita increase in the years since the end of World War I: "25 to 30 percent greater than in the prewar years." While this standard of prosperity did not divulge a numerical growth in unemployment among "non-agricultural salary and wage earners," Hansen's estimate of real wages, on a per capita basis, was confirmed by Paul Douglass of the University of Chicago in 1926, as well as in Mitchell's report on *Recent Economic Changes* in 1929.[15]

In 1929 Christine Frederick, a prominent business adviser, concluded that the "greatest idea that America has to give to the world" was "the idea that workmen and masses [should] be looked upon not simply as workers and producers but as consumers. Pay them more, sell them more, prosper more is the equation." President Hoover seconded the motion, declaring that "[h]igh wages" were the "very essence of great production."[16]

Some of this growth was puffery. "The vaunted high-wage philosophy of American industry," cautioned historian Irving Bernstein, "activated employers' vocal chords more than their purse strings."[17] To a limited extent, however, there was a growth of "real wages" throughout the twenties. The expansion of buying power among restricted sectors of the wage- and salary-earning population indicated that some businesses—mostly in the white-collar, sales, and service sectors—were following the "high-wage" logic.

But it wasn't increased income alone that was driving the mood of prosperity. This mood was also being generated by "finance companies" and "retail-credit associations" that extended a surfeit of previously unaccustomed consumer credit to encourage people to purchase mass-produced goods. "A forcible impetus was given to the expansion of credit by the automobile industry," explained Mowry and Brownell.

> Soon home appliances, radio sets, furniture, and even such luxuries as jewelry were being sold on the installment plan. By 1929, when apparently over 75 percent of the automobiles and probably more than half of all major household appliances were sold on time payments, total consumer credit, it has been estimated, had reached a peak of about $7 billion.[18]

A sentimental association between the "corporate boardroom" and the "consuming crowd" was being buttressed by other developments as well. One of these developments was a fundamental change in the capitalization of corporate enterprises. In the early years of large-scale industrialization, many of the mergers and trusts that came to dominate American economic life were the creations of small circles of wealthy individuals, industrialists and financiers who used their private fortunes to build immense business empires. The private and secretive nature of these holdings, along with their conspicuous lack of public accountability, encouraged an angry middle-class public to view corporate bosses as an unholy alliance of robber barons, men who had to be reined in for the common good of society.

By the 1920s, this situation had changed in fundamental ways. A growing number of large-scale enterprises were being transformed from "closely held private companies into publicly owned corporations." Though financial control of these corporations was still exercised by a tightly knit economic elite, and corporate accountants still provided little reliable public information regarding operations and profits, the savings of more and more Americans were gravitating toward securities that were being issued by these "public" concerns. David Hawkins, writing in the *Business History Review,* offered figures that dramatized the growing relationship between giant enterprise and the savings of a middle-class public. "As the years passed, particularly during the 1920s," he noted, "[t]he number of stockholders in the United States increased." In 1900, only half a million Americans were stockholders (about six-tenths of 1 percent of the population), including those who owned a small number of shares. By 1920, 2 million people owned shares in American corporations. By 1930, that figure had expanded fivefold, to 10 million stockholders.[19] With a growing share of the middle-class population invested in securities, their sense of well-being and of their own best interest was increasingly tied to the fate of big business.

With this linkage, the political affections of the middle class and of those who identified with that increasingly plastic sobriquet shifted decidedly to the right. A sector of the population that had—only a decade or so earlier—provided a political constituency for the energetic regulation of business now upheld the rhetoric of laissez-faire economics. For a nation of modern consumers, floating along on a tide of credit, and among an expanding aggregate of corporate shareholders, wrote Hawkins, "[b]usinessmen were regarded with a new respect."

Among those able to afford the lifestyle of the "comfort class," wrote Columbia University economist Rexford G. Tugwell in 1925, money was being spent to emulate the "possessions and enjoyments" of America's economic elite. Whereas ostentatious wealth had—only shortly before—been viewed as a sign of social impropriety, during the twenties it became a polestar for middle-class aspiration.

A family on the comfort level will often sacrifice much—perhaps even mortgage its house—to possess an automobile of respected make, not only because it enjoys riding, but because a wealthier neighbor has one.[20]

The political life of the twenties followed suit. With many eyes bedazzled, and opposition voices grimly silenced, commercial boosterism became the order of the day, and Republican presidential administrations were elected in 1920, 1924, and 1928, all by considerable margins.[21] As he ran for president in 1920, Warren G. Harding called for a "return to normalcy." This phrase meant, he explained, "less government in business and more business in government."[22] This was more than empty rhetoric. Upon his election, Harding appointed Andrew Mellon, "one of the two or three richest men in the country," secretary of the treasury.[23]

An era of unregulated business enterprise was under way and proceeded through the end of the decade, initially under Harding, then Calvin Coolidge and Herbert Hoover. Coolidge, explaining the miracles of his laissez-faire administration to the public, rhapsodized on ways that tax cuts and unencumbered assistance to business enterprises were promoting a state of well-being that reached, without exception, throughout American society.

> This policy has encouraged enterprise, made possible the highest rate of wages which has ever existed, returned large profits, brought to the homes of the people the greatest economic benefits they ever enjoyed, and given to the country as a whole an unexampled era of prosperity.[24]

As Coolidge delivered his State of the Union Address on December 4, 1928, his last year in office, he reported on a vigorous American economy that was on the brink of establishing universal abundance as a new standard of living:

> The great wealth created by our enterprise and industry, and saved by our economy, has had the widest distribution among our own people, and has gone out in a steady stream to serve the charity and the business of the world. The requirements of existence have passed beyond the standard of necessity into the region of luxury. Enlarging production is consumed by an

increasing demand at home and an expanding commerce abroad. The country can regard the present with satisfaction and anticipate the future with optimism.[25]

Meanwhile, Herbert Hoover—Coolidge's secretary of commerce before becoming president—encouraged the development of trade associations, corporate groups that followed the paradigm of the NELA and served to quicken the "concentration of industrial control" in fewer and fewer hands.[26] These associations were themselves public relations bodies, groups that provided an ongoing and ubiquitous public voice, speaking in neighborly terms on behalf of immense combinations of capital. This voice, argued economic historian Thomas Cochran, tended to dominate or drown out all others.

> So profoundly pro-business was the national temper and so successful were business efforts in keeping the favor of the public, that other groups might combine, publish, speak, and vote, and still industrial business could assert itself above all competitors for public favor. . . . [B]usiness associations were so powerful in the twenties that none of these groups could withstand them. Business had, as [Roger] Babson said, "the press, the pulpit and the schools."[27]

The commercial mass media, direct beneficiaries of a pro-business and pro-merchandising culture, provided an assenting chorus. Prosperity and its effervescent energies became an ongoing theme in magazines, movies, books, and the press and on radio. Bruce Barton's 1925 best-seller, *The Man Nobody Knows,* was but one ardent example of a mass culture in which a gospel of business was assembling adherents. In its pages, the life of Jesus Christ was presented, but here Jesus appeared as the hero of an entrepreneurial success story, a poor country boy who made it big as a public relations practitioner and the founder of a thriving business organization.

Surveying the rise of the new, pro-business creed in the 1920s, it is difficult to draw distinctions between the direct influence of public relations practices and the part played by a constellation of simultaneous social developments. It is difficult to do so in part because public relations practices are habitually secretive, but also because in the 1920s a culture of promotionalism became so implanted and widespread as to make the lines of demarcation more and more obscure.[28]

Whatever the case, one thing is clear. All these changes combined to constitute a significant "structural transformation of the public sphere," to lift a phrase from Jürgen Habermas. A middle-class public that had, in the Progressive Era, defined itself and its publicity in opposition to giant enterprises was being transformed into one that was increasingly defined by boosterism and by the consumption of products and ideology generated by institutions they had formerly opposed.

Some tenacious Progressives expressed disaffection. "Business is the order of the day," objected John Dewey in his 1927 book, *The Public and Its Problems*. The "attempt to stop its course is . . . futile." The word "prosperity," he added with disapproval, "has taken on religious color."[29] Two years later, in a subsequent jeremiad, Dewey described Americans as "living in a money culture. Its cult and rites dominate." Remarking on social trends epitomized by Barton's bestseller, he then added:

> [N]owhere in the world at any time has religion been so thoroughly respectable as with us, and so nearly totally disconnected from life. . . . The glorification of religion as setting the final seal of approval on pecuniary success . . . and the adoption by the churches of the latest devices of the movies and the advertiser, approach too close to the obscene.[30]

Elsewhere in the nation—at least for a time—there was little visible protest. "The business of the United States is business," President Calvin Coolidge evangelized, and an evanescent assembly of modern consumers genuflected in pious agreement.[31]

Yet tarnishing the exuberant celebration of "pecuniary success," there were a number of developments afoot that would shortly reveal a darker side of the "money culture." The first of these developments provided a discordant accompaniment to the hymn of "high wages." Though wages grew throughout the twenties, even during a business depression that took place in 1921 and 1922, there was, over the same period, an attending rise in the number of people who were unemployed. "By the later years of the decade," explained economic historian William J. Barber, "there were some disturbing signs that high wages were indeed tending to price labor out of the market.

> High wages were costing jobs by pushing employers to substitute capital [technology] for labor. In manufacturing, mining, and the railroads, for example, it could be established that employment had shrunk while wages had risen.[32]

Barber's reading of the situation mirrors Wesley Mitchell's findings in 1929. Though Mitchell also described a rise in wage levels, he provided an interpretation of the data that suggested that they tended to "minimize the seriousness of unemployment." "While our economic progress has meant larger per capita earnings for all workers taken together," he concluded, "it has imposed severe suffering upon hundreds of thousands of individuals."

In certain pivotal industries, as well, wages dropped precipitously. If the twenties was a period when the spread of mass-produced fashions and of fashion consciousness were becoming conspicuous features of a modern consumer culture, it was also a time when workers who were involved in the production of these goods experienced severe economic hardship. To lower their production costs, textile companies gravitated south en masse. The price of this move was paid for by textile workers. "Wages in southern mills," reported labor historian Samuel Yellen, "were roughly one-third below those in [the] New England mills" where most American textiles had been formerly produced.[33]

The consequence of these disparities was considerable. Despite a statistical rise in wages, the upgrade was not experienced evenly throughout the population; the distribution of income was extremely unbalanced. While some wage earners were beneficiaries of the new economic bounty—were elevated to the status of consumers—a vast number of workers continued to be caught in old patterns of existence. Amid the widespread implementation of mass-production methods, their livelihoods became even more unstable; with an intensifying substitution of capital for labor, many were victims of "technological unemployment."

It was not only the working class that bore the burdens of prosperity during the twenties. As "the concentration of industrial control proceeded almost unchecked," Soule recounted, local businesses and small manufacturers were being swallowed up in enormous gulps.

> Between 1919 and 1930, more than eight thousand separate business establishments in manufacturing and mining disappeared as separate entities either by being combined with or acquired by another company. Before 1928 nearly five thousand public utilities so disappeared. By 1929 chain stores sold 27 per cent of the food of the country, 10 per cent of the drugs, 30 per cent of the tobacco, 27 per cent of the apparel, and 26 per cent of the general merchandise. . . . It was estimated that by the end of 1929 the two hundred largest business corporations possessed nearly half of the corporate wealth of the country, 38 per cent of the business wealth, and 20 per cent of the total national wealth.[34]

Along the way, the mythic pillars of American communities—small shopkeepers and entrepreneurs—were becoming symbolic remnants of a fading way of life.

Poised above these instances of painful experience, however, it was the dematerializing character of the economy itself that posed perhaps the greatest threat to the general welfare. If public relations, advertising, and other agencies of persuasion were becoming increasingly adept at generating seductive—though ethereal—representations of reality for public consumption, this tendency was mirrored in the economy more broadly. Throughout the decade preceding 1929, much of the widely trumpeted prosperity was itself built on vaporous abstractions. Business, overall, was becoming more and more dependent on a play of symbols, on insubstantial representations of value.

This tendency was evidenced in the $7 billion of consumer credit that was extended throughout the decade and in the reckless loans that became standard banking practice. Banks and other financial institutions were lending money they could not recoup. People were buying products with money that they had not yet earned. At the center of each debt and each purchase stood a delicate act of faith, a belief that improved living conditions bought on the installment plan would be self-fulfilling and—in the long run—look after themselves.

Even more ethereal than consumer credit, which was at least used to purchase actual goods, were the monumental combinations of wealth that were driving the buoyant culture of prosperity. A declining number of corporations was engaged primarily in the production of goods or services. Many concerns existed for purely speculative purposes as "pyramided holding companies," edifices constructed of thin air whose raison d'être was to make money.

By the late twenties the demand for new speculative opportunities had become so great that holding companies and investment trusts were able to sell more than a billion dollars' worth a year in stocks and bonds that had little but other common stock behind them. Even then the supply of securities remained insufficient, and prices soared almost out of sight as intense buying continued.

Such companies, wrote Thomas Cochran, "would have delighted the great promoters of earlier days. Their appearance was delayed," however, "because their formation required a great congregation of security speculators." The middle-class consumer—often using credit here as well—supplied the requisite golden goose, as more and more people scrambled for their piece of prosperity.[35]

The speculative approach to capital accumulation was hardly a sporadic phenomenon during the twenties. Holding companies, organized chiefly to make money, were becoming a business norm. Soule provided a revealing lay of the land:

Concentration of control, which began to run far beyond any conceivable purpose of exercising influence on productive or managerial efficiency, was undertaken for financial gain of the promoters. . . .

In general industry, out of the ninety-seven largest corporations at the beginning of 1929, twenty-one were purely holding companies, five were parent companies primarily for holding purposes, eight were parent companies devoted about equally to holding and operating, and fifty-nine were parent companies primarily concerned with operating. *Only four of the ninety-seven were strictly operating companies.*

Among his 1929 specimens of "the pure holding company," Soule cataloged Allied Chemical, Eastman Kodak, and United States Steel.[36]

In large part, these agglomerations were paper mazes. They served to attract investment capital and amassed fleeting fortunes for some, but they also represented a zone where the "symbolic economy" and the "real economy" of goods and services were growing further and further apart. Corporate accounting practices were skewed to uphold the separation. Little fiscal information was provided. When it was, it constituted a new literary genre. Whimsical values were assigned to stocks that were then bought and sold exclusively for the purpose of profit. The power of images, an epistemological cornerstone of modern public relations thinking, was becoming the more general underpinning of economic success.

Parallel dynamics drove the "real estate boom" of the twenties, as well. A surfeit of buildings that went up throughout the twenties were, according to architect Frederick Ackerman, financed by real estate bonds that were floated with little regard to housing or office needs. "During the last decade," Ackerman reflected in 1932, "need and effective demand played little or no part in the promotion of structures representing in total an investment of billions of dollars." In spite of the widespread palaver about the creation of new and prosperous communities for consumers, much of the real estate growth of the twenties, he concluded, was driven by "the exigencies of speculation."[37]

The conflict between real estate development and social needs is particularly evident when one inspects patterns governing the housing industry during the twenties. During that period, reported housing historian Nathaniel Keith, "three-fourths of the housing production . . . was marketed to the top one-third of the household income spectrum and there was no production for the bottom one-third."[38]

Behind the bright apparition of prosperity, there were perilous realities. Along with the unemployment and deep-seated poverty that persisted for millions, the widely publicized middle-class abundance was itself disastrously fragile. Soaring security values were commercially created fictions more than representations of substantial economic growth. There were perilous levels of unrecoverable debt. And while wages had improved for some, the distribution of income was still lopsided. Markets for consumer goods were not yet large enough to absorb the prodigious productive capacity of overcapitalized mass-production industries. An "underconsumption" emergency loomed.[39] (This emergency hit the home-building industry quite early, by 1925, as a housing market skewed to attract the upper economic third of the population neared saturation.)[40] In a society in which the promotion of "prosperity" had become public policy, however, these realities were largely ignored; they were neither analyzed nor responded to.

Civic indifference to these issues, however, did not alter the fact that the widely touted affluence was a house of cards. Administered by a pervasive and increasingly sophisticated machinery of representation, buttressed, in large part, by fabrication and blind faith, when the house was jogged, it collapsed.

As unemployment rose, people began to lose their homes and debts went unpaid. In a laissez-faire environment, there was no effective machinery of response. Then, in October 1929, the bottom fell out, beginning with the stock market crash and followed by crack-ups in other markets. The habitually reserved *New York Times* narrated the "disorganization, confusion and financial impotence" in the following terms:

> Stock prices virtually collapsed yesterday, swept downward with gigantic losses in the most disastrous trading day in the stock market's history. Billions of dollars in open market values were wiped out as prices crumbled under the pressure of liquidation of securities which had to be sold at any price. . . .
>
> From every point of view, in the extent of losses sustained, in total turnover in the number of speculators wiped out, the day was the most disastrous in Wall Street's history. Hysteria swept the country and stocks went overboard for just what they would bring at forced sale.
>
> Efforts to estimate yesterday's market losses in dollars are futile because of the vast number of securities quoted over-the-counter and on out-of-town exchanges on which no calculations are possible. However, it was estimated that 880 issues, on the New York Stock Exchange, lost between $8 billion and $9 billion yesterday. . . .

The market on the rampage is no respecter of persons. It wasted fortune after fortune away yesterday and financially crippled thousands of individuals in all parts of the world. . . . The market has now passed through three days of collapse, and so violent has it been that most authorities believe that the end is not far away.[41]

In human terms, the debacle would be devastating and enduring. For millions, the image of prosperity was washed away almost instantaneously. They were forced to recognize what had been there all along, but so effectively hidden from view. A gaping hole had opened up in the pavement along Easy Street, and in the sobered minds of multitudes, business and businessmen, speculators and plutocrats— the cult heroes of the twenties—soon became objects of scorn.

Bernays notwithstanding, *friendly giants* were becoming ogres once more. A new publicity machinery that would arise in response to the wreckage would only add to that impression.

12
The Greater Good

THE STOCK MARKET crash was but the overture to an extended period of economic devastation. In 1931, the bond market plummeted. A year later, the mortgage market succumbed. By the fall of 1932, both industrial production and national income had fallen precipitously. Steel plants were running at only 12 percent of capacity. Industrial construction had declined to a mere 7.7 percent of its 1929 level. Institutional figures, viewed together, are overwhelming:

> Between 1929 and 1933 the GNP fell from $103.1 billion to $55.6 billion. . . . Between 1929 and 1932 more than one hundred thousand American businesses failed, the total net profits of private corporations dropped from $8.4 to $3.4 billion, and total industrial productivity fell off 51 percent. From 1929 to 1932 the value of both American imports and American exports declined by more than two thirds.[1]

Beneath the surface of these statistical catastrophes, the human toll was enormous. The industrial labor market had evaporated, and by 1932 between 12 million and 17 million people—a quarter to a third of the American workforce—were out of work. Among those still employed, many held part-time jobs at reduced wages, enduring a state of relentless insecurity. Farm income, which had been severely depressed throughout the twenties, was decimated even further, falling from $11 billion to $5 billion nationwide between 1929 and 1932. Banks were failing, and with them, a multitude of life savings became irretrievable. Many people who had ridden the bubble of prosperity during the twenties were now plunged into desperate times. Homeless and hungry, legions of Americans gravitated to shantytowns, scavenging for food. "Never in modern times," remarked economist Rexford G. Tugwell in 1932, "has there been so widespread unemployment and such moving distress from sheer hunger and cold."[2]

The cant of prosperity and the celebration of laissez-faire capitalism—so boisterous only a few years earlier—had vanished. "Each of the failures made it harder for some large public group to get a living," observed S. H. Walker and Paul Sklar, a pair of business reporters. "In the end a majority of the citizens had been more or less severely hurt by the collapse of the economic machine." With these reversals, business enterprise, which had served as a spiritual lodestar during the twenties, fell into widespread disrepute. "[T]he people sought to fix the blame for what was happening," noted Walker and Sklar, "and by and large they blamed business. Those who did not grow actively hostile to business, they added, "came to distrust business as a trustee of the national economy."[3]

Callous to the growing misery around them, business leaders did little to neutralize these sentiments, nor did many grasp the hazardous social precipice upon which they themselves were perched. As millions suffered, many corporate masters continued to bring home exorbitant salaries and bonuses, at the same time contributing little in the way of taxes. Meanwhile, in public pronouncements they scolded the government for spending too much money on relief and called for cuts in already glaringly insufficient social spending.

Amid the cataclysm, few businessmen assumed any obligation to deal with the social destitution, nor did they wish to see any energetic governmental response. Walter Gifford, the head of American Telephone and Telegraph spurned the notion of federal aid to the unemployed as a violation of America's tradition of unregulated enterprise. "Federal aid would be a disservice to the unemployed, or might be a disservice to the unemployed" he declared before a Senate subcommittee in 1931. "[T]here is a grave danger," he warned, "in taking the determination of these things into the Federal Government. I think the country is built up on a very different basis."[4]

This was standard fare from American business. As the Committee on Labor of the House of Representatives debated the possibility of establishing a national old-age pension system—to provide pressing relief for elderly Americans—John Edgerton, president of the powerful National Association of Manufacturers (NAM), huffed that his organization refused to bow to "social and political pressures."

Today we have before Congress groups advocating the passage of Federal Public Old Age Pensions to be supported by national appropriations. And this at a time when factions in individual states are agitating for pensions, old-age compensation, or similarly-termed dole for the indigent aged.

The National Association of Manufacturers, for the organized industry of the country, has made representations to Congress against the social advisability . . . of such national measures. It maintains in the first place that such a pension scheme is not within the province of Congress under the authority given by the Constitution; and, additionally, that such a system of doles, from the economic value-point, is an unwarrantedly weakening drain on industry, a deterrent of individual initiative, and a menace to our competing strength in the marts of the world.[5]

Later that year, Edgerton confided to NAM members that homeless and jobless Americans had only themselves to blame for their predicament. Their cruel conditions, he instructed, were simply the result of their not having dutifully practiced "habits of thrift and conservation." "[I]f they gamble away their savings in the stock market or elsewhere," he added disdainfully, "is our economic system, or government, or industry to blame?"[6] Amid widespread economic distress, pronouncements such as this only quickened the spread of anti-business feeling.

With the fall of big business' public image, rancor gravitated toward the Hoover administration as well. Though the president did sanction some exploratory investigations into the causes of the breakdown—some of which revealed egregious cases of financial manipulation and corruption—he was seen, by and large, as ineffectual, dispirited, and unresponsive to the wretchedness around him. As shantytowns multiplied in cities throughout the United States, they acquired the popular sobriquet of "Hoovervilles," a bitter encomium to a president whom many held accountable for their woes.

As the economy slid, Hoover's relations with the press did little to improve his reputation in the public mind. Earlier in his career, particularly during his years as secretary of commerce under Harding and Coolidge, Hoover had been relatively proficient in dealing with the press, routinely dispensing evidence—in the form of press releases and official reports—designed to demonstrate the widely hailed prosperity. In the process, he gained media celebrity as an able "engineer" of industrial progress, a builder and promoter of economic growth.

As president, Hoover was less accessible, in keeping with the customary bearing of his office. On occasion he agreed to answer reporters' questions, but only if they were submitted to him—in written form—beforehand.[7] With the breakdown of the economy, however, Hoover completely withdrew. He was seen as "uncommunicative, hostile . . . all but totally estranged from the press."[8] By the fall of 1931, with the economic situation worsening, his relations with Washington correspondents had, according to one of them, achieved "a state of unpleasantness without parallel during the present century."[9]

Hoover's public undoing reached its culmination in 1932, when he called out army troops, which violently dispersed a peaceful assembly of unemployed World War I veterans who had marched on Washington to claim bonuses promised them as a pay adjustment for their service in the First World War.[10] When the ragged multitude of bonus marchers was driven from its encampment amid a fusillade of fire and gas bombs, Hoover's public standing reached a low from which it did not recover. The suffering of the depression was far too general—and the Committee on Public Information had done its job too well during the war—for many Americans not to see the attack on the Bonus Army as an attack on themselves.

The assault on the Bonus Marchers was the deed of a leader who was glaringly out of touch with the people and their needs; it accentuated an already perilous leadership vacuum at the top. Meanwhile, the population was becoming progressively more jittery. In Europe, similar conditions provided a breeding ground for fascism. In the United States, they paved the way for a resounding Democratic victory in the 1932 presidential election and for the emergence of Franklin D. Roosevelt (FDR) and of the "New Deal" that he promised all Americans.

■　■　■　■　■

When Roosevelt took office in March 1933, bad times had gotten worse. "The interval between Roosevelt's election in November, 1932, and his inauguration in March, 1933," noted historian William Leuchtenburg, "proved the most harrowing four months of the depression. Three years of hard times had cut national income more than half; the crash of five thousand banks had wiped out nine million savings accounts."[11]

Tugwell, who left his professorship at Columbia University to become a member of Roosevelt's inner circle of advisers—his Brain Trust—described the United States, at the time of FDR's first inauguration, as a society nearing the brink of popular rebellion. "I do not think it is too much to say," he wrote in his journal, "that on March 4 we were confronted with a choice between an orderly revolution—a peaceful and rapid departure from the past concepts—and a violent and disorderly overthrow of the whole capitalist structure."[12]

Informing Roosevelt's obvious preference for "orderly revolution" were economic ideas that had begun to emerge during the twenties, ways of seeing that were at odds with the triumphal canon of unfettered free enterprise. No one advanced such ideas more effectively than British economist John Maynard Keynes. In a 1926 essay, "The End of Laissez-faire," Keynes made a conspicuous break with prevailing assumptions of bourgeois economic thought. Though he allowed that capitalism might indeed be "more efficient for attaining economic ends than any alternative system yet in sight," he also argued that capitalism—as a social system—was "in many ways extremely objectionable."[13] Countering notions that business enterprises should be permitted to proceed without governmental intervention and rejecting the idea that unrestrained profit taking would ineluctably generate social and material benefits, Keynes proposed a vision of political economy that presupposed an elemental conflict between private enterprise and the general good.

"The world is not so governed from above that private and social interest always coincide," he observed. "It is not a correct deduction from the Principles of Economics that enlightened self interest generally is enlightened."[14] Repudiating the twenties' pipe dreams of prosperity, Keynes described capitalism as an economic system that routinely and congenitally benefited from human failure and defeat.

Many of the greatest economic evils of our time are the fruits of risk, uncertainty, and ignorance. It is because peculiar individuals, fortunate in situation or abilities, are able to take advantage of uncertainty or ignorance, and also because for the same reason big business is often a lottery, that great inequities of wealth come about; and these same factors are also the cause of the unemployment of labour, or the disappointment of reasonable business expectations, and of the impairment of efficiency and production.

The remedy for these deleterious tendencies, Keynes concluded, would not come from the unregulated activities of individual businessmen. In fact, he added sharply, it is often in the economic interest of private entrepreneurs "to aggravate the disease."[15]

The role of government, Keynes proposed, was to intercede as an agent on behalf of the social body, to ensure the "social interest" of the community in those circumstances where the normal functioning of business fails to do so.

> The most important *Agenda* of the state relate not to those activities which private individuals are already fulfilling, but to those functions which fall outside the sphere of the individual, to those decisions which are made by no one if the state does not make them. The most important thing for government is not to do things which individuals are doing already . . . but to do those things which at present are not done at all.[16]

His was not an argument for the abolition of capitalism; Keynes continued to place a high value on "private initiative and enterprise." He was, however, suggesting that government was the "appropriate organ of action" through which society could, if required, exert "directive intelligence . . . over many of the inner intricacies of private business." A "co-ordinated act of intelligent judgement," in short, was necessary to balance the interests of "the community as a whole" against the "money-making and money-loving instincts" that were the motor force of business.

In 1926, Keynes had relatively few takers in the United States. The priests of prosperity continued to condemn the evil of governmental regulation. When FDR assumed office seven years later, however, the "social interest" of the community lay in a state of irrefutable ruin, and Keynes's ideas had gained ground. Too many urgent decisions were being made by *"no one."* Too many pressingly needful things were not being *"done at all."* It seemed time for the "directive intelligence" of government to step in.

The architects of the New Deal were guided by more than Keynesian economics, however. They were also inspired by older, more American visions, drawn from memories of the Progressive Era. As encountered in Edward Bellamy's *Looking Backward* and fleshed out over several decades in the writings of Henry George, Simon Patten, George Gunton, Charlotte Perkins Gilman, John Dewey, Edward Filene, and Lewis Mumford, this train of thought argued that mass-production methods augured the potential for unprecedented, universally attainable, material abundance. Questioning ancient assumptions that scarcity and poverty were inescapable features of the human condition, these modernist visionaries maintained that industrial society stood on the threshold of general well-being and was heading toward a new epoch, in which democratic egalitarianism would be reinvigorated and mass-produced consumer goods would be available to all.

In its own way, the gospel of prosperity that flourished during the twenties had served to sustain and popularize such imaginations. The dramatic growth of consumer industries and an increasingly pervasive culture of advertising had proudly publicized an oath of abundance that suggested that all would benefit from the fruits of economic expansion. Though millions had not tangibly benefited from the merchandising revelries of the 1920s, a consumer-oriented vision of *the good life*—the centerpiece of a new American birthright—had been proposed and would inform the aspirations of a generation.

As Roosevelt and his Brain Trust of progressive-minded social thinkers and activists formulated game plans for their "orderly revolution," the Progressive concept of industrially fired material well-being—the idea of *the people as consumers*—along with the Keynesian idea of the state as an indispensable force of "directive intelligence," were close at hand. So, too, was a belief in the importance of publicity.

In "The End of Laissez-faire," Keynes had prophetically anticipated the importance of this dimension within his vision of economic reform. While the essay focused primarily on the need for the state to impose direction on the private sector, Keynes also maintained that "full publicity"—the incessant propagation of information "on a great scale"—was essential to the success of his plan.

In part, the idea of "full publicity" was about making "all business facts which it is useful to know" available to those who were directly involved in analyzing problems and making decisions.[17] But it was more than that.

"[T]he fiercest contests and most deeply felt divisions of opinion," Keynes had predicted in 1926, will not boil up "around technical questions, where the arguments on either side are mainly economic." For most people, he declared, battles will be waged around questions that "for want of better words, may be called psychological or, perhaps, moral." To bring about economic change, then, it was necessary to nurture a psychological and moral renovation in society.[18]

No one was more suited to this task than FDR. It wasn't him alone, of course. The New Deal was a collective creation, the invention of a generation of Americans who were alarmed and outraged by the rampant destructiveness of "free market" capitalism and were looking to establish an alternate arrangement of social and economic priorities. Sometimes FDR was their leader, sometimes he was dragged along by them. But in his prodigious capacity to shepherd and embolden the public mind and in his ability to engage the thinking—as well as the sentiments—of the nation, no previous president had revealed a greater aptitude. A natural publicist, FDR challenged the intrinsic dualism that had guided the practices of public relations since the turn of the century.

From 1900 on, public relations thinking had vacillated between two poles of epistemological understanding. At one end there was the Progressive democratic faith, which assumed that people were essentially rational beings, that they could be most effectively persuaded by a publicity of factual, logically framed argument. At the other end was the perspective that had gained a legion of converts during the Great War. This view held that human nature was essentially irrational and maintained that "opinion" was most efficiently shaped by scientifically informed subliminal appeals to unconscious urges and instinctual drives. This outlook embraced a rhetoric of symbols, and under its influence the image had begun to displace the word as the favored language of public address.

In FDR's mind, things were less absolute, more textured. His approach to publicity moved beyond the myopic essentialism that had previously shaped public relations debates. In some ways FDR was a Jeffersonian publicist, an eighteenth-century democrat, committed to ongoing "civil instruction," believing in the possibility of informed public debate. At the same time, FDR was a prototypical twentieth-century persuader, intuitively sophisticated about public psychology, remarkably attuned to the modern media apparatus and to the powers of visual communication.

Roosevelt's Jeffersonianism was informed by historian Claude Bowers's 1925 book on Thomas Jefferson and Alexander Hamilton, a study that presented the men as the sires of two antagonistic yet persistent political traditions.[19] At one end stood the egalitarian principles of Jefferson, whose faith in the common man and commitment to popular democracy were inspirational to Roosevelt. At the other stood the Hamiltonian persuasion, a patrician perspective that discounted the opinions of "the average man" and mistrusted the ideal of "popular government." This to Roosevelt was the vantage point of vested wealth.[20]

Bowers's book focused on political struggles that marked the life of the early republic, but for FDR its implications were remarkably up-to-date. Representing the outlook of economic elites, Hamilton anticipated—in Roosevelt's mind—the pro-business boosterism that governed the politics and culture of the 1920s. Against the modern Hamiltonians, Roosevelt espoused the optimism of Jefferson, the true democrat who dared to rally the energy of "the masses against the aristocracy of the few."[21]

FDR pictured America in the twenties as "a period similar to that from 1790–1800, when Alexander Hamilton ran the federal government for the primary good of the chambers of commerce, the speculators and the inside ring of the national government."[22]

To counteract this tendency, Roosevelt argued that the "line of demarcation which differentiated the political thought of Jefferson on the one side, and of Hamilton on the other, must be restored." The Democratic Party, he declared as he moved toward his run for president, "must make it clear that it seeks primarily the good of the average citizen through the free rule of the whole electorate, as opposed to the Republican Party which seeks a moneyed prosperity of the nation through the control of government by a self-appointed aristocracy of wealth and of social and economic power."[23]

Central to FDR's Jeffersonianism was a belief in publicity as an indispensable instrument for promoting democratic dialogue. "Jef-

242 BATTLES FOR THE "AMERICAN WAY"

ferson brought the government back to the hands of the average
voter, through insistence on fundamental principles, and *the education
of the average voter*. We need a similar campaign of education," he
insisted. As he evolved from candidate to president, he reiterated this
theme again and again:

> Jefferson realized that if the people were free to get and dis-
> course all the facts, their composite judgment would be better
> than the judgment of a self-perpetuating few.[24]

To invigorate popular democracy, and to uphold the interests of "the
forgotten man," political leaders must commit themselves to fostering
public education and public conversation. "The constant free flow of
communication among us—enabling the free interchange of ideas—
forms the very blood stream of our nation."[25]

To ensure this flow and to further his commitment to "Jeffersonian" principles, Roosevelt would promote the federal government
not merely as an instrument of "directive intelligence," but as a
"clearing house for the exchange of information and ideas, of facts and
ideals, affecting the general welfare."[26] The government would gather
opinions from around the nation, he pledged, and disseminate ideas
for the greater good. In a historic battle between the vested interests
and the forces of democracy, FDR was looking for a "modern substitute for the old town meeting, and the talk around the stove."[27]

Alongside his respect for eighteenth-century democratic ideals, however, Roosevelt was also a man of his moment. His magnetic personality
and his uncanny understanding of the mass media as instruments for
mobilizing public opinion responded to the demands of the modern age.

Roosevelt's apprenticeship as a modern publicist began early in
his political career. Running for the state Senate of New York in
1912, he chose Louis McHenry Howe—a sympathetic reporter for
the *New York Herald*—to direct his campaign. A seasoned journalist,
Howe provided Roosevelt with techniques for getting his name in the
newspapers and for keeping it there by cultivating "national press
attention." Historian Betty Houchin Winfield elaborated:

> Howe devised a campaign strategy to send thousands of "per-
> sonal" letters from Roosevelt to farmers throughout the dis-

trict, publish large newspaper advertisements, and mail ready-to-print boiler-plate articles emphasizing specific Roosevelt proposals.[28]

Howe would become Roosevelt's closest political adviser into the White House years. Throughout, his overarching game plan was to manage news coverage strategically. Howe's approach was simple and relentless. "If you say a thing is so often enough," he instructed, "it stands a good chance of becoming a fact."[29]

Howe also encouraged Roosevelt to mingle with ordinary people. When FDR was assistant secretary of the navy, for example, Howe prodded him to go out and talk with workers in the navy yards, to thrash out the pros and cons of their "labor conditions." From these encounters, Eleanor Roosevelt later recalled, FDR "developed a political flair" with people, an ability to connect that would characterize his leadership style through the remainder of his life.[30]

While governor of New York, FDR continued to learn from Howe's expertise, gaining a serviceable understanding of the ways that facts, events, and circumstances evolve into something known as "news." In presenting his gubernatorial program to reporters, for example, FDR dished it out piece by piece, in readily digestible packages that were dispensed over a period of days or weeks. This technique made the program easy to report on; extended the life of the story; and, most important, made it easier for readers to understand. Roosevelt was also encouraged by Howe to experiment with the medium of radio as a means of skirting the customary watchdogs of truth—the newspapers—in order to chat directly with the people. In a political world that was still defined by habits of aloofness and ceremony, this was an unprecedented move toward accessibility and intimacy. For a man committed to the Jeffersonian ideal of "civil instruction," FDR was in the process of becoming, by the end of the twenties, a master educator.

If Howe's mentorship was key to Roosevelt's development as a publicist of *the word*, it was a personal crisis—a life-altering bout with poliomyelitis—that honed his skills as an image maker. In August 1921, at the age of thirty-nine, FDR was stricken by the virus. Though he struggled to recover and would spend the rest of his life looking for a remedy, his legs were permanently paralyzed.

This condition presented an enormous challenge. Beyond the private difficulties faced by a vigorous man who was now, suddenly, a paraplegic, Roosevelt's condition also threatened to nullify his public aspirations. Could a man in a wheelchair communicate the aura of strength that people expected of their political leaders? Fearing the worst, Roosevelt's mother encouraged her son to accept an invalid's asylum.

Roosevelt rejected this counsel; his desire to remain in politics presented him with one of his greatest challenges, to expel all visible evidence of his infirmity from the public mind. During the early weeks of the affliction, Howe repeatedly declared to reporters that his boss was only mildly ill, that full recovery was expected. FDR also labored to keep his name and political viability alive during his recuperation, contributing regular columns to newspapers in Georgia (where he was convalescing) and New York.[31]

When the acute phase of the illness passed, Roosevelt needed to project an image of himself as a man fully capable of withstanding the rigors of public life. Running for governor of New York in 1928, he perfected a way of conveying the impression that he was able to walk, using his strong upper body to shift his weight back and forth between a cane on one side and his son Elliott on the other. Though he could not actually move his legs, this arduously staged illusion permitted FDR, the campaigner, to portray himself as a man who had beaten the curse of a disabling disease.[32]

To bolster the image of vigor, Roosevelt seized upon other public relations techniques. Contemplating a run for president in 1931, for example, he pulled a preemptive publicity stunt to refute those who might question his candidacy on the basis of poor health. He "ostentatiously took out over half a million dollars of life insurance through twenty-two companies," relates James MacGregor Burns, "and saw that the highly favorable medical report was well publicized."[33]

Methodically cultivating the picture of a person who was back on his feet, FDR was able to enlist the willing cooperation of the press corps. Hugh Gregory Gallagher, who chronicled FDR's "splendid deception," described an implicit pact struck between Roosevelt and photojournalists, initially in Albany as governor and later in Washington while president.

FDR had made it a rule, during his first campaign for governor, that photographers were not to take pictures of him looking crippled or helpless. His actual words, said to some newsreel cameramen taking his picture as he was being helped out of a car in 1928 were, "No movies of me getting out of the machine boys." And from then on . . . no such pictures were taken. It was an unspoken code, honored by the White House photography corps. If, as happened once or twice, one of its members sought to violate it and try to sneak a picture . . . one or another of the older photographers would "accidentally" knock the camera to the ground or otherwise block the picture. Should the President himself notice someone in the crowd violating the interdiction, he would point out the offender and the Secret Service would move in, seize the camera, and expose the film.[34]

This system of "voluntary censorship was rarely violated," and it has shaped the visual record of FDR's remarkable political career to this day. Of the more than "thirty-five thousand still photographs of FDR at the Presidential Library," Gallagher reported, "there are only two of the man seated in his wheelchair. No newsreels show him being lifted, carried, or pushed in his chair. Among the thousands of political cartoons and caricatures of FDR, not one shows the man as physically impaired."[35]

Roosevelt's genius in erecting a spectacle of mobility—over a period of nearly twenty-five years—was essential to his political ascendancy and testimony to his monumental personal strength. His ability to present a seamless semblance of physical vigor consigned his paralysis to the position of a nonissue and made room for him to guide the far more significant and comprehensive governmental public relations campaign that characterized his presidency and the New Deal more generally.

■   ■   ■   ■   ■

The success of New Deal publicity was predicated on a number of elements. There was Roosevelt's remarkable aptitude as both a student and a leader of public opinion and the ingenuity and talent of many who went to work in his administration. Bordering all this—an element that cannot be discounted—was the dire social emergency of the Great Depression, a tear in the fabric of society that compelled many to question and reconsider the defining values of American life.

Programmatically, there were two ways that Roosevelt and the New Dealers tried to resuscitate American society. On the one hand, their critique of laissez-faire capitalism led them to launch programs that would use the government to modernize American business standards, to intervene in speculative practices that had damaged the economy, and to secure the wobbly position of the middle class.[36]

At the same time, the New Deal sought to establish channels through which historically disadvantaged Americans—farmers, industrial workers, the elderly, the sickly, and the destitute—might gain guaranteed access to the material ingredients of a more comfortable life. Here, FDR's programs went head-to-head with the religion of private enterprise, proposing that the government might create the means to improve social conditions where private enterprise—which routinely jockeyed prices and production to maximize profits—had congenitally failed.[37]

Responding to rife feelings of social anxiety, the New Deal also sought to institutionalize social welfare assurance, to provide a reliable system of security for people in need. Unemployment insurance was established to provide subsistence and relief to those who were temporarily out of work. Against protests from the NAM and other stubborn business interests, the Social Security Act established the principle of universal old-age insurance. The promise of guaranteed universal health care was also placed on the agenda, though this aspect of social insurance has never been fulfilled.

In short, the core of New Deal politics was predicated on a fundamental shift in the balance between economic practices and social life. If laissez-faire sermonizers had preached that the free market economy was sacred and that it was the duty of society—and its inhabitants—to surrender all other considerations to the supremacy of the market, the New Deal proposed a different formula, one that evaluated the market in terms of its ability to support the greater good of society. When the market failed to do so, New Dealers reasoned, economic institutions and practices had to be adjusted to respond to social need. This realignment of social priorities explains both the wide popular appeal of New Deal programs and the anti–New Deal sentiments that began to mount early on in many of the boardrooms of American businesses.

13

The New Deal and the Publicity of Social Enterprise

A SIMPLE LIST OF New Deal programs, however, does not adequately explain the extent to which the New Deal, over a period of years, was able to alter the ways that Americans saw themselves and their world. Throughout the twenties, a sunny portrait linking an ideal of public welfare to the principle of unfettered private enterprise had been diligently painted by a modern corporate publicity apparatus. As the daydream vanished, Franklin D. Roosevelt's remarkable dexterity in restoring public optimism—around a spiritual covenant linking the general welfare with governmentally insured social enterprise—was founded largely on his own ingenious instincts as a publicist. As much as any particular New Deal program, it was the protocols of publicity that served to fortify the public mind, leading it beyond the conceits of laissez-faire capitalism.

From the beginning of his presidency, Roosevelt placed a high priority on public relations. Louis Howe, his chief council, assembled a daily press summary—nicknamed "Howe's Daily Bugle"—that kept the president apprised of news coverage and editorials that appeared throughout the nation. This kind of information, capsulizing views from around the United States, was essential to the president. "Franklin reserved certain periods for his study of the press, particularly the opposition press, and, at least while Louis Howe was with him, he was always closely informed on all shades of opinion in the country," recalled the First Lady, Eleanor Roosevelt.[1]

Roosevelt's dealings with the press were aided by a team of seasoned reporters who served as his public relations advisers. Beyond Howe, there was Marvin McIntyre, a former city editor of the *Washington Times* and a graduate of the Committee on Public Information. There was also Stephen Early, who, in 1933, became the first to occupy the newly created office, presidential press secretary.[2]

It was FDR himself, however, who played the starring role in White House press relations. Previously, direct interactions between presidents and the press were largely ceremonial. Calvin Coolidge communicated with reporters almost exclusively through an official "spokesman." Herbert Hoover occasionally responded to reporters' questions, but only when they were submitted to him beforehand, in writing.

With the coming of the New Deal, these rituals were scrapped. Never before had correspondents had such unrestricted access to a president, and they reveled in it. "Mr. Roosevelt's impact on the Washington correspondents was galvanic," observed Leo C. Rosten in 1937. "Precedents were brushed aside, formalities ignored, the hocus pocus of Presidential aloofness forgotten."

A naturally sociable man who had acquired a good deal of experience bandying with ordinary folks, FDR schmoozed with the press enthusiastically. He enjoyed the interchange, and his empathic personality provided a democratic tone to press conferences and other public functions.

> Mr. Roosevelt announced that the correspondents would be free to ask direct oral questions. . . . No President had submitted to the hazardous practice of oral questioning en masse. Roosevelt did—and won the press corps by his skills.[3]

Reporters experienced FDR's personal charm with friendly fascination. For the most part, they were thoroughly enchanted. One reporter's glowing recollection offers a rich portrait of the process.

> I knew him, I'd been introduced to him. When I was a newspaper man I used to see him three times a week in press con-

ferences. He was a genius in handling the press; in knowing a lot and in being able to answer questions from the press. [Even though] most of the press . . . was editorially against Roosevelt, and fiercely so, the journalists were all for him. There were a few reporters who were considered real oddballs, who were personally critical and inimical to him. They could ask questions too. And he was . . . usually very delightful. Accessible. Oh yes, oh boy. He shaped the press conference. [Before FDR became president] there was no such thing.[4]

Roosevelt also established the routine of inviting reporters to be guests at state dinners and other receptions. This had never been done before. Early worked with Eleanor Roosevelt to ensure that the roster of Washington correspondents was divided evenly by the number of White House functions to be held each season. This system assured that every reporter, along with a spouse, experienced the tribute and flattery of a White House invitation. Employing first-name familiarity with his guests, comfortably intermingling them with heads of state and other notables, Roosevelt encouraged reporters to feel they had undergone an unprecedented advance in social status.[5]

This was the key to FDR's magnetism: his ability to make ordinary people feel that they were, in his sincere estimation, extremely important. Because of this ability, at least in part, the president made conventional elites—those who thrived on now frayed customs of deference—uneasy. The personal style of FDR, an aristocrat by birth, an easygoing democrat by conviction, both embodied and contradicted the standards by which Americans had historically gauged their presidents. As Julius C. C. Edelstein, a reporter for Drew Pearson's column, "The Washington Merry-Go-Round," described him:

He was the one who was hated by the aristocrats as a traitor to his class. And yet his personality and his style and his manner . . . the way he held a cigarette . . . his graces. He was just First Family. And this was very much appreciated by the people. He spoke of ordinary people in a sort of highly educated Bostonese . . . a Harvard accent . . . and they lapped it up.[6]

The reporters' soaring sense of access and of heightened status was, in large part, accurate. The reporters interacted with a president as never before, and in their news reporting—which was predominantly favorable—they served as esteemed ambassadors of political innovation. A number, in fact, moved from the press corps into the White House to work as speech writers or publicists.

Though FDR ardently romanced working journalists, it must be inserted that his attitude toward their employers—the newspaper publishers—was openly and deliberately hostile. Denouncing the elitist bias of the nation's editorial pages, he routinely asserted that 85 percent of American newspaper publishers were opposed to the New Deal.[7]

To a certain extent, FDR's regular attacks on newspaper publishers must have been strategic. Painting the publishers as latter-day Hamiltonians, FDR was also steeling his administration against an ideological counterattack that—if the historic zeal of the free enterprisers was any index—was certain to come. If his rapport with reporters served to keep his message in the news columns, Roosevelt's concomitant attack on the publishing giants was designed to alert Americans to the untrustworthy nature of commercially manufactured information and opinion. Counting newspaper owners among the "economic royalists" who had carried the country to ruin, Roosevelt warned that they and their editorial opinions must be vigilantly and continually questioned. Implicitly, he was laying the way for the New Deal administration and its various publicity agencies to be seen by the public as more reliable sources of information.

In his frequent and friendly dealings with print journalists, FDR borrowed from public relations know-how that had been evolving since the turn of the century. Yet New Deal publicity reached far beyond newspapers. It also sought to open up new channels of communication in order to circumvent the power of the historically conservative commercial press. With this aim in mind, the New Deal administration assumed the functions of a sophisticated publicity apparatus, working overtime to exert a direct influence on the public mind. This strategy was applied in a wide range of venues.

One of the most prominent was the New Deal's innovative use of radio, a medium that, according to Early, the presidential press secretary, was preferable to newspapers as a publicity device. "It cannot misrepresent nor misquote," he observed at a time when radio was still, for the most part, live. "It is far reaching and simultaneous in releasing messages given it for transmission to the nation or for international consumption."[8]

FDR's ability to employ radio in the thirties was lubricated by a number of factors. First, there were deep personal relationships that existed between the White House and the two major broadcast networks—NBC and CBS. Henry Bellows, head of CBS's Washington bureau, had been Roosevelt's classmate at Harvard. George Holmes, the chief Washington correspondent for NBC, was Early's brother-in-law.[9]

Yet there were other considerations that encouraged the radio industry to be particularly cooperative. Unlike the commercial print media, which enjoyed the sanctuary of the First Amendment, broadcasting was legally more vulnerable to governmental intervention. As Erik Barnouw and, more recently, Robert McChesney have ably demonstrated, the twenties and early thirties witnessed pitched battles over the control of broadcasting in the United States. Many questioned the advisability of commercializing the airwaves, arguing that radio must be maintained on behalf of the "public interest." They saw radio as too invasive, potentially too dangerous to be entrusted to the control of unregulated private interests.[10]

By the mid-thirties, these battles were virtually over. The commercialization of American broadcasting had been settled as an indelible fact. Nonetheless, the principles of "public interest" and governmental oversight still lingered and had been written into communications law. As part of the "public interest" component, for example, the Federal Communications Commission charged all radio stations to offer a measure of "educational" programming.

Given their concerns that the government would interfere with license renewals or might initiate antitrust litigation against the networks, leaders of the radio industry labored to foster a spirit of accommodation with the administration. "The close contact between you and the broadcasters," CBS's Henry Bellows told Press Secretary Early, "has tremendous possibilities of value to the administration, and as a life-long Democrat, I want to pledge my best efforts in making this cooperation successful."[11] In the spirit of this cooperation, the networks produced a number of programs that roundly praised the New Deal and its policies. In 1935, for example, CBS produced a program entitled "Of the People, By the People, For the People," celebrating "the New Deal's second anniversary." On it, "professional actors recreated great moments in the administration's brief history, the 'actual participants' discussed the events depicted." Historian Richard Steele added that "CBS arranged through the Office of Education to have civics and government classes listen to the two-hour program and even provided supplementary reading materials."[12]

Beyond network-produced programming, the radio industry also handed over a large measure of network airtime for government-produced programming. While newspapers resisted requests to carry news of governmental operations without editorial comment, the radio industry submitted with gusto, and the New Deal publicity apparatus became a conspicuous supplier of mandated educational programming.

> Everything the administration had to say went over the air-waves without the intercession of reporters, editors, or publishers. Not only did radio carry the government's message without adulteration, it carried it farther, more immediately, and more effectively than newspapers. A nationwide "hookup" simultaneously reached millions, including many never touched by newspapers. And, given the proper speaker, it reached them in a form more readily understood than the printed statement.[13]

The administration was not lacking in "proper speakers." The First Lady and cabinet members took to the air. Howe had a weekly radio series of his own. "Special" informational programs and "spot" announcements were offered airtime as well.[14] But it was the president whose mastery in communicating effectively through a radio microphone was the most profound.

During the first ten months of his administration alone, Roosevelt spoke directly to the nation on twenty occasions.[15] He saw radio as a medium that could help him reinvigorate democratic ideals. It could, he thought, "restore direct contact between the masses and their chosen leaders."[16]

Nowhere is FDR's use of radio more illuminating than in the thirty-one "fireside chats" that he delivered over the course of his presidency. Meticulously conceived radio talks through which he forged a lasting and intimate bond with his constituents, they power-fully illustrate his skills as a publicist, his Promethean capacity to mix Jeffersonian ideals of democracy with modern media know-how. Though the chats were carefully scripted by policy advisers and then finely polished by the playwright Robert Sherwood, everything about Roosevelt's delivery suggested a tone of straightforward conversation and neighborly intimacy.[17]

Having witnessed him delivering his chats, FDR's Labor Secre-tary Frances Perkins provides the most graphic firsthand account of his media style. His gift, according to Perkins, was in his ability to shut out his own environment, to visualize his audience as real people sitting in their homes, and then to project himself out into the ether as a disembodied spirit sitting among them.

> He did not and could not know them all individually, but he thought of them individually. He thought of them in family groups. He thought of them sitting around on a suburban porch after supper of a summer evening. He thought of them gathered around a dinner table at a family meal. He never thought of them as "the masses."
>
> When he talked on the radio, he saw them gathered in the little parlor, listening with their neighbors. He was conscious of their faces and hands, their clothes and homes.
>
> His voice and his facial expression as he spoke were those of an intimate friend. After he became President, I often was at the White House when he broadcast, and I realized how unconscious he was of the twenty or thirty of us in that room and how clearly his mind was focused on the people listening at the other end. As he talked his head would nod and his hands would move in simple, natural, comfortable gestures. His face would smile and light up as though he were actually sitting on the front porch or in the parlor with them. People felt this, and it bound them to him in affection.

Tours of the heartland confirmed Perkins's perspective.

I have sat in those parlors and on those porches myself during some of the speeches, and I have seen men and women gathered around the radio, even those who didn't like him or were opposed to him politically, listening with a pleasant, happy feeling of association and friendship. The exchange between them and him through the medium of the radio was very real. I have seen tears come to their eyes as he told them of some tragic episode . . . of the poverty during unemployment . . . and they were tears of sincerity and recognition and sympathy.

I have also seen them laugh. When he told how Fala, his little dog, had been kicked around, he spoke with naturalness and simplicity. He was so himself in his relation to the dog, based on the average man's experience of the place of a pet in his home, that the laughter of those gathered around radios of the country was a natural, sincere, and affectionate reaching out to this man.

To Perkins, FDR's skill in transcending the encumbrance of spatial distance, in establishing what Gabriel Tarde had termed the "mental cohesion" of a "spiritual collectivity," was the key to FDR's dexterity as a leader.

The quality of his being one with the people, of having no artificial or natural barriers between him and them, made it possible for him to be a leader without ever being or thinking of being a dictator. . . . It was this quality that made people trust him and do gladly what he explained was necessary for them to do.[18]

Yet beside his avuncular style and the rapport he was able to establish with his listeners, FDR's use of radio also exemplified his Jeffersonian convictions. Reading over the texts of his fireside chats, one cannot help but be struck by their substance, by the sophisticated political arguments they routinely presented. More than their capacity to transmit an aura of familiarity, the chats were also a repudiation of the accustomed disdain for the public mind that had framed public relations thinking since the end of World War I.

FDR chats with his friends. U.P.I./BETTMANN

In Roosevelt's words there was the clear intention to educate; to reason with his listeners; to make issues more comprehensible, not less. This intention was evident in his first fireside chat, which aired on March 12, 1933, only a week after his inauguration. Here FDR's objective was to explain actions being taken to resuscitate the incapacitated banking system. From his first sentence, an inflection of genuine concern was combined with the teacherly promise that, as president, he would work to keep the public informed, so people might fully grasp the circumstances that weighed on their social and economic lives. Unspoken, but evident, was a determined and unaccustomed faith in ordinary people's ability to make sense of things.

My friends, I want to talk for a few minutes with the people of the United States about banking—to talk with the comparatively few who understand the mechanics of banking, but more particularly with the overwhelming majority of you who use banks for the making of deposits and the drawing of checks. I want to tell you what has been done in the last few days, and why it was done, and what the next steps are going to be.

What followed was a well-organized national civics lesson, a patient account of the way that a modern banking system operates. For those suckled by an age of hype, FDR's palpable regard for his listeners' intelligence and the straightforwardness of his explanation are nothing short of astonishing. They provide an uncommon glimpse at a moment when American political life was, for a time, energized by the ideal of an informed and conscious citizenry.

> First of all, let me state the simple fact that when you deposit money in a bank the bank does not put the money into a safe deposit vault. It invests your money in many different forms of credit—in bonds, in commercial paper, in mortgages, and in many other kinds of loans. In other words, the bank puts your money to work to keep the wheels of industry and of agriculture turning round. A comparatively small part of the money that you put into the bank is kept in currency—an amount which in normal times is wholly sufficient to cover the cash needs of the average citizen. In other words, the total amount of all the currency in the country is only a comparatively small proportion of the total deposits in all the banks of the country.

He then proceeded to clarify the events that, in February and early March of that year, had caused banks throughout the country to topple like dominos.

> Because of undermined confidence on the part of the public, there was a general rush by a large portion of our population to turn bank deposits into currency or gold—a rush so great that the soundest banks couldn't get enough currency to meet the demand. . . . By the afternoon of March 3, a week ago last Friday, scarcely a bank in the country was open to do business.

He closed his exegesis with a reasoned explanation of the "national bank holiday," a temporary closing of banks in order to arrest the run on deposits and to reinforce "our financial and economic fabric."

Yet beyond the rational tone and the detailed explanation, there was something else about this talk that broke from publicity thinking of the recent past. Throughout the twenties, the public had increasingly been seen as an inanimate entity, as protoplasmic raw material to be molded by impression managers. In Roosevelt's approach to public conversation, all this changed. *The public* reentered the stage of history as a subject, an active and thoughtful force.

Throughout his exposition on banking, for example, the importance of *the people* as participants in a bold national effort was paramount. The need to fortify public courage, to rest the efforts of government on the active support of the people, was unmistakable in his tone. "Let us unite in banishing fear," he enjoined his listeners. "We have provided the machinery to restore our financial system . . . it is up to you to support and make it work. It is your problem, my friends, your problem no less than it is mine. Together," he concluded with a measure of confidence that had been absent from many people's lives, "we cannot fail."[19]

In subsequent chats, Roosevelt's notion of an engaged public grew in importance. He challenged Americans to discredit the contemptuous wisdom of the compliance engineers like Walter Lippmann, who for a decade-and-a-half had asserted that the public was inherently incapable of informed political understanding, unfit for reasonable decision making. "It is time," Roosevelt encouraged his listeners on April 28, 1935, "to provide a smashing answer for those cynical men who say that a democracy cannot be honest, cannot be efficient. If you will help, this can be done."

This was not simply rhetoric. As powerful business interests became steadily more hostile to New Deal policies, Roosevelt believed that ordinary citizens had to be mobilized. They had to become politically active, and believe in themselves as politically powerful to counterbalance the substantial weight of unfriendly corporate and financial interests.

For a publicist this was an unfamiliar kind of reasoning. With the decline of radical progressivism, public relations had evolved into an instrument of vested power, a necessary antidote to a critical public and a restless crowd. PR was seen as the tonic that could cure perilous democratic ideas that had boiled up among the "lower strata" of society. In his uses of publicity, on the other hand, FDR struck a bargain with popular activism. Exhibiting trust and affection for the public, not fear, he encouraged ordinary people to examine even his own New Deal programs and to provide suggestions—if required—for more suitable actions to be taken.

> I . . . hope you will watch the work in every corner of the nation. Feel free to criticize. Tell me of instances where work can be done better, or where improper practices prevail. Neither you nor I want criticism conceived in a purely fault-finding or partisan spirit, but I am jealous of the right of every citizen to call to the attention of his or her government examples of how the public money can be more effectively spent for the benefit of the American people.[20]

Given the overarching principle of "the greater good," this was also an implicit invitation for every citizen to question any institution—public or private—whose policies or activities impacted on the terrain of social life.

The fireside chats also offered an opportunity for FDR to articulate a vision of an American way of life that was distinct from the religious equation between democracy and "free enterprise" that had been promulgated throughout the twenties. Such business-oriented renderings of democracy—FDR charged in his radio talk of June 28, 1934—serve only to benefit "the comparative few who seek to retain or to gain position or riches by some shortcut which is harmful to the greater good."

A more humane democratic standard was necessary, he urged, one that "seeks the primary good of the greater number" as its supreme objective. Toward this end, he proposed a new social compact—a foundation of three inviolable social principles, each of which linked the needs of individuals to the notion of governmental stewardship on behalf of "the greater good."

> That security involves added means of providing better homes for the people of the nation. That is the first principle of our future program.
>
> The second is to plan the use of land and water resources to the end that the means of livelihood of our citizens may be more adequate to meet their daily needs.

And . . . the third principle is to use the agencies of government to assist in the establishment of means to provide sound and adequate protection against the vicissitudes of modern life—in other words, social insurance.

Distancing these principles from the label of "socialism," perennially a foreign idea to the minds of many Americans, FDR asserted that they were simply a reanimation of America's honorable democratic roots, a return to principles that had gotten lost amid an inferno of commercialism.

We seek the security of the men, women, and children of the nation . . .

. . . I believe that what we are doing today is a necessary fulfillment of what Americans have always been doing—a fulfillment of old and tested American ideals.[21]

Yet as Roosevelt evoked the grail of venerable democratic principles, he also carried those principles to a level unprecedented among presidents. The "men, women, and children" for whom he spoke constituted a far more inclusive public than had heretofore been seen.

The Declaration of Independence had elevated the principle of universal equality, but its author and its adherents were enmeshed in social and economic structures that ensured that the ideal of general rights could not be realized. The sovereign public of the late eighteenth century had been limited to white—primarily Anglo-American—men, property holders at that.

Even the early-twentieth-century Progressives, who pointed the way for many New Dealers, held to a notion of the public that was extremely limited in membership. While they boldly condemned the excesses of private enterprise, they were also consumed by a relentless anxiety over the ungovernable passions of an alien and dangerous crowd. Their public was still—for the most part—restricted to the company of the Anglo-American middle class.

With the coming of the New Deal, however, the prevailing conception of the American public became more inclusive than ever before. To a large extent, this expanded view of America reflected dramatic shifts that had altered the makeup of the electorate. During the New

Deal period, noted historian Steven Fraser, the public increasingly included among its ranks "legions of new voters from among the new immigrant working class."[22]

For Roosevelt, customary distinctions between *the public* and *the crowd* served no political purpose. If anything, they accentuated divisions that, if cynically exploited, could serve to erect a protective middle-class barrier between the very rich and the very poor. In Roosevelt's fireside chats—along with other arenas of New Deal publicity—the crowd was unified with the public under the common appellation of *the people*. Though FDR would strategically throw swipes at the "kidnapers, bandits, and malefactors of great wealth" who opposed his programs, he painted a picture of the American Way in which class distinction, of any kind, had no place.

This egalitarianism became increasingly evident as FDR approached the 1936 election, a time when business opposition to the New Deal had grown fierce. Accepting his party's nomination that summer, Roosevelt had excoriated "the royalists of the economic order" who, while they grant "that political freedom [is] the business of the Government," at the same time maintain that "economic slavery [is] nobody's business."

> They granted that the Government could do anything to protect the citizen in his right to vote, but they denied that the Government could do anything to protect the citizen in his right to work and his right to live. Today we stand committed to the proposition that freedom is no half-and-half affair. If the average citizen is guaranteed equal opportunity in the polling place, he must have equal opportunity in the market place.[23]

In his fireside chat of September 6, 1936, a pre-election appeal for the votes of farmers and laborers, he built upon this campaign theme.

> In this country we insist, as an essential of the American way of life, that the employer-employee relationship should be one between free men and equals. We refuse to regard those who work with hand or brain as different from or inferior to those who live from their own property. We insist that labor is enti-

tled to as much respect as property. But our workers with hand and brain deserve more than respect for their labor. They deserve practical protection in the opportunity to use their labor at a return adequate to support them at a decent and constantly rising standard of living, and to accumulate a margin of security against the inevitable.

Realizing that such egalitarian rhetoric would surely alarm the propertied classes and set their own propaganda machine into motion—condemning the president as an instigator of class conflict—Roosevelt argued that it was the intractable stance of vested property that actually jeopardized the social order. Efforts to oppose workers' rights, he warned, will not protect America from conflict, but bring it to ruin. Events overseas, he testified, were already providing a cautionary lesson.

It is those . . . who . . . would try to refuse the worker any effective power to bargain collectively, to earn a decent livelihood, and to acquire security. . . . not labor, who threaten this country with that class dissension which in other countries has led to dictatorship and the establishment of fear and hatred as the dominant emotions in human life.

Against the threat of these possibilities, Roosevelt proposed the idea of a more providential society, in which the oath of universal equality was the guiding principle. "There is no cleavage," he told his radio audience, "between white-collar workers and manual workers, between artists and artisans, musicians and mechanics, lawyers and accountants and architects and miners."

To emphasize his message, FDR turned to the question of familiar American rituals and their meanings. It was the evening before Labor Day as he spoke, and he seized the occasion to encourage listeners to think of the holiday as something more than a simple tribute to working-class people. "Anyone who calls it a class holiday," he intoned, "challenges the whole concept of American democracy." He then explained, offering a lesson in democracy that spoke powerfully to the needs of millions of Americans while repudiating the prevailing ideology of the free enterprisers:

The Fourth of July commemorates our political freedom—a freedom which without economic freedom is meaningless indeed. Labor Day symbolizes our determination to achieve an economic freedom for the average man which will give his political freedom reality.[24]

This widely publicized idea—that in order for Americans' political rights to mean anything, Americans' economic well-being must be likewise guaranteed—was the glue that brought a nation together at the height of the Great Depression. It was a promise that as America moved toward the future, the activities of private enterprise would be tolerated only insofar as they sustained the general welfare of all Americans. When they didn't, it would be the social enterprise of government to ensure that the precept of "the greater good" would be enforced.

A reconfigured portrait of America—and of American democracy—was a persistent element in Roosevelt's public oratory, but it was also a vision that reached far beyond his personal talents as a publicist. It permeated the New Deal's approach to doing politics, to building and maintaining popular support.

More than a set of programs or a purposeful gathering of individuals, the New Deal was a huge publicity apparatus, grander in scale and far more effective and beloved than George Creel's Committee on Public Information. Its impact on the American political imagination was so extraordinarily durable that only in the last two decades of this century has a business-sponsored and extravagantly financed counterattack (which commenced in 1935, as recounted in Chapter 14) been broadly, if perhaps impermanently, triumphant.

The means by which the New Deal administration transmitted its ideas were inventive and varied. Some techniques were but ingenious extensions of conventional PR practices, whereas others employed the creative labor of the nation to erect a new and compelling tableau of America, its people, and their ill-met needs.

In terms of the former, for example, both Early and McIntyre—over and above their experience in print journalism—had spent time working in the newsreel industry during the twenties. These contacts meant that the White House had ready access to movie theater newsreels that complemented its positive image in news columns and on radio.[25]

Yet to a number of influential New Dealers, relations between the White House and the commercial news and entertainment industries were not enough. Particularly in the years between 1935 and 1937, as corporate interests became increasingly unhappy with New Deal policies toward the entitlements of privately held wealth, the government began to take steps to bypass the conventional commercial manufacturers of truth. To establish open corridors linking the administration's activities with the general public, a number of governmental agencies— most notably the Works Progress Administration (WPA) and the Resettlement Administration (RA), later called the Farm Security Administration (FSA)—moved toward the deployment of independent communication strategies that mobilized a diversity of creative arts on behalf of New Deal programs, generated their own communications channels, and promoted and advanced an inclusive vision of America.

The range of these enterprises was enormous; together, they contributed to the way that people continue to envision the period of the Great Depression and the New Deal. They included the WPA's Federal Writers Project and other programs that employed artists to paint murals in post offices and other federal or federally funded facilities. There was also a Federal Theatre Project whose documentary-style "Living Newspapers" addressed the fact and drama of pressing social realities.

There were also documentary motion pictures, most notably Pare Lorentz's *The Plow that Broke the Plains* (1936) and *The River* (1937), a poetic tribute to the Mississippi River as the blood supply of a nation in crisis. In the latter film, the river assumed the role of a heroic and tragic figure. It was the historic source of America's wealth, carrying cotton, lumber, and the products of American industry that clothe, house, and feed the world. At the same time, it unbosomed the onerous costs of American industrial expansion: the deforestation, soil depletion, and flooding that threatened the survival of ordinary Americans.

Behind this visual epic of industry, riverboats, billowing clouds, and a river swollen with tree trunks, intercut with shots of depleted land and devastated forests, lay an argument about recent American history, connecting unregulated economic growth with undeniable evidence of natural wreckage. At the same time, *The River* provided an argument on behalf of the land-reclamation activities of the FSA, the New Deal agency that had sponsored the production of the film.

In many ways, the FSA—and its predecessor, the RA—offer a paradigmatic look at New Deal publicity. In the nearly 80,000 photographs that were produced and disseminated under the auspices of these agencies, one gets an illuminating look at the ways that New Deal publicity served to broadcast a new and unaccustomed picture of America, of the American people, and of the American way of life.[26]

Thematically, the photographs offered arguments akin to those encountered in the rhetoric of the fireside chats. In his radio addresses FDR had spoken of *a third of a nation ill-housed, ill-clothed, and ill-nourished.* He had proposed a concept of democracy that joined the promise of economic security to that of political rights. He had argued that business profits must be linked to the touchstone of the greater good and that it was the role of the government to ensure that outcome. In an empathic tone, the president had expanded the bounds of citizenship. If the fireside chats had provided a verbal argument on behalf of a redefined America, however, it was through the innovative photography of the RA and FSA that this ideal was most eloquently visualized.

The RA's and FSA's enterprise in photographic publicity was the offspring of two men whose lives, by the mid-thirties, had been connected for more than a decade. One was Rexford G. Tugwell, the brain truster and former economics professor, who was named to head the RA in 1935; the other was Roy Stryker, son of a radical populist farmer from Kansas, who had been a student of Tugwell at Columbia University in the early 1920s.

As a freshman in Tugwell's course on utopian socialism and in other courses, Stryker was transported by his professor's iconoclastic social views and his inventive approach to pedagogy. While many American intellectuals had become witting mouthpieces for a dominant faith in "prosperity," Tugwell rejected the prevailing doctrines of the period. His investigations fastened on the egregious deficiencies of economic life, on the millions of Americans who continued to be plagued by conditions of social and economic deprivation.

In his approach to teaching, Tugwell also repudiated the ruling dogma. Dissatisfied with the abstract predilections of most academic economics—which, he believed, only distanced students from a true appreciation of society and its problems—Tugwell embraced a pedagogy designed to make ordinary people's lived experience the foundation of economic thinking.[27] To accentuate the experiential dimension and consistent with the image-oriented approach to persuasion that characterized the postwar period, Tugwell made innovative use of "visual aids as an adjunct to learning." F. Jack Hurley, who chronicled the collaboration between Tugwell and Stryker, elaborated:

> Tugwell believed strongly in descriptive economics. He felt that it was important for students to have visual contact with the economic institutions they were studying. What did a bank look like? What did a cotton farm look like? How did it differ from a rice farm?[28]

Through Tugwell's freshman course, Introduction to Contemporary Civilization, many Columbia students were touched by his novel approach to teaching, but none more than Stryker. Under Tugwell's tutelage, Stryker became obsessed with the problem of how to communicate social and economic realities visually. In 1924, Tugwell offered Stryker—now his graduate teaching assistant—the position of "joint author" in exchange for selecting images and preparing captions for an economics textbook he was preparing. Stryker's fascination with the problem of visual communication now had a perfect outlet.

Published in 1925, the book, *American Economic Life and the Means of Its Improvement,* foreshadowed the social radicalism of the New Deal in general and the photographic publicity of the RA and FSA in particular. Written when the religion of money was at its height and images were routinely employed to aggrandize the cult of prosperity, the book provided a refreshingly subversive mix of words and images, one that stressed the economic hardships and social contradictions that lurked beneath the surface of *the good life.* While the book echoed Simon Patten's optimistic faith that industrial civilization had the potential to bring about a new and universally improved standard of living, its assessment of the present was that this promise remained largely unfulfilled. Against the widely promoted idea that America was a land of general prosperity, the authors of *American Economic Life* dissected American society into woefully unequal thirds.

At the top of the heap were the wealthy, the 1 percent of the population that garnered 12 percent of the national income—often without even working—and whose assets constituted an even larger percentage of the nation's wealth.

Below these people stood an intermediary group—13 percent of the population, according to Tugwell—who were defined as those living at the "comfort level." These were the middle class who, occasional difficulties notwithstanding, enjoyed a "regular money income" and who, in the 1920s, benefited from the proliferation of modern consumer goods.

Beneath these two groups were that 86 percent of the population whose lives were mired in poverty and whose social lives were marred by a combination of "discontent and crime." This group comprised rural and urban working people who, despite their often arduous labors, earned only a "bare subsistence." It also included the growing number of unemployed people.

In the face of these potentially explosive social divisions, *American Economic Life and the Means of Its Improvement* offered a number of proposals designed to promote the "economic progress of society as a whole." These proposals included the modernization and improvement of living conditions in cities and the depressed agricultural heartland, a more just distribution of income, the establishment of collective bargaining rights, and comprehensive social and economic reorganization and planning. In an era of laissez-faire, it was an argument for energetic economic interventionism.

Written by Tugwell, the book's text relied on a range of eloquent sources to make its points, but it was the photographic element of the book, concocted by Stryker, that stood out as its most articulate feature. None of the pictures were taken by Stryker, nor did he commission anyone to take new photographs for the volume. His approach to the pictorial ingredient of the book was essentially curatorial; he collected pictures and wrote captions for them.

Locating the photographs that would provide a picture of social conditions and would elevate social consciousness, however, was not an easy task. As historian Jack Hurley noted, most serious photographers of the period—people like Edward Steichen or Edward Weston—were exploring the camera as an artistic instrument, and most of the mass media were using photographs "to present an idealized view of life as it ought to be, rather than life as it was."[29]

In response, Stryker went to three sources for his photographs. When appropriate—to depict a rural setting, for example—he used

Life as It Ought to Be: In advertisements during the 1920s, photographs were often used to present people with a picture of *who they could become* if only they purchased and used the right product. In this 1926 ad for LUX Toilet Soap, Hollywood starlets are the models against which ordinary women are expected to measure themselves.

photos from stock photography agencies like Ewing-Galloway. To document manufacturing processes and to portray new consumer goods available to the comfort class, he procured photos from the publicity departments of a number of companies.

In his effort to represent the deplorable disparities of American life, however, he turned to a man who, during the Progressive Era, had pioneered in the field of social photography, Lewis Hine. Stryker's debt to Hine is evident throughout the book. Despite the fact that many of the pictures were now twenty years old, more than a third of the photos included in the book had been taken by Hine, who obligingly opened his files to Stryker.[30]

Beyond his reliance on Hine's images, however, Stryker also drew on the photographer's wisdom about the ways that photographs might be used to offer social arguments. Of particular advantage was Hine's thinking on the use of "social pen pictures," compelling captions to accentuate a photograph's appeal.

In *American Economic Life,* Stryker carried the social pen picture, as an instrument of persuasion, to an unprecedented—often thoroughly manipulative—level. Pictures that, without words, might have been open to a wide range of interpretations were marshaled for singularly didactic and frequently melodramatic purposes.

A photograph of a pastoral rural landscape, with the added caption "An isolated region—where roads are poor and neighbors few," for example, became an argument against the dulling solitude that, in Stryker's mind, hobbled the lives of many Americans.[31]

Other captions were aimed at evoking for a reader the experience of terrible working conditions. A picture of children picking cotton in Texas is punctuated by the words "The sun is hot, hours are long, bags are heavy" and by the sardonic observation that some cold-hearted people actually see the "discipline of work like this" as just "what children need!"[32]

A picture of a Bowery bread line was reinforced by a historical commentary addressing the cruel ironies of an industrial civilization that, though capable of producing plenty, continues to harbor want.

> To beg for bread has been the ultimate degradation throughout human history. Men and women will suffer most indignities and survive most shames before they come to this. In an age of surplus the bread line still survives, though shrunk in numbers.[33]

A woman sitting on a sidewalk, her head buried in her hands, is explained by the eulogy: "Despair—an unrecognized by-product of industry."[34] A close-up of a young man working at an industrial loom is described as "A youthful machine-tender in an immense impersonal factory." A similar picture, this time with a young girl, is presented to emphasize that there was "Neither joy nor interest in this monotonous work."[35]

With each caption, Stryker sought to emphasize the often unrecognized social forces that were at play in the everyday experiences of ordinary individuals. This intent didn't only guide his delineation of poverty, it was his overarching approach to representation throughout the book.

As applied to those living at the "comfort level," for example, Stryker's "descriptive economics" provided a powerful rejoinder to his portrayals of poverty. A well-dressed mother and her two children, seen at the front door of their suburban home, provided an opportunity for the reminder that "Mothers and children have a better chance on the comfort level."[36]

A picture of a prosperous young couple, sitting in their well-appointed living room, was used to instruct readers that the maintenance of such a setting "is dependent upon a regular money income."

Captions also contrasted the subjective lives and spiritual fulfillment of people living at different social levels. A portrait of a gray-haired man wearing eyeglasses and a jacket and tie, for example, provided a chance to contemplate the divergent patterns of aging that mark different strata.

> A member of the professional group—neither tired of his job nor tired by it; still keen and alert, his greatest usefulness just beginning at an age when wage-working men and women are beginning to wonder what luck old age holds in store for them.[37]

A picture of a middle-class "musician in his studio" was interpreted by the doleful observance that "genius is not always permitted such favorable surroundings."

If pictures of people at the "comfort level" were employed to visualize a beneficial way of life, a standard for all Americans, the lives of "the rich" were framed by an aversion rarely encountered during the 1920s. A hotel in Palm Beach was described simply as "a place where rich men idle."[38] A picture of a mansion in New York City, its "windows and doors boarded up," provided the opportunity for a discourse on the yearly migration patterns of plutocrats. The house, the caption explained, "will no doubt remain in this condition except during a few weeks in the fall, when its owners come back for an interval between

Neither joy nor interest in this monotonous work. (Courtesy National Child Labor Committee. Photo Hine)

Despair—an unrecognized by-product of industry. (Photo Hine)

To beg for bread has been the ultimate degradation throughout human history. Men and women will suffer most indignities and survive most shames before they come to this. In an age of surplus the bread line still survives, though shrunk in numbers. (Photo Hine)

Mothers and children have a better chance on the comfort level. (Photo Hine)

Poverty self-perpetuating. It can more readily be comprehended when one contrasts these two pictures. Left.—Mother and child of the comfort group. Right.—Widow and her nine children. (Photos Hine)

An illustration of what it means to live without surplus above immediate needs. (Photo Hine)

The New York City home of one of the wealthy class—with doors and windows boarded up. It will no doubt remain in this condition except during a few weeks in the fall, when its owners come back for an interval between shore or mountains in the north and shore or mountains in the South. It is interesting to note that within a few blocks of this house is one of New York's most crowded sections. (Photo Hine)

A member of the professional group—neither tired *of* his job nor tired *by* it; still keen and alert, his greatest usefulness just beginning at an age when wage-working men and women are beginning to wonder what luck old age holds in store for them. (Photo Hine)

A musician in his studio—genius is not always permitted such favorable surroundings. (Photo Hine)

In assembling the images and captions for *American Economic Life,* Roy Stryker used pictures and words to illuminate the social inequalities and, for many, the spiritual deterioration of life during a period of so-called prosperity. AMERICAN ECONOMIC LIFE, 1925

shore or mountains in the north and shore or mountains in the south. It is interesting to note," the caption adds, in reference to the spaciousness of this sporadically inhabited dwelling, "that within a few blocks of this house is one of New York's most crowded sections."[39]

• • •

Though prepared as a course text, initially for freshmen at Columbia University, *American Economic Life and the Means of Its Improvement* pointed to a pictorial publicity that veered dramatically from the visual thinking of its time. While Stryker's pictures were arranged to strike an emotional nerve, their claim was toward an objectivity—a documentary realism—that had, in large part, been abandoned by modern picturizers. Unlike the overtly idealized imagery, the psychologically inclined "masturbation of the eye" that had gained prominence throughout the 1920s, these pictures with aphoristic captions offered to illuminate actual social experiences, to present verifiable social facts.

In the twenties, this approach to visual publicity stood at the margins of society. It was a technique used by a team of radical economic thinkers to examine social and economic trends, to challenge the establishment, and to question prevailing notions of "prosperity." It was also employed to propose a vision of democracy that would extend to a greater number of Americans. Part of what is remarkable about the book, even today, is its spirited dissent from the ethic of commercial boosterism. In the context of the Great Depression, however, and backed by a government that was putting many of their once heretical ideas into action, Tugwell and Stryker's publicity of "descriptive economics" began to exert an influence on the countenance of American political culture itself. Though boosterism would continue to inform the inflection of commercial advertising and sumptuous products and settings were a typical aspect of escapist films in the thirties, a more critical eye was advancing into the American mainstream.

The time was 1935 and the place was the RA, an independent New Deal agency with Tugwell at its head. The RA was engaged in a range of activities designed to reconstruct depressed rural areas. In addition to "land-use" programs and "loans and grants to individuals and groups of farmers," the RA also sponsored a number of social experiments, including federally funded suburban communities, "Greenbelt towns" as they were called, and "several experimental communal farms for rural families that had suffered displacement."[40] It was these experiments, explicit challenges to the religion of private enterprise, that prompted Tugwell to set up an "Information Division" to tell the RA's story and to combat anticommunal, antigovernment propaganda that was sure to come from the commercial press and from an increasingly nervous business community more generally. Following a guiding precept of public relations thinking that dated to the turn of the century, the Information Division was Tugwell's apparatus for winning the hearts and minds of middle-class Americans to the RA's social democratic cause. But unlike progressivism, the appeal reached beyond the middle-class toward an expanded—largely immigrant and working-class—electorate that constituted the base of FDR's support. Like other components of New Deal culture, the Information Division endeavored to build a cross-class united front.

The Information Division was a multimedia enterprise, generating radio programming and—as was mentioned—films. At its center, however, stood something called the Historical Section, headed by Tugwell's old friend Stryker, which was charged with the job of producing and disseminating a photographic record of the RA and its mission.

In this regard, it was remarkably successful. Between 1935 and 1943, when the Historical Section (by then a part of the Office of War Information) was disbanded, Stryker's uncanny ability to tell stories through pictures would condition the ways that many people understood not only the hardships of the depression, but themselves, their fellow Americans, and their society. This time, with the federal government subsidizing his visual appetites, Stryker no longer had to rely on previously taken photographs. He could parent his own images, shot with the programs of the RA, and then with the FSA, in mind.

Abetting Stryker in this enterprise was a band of men and women—some with minimal prior experience as photo documentarians—many of whose names would become celestial in the annals of American art: Walker Evans, Ben Shahn, Dorothea Lange, Carl Mydans, Russell Lee, Arthur Rothstein (also a former student of Tugwell at Columbia), Marion Post Wolcott, John Vachon, Jack Delano, John Collier, Sheldon Dick, and others.

In certain ways, the work of the Historical Section was a continuation of efforts begun with the publication of *American Economic Life*. Yet since Stryker was now able to commission his own photographs and was in a position to guide the process of their creation, he felt less obliged to explain them with words. FDR—in his fireside chats and elsewhere—was already furnishing stirring captions. Breaking from the double-barreled tactic of image and caption that had been employed in his and Tugwell's textbook, this time Stryker threw his confidence squarely behind the eloquence of images. Captions were terse when provided, simply identifying a subject.

Barely a year after Stryker's RA service began, the writer James Agee—whose collaboration with photographer Walker Evans, *Let Us Now Praise Famous Men,* would emerge as a classic piece of New Deal culture—baptized the camera as "the central instrument of our time." In words recalling those of Walter Lippmann in *Public Opinion,* Agee observed that "the camera can do what nothing else in the world can do: . . . perceive, record, and communicate, in full unaltered power, the peculiar kinds of poetic vitality which blaze in every real thing and which are in great degree . . . lost to every other kind of art."[41]

More than any other medium, he judged, the camera could simulate the impact of a face-to-face encounter. It could exert what Lippmann had termed an unparalleled "authority over the imagination." At the tiller of the Historical Section, Stryker went forward with the same assumptions. He believed that a photographer, adequately instructed, could guide the process of interpretation by a viewer and could encourage a better understanding of the world existing beyond the frame. "If a photographer understands the social forces present in a scene," he maintained, "the resulting photograph should be a satisfactory pictorial representation."[42] Properly formulated, Historical Section photographs should require no additional words to communicate relevant social and economic realities. With this idea in mind, Stryker provided his photographers with straightforward instructions for their assignments. As Dorothea Lange prepared for her first RA photo excursion in 1936, for example, Stryker requested:

> Would you, in the next few days, take for us some good slum pictures in the San Francisco area. . . . We need to vary the diet in some of our exhibits here by showing some western poverty instead of all south and east. . . . When you get to Los Angeles, I think it might be worthwhile to see if you can

pick up some good slum pictures there also. Do not forget that we need some of the rural slum type of thing as well as the urban.[43]

In a 1938 letter to Sheldon Dick, briefing the photographer for a trip to Pennsylvania's coal region, Stryker was even more explicit, revealing his ability to identify the "social forces present in a scene."

The specific things I noted when I was there were that the town dropped down into a Pennsylvania mountain valley. Everywhere you look is man-made desolation, waste piles, bare hills, dirty streets. It is terribly important that you in some way try to show the town against this background of waste piles and coal tipples. In other words, it is a coal town and your pictures must tell it. It is a church dominated place. . . . The place is not prosperous, people are loafing in saloons and around the streets. You must get this feeling of unemployment. There are many unpaved streets. . . . The houses are old and rundown. The place is devoid of paint. I am sure lots of cheap liquor is consumed for no other reason than in an attempt to blot out the drabness of the place. When you are ready to shoot people try to pick up something of the feeling on the side of youth. Try to portray the hope-lessness of their position. . . . youth's confusions—liquor, swing, sex, and more liquor. The actual details will have to be worked out by yourself.[44]

Not all the photographers accepted their instructions with equa-nimity. Tensions between Stryker and Evans, in particular, were leg-endary. Yet as one approaches the thousands of photographs assembled under the auspices of the RA and FSA, one is struck by the extent to which the images conform to a distinct set of guidelines and the degree to which, together, they constituted a coherent pub-licity on behalf of a renegotiated picture of America, a picture that clashed, eloquently, with what had governed America's national cul-ture in the 1920s and beforehand.

First, most RA and FSA pictures were shot with black-and-white film. In preceding decades, the availability of modern synthetic dyes

(ABOVE AND OPPOSITE) RA and FSA portraits: Introducing America to Americans.
LIBRARY OF CONGRESS

and color photography had increasingly defined the window dressing of American industrial society; colorful products and representations of products had become part and parcel of visual culture in general and merchandising in particular. The choice of black-and-white film, then—as historian Sally Stein persuasively argued—embodied a decision to present a reality that contrasted with that seen in the commercial sphere. Against the color-coded daydreams of advertising, black-and-white photography claimed to reveal a truer, more sobering reality, more in synch with the lives of real people.[45]

Yet beyond this socioaesthetic consideration, there were also recurrent—often overlapping—subjects and themes that unified the pictures of the FSA as a publicity campaign. Many of the photographs were simply portraits of people, alone or in groups: portraits of Americans. Other photographs drew attention to the arduous social, economic, and environmental circumstances faced by these people, conditions that the RA and FSA sought to remedy. A third group might be said to comprise a portrait of America as a place, doc-

umentations of everyday life: the homes, the land, and the towns where ordinary Americans lived.

The portraits of people, one after another, stand at dramatic odds with traditions of portraiture that had dominated to that time. William Stott wrote that FSA documentary was "a radically democratic genre" that uplifted the ordinary while diminishing the importance of the high and mighty.[46] This standard was continually borne out by the images. Against a history that had habitually damned poor people as belonging to a faceless, often loathsome *crowd*, FSA portraits accentuated the humanity and dignity of those who suffered in America's dust bowl. If most earlier photo portraits of poor people were either condescending and clinical or were marked by the attempt to fashion—in a studio setting—a decidedly middle-class facade, these were portraits that dignified and emphasized hard work and suffering as a credential of one's humanity.

This was the "salt of the earth." It was not simply *poverty* being portrayed, it was people. Tugwell had instructed Stryker, "Roy, a man may have holes in his shoes, and you may see the holes when you take the picture. But maybe your sense of the human being will teach you there's a lot more to that than the holes in his shoes, and you ought to try to get that idea across." In the strong but weary gaze of Lange's "migrant mother" and in scores of other pictures, this teaching was expressively realized.

When Stryker claimed that the Historical Section "introduced America to Americans," he underlined the extent to which the photographs presented a portrayal of America and of the American people that had, to that point, been largely invisible in a national, mass-mediated culture. Poor white tenant farmers from Alabama; black cotton pickers on a plantation in Mississippi; children without shoes; flood refugees; unemployed miners; "Okies" on the road seeking a better life; breast-feeding mothers with worried looks in their eyes; migratory Mexican field workers; furrowed and callused hands; men on a chain gang or a county farm; a black teacher in a dilapidated rural school, using chalk on a broken slate in her struggle to enlighten the children; community sings; and a small town meeting in Texas. These were the diverse portraits of Americans that challenged the hegemony of middle-class Anglo-America, and they set the stage for battles over *American identity* that even now, at the edge of a new millennium, are still with us.

In the 1930s, this was a picture of the nation that the American middle class—for whom the photographs were, in large part, being produced—had not seen before, certainly not in publicity coming from the federal government. In most prior representations of the poor, the character of their otherness was conspicuous. "These are not people like you," most pictures had silently declared; "these are people to be feared." Messages like these had helped to erect a polit-

(OPPOSITE) FSA photographs illustrating social, economic, and environmental conditions. Arthur Rothstein's 1936 photograph of a steer's skull on the parched earth of Pennington County, South Dakota, provoked a controversy over the authenticity of FSA images when it was discovered that it was only one of a series of pictures of the skull, each shot against a different terrain. Anti–New Dealers pointed to Rothstein's picture as a sign that FSA pictures couldn't be trusted. LIBRARY OF CONGRESS

ical barrier between the middle and lower classes, even during the Progressive Era. More recently, from the mid-teens through the twenties, the silent eloquence of images had been used to forge a psychological bond between middle-class Americans and large corporations.

The political success of the New Deal, however, required a different argument, one that transcended the impediment of *otherness* that divided a photographic subject from the audience and, more important, one that encouraged a process of identification between the viewer and the viewed, between the middle class, new working-class voters, and the poor. Stryker's old school mate Arthur Rothstein had argued that "the lens of the camera is, in effect, the eye of the person looking at the print."[47] In the hands of Rothstein and other RA and FSA photographers, this understanding gave rise to a portraiture in which the subjects and the audience entered into close eye contact. These portraits did not afford the spectator the luxury of safe distance; they consciously asked the viewer to project himself or herself into the reality being portrayed, into the everyday lives of the people in the pictures. In the depths of the Great Depression, a middle class that was itself enduring considerable pain had grown uncharacteristically responsive to this call.

The FSA portraits were unquestionably influenced by the eye of Hine, but they also represented Stryker's detachment from the world-view of the celebrated Progressive documentarian. In preparing *American Economic Life* in the mid-twenties, Stryker had been deeply affected by—and heavily dependent on—Hine's visual sensibility. As a result, although the book devoted a great deal of attention to the problems of agricultural poverty, its visual idiom was strikingly urban and industrial. This urban industrialism made sense. Much of Hine's work focused on factory workers and miners, on cityscapes. At the height of the great migration, many of his subjects were distinctly immigrants. The RA and FSA photos, on the other hand, while they were conversant with Hine's approach to "social photography," presented a vision of *the people* that was quite different; overwhelmingly rural, stridently *American*. This vision was probably essential to their broad appeal. Though the people portrayed were markedly diverse, their framing was mythically Jeffersonian. The weathered faces and the callused hands evoked those of heroically self-sufficient pioneers,

FSA pictures of everyday life. On the walls of broken hovels and along the dusty roads, the promises of the consumer culture furnished stunning proof of their own emptiness. LIBRARY OF CONGRESS

now in need of help. They seemed to be awaiting Henry Fonda to portray them, and he would.

If the portraiture provided "handles for identification" between spectators and subjects, other photos furnished dramatic visual metaphors by which social, economic, and environmental problems, primarily those afflicting America's heartland, were made legible to the urban middle class. In a grainy print, a man and his son are seen "Fleeing a Dust Storm" in Cimarron County, Oklahoma. A family—its worldly possessions piled in a small wagon—trudges along a barren highway, graphic evidence of social displacement. A hastily dug grave with a rough-hewn headstone, a common dinner plate atop the mound of dry, recently shoveled earth, provides silent testimonial to a casualty along the road. A ramshackle triple-decker building with a muddy backyard presents a vivid demonstration of substandard housing. A crude sign for a twenty-cent flophouse becomes a marker of general want. A black man sipping from a "colored" water barrel in the South points to the legacy of embedded racial segregation that—with proper attention—might also be remedied. A "Christmas Dinner in Iowa," captures four raggedy children, sitting in a leaky cabin, eating their scanty holiday meal out of a rusty, chipped bowl.

Contextualizing the portraits of people and their dire circumstances were photographs that collectively amplified a broad panorama of everyday life. Many were of exteriors that told important American stories: decrepit cabins and outbuildings on a plantation where children and grandchildren of slaves continued to live, street scenes in small towns where unemployed men wiled away their days, rural churches where the forgotten kept their faith and gave their thanks to God, dilapidated small-town general stores where both merchants and customers eked out a bare living, and local cafés where ordinary people came to eat and socialize.

Other photographs were of interiors, places where people lived and assembled their material culture. Evans produced many portraits of the simple implements of life—a washstand and kitchen table, a bucket, a chair, a bed, a fireplace, tin plates, laundry, a broom, and the decorations that poor people put on their walls. Despite the meagerness of these places and objects, Evans's camera offered them an almost reverential status as marks of authenticity.

What is striking about these images of everyday life—particularly when viewed in relation to the commercial imagery that had dominated in the twenties—is the marginal, sometimes ironic status of the commercial culture within them. The jerry-built shops that are seen in many street scenes, for example, display the signage of big business—GULF Oil, Coca-Cola, NEHI sodas, Dr. Pepper, Budweiser, "Grand Prize"—but in these photographs the signs were divested of their merchandising luster. In their black-and-white positiveness, they now testified to the extent to which the culture of prosperity and its once buoyant symbols stood in a state of disrepair.

In many of the interiors, as well, symbols of the commercial culture—magazine advertisements or promotional calendars—are revealed as tattered debris, scraps of paper pasted on the wall to keep inclement weather from leaking through cracks between the timbers or in a makeshift gesture toward decoration. Against the walls of broken hovels, the promises of the consumer culture furnished stunning proof of their own emptiness. These pictures served to underscore bitter distinctions between commercially promulgated ideals and the realities of peoples lives.

The visual ironies, like the diverse portrayal of Americans themselves, provided a defining thread in much FSA photography. These pictures' visual style employed a language of contradiction. The photographs celebrated America while rejecting an American national culture based on the religion of "prosperity" and commercial images. In short, they encouraged people to rethink what business as usual really meant.

■　　■　　■　　■　　■

In the early 1920s, Lippmann had theorized that people's worldviews were framed by illusory "pictures in their heads." These pictures, he argued, were guided by culturally determined stereotypes—mental templates that gave form and meaning to people's experiences. Throughout the twenties, such thinking had guided an exuberant generation of image managers, publicists who industriously erected a stereotype of democracy that was founded on the ideas of *consumer choice* and *middle-class prosperity.*

By the mid-1930s, in the wake of economic collapse and fostered by a generation of revisionist image makers, the prevailing stereotype of American democracy had changed. It was more inclusive, it upheld an ideal of universal rights, and it cited the dire needs of regular people—poor farmers, industrial laborers, the unemployed—as the ultimate index of the common good.

With this change in stereotype, the idiom of visual publicity itself had been transfigured. If twenties publicists had mounted elaborate retail dramas, with new consumer goods occupying center stage, the dramas being staged by New Deal publicity were human dramas, with unadorned and ordinary people at their center. In the twenties, image makers had consciously exploited the realm of fantasy; the new generation used images to evoke a sense of the real, albeit a real that was deliberately devised to deliver a powerful emotional punch.[48]

This new social aesthetic was not simply the creation of RA/FSA photographers. Like the visual oratory of prosperity, it was a product of its time. It derived from the overwhelming realities of the Great Depression. But from 1935 onward, the photographs coming out of the Historical Section increasingly created poignant opportunities for Americans to see themselves and their needs anew.

The simple existence and style of the images, of course, did not create these opportunities. A basic element of Stryker's mission was the wide dissemination of his agency's photographs, particularly aimed at the middle-class electorate whose sympathies were essential to the political viability of New Deal policies.

At first, the taking and collecting of photographs took precedence over their exhibition. Within a year, however, display had become a prime objective.

The first major exhibition of the photographs came at the 1936 Democratic convention. With the New Deal under continuing attack from business and the political Right, the pictures' outspoken depiction of a devastated heartland and their remarkable pathos forcefully seconded a radically democratic party platform that declared:

> We hold this truth to be self-evident—that government in a modern civilization has certain inescapable obligations to its citizens, among which are: (1) Protection of the family and the home; (2) Establishment of a democracy of opportunity for all the people; (3) Aid to those overtaken by disaster.[49]

The national attention began to snowball. At an annual photo exhibition sponsored by U.S. Camera in 1936, four pictures by Historical Section photographers were included. Shortly, the College Art Association, a national organization of art educators, sponsored a traveling collection of the pictures.[50] The photographers were becoming prominent, and their pictures were being venerated as important works of modern art.

At no time was this artistic celebration more evident than in April 1938, when the First International Exposition of Photography was held at the Grand Central Palace in New York. In the show, organized around the theme, "How American People Live," a selection of FSA photos were prominently featured. Among the seven thousand visitors on the first day, the impact of these pictures was clearly overwhelming. One after another, in written responses to the show, visitors cited the power of the pictures, their ability to convey what one visitor termed the "real life of a vast section of the American people."[51]

A growing number of institutions were making use of the FSA pictures. Post offices exhibited them as symbols of the government's compassion. Libraries offered them as educational materials for readers. Museums displayed them as art. University classes in economics and sociology employed them as instructional tools. As the success of the photographs became evident, FSA staffers were asked to take on publicity assignments on behalf of other governmental agencies.[52] Stryker's operation was providing a visual standard for the New Deal's rendition of American society.

The impact of the FSA, however, reached beyond institutions of art, education, and government. Between 1938 and 1940, the photographs began to appear, more and more, in the commercial media, often without credit. Among the national magazines with large middle-class readerships in which FSA pictures appeared were *Time, Life, Look, Newsweek, Saturday Evening Post, Survey Graphic, Colliers, McCall's, Fortune, Nation's Business, Today, Literary Digest,* and *Current History,* among others. The photos appeared in more specialized journals, like the *Birth Control Review* and *Junior Scholastic,* as well. They showed up in big-city dailies—the *New York Times* used the pictures routinely—and in small-town weeklies.[53] Even if it was often unattributed, FSA's visual epic of America was becoming a conspicuous element in the culture-at-large.

Stryker's lack of proprietary instinct assisted this progression. Whereas a leader of a *commercial enterprise* might have fought to keep his company's product from being used without proper identification, Stryker's sense of *social enterprise* led him in the opposite direction. "The basic need was to get the pictures before the public," explained Hurley, "direct publicity for his own group was a secondary consideration." This stance, Stryker's willingness to see FSA photos stand as nothing more than social facts, clearly assisted in the dissemination of the FSA's rendition of America.

In many ways, the American mass media actively participated in the promulgation of the FSA way of seeing. Magazines not only used FSA images directly, they also began to hire FSA photographers or photographers with an akin sensibility to produce photo essays for their pages. Evans and Agee's *Let Us Now Praise Famous Men*, for example, began as an assignment for Henry Luce's *Fortune* magazine. Margaret Bourke-White, who became a celebrated *Life* magazine photographer, had taken pictures for a 1930 reissue of Tugwell and Stryker's *American Economic Life*. Many of her late-thirties images, as well, simulated an FSA aesthetic.

An FSA-like portrait of America also seeped into Hollywood films to some extent. Even before Stryker's work at the RA commenced, documentary-style portrayals of destitution were beginning to appear. Mervyn LeRoy's 1932 classic, *I Am a Fugitive From a Chain Gang*, has the feel of the FSA photos, and LeRoy and Busby Berkeley's *Gold Diggers of 1933* ends with a mournful tribute to "the forgotten man." King Vidor's 1934 film, *Our Daily Bread*, not only anticipated the Historical Section's visual style but, in its receptive depiction of an agricultural cooperative, corresponded with some of the RA's and FSA's utopian experiments. Fritz Lang's *Fury* (1936) and Mervyn LeRoy's *They Won't Forget* (1937) both wrestled with the problem of southern lynchings using a naturalistic style. In 1940, *The Grapes of Wrath*—in which Henry Fonda and the salt of the earth would finally meld—borrowed conspicuously from the FSA in its focus on rural displacement and in its aesthetic intonation. *Sullivan's Travels* (1941) and other films bore the imprint of Stryker's enterprise.

What Steichen termed the "simple blunt directness" of the FSA photos, however, was undeniable. The photos' ability to leave a viewer with what he defined as the "feeling of a living experience" magnified the impact of photojournalism. Ironically, in a business in which attracting readership was the name of the game and in an environment in which the FSA's kind of photography spoke to readers, it is little wonder that these problematically subversive images began to impregnate the establishment culture.

For many in the upper echelons of corporations and for the political Right, the combined impact of New Deal publicity was alarming—even more so than its precursor in the Progressive Era. During that earlier time, an anxious middle class served as a defensive buffer between corporate power and the wrath of the masses. This protection had solidified during the twenties, when the growth of consumer industries and the spirit of boosterism tied middle-class ideals to the hitching post of business. Now, it seemed, the fragile middle class and the "Hoe Man" had become allies, joined by the power and publicity of the federal government.

14

Money Talks:
The Publicity of
Private Enterprise

IN *The Age of Extremes,* his sweeping chronicle of the years between 1914 and 1991, Eric Hobsbawm argued that the Great Depression—like no episode before or since—posed an emergency for world capitalism that appeared to imperil its survival as an economic system. There had been grave economic disruptions before then, to be sure, but "[i]n the past, waves and cycles, long, medium and short, had been accepted by businessmen and economists rather as farmers accept the weather, which also has its ups and downs."

> There was nothing to be done about them: they created opportunities or problems, they could lead to bonanzas or bankruptcy for individuals or industries, but only socialists ... believed that [these] cycles were part of a process by which capitalism generated what would in the end prove insuperable internal contradictions.

In spite of acute periodic ruptures, the presumption that the market economy would only continue to progress was, at least among business leaders, sacrosanct.

The depression that started in the late twenties, however, was different. "[P]robably for the first, and so far the only, time in the history of capitalism," Hobsbawm observed, "its fluctuations seemed to be genuinely system-endangering."[1] Internationally, he added, the deflation of capitalist confidence was only accentuated by the mounting "spectre of communism" in the USSR.

> The trauma of the Great Slump was underlined by the fact that the one country that had clamorously broken with capitalism appeared to be immune to it: the Soviet Union. While the rest of the world, or at least liberal Western capitalism, stagnated, the USSR was engaged in massive ultra-rapid industrialization under its new Five Year Plans.[2]

In the United States—the epicenter of the crash—the sense of "catastrophe and disorientation" among many businessmen, economists, and conservative politicians was particularly severe.[3] The trend toward governmental intervention heightened these anxieties, of course. But as much as the New Deal's economic policies worried the business community—particularly its program to "tax the rich"—it was the popular success of the New Deal's publicity apparatus that was one of the most rankling causes of alarm.

"Never before has the Federal Government undertaken on so vast a scale and with such deliberate intent, the task of building a favorable public opinion toward its policies," shuddered E. Pendleton Herring, a conservative Harvard political scientist, in 1935. Assessing the New Deal's uncanny ability to manage the news process, Herring described a national media that was being overwhelmed—and effectively controlled—by an endless tide of governmentally manufactured information.

> News comes out of the Federal bureaus in a flood. Today's mistake is washed away by the plans of tomorrow. Sifting out the news from the mass of prepared official statements is a task which discourages further curiosity for more detail on the part of the busy journalist. . . .
>
> The present system insures that a favorable presentation of all news concerning the Government is available to the newspaper. For the newspaper men, the easy course is that of acceptance without further investigation.

These developments, Herring warned, posed "[d]ire implications for democracy. Deliberately and legally establishing agencies for the creation and stimulation of favorable opinion seems to strike at the basic concepts of popular government. Can one speak of government by consent," he asked, "when this consent is manufactured by official press agents?"[4] To stave off this trend toward "dictatorship," Herring recommended that it would be necessary for the "minority" Republicans to deploy their own "publicity division" to maintain a viable "opposition" voice.[5]

As the thirties proceeded, a growing chorus of business champions raised similar concerns. T. J. "Tommy" Ross, former partner of the recently deceased Ivy Lee, deplored the extent to which "government by publicity" was becoming "the order of the day," while S. H. Walker and Paul Sklar—two reporters who served as mouthpieces for big business—noted the unsettling extent to which the Roosevelt administration had both galvanized and united with popular "resentment, hostility, and distrust" toward business.

Compounding the threat of New Deal programs and publicity, a medley of indigenous social movements were becoming increasingly vocal in their opposition to business practices during the depression years. If businessmen throughout the twenties had upheld a vision of the public that was composed of obedient consumers—slavishly adhering to the honored laws of social psychology—the American public of the thirties was increasingly composed of activists. Intrinsic to the New Deal era, and often with government encouragement, mass mobilizations were under way that, from a variety of quarters, were undermining the habitual domain of big business.

The most well-known mobilization, of course, was the unprecedented organization of industrial laborers that occurred during the thirties, largely under the leadership of the Congress of Industrial Organizations (CIO). Enabled by the federal endorsement of collective bargaining, this was the moment when the ranks of organized labor swelled and when the rights of working people took flight as a sacred national principle.[6]

Popular mobilization, however, reached far beyond organized labor. Following a decade when consumers were routinely characterized as eager shoppers, submissively awaiting the newest product or style, the thirties witnessed the rise of an organized and fairly militant consumer movement. Bolstered by various New Deal agencies (particularly the National Recovery Administration [NRA] and the Agricultural Adjustment Administration), the movement actively challenged the status quos of production, distribution, and merchandising.

Contesting a growing trend toward national chain-store businesses, for example, a vocal coalition of consumers, farmers, small-businessmen, and New Deal politicians arose in the thirties that sought to restrict the power of chains like the Atlantic and Pacific Tea Company (A&P) or Kroger.[7] As gargantuan "middle men" purchasing in enormous volume, merchandising chains had seized control of entire producer markets, causing a precipitous decline in farm prices. As national retailers—buying and selling in volume—they were also contributing to the rapid eradication of locally based businesses. This goal having been largely achieved, consumer advocates argued, the chains now held the customer by the throat. The antichain movement, which had started to simmer even in the late twenties, sought to rectify this situation, to protect the interests of farmers, local and regional businesses, and consumers alike.

Along parallel lines, the thirties also witnessed the growth of consumer purchasing cooperatives. By 1936 co-ops were a visible feature on the economic horizon and were receiving New Deal support.[8] The Cooperative League, a coalition of co-ops, was producing its own "string of private brands" of canned and packaged goods and was contemplating the manufacture of appliances. Even the conservative American Federation of Labor endorsed the co-op movement as a natural complement to trade unionism.

> The cooperative movement is the organization that is designed to protect the workers in their (consumer) relations with business men in the same sense that the trade union movement protects them from the employers. . . . The American Federation of Labor is ready to work with any constructive movement for consumers' cooperation.[9]

Alongside these organizational developments, the questioning of embedded business practices was becoming widespread. While businessmen railed against New Deal publicity, for example, corporate publicity was falling more and more under the public microscope. Bolstered by arguments that advertising fostered monopolies by driving those who couldn't afford to pay for it out of business or that advertising—a deductible business expense according to 1919 income tax law—offered corporations an attractive loophole for not paying taxes, anti-advertising campaigns were growing on college campuses and among consumer organizations.[10] Recognizing the spreading influence of the consumer movement, a downcast writer in *Printers' Ink* observed that the popular belief that "honesty and advertising just can't mix" threatened to spread to "thousands of classrooms in colleges all over the country."[11]

Rather than addressing members of the public as individual customers—the preferred approach of the twenties—businesses were now facing consumers en masse, organized as political-economic bodies. The notion that businesses could control the public mind, an arrogance that prevailed in commercial circles throughout the twenties, had faded. Amid the clamor of the time, the long-term balance of power seemed to be shifting perilously away from businesses.[12] Among anxious corporate leaders and their public relations advocates, the survival of capitalism—its place in America's future—seemed much in question.

This sense of jeopardy drove the development of corporate PR during this period. Responding to this crisis of legitimacy, a wide array of business leaders began to see public relations as a paramount concern of management. This perspective provided fertile ground for the general growth of independent public relations practices. The firms of Edward Bernays, Ivy Lee & T. J. Ross, Carl Byoir and Associates, Whitaker & Baxter, Hill and Knowlton, and Bernard Lichtenberg's Institute of Public Relations, among others, gained prominence during this precarious period.

To some extent, public relations activities proceeded as they did during the years prior to the depression. Particular products continued to be hyperbolized; individual corporations or industries defended themselves against immediate or impending attacks.

Developments in the chain-store industry provide a clear picture of the latter. In 1935, with national grocery chains under assault, a major food industry powwow held in New York established a front group, the National Food and Grocery Committee, to argue the public advantages provided by national chain supermarkets.[13] In 1938 the California Chain Stores Association followed suit, establishing a paper organization, The Foundation for Consumer Education. Its connection to the chain association unacknowledged, the foundation presented itself as an ostensibly neutral clearing house of information to benefit "the welfare of consumers."[14] Along similar lines, in 1938, Carl Byoir—whose credentials included representing Hitler's Third Reich in the United States—was brought in by the A&P to erect a credible charade of public support against the threat of federal taxes on chains.[15] Through these combined efforts, antichain legislation, at both the national and local levels, was—in a number of critical instances—successfully frustrated.[16]

Targeted campaigns were mounted at other politically charged crossroads as well. In 1935, The Associated Advertising Agencies of America engaged in a public relations effort designed to defend their industry against "muck-raking authors and others who attempt to destroy . . . public confidence" in advertising.[17] On other fronts, relatively inexpensive co-op products, which threatened to challenge the hegemony of the "name brands," were widely attacked as being of poor quality.[18] The steel industry, hit by a wave of CIO organizing, actively engaged in PR to clear the name of Big Steel.[19] Southern textile mills, whose reputation was damaged by critical images of the rural South, mounted photographic campaigns calculated to demonstrate that "not all Southern mill villages are the living hells" that Resettlement Administration and Farm Security Administration (FSA) photographs suggested.[20]

Yet to many businessmen and PR specialists from the mid-thirties onward, these scattershot activities were not sufficient to deal with the acute public relations crisis that was plaguing capitalism overall. With a skeptical public questioning corporate commitment to the common good and the president assailing big business as "a concentration of private power . . . a cluster of private collectivisms . . . masking itself as a system of free enterprise," a growing number of business strategists were convinced that a more comprehensive public relations campaign—to resurrect the power and ensure the future of the business system itself—was essential.[21]

Chiding many businessmen's failure to grasp the urgency of the moment, Edward L. Bernays summarized the task that stood before businessmen in 1936. Simply put, they needed to look beyond their individual corporate ledger books in evaluating their collective self-interest:

> Industry and business have not yet seen that they need to consolidate their position; that that is a deeper and more vital problem of existence than that of raising the quota of sales of a specific company.[22]

A year later, in a brand new magazine, *Public Opinion Quarterly,* PR specialist Morton Long reinforced the idea that past thinking was insufficient as a way of coping with the political realities of the time. The "old easy reliance on the professionals of politics to temper the tides of popular unrest," he observed, "has become increasingly untrustworthy" as a way of handling antibusiness sentiment. "The dominant popular ideology," as he termed New Deal politics, "has become increasingly incompatible with the emerging character of modern industry." It was essential, he concluded, for business, as a whole, to come to its own defense.

A similar refrain was heard from T. J. Ross. "No corporation can any longer consider itself an economic entity sufficient and responsible unto itself alone," he cautioned. "It is a unit of the industry of which it is a part" and is an extension of "the whole of private enterprise." In the face of antibusiness turmoil, he argued, businessmen could no longer afford to remain aloof. They must study the "trends of popular thought," take advantage of up-to-date social scientific tools, and learn to act accordingly.

> If industry is to be successful in dealing with public opinion . . . it must learn the language of the people, it must consider the study of public opinion as important as any phase of its operations. It must recognize that public opinion can be measured, and utilize the increasingly scientific methods developing today for gauging it.[23]

Others were more apocalyptic in their descriptions of the crisis and in their call to arms. "American industry—the whole capitalist system"—wrote Byoir in 1938, "lives in the shadow of a volcano. That volcano is public opinion. It is in eruption. Within an incredibly short time it will destroy business or it will save it."[24]

Carl W. Ackerman, dean of the Columbia School of Journalism, seconded the thought. "Every citizen in the United States today," he announced, "is participating in a world war of ideas. This war may be as destructive of property rights, individual freedom, institutions and family life as a war involving material resources. In this modern warfare," he concluded, "the printed and spoken word . . . [is] the decisive weapon."[25]

Writing in *Public Relations* magazine, Colby Dorr Dam voiced his concern that American business was losing the *war of ideas.* "The present news situation," he contended, "is a clear threat to the life of capitalism." Echoing Ross's argument that corporations needed to learn to speak plainly in the people's language, Dorr Dam cited the problematic way that business news was customarily reported.

> Profits are news; and millions of wage earners read this news. Financial news is written from the stockholder's rather than the mass man's point of view. . . . These stories give little attention to profit for labor or the average consumer. Wherever finance is mentioned the stockholder is king. As a result both organized labor and the mass man too often think of large industry as a bottomless gold mine.[26]

Suggesting a strategic shift in rhetoric, *Fortune* magazine editorialized that big business should begin to frame itself less as a money-making apparatus and more as a "public utility," a battery of institutions that exists primarily to serve the needs of society. The corporate sector needed to persuade people that "Business is not just a phenomenon on the surface of American life: that it is American life; that it is to the people essentially what the Conquest or the Church was to people of other ages."[27]

Business journalist Glenn Griswold, writing in *Public Opinion Quarterly,* argued that businessmen must abandon their pie-in-the-sky hopes for the public becoming conservative again and electing a Republican president, for rolling back "social legislation," and for "turn[ing] the clock backward [to] abolish bureaus [and] return[ing] some considerable distance toward the economic simplicity of the past."[28]

What was needed, Griswold maintained, was for business to take on the New Deal on its own ground. Businesses, he counseled, should claim the social values of the New Deal as their own. They must also present, and provide tangible evidence for, the argument that corporate America—not the government—was the surest route to safeguarding the general well-being of society. A public relations program must be established, he wrote, "which truly brings corporations in team with public welfare and a sense of obligation to employees, home community and stockholders."[29]

Another approach to corporate PR was suggested by Raymond Moley, a former member of FDR's Brain Trust. In the Roosevelt administration, Moley had always been a conservative voice.[30] He believed, wrote historian James MacGregor Burns, "in a kind of benevolent partnership between government and business that would leave capitalists with power and status while achieving efficiency through national planning, and ending the aimlessness and wastefulness of free competition and rugged individualism."[31] As Roosevelt moved to the left, assuming a more censorious tone toward business, Moley had indignantly resigned from the administration and become an advocate for corporate America. "Business," he wrote, "can be induced to promote vital challenges to government in the forward march of social and economic well being." To do so, however, business needed to advertise "a broader social vision," one that would "again and again make it clear that our economic system and our political system are essentially opposite sides of the same coin." Toward this end, Moley suggested that advertising and public relations campaigns must be staged that continuously demonstrated a connection between business enterprise and democracy, between corporate enterprise and the social needs of the community.[32] In brief, the task before capitalism was to learn to use what one PR specialist described as "words and phrases which summarize the unspoken impressions and hopes of millions."[33]

■　　■　　■　　■　　■

By 1937, this kind of thinking was becoming commonplace. When Paul Nystrom, professor of marketing at Columbia University, surveyed 442 industrial leaders that year, he discovered that "economic research and public relations now outweigh the other branches of research" going on in American corporations. "Public relations," he inferred from his study of business opinions, "is easily the most important field of study for most of the large corporations at the present time."[34]

In an effort to gain a better understanding of the public mind for corporate clients, the opinion research industry—relatively small to that point—began to thrive and was on the verge of becoming a diagnostic fixture of American life. The appearance of *Public Opinion Quarterly*—founded in 1937 by Professor Harwood Childs of Princeton—was another reflection of a growing interest in the study, measurement, and management of public opinion.

"Business smells bad to the public," declared a writer in *TIDE*, an advertising, public relations, and merchandising trade journal. By November 1937, however, things were changing; "there was evidence everywhere that business had finally gotten on the ball."[35] In a special "Report to Executives," *Business Week* concurred and emphasized the significance of this development:

> Out of the news, week by week, comes evidence of the importance of sound public relations in American corporate business and of the awakened interest of its executives in the problem of gaining public good-will. . . . Read thoughtfully, this evidence shows that a solution of the problem is vital not merely to sales but to the existence of our present system. . . .
>
> The public mass is in a resentful mood. Politicians of all colors are ready to manipulate this feeling for vote production and a crackpot fringe is biding its time again to drum up the fuzzy-wuzzies.
>
> Business cannot afford to allow these forces to operate unchecked. This involves actions proving consideration for the public, not merely words professing solicitude.[36]

A sampling of this newfound religion can be gleaned from the words of Lewis H. Brown, president of the Johns-Manville Corporation, who talked of the need to cultivate in children a vision of corporate America as the key to America's past and its future. "We must, with moving pictures and other educational material," he implored, "carry into the schools of the generation of tomorrow an interesting story of the part that science and industry have played in creating a more abundant life for those who are fortunate to live in this great country of ours." Business, he maintained, can only blame itself if this message isn't being sent.

> After all, it is our own fault if three-fourths of the teachers in our schools and colleges have never been inside a factory. It is our fault if all they know about business and industry is what they read in books . . . [by] Karl Marx or Henry George.[37]

A similar sense of precariousness was evident in the words of Paul Garrett, who headed General Motors'(GM's) increasingly busy Public Relations division. Facing widely publicized sit-down strikes by workers against GM plants, Garrett spoke of the need for business to build bridges that would encourage middle-class consumers to see an identity of interests between themselves and American industries.

> The challenge that faces us is to shake off our lethargy and through public relations make the American plan of industry stick. For unless the contributions of the system are explained to consumers in terms of their own interest, the system itself will not stand against the storm of fallacies that rides the air.[38]

An example of what Garrett meant when he called for publicity that would underscore "the contributions of the system" was GM's traveling exhibit, "Parade of Progress," which made a 20,000-mile tour of the United States in 1936. Organized at every stop by GM dealers and the local chambers of commerce, the caravan offered a rendition of America's past and future that equated progress and social change with the emergence of new technologies. At a moment when many looked toward "the people" and "government planning" as the forces that would guide America's future, the "Parade of Progress" dramatized a picture of things to come that would be technologically determined, engineered by the genius of corporate science. *Previews of Science*, a film show—featuring the familiar voice of radio commentator Lowell Thomas—tied the whole exhibit together with an inspirational narrative of America's future. This future was not defined by governmental programs or by systematic economic planning, but by the unregulated and beneficent activities of American corporate enterprise. Big business became the hero in this epic tale of progress.

GM was not alone. Public relations efforts, offering an implicit defense of the free enterprise system and linking business with the public interest, were simultaneously being mounted by other giants of American industry: E. I. DuPont; General Electric; Goodyear; the Aluminum Company of America; IBM; Westinghouse; and, of course, American Telephone and Telegraph, the company that discovered the value of PR at a time when most other corporations were still damning the public.[39]

This novel trend was noted at the time by Walker and Sklar, the two *TIDE* magazine reporters who became corporate America's Boswell as business moved to embrace the idea of public relations. Their 1938 book, *Business Finds Its Voice: Management's Effort to Sell the Business Idea to the Public,* continues to be the most fully itemized contemporaneous account of big business' public relations activities during these critical years of change.

Co-opting the vernacular of political activism that marked the New Deal period—as in the labor *movement,* the consumer *movement,* and the cooperative *movement*—Walker and Sklar entitled the shift in business thinking the public relations *movement.* Through linguistic analogy, they sought to portray a bond of social concern that connected big business' PR activities with the activities of Americans who were engaged in a politics that was, as a rule, diametrically opposed to customary corporation policies.

The attempt to establish a synergy between corporate enterprise and popular aspiration moved far beyond the public relations efforts of individual corporations. From the mid-thirties onward—particularly following FDR's overwhelming reelection in 1936—the need of businesses to "consolidate their position," as Bernays had put it, spawned public relations efforts in which corporations looked beyond their own parochial interests and joined together as a united front. The guiding force behind this corporate collaboration was the

National Association of Manufacturers (NAM), an industrial trade organization that figured heavily in Walker and Sklar's story.

NAM was not a new organization. Founded in January 1895, the group had been the conservative voice of business for decades. During that time, NAM had done little to smooth relations between big business and the public. If anything, it was contemptuous of the public, reliably opposed to unions, old-age pensions, health care programs, and governmental relief programs of any kind. Even as the Great Depression drove millions into destitution, NAM president John Edgerton continued to issue public statements that typified the image of the insensitive businessman. When municipal governments considered establishing relief programs following the crash, all that NAM worried about was the extent to which these efforts might expand the powers of government and, hence, encroach on the privileges of private wealth. At its national conference, held at New York's Waldorf Astoria Hotel in October 1930, the following proclamation suggests the standard contempt the organization expressed toward the suffering of the average American.

> The popular mind does not readily grasp the fact that the appetite of government for power expands with feeding far faster than do its muscles develop for the increasing weights of responsibility. The crowds who clamor for "hand-outs" in various forms from the public pantry are made to believe that it is all at the expense of the very rich and is therefore, a legitimate and just process of redistributing wealth and equalizing opportunity. They do not see the bejeweled hand of greed and graft concealed in the deceiving glove of imitative human interest.[40]

Statements such as this drove NAM to the brink of extinction. Whatever their inner convictions, few businessmen were interested in publicly associating themselves with such pronouncements in the midst of so much social misery.

At the gate to the graveyard, however, a palace revolt began, breathing new life into NAM. In December 1931, as business historian Richard Tedlow recounted, Edgerton was ousted by a group of industrialists—members of a private dinner club, the Brass Hats—

who were concerned that because of the economic collapse, "radicals" and "demagogues" threatened to seize control of the nation. They determined that action needed to be taken and NAM needed a new direction.

One of the group, Robert L. Lund—president of Lambert Pharmaceutical Corporation, the makers of Listerine mouthwash replaced Edgerton as president. Familiar with techniques for masking foul odors, Lund was convinced that the aroma of American business demanded improvement. Breaking from the organization's past in September 1933—only six months into FDR's first term—Lund and the new NAM leadership made the decision to launch a public relations campaign to defend business against the growing uproar of criticism.[41] Explaining this decision at NAM's convention in December of that year, Lund evidenced a new awareness of the problem of public opinion that would consume NAM over the next two decades.

> Industry must educate public opinion . . . [A]ny cause must have public opinion behind it to succeed, and while it has such support, any cause is virtually invincible. Industry for years has stood satisfied in its own power and has totally failed in seeking the favor of public opinion. We have nothing to gain by being inarticulate. . . . We must come back to the fundamental fact that unless we reach the people, others will, and the prejudice they create is more than likely to be injurious.

For business to succeed in this public appeal, Lund continued, companies could no longer view themselves as individual economic entities. Inasmuch as the opposition was becoming more and more consolidated—assisted by the agency of the New Deal—it was essential for corporations to meld as a force, to act as one under the banner of "free enterprise." They must see themselves as part of a coherent system.

> [I]t is of paramount importance that industry and commerce pull together, and that close cooperation be set up in order that business as a whole will be able to do its part in setting up sound governmental and economic policies. This means that competition between commercial and industrial organi-

zations must be stopped, and all friction and overlapping effort must be eliminated, and that an authoritative contact be sustained so that it will be of certain these things will be done.[42]

Over the next two years, however, little was done to implement this vision. Relations between business and the Roosevelt administration had not yet reached bottom, and old-guard thinking continued to survive among NAM's membership. By the end of 1935, however, the terrain had significantly shifted. The Supreme Court had ruled the NRA—the centerpiece of New Deal legislation—unconstitutional, and FDR was becoming considerably less conciliatory toward a business establishment that he had hoped would participate under the banner of the NRA's Blue Eagle.

The divisions in American society were growing. The president's oratory assailed the money changers in the temple while it fired hope for the future among ordinary Americans. The peril to the business system, as it had customarily operated, was becoming more palpable.

Resuscitating Lund's idea, his successor as NAM's president, Colby Chester (chairman of the board of General Foods), made the consolidation of corporate America around the issue of public relations his number one priority. Speaking to the Congress of American Industry in 1935, NAM's general counsel, James A. Emery, echoed this imperative and called upon his legions.

This representative gathering is a call to arms. Not to resist physical assault but the march of ideas and theories that steal into the minds of men like a thief in the night. . . . Never before has every form of business been so continuously threatened with the shackles of irrational regulation or back-breaking burdens of taxation.

Do we believe in and intend to retain a system of private enterprise as the best means of social progress? . . .

. . . We live under a government of opinion. Let us enter the lists. . . . Then let us appeal with confidence to every stockholder, every employee, every man and woman who carries the burdens of this hour and lives in the shadow of its great uncertainties, to join in the general assault upon these alien invaders of our national thought that menace the security of our common future.[43]

Industrial leaders, it appears, were listening. Given the severity of the crisis and the growing recognition that something needed to be done to defend their interests, NAM's membership began to grow. Between 1935 and 1941, according to *Fortune* magazine, membership in the organization expanded more than threefold, from 2,500 to 8,000 companies.[44] Beyond "individual company memberships," *Business Week* reported in 1937, NAM had affiliates in twenty-four states and subsumed "several hundred local manufacturers' organizations and many national manufacturing trade associations."[45] Over a six-year period NAM's public relations budgets would escalate from $500,000 to $1 million per year, a tidy sum in those days.[46] This money, it should be added, did not include enormous financial and in-kind contributions from member companies and trade organizations. The phrase *Corporate America* was becoming something more than a theoretical fantasy. Under the leadership of NAM, the management of American businesses—GM, Chrysler, Big Steel, General Electric, Sylvania, E. I. DuPont, Curtis Publishing, General Foods, and so forth—were consolidating into a functional apparatus. Its august mission: to combat the evil of New Deal propaganda, to derail the idea that governmental programs can help bring about social welfare, to win the hearts and minds and imaginations of the American people, and to save the capitalist system.

NAM's task was described this way in a 1936 internal memorandum on NAM activities, coming out of the East Central Regional Office in Detroit.

Public sentiment is everything—with it nothing can fail; without it nothing can succeed! Whether we continue to have a competitive economy depends on what the folks along Main Street think and believe about industry. Right now Joe Doakes—the average man—is a highly confused individual. . . . Industry . . . is faced with the job of re-selling all of the individual Joe Doakes on the advantages and benefits he enjoys under a competitive economy. Talking among ourselves

won't alter public sentiment one iota. We must talk earnestly
about our hopes, achievements, and problems with the man in
the street—in every day language he will understand.[47]

The man who would take charge of this effort was not a traditional captain of industry. He was not a "banker" or a "production
man" or a "lawyer" or an "engineer," as Bruce Barton said, but "a
great showman and trade-association specialist."[48] When Walter
Weisenburger assumed NAM's executive vice-presidency in 1934, the
elevation of "public relations men" to the highest levels of industrial
policy making, had begun. He was the general who would lead the
holy war.

Launched with the assistance of the U.S. Chamber of Commerce—representing small-business and professional men, as NAM
spoke for large manufacturing interests—the war was entitled the
campaign for the "American Way." At the heart of this endeavor stood
the desire to challenge the fundamental social assumptions of the
New Deal and to project a picture of American business as a system
that—through its normal routines—responds to and meets the concerns and aspirations of ordinary Americans. The key was to present
a case for American business not from the customary vantage point
of the stockholder, but from "the mass man's point of view."

An early advertisement, produced for the American Way cam-
paign in 1936, offers a snapshot of NAM's efforts at its inception.
Commandeering the ideal of the "greater good," a central element of
New Deal politics, the ad translated that goal into corporate terms.

WHAT IS YOUR AMERICA ALL ABOUT?
. . . Our American plan of living is simple.
Its ideal—that works—is the greatest good for the greatest number.
You . . . are part owner of the United States, Inc. . . .
Our American plan of living is pleasant.
Our American plan of living is the world's envy.
No nation, or group lives as well as we do. [49]

Despite this sunny rhetoric, NAM had an apocalyptic vision of
American society standing at a fateful juncture, engaged in a battle
between two opposing ideas of democracy, two irreconcilable ways of

life. A 1936 NAM pamphlet—*What Is Your American System All About?*—described the moment as one in which Americans faced a choice between "two kinds of government." In one, "the citizen is supreme and the government obeys his will"; in the other, "the state is supreme and controls the citizen."

> The first is individualistic, the second is collectivistic. In the first, man creates machinery to look after him as a separate, individual entity, and retains the power to run the machinery. In the second, man is but a small cog in the machinery; his desires and will are sacrificed to the state.

Like the New Deal, the American Way laid claim to "the greatest good for the greatest number," but within NAM's ideology, a consequential shift in emphasis had occurred. While New Deal politics maintained that the economic interests of individual businessmen—or of fictive "individuals," such as corporations—must not be permitted to trample the broader needs of the community, NAM's priority was to invert that formula. The individual and individual rights were upheld as society's raisons d'être, while the social interest of the community was relegated to a subordinate status. In NAM's pronouncements "the common good" became a consequence, rather than the goal, of social life.

> Socially, this system preserves freedom of opportunity for the individual to strive, to accumulate, and to enjoy the fruits of his accomplishments. Politically, it results in what we call a "democracy" but what really is a rule of limited powers granted by individuals, through written constitutions, to state and federal governments.[50]

Democracy—which for New Dealers was founded on the precept that government *of the people* must balance economic life to protect the interests of the common good—was being presented in terms that championed the prerogatives of individual entrepreneurs while providing lip service to the interests of society as a whole.

To mount an army to withstand this "collectivistic" current, maintained George Sokolsky, a prominent association spokesman, NAM must reach out and awaken the passions of the middle class.

Your job in crystallizing public opinion nationally is to fight every day, uncompromisingly, fight even if you have to fight your own people, but go out and win the support of the great middle class of Americans who want to be in this war. And who are they? They are the businessmen, small and large. They are the bulk of our clergymen; they are the bulk of our teachers; [and, he added] . . . they are the bulk of our workers.[51]

"The fight must go on, and it must go on until it is won—the fight for private enterprise and liberty for the individual," Sokolsky harangued his audience. But questions lingered as to how this "great middle class of Americans" would be brought to tow, how this "world war of ideas" would effectively be waged. Behind the bombast of "free enterprise" and "individualism," what broad objectives must be most vigorously pursued? What organizational structure would best serve these objectives? What avenues of communications should be employed? And finally, how might NAM devise an effective rhetoric for business to combat the drift of New Deal politics and right itself in the public mind? As the American Way campaign gathered momentum in 1936, it was propelled by a grudging recognition that prior NAM efforts had done little to answer these questions.

■   ■   ■   ■   ■

To cure the middle class of its growing antagonism toward business, NAM's first general objective was to publicize the idea that there is a harmony of interests linking corporate America with the majority of ordinary Americans. An essential element here would be an attempt to use public relations techniques to provoke involuntary mental associations regarding the "inter-relation and inseparability" of the economic principle of "free enterprise" and the political principle of "democracy." As recounted at a NAM Public Relations conference in 1939, the task was to "link free enterprise in the public consciousness with free speech, free press and free religion as integral parts of democracy."[52]

A second objective was to redirect current public thinking about taxes. Since the late eighteenth century, mainstream American society had often been defined by a profound ambivalence toward taxation. "No taxation without representation," of course, had been the battle cry of the Revolution. In the crucible of the New Deal period, however, things had changed. The idea of a progressive income tax, one that assessed taxes according to income—the poor paying less, the rich paying more—had gained ground as a democratic principle. FDR's program to tax the rich underlined the idea that it was the government's role to intervene on behalf of the people, even if that meant encroaching on wealthy Americans who often, in the past, had succeeded in avoiding their share of the burden.

Here, NAM's basic tack would be to refute the notion that taxes were levied primarily at the expense of the rich. "Surveys show," NAM officials reported, that "a tremendous proportion of the people do not realize they pay taxes at all but that, where people do recognize the tax burden, taxes are . . . unpopular." It was necessary, then, to take actions that would "add fuel to the growing fire of resentment" against taxes. This meant talking less about how taxes hurt businessmen and more about the iniquity of "hidden taxes" that hurt everyone—sales taxes and taxes that are passed on to consumers in the prices they pay for goods.[53]

A third objective of the campaign was to deal with the troublesome problem of organized labor. Given the improved footing of unions during this period and the growing public acceptance of collective bargaining rights, NAM had to abandon its vocal animosity toward labor unions in general. A general attack on organized labor would give way to a focus on the problems of "unscrupulous unionism and radicalism," problems that, according to NAM, posed a formidable threat to the American Way.[54]

The fourth broad objective—perhaps the most important of all—was to do battle over the idea of *the future*. By 1936, there was a growing urgency surrounding this issue. Many Americans believed that a process of "socialization" was inevitably under way—that America's future, the future of democracy, and the dream of universal equality all depended on government-assisted social and economic planning. Even in the business community, there were voices arguing that corporate America must accept "whatever measure of socialization has been accomplished and adjust to living with it."[55]

Facing defeatism in their own ranks, NAM's public relations leadership decided it must address the question of history: the history of the future and the forces that would drive it. The problem of the future would be addressed on two levels. First, NAM would have to project images of the future in which capitalist industry, not government, was positioned as the motor force of change. This task needed to be performed with an eloquence capable of competing with the New Deal vision of the future.

Second, with so many young Americans leaning toward the left, it was important to make special efforts to reach out to "the oncoming generation," to convince them "that people who preach that opportunity [through private enterprise] is gone are wrong."[56]

"The high school and college graduates of today will shape the future economic and social structure of our country—will decide 'Which Way America?'" explained a 1936 pamphlet from NAM's Detroit Regional Office.[57] With so much at stake, another NAM publication spelled out, school programs, which were designed to impress "youthful minds in the formative stage," would be indispensable.[58]

To promote these objectives, it was necessary to build an organization that would operate simultaneously on two important fronts. On the one hand, it was essential for NAM to convince its corporate membership to buy into the importance of public relations and to participate in the planning and deployment of the American Way endeavor. A second organizational task was to establish local mechanisms for NAM to filter its campaign into communities throughout the United States. Strategies on both fronts were instructed by experiences gained during the First World War.

In terms of mobilizing industrial corporations behind a common cause, the closest available model was the War Industries Board, which had coordinated industrial production as the United States entered the war. Established by Chester (of General Foods) in 1938, NAM's Public Relations Advisory Board performed a similar function.

Made up of representatives from the nation's major corporations—GM, General Foods, Standard Oil of New Jersey, Armstrong Cork, R. J. Reynolds, Eastman Kodak, E. I. DuPont, McGraw-Hill Publishing, American Cyanamid, Lambert Pharmaceuticals, the Canada Dry Corporation, and so forth—the committee was designed to ensure that NAM and its powerful corporate members were all on the same page when it came to public relations strategy. Chaired by

GM's Paul Garrett and reporting to Weisenburger at their regular meetings, the Advisory Board carried on detailed exchanges regarding activities under way and plans for the future.[59] Never before had corporate America engaged in a comparable effort to coordinate and redirect the thinking of the nation.

The organizational approach on a community level took its inspiration from Creel's World War I Committee on Public Information apparatus. As outlined by James P. Selvage, the director of NAM's Public Relations Department and aide-de-camp to Weisenburger, the "organization and operation of a community program" began with the selection of a "Special Committee on Public Information" (CPI). Each local CPI should be made up of prominent business and professional leaders, "representative citizens known to be interested in the subject [of private enterprise] and who have the proper contacts to raise funds" to forward the campaign. The role of these leaders, he explained, would be to recruit those in their community who were not yet involved, and—in order to assist their efforts—to "[r]etain the services of a full time Public Relations Director" to oversee operations on a day-to-day level.[60]

Special CPIs, in short, were created to ensure that national efforts would be realized on a local level. It was the CPIs' responsibility, for example, to see that newspapers carried positive stories about local industries and to invite publishers, editors, and business writers to NAM-sponsored luncheons. The CPIs were also expected to arrange for nationally produced NAM media to be distributed on a community level.

Local educational institutions were also a domain of the special CPIs. The CPIs should see to it "that school libraries have material available for reading, the material presenting industry's viewpoint." The same held for "public libraries." In both settings, NAM materials geared toward young people should be distributed and displayed.

Beyond schools and libraries, a number of other local arenas for communicating the American Way were suggested. Following patterns established by the Four-Minute Men during the war, "Civic Clubs," "Women's Groups," "Negro Groups," "Foreign Language Groups," and "Motion Picture Theatres" were cited as appropriate venues for speakers to carry on the crusade. "Employer-Employee" relations groups should be encouraged, and businesses should hold

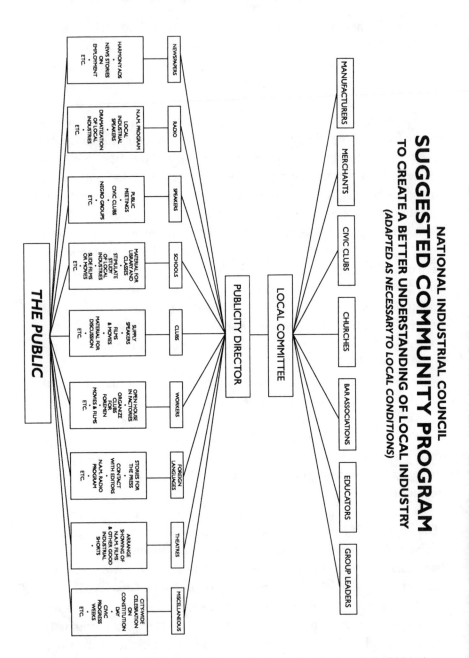

Facsimile of a 1937 instructional chart offering a plan for how to build local programs for preaching a pro-business gospel. The National Industrial Council was a public relations wing of the National Association of Manufacturers. COURTESY OF HAGLEY MUSEUM AND LIBRARY/YOFAXRAPS

"open houses" for the surrounding community. To influence the direction of informal discussions, CPIs provided "Industrial Facts" sheets to "people who supervise employees and labor" in factories. These fact sheets were designed to provide foremen with useful answers to "the average question" coming from the workers they supervised.[61]

Consolidating these local efforts, there was also a national media strategy. All available avenues were exploited: radio, motion pictures, slide shows with prerecorded narrations, newspapers and magazines, and even a World's Fair.

To combat the ethos of the New Deal effectively, NAM also had to employ new rhetorical styles. It needed to cultivate approaches to the public that would make its ideas not only palatable, but credible and appealing. The extent to which NAM's efforts succeeded, at least during the 1930s, is questionable. Yet an examination of this change in media presentation reveals new directions that, over a period of decades, would have a profound impact on American culture and society.

Before 1935, NAM's public rhetoric was essentially a rhetoric of assertion. In magisterial pronouncements and with little sensitivity to the broader human context, the organization repeatedly announced its unwavering commitment to the "Preservation of a Free Enterprise System." As the cult of prosperity vanished and new ways of thinking took flight, fewer and fewer Americans were listening.

While post–1935 NAM publicity continued to glorify the private enterprise system, its inflection began to change in consequential ways. To some extent, the change in tone reflected public relations thinking that had gained ground since the U.S. entry into World War I. Much of the material, for example, was of a visual nature. It also took rhetorical cues from the publicity work of the New Deal.

With new vigor and creativity, NAM pursued strategies for dealing with the press. Beyond a news service that distributed news stories with an "industrial viewpoint" throughout the country, the association established a multipronged syndication service that endeavored to place its feature materials in one newspaper in every town or locale throughout the country. These included a regular "philosophic-humorous . . . homespun" newspaper feature called Uncle Abner Says.[62]

Wealth of America More Widely Spread Than in Any Other Country

Distribution of Millions of Autos, Radios, Refrigerators and Homes Would Have Been Impossible Unless Bulk of Income Went for Wages

Observation shows that the productivity of the American worker, reinforced with power and with improved machinery, is the greatest in the world, and that the income thus produced has been widely spread among all classes of the population.

If this were not the case, the widespread distribution of millions of automobiles, electricity, refrigerators, telephones, radios, and individually owned houses which actually took place would have proved impossible. There would not have been the money to purchase them.

On the face of things, the absurdity of the mis-statements that 2 per cent of the people receive 60 to 80 per cent of our national income is apparent.

As a matter of fact, if such a poor distribution of wealth existed, the very mass-production and mass-consumption of goods, in which the United States has led foreign countries, would have been impossible. Our great plants, our millions of employed workers, would have been impossible.

In other words, the soap-box orators, who have been poisoning the public mind with false statistics, have been trying to explain away a plain truth.

And this truth is almost directly opposed to the false doctrines which they preach.

As the Brookings Institution of Washington has reported, those who work for a living receive as wages about 85 per cent of all the national income.

The remaining 15 per cent goes as a return on capital investments, MORE THAN HALF of which is owned by INDIVIDUALS OF MODERATE INCOME who own stock in our corporations. Some corporations have more small stockholders than employees.

The figures are proved by a study of the Federal income tax statistics.

As a matter of fact, those receiving incomes of $5,000 a year or more in 1933 got less than 10 per cent of the entire national income.

Those with incomes above $100,000 in 1932 and 1933 had less than 1 per cent of the national income.

It has further been figured that if in 1933 the entire income of all those receiving five thousand dollars and more had been confiscated by the government and redistributed evenly to the remaining 120,000,000 persons, each person would have received only $35 more each year.

Our real job is not of re-dividing national income, but of increasing the total of our wealth so that we will have more to divide. American experience shows that most of the increases in our national income will go into wages.

Before wealth can be distributed it must first be created. Every employed worker is a partner in the creation of this wealth. And any experiment which holds back recovery prevents the creation of new national wealth, cuts the returns to the employee and employer alike, leaves us less wealth to share, and prevents the return of the jobless to regular employment.

Sudden Shortening of Work Week Endangers All Jobs

Walk through a 10-cent store and see the amazing things you can buy for a dime, and try to remember what your grandfather paid for similar articles. Then ask yourself if you believe all these things can be made so much more cheaply that everybody who makes them can have a one-third boost in wages, on one day's notice, or even on a year's notice, and still make the things to sell for a dime.

Ask yourself if the goods you manufacture would stand such a hike in costs and still find consumers ready to buy.

Do you think automobiles can suddenly be made a third to a quarter cheaper? Or do you think that the result of sudden shortening of hours with the same pay basis would be to increase the price of the cars so that a great number of people would suddenly discover they could not afford to buy one?

That would mean that fewer cars would be made, which would mean that soon more people would be out of work, as the same effect was felt in other industries. We should be much worse off than when we started.

That is what would result from the suggested five-day, six-hour work week of 30 hours. If it came of a sudden instead of through normal processes as past cuts in the hours of work have come.

NOTE!

The article in the previous issue of this service, "Everyone Works for the Tax Collector," is available upon request in pamphlet form for direct distribution in response to a demand for preparation in this form.

Many Workers Are Owners

There is no such thing in America as an investors group, as a class distinct from those who work for a living. The reason it is impossible to make any such class distinction is that millions of citizens, wage and salary earners, also are investors.

They are owners directly through ownership of homes, real estate, bonds and stocks, or indirectly through savings bank accounts and insurance policies. Both the banks and the insurance companies invest in securities, and when securities are overtaxed or made worthless by legislation, then those who have bank accounts or policies are the sufferers. A number of our large corporations have more shareholders than employees.

These workers, through their thrift, are receiving, in addition to their wages and salaries, a share of the profits of industry. Damage industry and you hurt all who are dependent upon industry for a living.

Great Messages by American Patriots

Abraham Lincoln, who rose from a laborer to become one of the immortal figures of American history, said:

"The prudent, penniless beginner in the world labors for wages for awhile, saves a surplus with which to buy tools or land for himself, then labors for himself another while, and at length hires another new beginner to help him. This is the just and generous, and prosperous system, which opens the way to all, gives hope to all, and consequent energy, and progress, and improvement of condition to all."

These pro-business articles, already laid out for insertion in company publications, were distributed to employers around the nation by the National Association of Manufacturers during the late 1930s. Written to convince workers that unregulated capitalist enterprise was in their best interest, the articles responded to prevalent Depression-era issues, including the uneven distribution of wealth, antagonisms between the interests of the working class and those of the owning class, and so forth. COURTESY OF HAGLEY MUSEUM AND LIBRARY

A cartoon service, serving more than three thousand weeklies, disseminated cartoons that humorized a NAM way of seeing. In one cartoon, one encounters a picture of "the Forgotten Man," a popular symbol of those devastated by the depression. In criticizing the ways of big business, FDR—among others—often evoked his name. In this scene, however, the Forgotten Man is represented as a tattered and impoverished tax payer, his pockets completely fleeced. Fat cats reveling in the background, those who have picked him clean, are labeled "political spenders."[63]

There was also a Ripley's Believe It or Not-type feature called the Pocketbook of Knowledge. Boldly illustrated pages combined inter-

Two examples of *The Pocketbook of Knowledge,* syndicated as part of the National Association of Manufacturers's public relations efforts during the late 1930s. Amid a familiar "Ripley's Believe It or Not" kind of feature, amazing facts were presented about private enterprise and the American Way of Life. COURTESY OF HAGLEY MUSEUM AND LIBRARY

esting facts about the world ("THE FAVORITE SMOKE OF THE WOMEN OF BURMA IS THIS OVERSIZED CIGARETTE, TWICE AS BIG AS A CIGAR"; "THE 'SCOLD'S BRIDLE' WAS USED IN MEDIEVAL LONDON TO PUNISH WOMEN WHO GOSSIPED OR SCOLDED TOO MUCH . . . THE 'BRIDLE' FITTED SO CLOSE OVER THE MOUTH IT PERMITTED AN OFFENDER TO UTTER NOTHING MORE ANNOYING THAN A GRUNT"; and so forth) with facts calculated to present American private enterprise as the most advantageous economic system in the world: "CHILD LABOR? A RECENT SURVEY OF 1,572 LEADING MANUFACTURERS SHOWED THAT WITH A TOTAL EMPLOYMENT OF 2,900,000 WORKERS ONLY 28 CHILDREN UNDER 16 YEARS OF AGE WERE EMPLOYED!"; or "IN THE UNITED STATES THERE IS ONE AUTOMOBILE FOR EVERY 5 PEOPLE . . . FRANCE HAS ONE FOR EVERY 22; ENGLAND, ONE FOR EVERY 23; ITALY, ONE FOR EVERY 109. . . . POLAND CAN BOAST BUT *ONE CAR* FOR EVERY 1,284 OF ITS POPULATION!" Other amazing facts were intended to educate uninformed people about the "hidden taxes" they routinely paid: "IF YOU SMOKE ONE PACK OF CIGARETTES A DAY, THE FEDERAL TAX ALONE AMOUNTS TO ALMOST *$22.00 A YEAR*!"[64]

On the serious side, a team of six professedly independent scholars took turns writing a daily syndicated column on economics for 265 newspapers around the country. In the column, "You and Your Nation's Affairs," the six (who included faculty members from Princeton, Vanderbilt, NYU, Stanford, and the University of Southern California, as well as Ernest Minor Patterson, president of the American Academy of Political and Social Science) routinely blamed America's economic woes on misguided New Deal policies, arguing that unregulated business was the surest passageway to recovery. Paying heed to rules governing "third-party" PR strategies, NAM's hand in each of these features was not overtly acknowledged.[65] Newspaper publishers, many of whom were antagonistic to the New Deal, kept the secret and happily accepted these features for publication.

NAM also published a *You and Industry* series of booklets for distribution in schools, colleges, and public libraries. Guided by the dictum to "speak plainly, in the people's language," these booklets were, as NAM described them, attractively designed and "easy to understand." Aimed at the younger generation, the *You and Industry* series, as Weisenburger explained, exemplified "the heart and soul of the whole campaign"; they were meant to link the sentiments of "the individual with the industrial system."[66]

This was also the intent of a "newsweekly for boys and girls" that began publication in 1937. Disseminated with the cooperation of schools, *Young America* was a dramatic attempt to battle for the hearts and minds of America's young people. Articles, such as "Your Neighborhood Bank," "Building Better Americans," and "The Business of America's People Is Selling," offered children a weekly user-friendly portrayal of capitalism, a system that was portrayed to look after them, their families, their communities, and their interests.[67] With tens of thousands of individual subscribers and copies distributed in 70,000 schools, *Young America* was seen as a vehicle for carrying "the story of American industry into those places where the story is most needed—the school and the home."[68]

"Used by thousands of teachers for classroom assignments and collateral reading," NAM claimed, "it counteracts the radical propa-

ganda which is finding its way into our American institutions."
Explaining its purpose to prospective sponsors, *Young America* presented itself as the tonic that would lure children away from the trou-
bling political tendencies of the time in which they were growing up.

> Strange—that American industry worries about today's radi-
> cals—with never a thought of what today's youth will think
> about American industry TOMORROW. . . . One million
> youngsters will come of age this year. . . . A large percentage
> of these youngsters have no idea "what America is all about."
> Many have warped conceptions of the American system.
> Some are out-and-out communists . . . YOUNG AMERICA
> urges industry to tell its message to boys and girls—whether
> the medium be YOUNG AMERICA or several other juvenile
> publications. . . . [Y]outhful minds in the formative stage are
> more receptive to your message.[69]

Mimicking a documentary approach to communication that, as
William Stott argued, defined much of thirties culture, NAM also
engaged in the production of documentary films for distribution to
schools, movie theaters, and other public settings. Distributed by
Paramount Pictures, many of these films assumed a rousing inspirational tone. In ten-minute films like *America Marching On,* epochal
narrations by Lowell Thomas—and other conservative jawsmiths as
well—trumpeted the story of "America marching upward and onward
to higher standards of living, greater income for her people, and more
leisure to enjoy the good things of life as the greatest industrial
system the world has ever seen began to develop."[70] Here was a tale of
uninterrupted scientific progress, of a history driven by the genius of
American industry and by its stunning record of technological
achievements.[71] *The people,* who in much New Deal publicity were portrayed as the dynamic backbone of democracy, here assumed the role
of fortunate recipients, individuals who simply profited from the
largesse of a free enterprise system.

William Bird, a historian of film and television, wrote that during
the late 1930s, the propaganda of American businesses increasingly
moved from a "rhetorical" to a "dramatic" idiom. In their search for "the

most expeditious way of asserting their social and political leadership," more and more companies sought to convey "the personal meaning of corporate enterprise" through the vehicle of dramatic entertainments.[72]

In NAM's public relations activities from 1935 onward, the employment of dramatic formats was a conspicuous element. Much of NAM's publicity assumed the format of situation comedy and drama. To some extent, this general shift had been anticipated by theorists of social psychology going back to Gustave Le Bon.

"The imagination of crowds" Le Bon had argued in 1895, is most efficiently stirred when ideas are transmitted dramatically. "For this reason," he wrote, "theatrical representations . . . always have an enormous influence on crowds."[73] Walter Lippmann developed this idea in much greater detail in 1922. Inspired by the example of Hollywood, he maintained that drama is a powerful tool of persuasion because it supplies its audience with readily available "handles of identification," ways of seeing themselves in relation to the ideas being presented.

> We have to take sides. We have to be able to take sides. In the recesses of our being we must step out of the audience on to the stage, and wrestle as the hero for the victory of good over evil. We must breathe into the allegory the breath of life.[74]

In NAM's publicity from the mid-thirties forward, these ideas would come to fruition as an earmark of the way that big business would increasingly present itself to ordinary Americans. NAM's social philosophy, its long-standing commitment to unencumbered corporate enterprise, would continue, but it would be assisted by a highly personalized idiom, often through family dramas.

Roy Stryker, epitomizing the outlook of New Deal publicity, instructed his photographers to draw out the "social forces" that are "present in a scene." Within the lives of the ordinary Americans being photographed, Stryker believed, the overarching conditions of society would become more evident.[75] FDR, in his fireside chats, also painted in broad stroke. Though he assumed a personal tone with his listeners, he encouraged them to see themselves and their circumstances in relation to the world at large.

NAM's dramatic publicity proceeded from the opposite direction. It tended to reduce all questions to family and interpersonal situations. In its approach to telling business's story, it made the individual and the personal more prominent and diminished broader social ways of looking at the world. Even the division between wage labor and capital was likely to be presented as an easily resolved disagreement between a patient and understanding father and a well-meaning, but misguided son.

This penchant for burying social and economic issues under layers of highly personalized drama was palpable in *The American Family Robinson*, a fifteen-minute weekly radio program produced by NAM, beginning in 1935, and distributed, free of charge, to radio networks and local stations throughout the country. The program, it was explained at a March 1935 meeting of NAM's CPI, was intended to present "industry's principles against an entertaining background of family life and humor."[76] At that time, the program was already being carried by 211 radio stations, "48 NBC and Columbia chain stations."

The American Family Robinson chronicled the lives of an apparently typical American family. There was Luke and Myra Robinson and their two kids, Betty and Bob, and a number of stock characters (Dick Collins, Professor Broadbelt, Margolies, and others) who provided the program with its necessary political archetypes. A NAM rundown of the program identified some of the characters and enumerated their implicit dramatic objectives:

> Luke, the sanely philosophical editor of the Centerville Herald, espouses a fair deal for business and industry. There's Betty and Dick in love to bring romance in; Professor Broadbelt, prototype of the panacea peddler . . . and Mrs. Robinson who always brings to bear the leveling influence of a woman's judgement.

"All this," the text continued, "is made interesting, alive and tells industry's story so that it gets a hearing from the mass mind in understandable terms."[77]

An unpublished NAM scenario related one particular series of episodes:

> The comparatively peaceful life at Centerville is suddenly disrupted by a bad accident at Markham's furniture plant. Sev-

eral men are hurt and the occasion is seized by some as an opportunity for rioting. Bedlam breaks loose and the town is in an uproar. Markham doesn't know the cause of the accident and this . . . only serves to inflame the growing animosity against him.

Luke Robinson, editor of the *Centerville Herald*, comes forward as "Markham's only champion." For this, he is vilified by the community, "accused of being paid by Markham to hide the true facts of the accident." All Centerville is against Luke and Mr. Markham. The Bridge Club boycotts their weekly get-together at Mrs. Robinson's.

"The scene shifts to the meeting of the Friends of the Downtrodden. Bob [Luke Robinson's son] has prevailed upon his father to attend. Betty [Luke's daughter] is also there to hear Dick [her romantic interest] . . . deliver his paper on his idea of a future Utopia." Suddenly, Dick's presentation is "interrupted by Margolies, the society's chief trouble maker."

Margolies tears into Mr. Robinson for supporting Markham. "Robinson replies that all the known facts about the accident have been disclosed in the Herald but that the blame has not yet been determined." Margolies and the Friends of the Downtrodden accuse Robinson of being "a tool of the interests" (a euphemism for big money).

After much Sturm und Drang, the confrontation leads to a Saturday night "trial of Citizens of Centerville vs. Markham," held at the town hall. The issue of "the accident" has disappeared, and the trial is now about the oppression of Markham's workers. Miraculously, Markham is not only vindicated, but is revealed as a munificent benefactor. Though his "factory has been running at a loss for some time," he has continued to keep workers on the payroll. The town ends up giving Markham an ovation.

Following all this, Dick and Betty—who had had a spat over the Markham matter—are reconciled. Dick admits that "he has made a fool of himself" as part of the Friends of the Downtrodden and even comes to question whether "reform is a bad thing."

" 'No,' answers Robinson. 'There is a natural evolution of reform which goes on constantly—and reform is good when brought about slowly and under those 'rules of the game' which have proven good and true for three hundred years. But when you scrap the rules and try reform in the twinkling of an eye, a lot of people are going to get terribly and unnecessarily hurt.' "[78] With this statement, the story line ends with Betty and Dick in love once again.

Your Town, a NAM movie produced in 1939, provided a parallel narrative. In this one, "Jerry" gets into trouble with the law when, after joining a crowd to listen to soap-box radicals "shouting 'down with this—and down with that'" in front of the "Manson factory," people start having "fun" by throwing bricks. Later in the film, "Gramps" sits Jerry down for a heart-to-heart talk and sets the lad straight.

"I saw this town grow—I was a part of it all," he tells his grandson. Drawing on a sage memory, he recounts the town's history from the time it was a "vacant lot" until now.

> He recalled the time when Manson came to the little settlement seeking a factory site. He saw the factory constructed— and the town grow up around it. He told Jerry how every man, woman, and child had a stake in the success of that factory.

Jerry, viewers are advised, "learned some American fundamentals and was grateful."[79] As in the Markham factory story, father—or, in this case, grandfather—knew best.

In both stories one sees a fascinating cultural dynamic unfolding, one that remains with us today: the use of idealized renditions of the patriarchal family as a means of upholding and transmitting conservative values. To some extent, the dramatic content of *The American Family Robinson* radio soap opera and the film, *Your Town,* were a repackaging of Victorian morality for modern times. "The family" was reborn as a sentimental archetype, a safe haven from the slings and arrows of a dangerous world. But here, instead of sheltering the sensibilities of an anxious middle class—as had been the case in the late nineteenth century—the family came to the rescue of corporate America, which itself is portrayed as paternally benevolent.

NAM's dramatic personalization of political-economic issues went beyond its restaging of Victorian morality plays on radio and in film. *Flood Tide,* a filmstrip slide show with a synchronized recorded sound track, employed a day-in-the-life motif to instruct audiences about the evils of "hidden" taxation.[80]

A married couple, Paul and Maggie, are shown being inundated by "taxes, taxes, taxes," as the "Tax Grabber"—a froglike creature— "dogged them all day long." The narrator, Paul, describes their life as a perpetual governmental bombardment:

> Each morning a taxed alarm clock woke them up. They brushed their teeth with taxed toothpaste. At night they read by a taxed electric light, listened to a taxed radio.

It sounds as if they're trying "to tax us to death," Maggie sighs. "You can't even dodge taxes by dying," Paul informs her; "157 taxes are buried in your funeral bill."[81] Once again, the personal lives of ordinary Americans provided a serviceable medium for an industry way of seeing.

NAM's vast national billboard campaigns—built around the thematic slogans "There's No Way Like the American Way" and "What's Good for Industry Is Good for You"—offers another case in point. Funded by a $1.2 million gift from the Outdoor Advertising Agencies group (plus another $180,000 in in-kind posting costs from the Campbell-Ewald Company), this 1937–38 campaign put up 20,000 billboards in its first year and 45,000 in the second.[82] By 1938, every location in the country with a population of more than 2,500 had at least one of these signs. "The billboards are one part of the [American Way] campaign everyone sees," commented Weisenburger.[83]

Though the billboards were not narrative in form, each enacted an imaginary dramatic tableau. The posters with the common slogan, "There's No Way Like the American Way," used Rockwellesque family scenes as visual reinforcement for the economic points that were being asserted. One that claimed "WORLD's SHORTEST WORKING HOURS," for example, was illustrated by a family—a smiling mother and father and their two neatly dressed children (a boy and a girl)—enjoying a picnic outing by a pastoral meadow. In the distance, was the automobile that they drove to the outing. Another billboard, proclaiming "WORLD's HIGHEST WAGES," depicts the father kissing his little girl good-bye as the mother—in an apron—looks on admiringly from the door of their cozy suburban home. Perhaps the most well-known in the series—because it became the target of some caustic photographs by Dorothea Lange and Margaret Bourke-White—showed the delighted family tooling along the highway in their shiny new sedan, their little puppy sticking his head out the window. Here the tag line was "WORLD's HIGHEST STANDARD OF LIVING."

Again, as in the family dramas, an economic system was distilled into captivating and safe images of family life. Personalized pleasures in generically middle-class contexts offered a stark, if chirpy, contrast to the socioeconomic renditions of both wretchedness and possibility that formed the stock-in-trade of New Deal communications.

■　　■　　■　　■　　■

The American Way campaign is suggestive on two counts. First, NAM's public relations campaign was not just about NAM. Among NAM's leadership, on its Public Relations Advisory Board, and in the alphabet soup of trade groups that fronted for NAM (the NIC, or National Industrial Council; the NIIC, or National Industrial Information Committee; and so forth) were the leaders of America's largest corporations. Chambers of commerce throughout the country, local appliance and automotive dealerships, and fraternal organizations—the Rotary, for example—also participated in NAM's public relations endeavors. NAM's PR activities, then, provide one with a powerful keyhole through which one can witness the strategic thinking of corporate America, in coalition with a number of other conservative interests, at a moment of extreme crisis. Second, though the American Way campaign's success in reforming the public mind—at least during the late thirties—is arguable, the business-oriented worldview amplified by the campaign would become more and more prevalent in the United States in the period following the Second World War.

A supreme change in this direction came even before the war. It was the 1939 New York World's Fair, "The World of Tomorrow" as it was called. More than any publicity effort of the decade, the fair provided corporate America with a resounding opportunity to respond to the political hazards of the moment and to the nettlesome publicity of the New Deal.

In describing medieval carnivals, Mikhail Bakhtin maintained that these yearly revelries were characterized by what he termed a

arti•FACT

In 1937, the National Association of Manufacturers launched a nationwide billboard campaign designed to combat the New Deal's economic activism and to prompt mental associations between popular visions of *the good life* and the idea of an unregulated corporate enterprise system. The billboards were placed in every community in the United States with a population of 2,500 or more.

Dire social realities and persistent economic misery, however, contradicted the chirpy claims of the billboard campaign at every turn. These observable contradictions became a favorite theme of photographers who documented NAM's "There's no way like the American Way" billboards in settings that silently subverted the campaign's intended message. Figure 1, above right, is Margaret Bourke-White's famous *Life* magazine photo, "After the Time of the Louisville Flood." The other photograph, of a NAM billboard along a desolate stretch of Highway 99 in California [Figure 2, below right], was taken by Dorothea Lange on assignment for the FSA.

NOTE: As this book went into production, an ironically colorized version of "After the Louisville Flood" was created for use on the cover. In this computerized reinterpretation, the NAM billboard was cheerily colorized, while the stark reality of people on the relief line remained in documentary-style black and white.

Time Inc., which owns the original Bourke-White photograph (until copyright finally runs out in A.D. 2012), refused to grant permission for such use of their picture, citing it as one of the corporation's "most valued images" and noting that such images are never allowed to appear on covers of publications that are not produced by Time Incorporated. Colorizations of *Life* magazine photos, they added, are "not ever" sanctioned.

Conversely, FSA photographs—such as the one that now graces the book's cover—are, and have always been, "public domain." Produced under federal auspices on behalf of the American people, these pictures belong to everyone and may be used without restriction. In the genesis of this book's cover, at least, the platitude that the private enterprise system champions artistic creativity, and ensures the free flow of ideas, is thrown dramatically into question.

ARCHIE BISHOP

"double life." On the one hand, the festivities acknowledged and paid tribute to the hierarchy of the "official" order. On the other, within a highly ritualized symbolism, they made space for a worldview in which that hierarchy was turned on its head, where ordinary people and their utopian imaginations ruled. Amid the carnival, for a fleeting moment, there was an exhilarating aura of "change and renewal," a "temporary suspension of all hierarchic distinctions and barriers," a lifting of the "norms and prohibitions of usual life."[84]

This tension also characterized the 1939 World's Fair. Though situated in a world where social distinctions continued to be marked, much of the fair's rhetoric projected a fiercely democratic outlook. Seconding the New Deal's sociological symbolism, the World of Tomorrow presented itself—above all—as a celebration of the people, observed historian Warren Susman in an evocative essay on the fair. "It insisted it was the People's Fair and developed itself for the average American."[85]

In public pronouncements, Grover A. Whalen—the fair's president—stressed this point repeatedly. "This is your Fair, built for you, and dedicated to you," he informed visitors in his preamble to the *Official Guide Book*. "[T]he Fair was built for and dedicated to the people.

FIGURE 1. COPYRIGHT © TIME, INC.

FIGURE 2.

It was built to delight and instruct them," he would later assert.[86]

When FDR addressed the multitude at the fair's opening cere-
monies, this spiritual bond between the fair and the principle of the
greater good was there for all to see.

All who come to this World's Fair in New York . . . will receive the heartiest of welcomes. They will find that the eyes of the United States are fixed on the future. Our wagon is hitched to a star. But it is a star of good will, a star of progress for mankind, a star of greater happiness and less hardship, a star of international good will, and, above all, a star of peace. May the months to come carry us forward in the rays of that hope. I hereby dedicate the New York World's Fair of 1939 and declare it open to all mankind.[87]

Yet the World's Fair also lived a second life, one dominated by economic more than social considerations. The success of the fair depended upon the participation of exhibitors, and while planners spoke of a desire to be "fully representative of community interests," it was also true that most of these interests didn't have the means to build elaborate exhibits. "[T]he Fair should have included the cooperative movement, the granges and farmers' groups, the many useful and important social organizations that make up life in every community," fretted one fair administrator. "But you can't sell space to those folks. They haven't any money."[88]

Those who did have the money were America's large corporations, and the planners' efforts to attract corporate participation were energetic. In addressing the business community, the common good was not the primary selling point of the Fair Corporation. More than anything else in this regard, the World's Fair was offered as an opportunity for business to rescue itself from a profound political crisis. Exploiting its association with populist New Deal values, the fair presented itself as a strategic "public relations" opportunity for businesses to vindicate themselves in the public mind, to restake their claim on America's future, and to counteract the hegemony of the New Deal. This, in large measure, is what exhibitors attempted to do.

For the most part, previous World's Fairs had provided ritualized occasions for companies to show their technologies and products to a receptive middle-class public. Even the 1933–34 "Century of Progress" exposition, held in Chicago, had followed this formula. By the late thirties, however, it was apparent that, for business, a display of wares would not be enough.

The World's Fair's planners emphasized the importance of conveying social ideals. "We believe that the program of the Fair must have an underlying social objective," announced a statement of its founders.

> It must demonstrate the betterment of our future American
> life. It must stress the vastly increased opportunity and the
> already developed mechanical means which this twentieth
> century has brought to the masses for better living and
> accompanying happiness.[89]

"Other fairs have been chiefly concerned with selling products," explained Bernard Lichtenberg, director of public relations for the Fair Corporation. "[T]his one will be chiefly concerned with selling ideas." Characterizing the World of Tomorrow as "the greatest single public relations program in industrial history," Lichtenberg encouraged corporate exhibitors to approach the fair as a dynamic arena for battling the influence of the "New Deal Propaganda."[90]

Corporations should "take a lesson" from the "modern-day propaganda achievements" of the New Deal, Lichtenberg advised. "Just as the government is making use of such means as Pare Lorenz's *The River* on the screen, and the Living Newspaper on the New York stage to get across a message in an entertaining way," he told them, exhibitors must assemble their public demeanors with entertainment values in mind.[91]

It was not enough for big business simply to preach to people. It wanted to provide people with a recreational opportunity to imagine themselves as part of an engaging and futuristic spectacle. It needed to stage symbolic reconciliations between the egalitarian social objectives of the New Deal and the fundamental economic objectives of the commercial system. Before the gates had opened, as the business community primed itself for ideological battle, the commitment to entertainment, as a way of conveying an "underlying social objective," was evident.

Yet there were critical distinctions separating New Deal media from those that emerged from the corporate sector at the World's Fair. If the New Deal relied, primarily, on the idiom of social documentary, the fair's business-inspired entertainments were highly personalized family dramas mixed with miraculous techno-fantasies.

This new formula is manifest in *The Middleton Family at the New York World's Fair* (1939), a widely distributed promotional film produced by Westinghouse to trumpet the fair's commercial optimism in the American heartland.

The film had clearly taken some cues from *The American Family Robinson*. As with the Robinsons of Centerville, the Middletons of Indiana were characterized as a quintessential American family.[92] Also like the Robinsons', the Middletons' personal lives both contained and subsumed larger social issues. Reduced to amusing disagreements among family members, weighty social issues became the stuff of situational drama; simply presented, easily controlled, happily resolved.

As the story opens, the Middleton family has traveled east for a visit with Grandma and to make their pilgrimage to the New York World's Fair. Tom Middleton, a genial midwestern businessman, and Bud, his humorously pigheaded son, are engaged in a spirited debate over the world that awaits them in the future.

Reducing severe social divisions to simple generational misunderstandings, Bud's character sits in for—and disposes of—the misguided millions who have lost their belief in business' ability to provide meaningful opportunities for America's future. This lapse of faith, Tom patiently explains to his son, is why he has decided to bring his family to the World's Fair. "You've heard all the talkers," those who have disparaged industry's achievements, he informs his obstinate son. "Now you're going to see the doers."

Tom and Jane Middleton have another child as well, an older daughter named Babs, who's been living in New York with Grandma. As was the case with Betty Robinson, Babs's leanings are driven by romantic affection. As the story opens, Babs is infatuated with her art teacher, Nick Makaroff. Nick is a man, she tells her parents, who "knows the world like we know Main Street." As the story unfolds, his worldliness turns out to be a "fashionable" antipathy toward private enterprise. Even more literally than her little brother, Bud, Babs has been seduced by radical thinking.[93]

Their visit to the World's Fair is restricted to the Westinghouse Building, but this is enough to spur a religious conversion in both Middleton children. Led through the exhibit by Jim Treadway—a young Westinghouse tour guide who hails from back home—their wayward affections begin to change.

Thrilled by Elektro, a seven-foot talking robot who can count to five on its right hand; enthused by the experience of appearing on closed-circuit television; and enchanted by scores of other technological wonders that overflow the exhibit, Bud admits that the future might not look so bad after all. For Babs, the change is libidinally expressed. As Makaroff condemns the Westinghouse pavilion as a "Temple of Capitalism," Babs's passions shift from this rootless cosmopolite and cathect, instead, onto Jim Treadway, hometown boy turned missionary for the new-time religion.

Mother Jane, though not caught in the grip of radical politics, also undergoes a transformation of sorts. When she first gets to Grandma's, she isn't sure which excites her more: a visit to the World's Fair or a chance to savor Granny's great home cooking. She is metaphorically torn between an older and simpler way of life—represented by Grandma and her cooking—and the brave new world she is about to encounter. At the Westinghouse exhibit, this ambivalence is happily resolved. After witnessing a dish-washing contest between "Mrs. Drudge," who frenziedly hand washes her dishes, and "Mrs. Modern," who stands by tranquilly as her dishwasher performs the chore, the choice is clear. Even Grandma is convinced.[94]

While akin to the Robinson family, the Middletons were, at the same time, significantly different. The crises that were encountered by the Robinsons relied on Victorian values for their resolution; a strong father's moral teachings—advocating respect for customary values—acted as the primary medium through which new understandings were reached. With the Middletons, the father's authority was in question from the beginning. The agency of transformation for the Middletons occurred when they were offered an opportunity to imagine themselves in a marvelous technological future that would serve their every need. If the Robinsons preached a restraint born of scarcity and a strong sense of deference, the Middletons were propelled into a world of abundance, where consumers would be kings and queens.

In a rare moment of prophecy, the *New York Times* described *The Middleton Family at the New York World's Fair* as an illustration of "tomorrow's propaganda."[95] The same could have been said of the World's Fair as a whole. As a panoramic event, it foretold a world in which private corporations would exist primarily to serve the almighty consumer.

This principle permeated the World's Fair. The fair's entire physical ambience communicated a theatrical rendition of a corporately animated tomorrow in which hardship had disappeared.

This vision was cosmetically engineered by established industrial designers, men like Norman Bel Geddes, Walter Dorwin Teague, and others, specialists in the design of products and packaging, who were commissioned to assemble psychologically mesmerizing environments. The fair allowed them to work their magic on a vision of the future itself, to create a corporate theme park where private enterprise and popular notions of social progress would be aesthetically fused. Their objective, in short, was to turn power into beauty.

Teague, who drafted plans for a NAM pavilion in the fair's second year, explained:

> The objective of this exhibit should be to prove to the public the desirability of the American system of free individual enterprise, and the democratic way of life. . . .
>
> It must also be planned from the viewpoint of the visitor's interests, instead of reflecting only the exhibitor's viewpoint. . . . [T]he most commendable and educational exhibit will fail completely of its purpose unless it is presented in such a dramatic form that the people are interested, entertained; if possible, fascinated and delighted as they view it. The exhibit should be such that people will crowd to see it, give it their attention, and go away to disseminate enthusiastic reports of it. . . .
>
> . . . The exhibit should be designed as a unit—a single impressive show which can be seen in not more than twelve or fifteen minutes, built around the single theme stated above, and driving it home with the maximum of impact.[96]

While corporate exhibits celebrated New Deal principles of equal opportunity, economic security, and the greater good, they concurrently made the argument that it would be the free enterprise system—not an activist government—that would make these social ideals attainable.

Throughout the exhibits, popular entertainment and the aestheticization of commerce—usually disguised as science—were the guiding principles. GM's Futurama, designed by Bel Geddes, carried visitors into a futuristic America linked by electronically guided, accident-free highways. Whatever the uncertainties of the moment, trumpeted the exhibit, individual automobility—and the lubricated leisure that it affords—would persevere as the overriding precept of American life.

Throughout the fairground corporate idolatry ruled. Products assumed heroic proportions, reborn as sacred monuments. In tribute to the cash nexus, a giant cash register (National Cash Register Corporation), recognizable from a great distance, towered above fair goers' heads. There were immense Kodak cameras for recording personal memories, giant Underwood typewriters for making secretaries' lives more satisfying, and apparitionally lit automobiles hovering atop worshipful pyramids in tribute to the insatiable wanderlust of American motorists.

Amid the displays, through a silent eloquence of scale, the assumptions of New Deal culture were being embraced and—at the same time—implicitly disputed. If the FSA photographs had projected a vision of the world in which the lives and concerns of ordinary people dwarfed the tattered promises of a corporate consumer culture, within the World's Fair, this balance was overturned. Corporate research departments, not social planning, would propel America and consumers' needs forward; modern appliances, not social cohesion, would make life worth living; and prodigious boxes of Sunshine biscuits—baked by the happy little Sunshine Bakers scampering around its perimeter—would offer fairy-tale rejoinders to those who, like John Maynard Keynes, dared to wonder whether "private and social interest" necessarily coincide.

In its details, the corporate World of Tomorrow was designed to take the prototypical "Americans" of New Deal culture—farmers, industrial workers, and consumers—and present them with a future in which private enterprise would prevail not only economically, but ideologically; a future in which private enterprise would reaffirm its hold on the public mind and on popular horizons of possibility. In an overview of the fair, published by the merchandising magazine *TIDE*, these intentions were unmistakable.[97]

In an attempt to "turn farmers into friends," agribusinesses offered themselves as benefactors to a long-aggrieved agricultural population.

[The] Heinz Dome and the Beech-Nut Building make frequent references to the dependence on farm products. Swift & Co., always beleaguered by livestock raisers after better

(ABOVE AND OPPOSITE) Within the cosmology of World's Fair exhibits, giant enterprise was depicted as the source of both social progress and human happiness. The contrast with FSA photographs is marked. If FSA photographs emphasized the texture of human experience and minimized commercial ideals, the World's Fair photographs and exhibits tended to overturn this model: featuring corporate grandeur and trivializing all but commercial experiences.

prices, court their favor by showing how the company's promotions of unpopular cuts [of meat] create a broader demand. The railroads get in another lick by showing how they've helped the farmer take his products to market.

Responding to the much-heralded achievements of the Tennessee Valley Authority and other New Deal programs for rural electrification, Westinghouse, along with a number of privately owned utilities, engagingly demonstrated how their "all-electric" farms of the future would place the wonders of modern technology at the fingertips of long-suffering rural Americans.

Concerns of labor were also addressed. "That any of the exhibitors has ever been harassed by labor problems, many of them

still unsolved," commented *TIDE*, "no Fair visitor would ever guess." Companies proudly "point out how big a proportion of [their] expenses are for wages," and work conditions are depicted in inspirational tones. Retorts to common knowledge were everywhere to be found.

> U.S. Steel uses photo-murals to show its workers cheerfully toiling. . . . Ford's animated production chart . . . is full of gay little figures that never hint of assembly lines.

The "overall objective" of such theatrics, *TIDE* concluded, was "to knock down in general terms any conceptions that industry overworks and underpays."

To underscore their commitment to democracy and to propagate a corporate rendition of the future, a number of companies launched plans for bringing employees to the fair.

> One unique twist is Goodrich Tire's, who're using the Fair to better employee relations by helping workers finance Fair junkets. General Electric is reportedly considering a similar plan, and has, along with Goodrich and many others, dedicated specific Fair days to its employees. Johns Manville is one of those on the bandwagon with a special recreation room for the exclusive use of visiting employees and stockholders.

Even more resounding than customized entreaties to farmers and workers were public relations efforts at the fair that were intended to rebuild bonds with middle-class consumers who had become, like Dick in the *American Family Robinson,* "Friends of the Downtrodden." These people and their sentiments were essential to big business' political comeback, and in every corporate exhibit "the consumer" was heralded as the sovereign citizen and prime beneficiary of the world of tomorrow.

In big businesses' exorbitant celebration of "the consumer," one may discern critical ways in which New Deal values were simultaneously validated and transfigured in the fair's corporate environments. As the chosen beneficiary of industrial progress, this consumer spoke to a modernist imagination that saw society on the brink of universal abundance, approaching a time when democratic egalitarianism would be reinvigorated and mass-produced consumer goods would be available to all. This vision had been an elemental faith guiding many New Dealers.

The New Deal's version of the consumer, however, was activist and participatory. The consumer movement of the thirties was engaged in ongoing struggles for informative labeling and reliable grades and standards. It had targeted both advertising and chain stores as countenancing unfair monopolies. Some activists were even engaged in an effort to advance a noncommercial, consumer-run cooperative economy.

This rendition of the consumer contrasted sharply with consumers as seen in the corporate spectacles of the fair. If the New Deal's consumer was an active participant, the World's Fair proposed a consumer who was primarily a spectator, a person who was invited to watch himself or herself amid the dazzling bounty of a corporate future that waited just beyond the near horizon. If the New Deal's consumer was a historical subject, the corporately coded consumer was the exhilarated recipient of industrial largesse. History was made by corporate research departments.

To promote this commercial rendition of the consumer, however, the activist consumer needed to be marginalized. This condition was achieved in February and March 1938, more than a year before the World's Fair opened.

Ironically, the genesis of the corporately coded consumer came out of the fair's planners' early belief that—for the World's Fair to have legitimacy—the consumer movement would have to be represented in the World of Tomorrow. At the same time, the planners didn't want consumer participation to frighten away corporate exhibitors. The solution to this dilemma came with a decision to build a Consumer Building at the fair and to designate an Advisory Committee on Consumer Interests that would bring together people who often sat at opposite ends of the table. Hoping the committee would encourage chronic antagonists to find a common ground, the Fair Corporation appointed assorted "leaders of the consumer movement" and "trade association executives, advertisers, retailers, publishers." The committee began meeting in 1937.

Consumer activists had been hesitant to sit with mainstream commercial interests, but they agreed to do so with the following understandings. They were told that they could circulate an ongoing consumer questionnaire at the fair and that the exposition would include a consumer exhibit that would be noncommercial in outlook. They also believed that they would be permitted to supervise the consumer content of other exhibits. As time passed, however, these accords were violated. The businessmen who had agreed to finance the questionnaire decided that they would do so only if questions "of commercial value" were included on the survey. In short, they wished to exploit the questionnaire for market-research purposes; consumers' opinions were of value to them only insofar as they cul-

THE ENCYCLOPÆDIA BILLBOARDICA   966

Technology, Publicity & Social Progress

From the time of the industrial revolution many people have seen NEW TECHNOLOGIES AS THE KEY TO SOCIAL PROGRESS. Still with us today, this belief has informed conflicting strategies of public address over the course of the twentieth century.

The electric washing machine is fast replacing the old washboard and tub —saving time and energy which can be directed toward higher human purposes. (Courtesy N. Y. Edison Co.)

Figure 1: Publicity of Social Enterprise: Illustration and caption from *American Economic Life*, 1925.

Depending upon the motive and context of the publicity, however, interpretations of the relationship between technology and social betterment have differed significantly. These differences are observable if we compare the *publicity of social enterprise*, as articulated by Rex Tugwell and Roy Stryker in the mid-1920s, with the *publicity of private enterprise* that took flight at the New York World's Fair in 1939.

In *American Economic Life, and the Means to Its Improvement* (1925)—the economics textbook that served as a bridge between Progressive and New Deal approaches to visual communication—Tugwell and Stryker placed great emphasis on the emancipating powers of technology, but their interpretation of progress saw technology only as a means to a greater end. To these visionary publicists, new labor-saving products, such as the home washing machine [See Figure 1], were beneficial because they would allow people to spend their lives pursuing "higher human purposes."

In the corporate representation of technological emancipation that permeated the Fair, however, the notion of "higher human purposes" had been scuttled in favor of pure commodity fetishism. Throughout most of the Fair's exhibits, there was no higher human purpose than the joy derived from the purchasing of products. In publicity photos [Figure 2], commodities assumed the scale of religious monuments; consumers were depicted as adoring worshipers. In America's future—it was proposed—corporate exhibitors, always attuned to public desire, would serve as the ultimate arbiters of spiritual fulfillment.

Between these two visions lies an important question, one that remains with us still. ¿Will the future be guided by the yardstick of the common good, and be shaped by a belief in the diversity of human possibility? or ¿Will the future be defined in terms of new products to be consumed, and be ordained by the bottom-line wisdom of corporate enterprise?

Figure 1: Publicity of Private Enterprise: A promotional photo for the Eastman Kodak exhibit at the New York World's Fair, 1939

© BILLBOARDS OF THE FUTURE

minated in sales. There were other violations as well. Without their permission, the chair of the committee, Paul Willis (president of the Associated Grocery Manufacturers of America), exploited consumer leaders' names and organizations to lend authenticity to his committee, while noncommercial members of the consumer movement did not supervise the development of non-commercial consumer-oriented exhibits.

Convinced that the "Fair Corporation had welched on its original agreement," twenty-one consumer leaders on the committee publicly and bitterly resigned. By March 1938, there was no longer any consumer representation on the Advisory Committee on Consumer Interests.[98] The Consumer Building would be built and consumer issues would be mimicked, but "the consumer" had moved from being a participant in the fair to becoming one of its prefabricated products. In the second year of the fair, the Consumer Building was renamed the Fashion Building, perhaps an unwitting tribute to the ways that the World of Tomorrow had helped to transform the consumer from a thorn in the side into a marketable image.

Symbolically, the World's Fair would be inclusive. All faces—farmers, workers, consumers—would be seen within its venues. Few from among these groups, however, would be heard from. Enveloping a corporately controlled apparatus, a lavish spectacle of democracy emerged as a stand-in for democratic participation.

In 1927, Lippmann had written that the key to leadership in the modern age would depend on the ability to manipulate "symbols which assemble emotions after they have been detached from their ideas." The public mind is mastered, he continued, through an "intensification of feeling and a degradation of significance." In a variety of ways, the New York World's Fair served as the laboratory in which these ideas were tested in a popularly accessible form. Symbols that had come to the fore during the thirties—*the people, the farmer, the worker, the consumer, the greater good, economic democracy*—were detached from the issues and ideas that had propelled them forward and became credentials for corporate institutions against which many of these issues and ideas had, initially, been aimed. In a vast and buoyant extravaganza, feelings were uplifted; meanings were overthrown.

Early in the New Deal administration, FDR had tried to forge a working rapprochement between Keynesian economic planners and the business community on behalf of "the greater good." By 1935, when a conservative Supreme Court dismantled the National Recovery Administration, the attempt at reconciliation had failed. In the ensuing years, political bitterness ensued. FDR's rhetoric became increasingly antibusiness, while NAM denounced the New Deal as antithetical to the American Way.

In Flushing Meadow Park, the rapprochement that had failed organizationally reemerged, in altered form, on a grandiose symbolic level. The World's Fair provided a chance for ideas of the people, of socially motivated planning, and of private enterprise to come together in the form of one, colossal entertainment. Against the fractious black-and-white realism of New Deal documentary, a colorful corporate Oz had been invented. An optimistic vision of a society moving ever forward, improving everyone's lives, and unencumbered by social contradictions had been mounted on the boards of one great stage.

Though the entertainment would last only briefly and the cheer would be shattered by war, the fair's vision would continue, in the form of a promise, through the war years and into the postwar era. It would become the essential core of public relations thinking and of American commercial culture more generally.

PART 5

Commercializing
the Cosmos

15
Public Ultimatums

I N 1936, AS Adolph Hitler employed the cult of Aryan supremacy to draw the German masses toward the brink of total warfare, Walter Benjamin remarked that "[w]ar and war only can set a goal for mass movements on the largest scale while respecting the traditional property system."[1] In the intoxicating fervor of combat, Benjamin declared, irreconcilable tensions between capital and labor—chronic social and economic antagonisms—melt away beneath a sacred banner of national blood lust.

For corporate America, which had endured the humiliation of public scorn throughout much of the New Deal era, the United States' entry into the Second World War lent weight to Benjamin's judgment. As the mobilization for war forged a reconciliation between the Roosevelt administration and large-scale manufacturers, the reputation of big business began to improve and the corporate role in the defense of democratic principles gained increasing notoriety. Stark social disparities—which throughout the thirties had preoccupied the nation's attention—began to fade from public view as the federal government, giant enterprises, and the vast majority of the American people discovered common ground in a prodigious struggle to save the world from fascist aggression.

For business leaders and their beleaguered public relations counsels, the salve of war brought a welcome sense of relief. Many began to nurse the impression that the troublesome activism of the thirties was behind them and that new, more auspicious, priorities had captured the public mind. "[T]his is not the time to be promoting economic and general reform measures and everyone accepts that," reported Rex Harlow, a prominent public relations strategist, in

1942. The U.S. war effort, he boasted triumphantly, had finally checked the nation's disconcerting leftward drift.

> [T]he major interest of the administrative heads, in Washington, is winning the war, not making domestic changes. Some of the leftish groups have even complained that they were being forgotten, with the result that the President has had to reassure them that all social gains are not going to be abandoned.
>
> The influx of dollar-a-year men, and the ascendency of conservative Army and Navy people have changed the situation, too. There has recently been a noticeable change in the appreciation of business men's contribution to our national life.[2]

In business circles, there was a high-spiritedness that hadn't been seen since the late twenties. Addressing a National Association of Manufacturers (NAM) Executives Conference in Philadelphia in 1943, J. Howard Pew, president of Sun Oil, observed that industry's contribution to the war effort was already laying "the foundation for a better understanding of American business" among the public at large. "Slandered and vilified as it was in the thirties, subjected to crushing regulations and restrictions," he announced, corporate America was finally vindicating itself, serving "the nation and the world so well in this hour of peril."[3]

This renewed confidence inoculated public pronouncements from other commercial enterprises as well. "Not so long ago it seemed politically popular to smear bigness in business as unserviceable and something to be penalized," narrated a 1944 institutional advertisement for the Hearst Corporation, whose owner, William Randolph Hearst, was a well-known foe of Roosevelt's New Deal administration. "Then came the war," the ad related, and this kind of misbegotten thinking had happily disappeared. "Remembering the desperate need we had for weapons with which to fight for our country's life," it inquired derisively, "do you think now that any of our businesses will be too big for that?" The Hearst Corporation projected its logic forward. "Looking beyond war, and to the piled-up needs of the world and ourselves for more and better things, do you think that any of our businesses will be too big for that?"[4]

This sense of cautious optimism was not simply the consequence of corporate involvement in the production of weapons and other essential war materials. Just like the First World War, business involvement in a thriving propaganda campaign—this time with a legion of writers, broadcasters, moviemakers, publicists, and other mass media experts who were organized by radio newsman Elmer Davis's Office of War Information—had also emboldened private enterprisers with the conviction that they might, once again, gain mastery over the popular imagination.[5] War and the attendant need to stir feelings of national solidarity were, once again, supplying a state-of-the-art laboratory where business could experiment with the tools of ideological command. Conscientiously applied, many businessmen believed, the lessons of war might carry over into the peace.

W. J. Wier, of Chicago's Lord and Thomas advertising and public relations agency, offered a typical example of this hopeful way of thinking. "Here we sit with the greatest force for moving mass psychology that the world has ever seen," he proudly announced to his fellow publicists, picturing the vigor of America's war propaganda machinery. "Nothing that Goebbels has can hold a candle to it."

In the postwar era, Wier declared, popular sentiments should be redirected toward the vision of America that had debuted at the World's Fair, but had been dramatically postponed by the exigencies of war.

> We can awaken in the American people the dream they have been looking for and asking for and begging for since the turn of the century.
>
> We can explain why the American way of life—with its bathtubs and pop-up toasters and electric refrigerators and radios and insulated homes—is worth sacrificing anything and everything not only to preserve but to take forward in a future more glorious than ever.[6]

Yet not all projections were so sanguine. If war offered eloquent opportunities, it also underscored many of the problems that corporations had faced throughout the thirties. Heavy taxes and tight governmental regulation of businesses' wartime operations, for example, only hardened the corporate commitment to building a postwar America where the deep inroads of New Deal activism would be finally, and decisively, reversed. In widespread "planning for postwar" deliberations, business leaders repeatedly emphasized the need to elevate "Private Enterprise" to the consecrated status of a "Fifth Freedom," joining "Freedom of Speech, Freedom of Worship, Freedom From Want, and Freedom From Fear" in the pantheon of nonnegotiable democratic principles.[7] Behind such daydreams lay a desire to associate corporate ambitions with the social values of the New Deal while disabling the intrusive structures of regulatory control that had become business as usual throughout the thirties and into the war years.

Shepherding these efforts, as might be expected, was NAM, whose leaders were convinced that the postwar period would be a hazardous one for American business. "[W]e must not let the praise now being showered on industry blind us to the fact that our American way of life barely survived the onslaught against it in the thirties," Sun Oil's Pew reminded his NAM compatriots, and "this danger is not yet passed."[8]

Believing that "[i]ndependent business will live or die in the post war world," NAM leaders formed the Committee for Economic Development (CED) in October 1943 that convened under a "cloak of secrecy" and began to delineate "a post-war chart for American industry."[9] High on the CED's agenda lay the issue of "jobs for soldiers and war-workers" and the ability of manufacturers to sustain "as high a level of employment and production as possible" to ensure the conditions of social stability they so acutely desired.[10]

This objective was underscored by Frederick C. Crawford, NAM's president. "After the war," he cautioned NAM members, "the biggest task ahead of us will be to preserve all our historic freedoms, and to insure individual freedom of opportunity at home." This will be no mean task, he continued, enumerating business' social goals for the postwar era.

Political plans to besmirch business management are in the making. . . . Industry has a great story to tell, but it has failed miserably to bring a better understanding of our economic freedom. It has not emphasized in the public mind what that freedom actually means in terms of worker welfare, nor has it brought this important message directly to the worker. Only a clear knowledge of what our basic freedoms have meant in the development of our American way of life will enable us to preserve them. . . . As a molder of mass thinking, [then,] industry has a sacred obligation to perform. Either industrialists must take the lead to counteract those influences which would destroy our democratic system, or they must resign themselves to the inevitable loss of all those freedoms which have made America the envy of all mankind.[11]

On the calendar of the CED and in Crawford's clarion pronounce-ment, there was a pregnant shift from NAM's customary rhetoric. Previously, NAM's primary target audience for its PR efforts had been the Anglo-American middle class, people who were seen to have lost their way in the storm and stress of the Great Depression. Even in the depression, NAM evinced a congenital disdain for working-class demands. In the crucible of war, however, and amid an economic recovery kindled by war production, NAM leaders began to speak of America's workers—many of them from immigrant backgrounds, who were now soldiers or munitions workers—with mounting concern. It was these people who would be returning to peacetime with a powerful set of democratic expectations, and it was they who must be appeased to safeguard the interests of American business.

One way that business began to address these groups was through its wartime advertising. A shortage of consumer goods—exacerbated by government-imposed rationing—made product advertising point-less at the time. Companies instead produced "public relations" ads that highlighted corporate participation in the war effort, while pre-senting exuberant pictures of postwar America as a society where a cornucopia of wondrous new products (televisions, washing machines, and other modern appliances, for example) would be the birthright of all Americans. Fictitious and generic American families, like "the Smiths" and "the Browns," showed up in a wide range of advertise-ments, providing graphic and alluring depictions of a consumption-defined "good life" that would be available to all after the war. In their vow to bring about a limitless, product-laden bounty, these commercial communiqués offered a picturesque alternative to social democratic ideas of the "greater good" that had gained currency during the New

This 1945 advertisement from the Ford Motor Company is but one illustration of a promising, product-defined vision of the American future that was proposed by much wartime advertising. NEW YORK PUBLIC LIBRARY PICTURE COLLECTION

Deal period. Private industry, the ads affirmed, would provide the fountains by which America's material thirsts would be quenched.

At the same time, corporate leaders were also agitated by the mass mobilization against "the traditional property system" that had grown throughout the thirties and that, they feared, might reappear when the war ended. The unprecedented power and legitimacy of labor unions made this concern all the more real. In response to these contingencies, they reasoned, the promise of newfangled commodities would not be enough. Private enterprise—unfettered by governmental intervention—would also need to paint a picture of itself as the only system through which democratic values and aspirations would be adequately met. The threat of a mobilized public would require business to package itself as a pure expression of the people's will. "You can no longer tell your employee what to do," exclaimed a writer in *Printers' Ink,* "you must sell them."[12]

This task of selling the business system was seen by many as one that demanded careful public relations planning, and opinion researchers—including Elmo Roper, Claude Robinson of the Opinion Research Corporation, and Henry C. Link of the Psychological Corporation—launched statistical surveys designed to plumb the depths of the public mind. Questioning the appeal of the concept, "free enterprise," for example, Link found that most Americans failed to respond to the idea. The "great public," his study concluded, "neither fears nor understands State Socialism nor does it crave or understand our system of free enterprise." For business effectively to forge an identity of interests between itself and ordinary working Americans, Link advised, "a new and more realistic vocabulary" of persuasion, attuned to the outlook of the public mind, must be invented.[13]

Behind the quest for a *new vocabulary*—an enterprise that would advance dramatically as the war came to an end—lay one overarching public relations objective. "In the reconversion period" from a wartime to a peacetime economy, as W. W. Suitt—director of sales development for a large manufacturing concern—worded it, there must also be an accompanying "reconversion of thought."

> The thinking of the general public must turn from acceptance of controls, restrictions and regulations placed as a war-time exigency on business as well as individuals, to a demand on the part of the voter for a return to a system where a work economy can function—where business can seek its own level in a free competitive enterprise.[14]

As explained in the forward to the *Proceedings* of NAM's 1944 national conference, members had to expand their expertise beyond the workaday "techniques of production and distribution." More than knowing about "the material needs which it supplies to the people," business must also develop a greater sensitivity to "the personal feelings of the public toward industry as a whole and in particular." The apparition of a perpetually polled public—repeatedly having its temperature taken to provide businessmen and politicians with a suitable rhetorical spin—was beginning to loom over America's horizon.

As the Second World War moved toward a conclusion, reflections on public-opinion management became increasingly routine. The War Advertising Council—which had generated a mountain of publicity under the auspices of the Office of War Information—encouraged war propagandists to maintain their state of mobilization after the peace. "This country's wartime information mechanism," they reported, "was powered almost entirely by American business." During the war, they explained,

> [b]usiness assumed the public information job—and the public has been conscious of that fact. Having assumed this responsibility, can business now drop it completely?
>
> . . . It seems overwhelmingly to the interest of business and the people to continue it.
>
> Wartime public opinion polls confirmed the rising popularity of business. . . . good opinion universally held for the advertiser who enlisted in the public service.
>
> Given these circumstances, the Advertising Council argued, business could ill-afford to abandon the powerful advantage spawned by the image of this "unselfish" contribution to the war effort.[15]

■   ■   ■   ■   ■

Despite business's renewed sense of aplomb, as the war ended there was still trouble in Babylon. Phantoms encircled the American military-industrial triumph. Anxiety about the future continued to occupy business leaders. Public relations agendas, inspired by a horrific—still fresh—memory of the decade-long "onslaught" against business, were markers of corporate unease.

Amid the confetti of victory, recalled Leo Bogart—who participated in high-level public relations discussions during the mid- to
late-forties—there was a belief among many of America's corporate
elite that they were stepping into "a very perilous and uncertain
period."[16] Despite an economic recovery fueled by the war and an
ostensibly recuperated public reputation, there was a sense of foreboding. With the war now over, nervous recollections of a seething
popular antipathy toward giant enterprises returned to haunt the
reveries of business leaders. In the citadels of power, men who had—
not long before—been vilified as "economic royalists" were concerned
that a restive populace might, once again, clamor at their gates. In
ways hard to fathom from the vantage point of the market-governed
world in which we live, the New Deal, its aggressive social Keynesianism, and a decade of popular mobilization had considerably intim-
idated corporate America.

Nowhere was this situation more apparent than behind the gates
of the Westchester Country Club, one of the country's venerable—
and restricted—monuments to Anglo-American rule in the United
States. There, in a sequestered meeting hall in November 1945, an
inner circle of powerful men met to discuss the social contingencies
faced by capitalist enterprises, hoping to arrive at decisions that
would protect their considerable interests and redirect the future life
of the nation.

This landmark occasion was the first in what would be a series of
Public Relations Conferences convened by the Standard Oil Company
of New Jersey (SONJ) and its affiliated companies. Attending the
meeting were top executives of the New Jersey holding company
(known today as Exxon), several key representatives from Standard's
recently established public relations department, and a prominent
group of outside advisers from a variety of relevant fields.

If any company needed to address a public relations crisis it was
Standard Oil. For three-quarters of a century, no other corporation
had attracted an equivalent amount of public contempt. Founded by
John D. Rockefeller in the early 1870s, the Standard Oil Trust soon
seized control of the American petroleum industry, combining
schemes of financial consolidation with a ferocious overpowering of

smaller, localized producers.[17] Rockefeller's predatory manipulations began to attract public scorn when they were described by Henry Demerest Lloyd in "The Story of a Great Monopoly," published in 1881.

Following a decade of governmental investigations and stillborn lawsuits against the petroleum giant, in 1902 Progressive journalist Ida Tarbell published a series of articles detailing the trust's myriad corrupt practices. Growing public indignation laid the way for a spectacular—though basically inadequate—antitrust decision in 1911, which proposed to dissolve the monopoly.

In ensuing decades, despite the efforts of Ivy Lee, Standard Oil—and the Rockefeller name—became widespread symbols for reckless, socially irresponsible corporate greed. As oil executives converged at the Westchester gathering, these harsh judgments continued to taint the company's name. In a candid "Review of Public Opinion Particularly Affecting Standard Oil," Frank Surface, assistant to the president of SONJ, matter-of-factly recited the tale of public disaffection. "The history of Standard Oil in its relations with the public has not been too fortunate," he began.

> Back in the days after the turn of the century, in the "trust busting" days of Teddy Roosevelt, Standard Oil was regarded as the prime example of a powerful, grasping, iniquitous business organization. Ida Tarbell's book, the dissolution suit, and so forth confirmed this idea of the company.

"In the thirty years or more that followed," Surface conceded, "very little was done to offset this idea of the company."[18]

By 1945, as the Public Relations Conferences began, another more recent cloud darkened Standard Oil's future. In March 1942, a Senate committee chaired by Harry Truman—while investigating concentrations of economic power—had stumbled upon a particularly damaging bit of information. The committee learned of a series of patent and process-exchange agreements—for synthetic "Buna" rubber—between SONJ and the notorious German chemical cartel, I. G. Farben. Later it would be revealed that these agreements persisted even after the United States had entered the war.[19]

Accusations of treachery spread through the mass media. A corporation with an already dubious past was now shaken by a new onslaught of public condemnation. The I. G. Farben scandal, Surface reported to his colleagues, hit the company "like a small atomic bomb." Embarrassed executives, for the first time, "really awakened to the necessity of doing something about public opinion."[20]

By the middle of 1943, a new public relations department had been created, which began by devoting nearly all its energies to "defending the company against charges of collusion with the Germans."[21] Now, as SONJ executives—and a number of pertinent others—conferred at the Westchester Country Club, the specific fallout of the I. G. Farben connection gave way to a more sweeping sense of emergency.

On the morning of November 19, following a greeting by George Freyermuth, who managed SONJ's public relations outfit, Elmo Roper stood to address the gathering. Roper was one of the country's leading experts on public opinion in 1945. During the 1930s, Roper had distinguished himself conducting surveys for *Fortune* magazine. He would later go off on his own, conducting the Roper poll. Until George Gallup scooped the survey-research community by correctly forecasting a Roosevelt victory in 1936, Roper was America's most highly regarded opinion analyst.

Roper was not a disinterested student of public opinion. Like most pollsters, he pondered public opinion for strategic purposes, to provide those who paid for his services with an advantage over those whose thoughts were being methodically mapped.

Though Roper was never trained as a social scientist, his ability to read the public mind, as well as his authoritative bearing, had impressed a wide number of corporate clients. He had the personality to command their attention and the knowledge and ability to advise them on important policy decisions. Bogart, who participated in SONJ's early PR meetings, described Roper as a man who instilled enormous confidence in those who employed him.

He was a man of great poise, a tremendous sense of humor. [He] did not suffer fools gladly [and had] no tolerance for bullshit, though he could sling a little bit himself. [He was] very articulate, very charming, [and had] a great ability to get to the kernel of what was actionable in survey data. [He was] not a technician, never pretended to be. He left that to the people around him. [He had a] great interest in politics, and a strong personal political sense in his handling . . . of clients and other people.[22]

At this Public Relations Conference—and in subsequent meetings—Roper was called on to synopsize the general "mood of the American people." His report was dire, not just for a company that had habitually disregarded the winds of public opinion, but for all who desired to uphold the principle of unregulated private enterprise. Employing a jargon that revealed the extent to which theories of social psychology had informed his profession, Roper described a population that was extraordinarily jittery and potentially explosive, one that had just experienced "fifteen years of emotional crisis." He went on:

They had ten years of depression, with all of the emotional disturbance that goes with not knowing where your next meal is coming from, or whether or not you are shortly to reduce your scale of living.

They were plunged out of practically ten years of the kind of emotional crisis that goes with a depression into roughly five years of a different kind of emotional crisis, a war, where everyone was worried about what was going to happen to his son, or his brother, or her husband.

So we have today tired, somewhat frustrated and emotionally disturbed people.[23]

Roper then moved from a psychological to a political-economic plane. During the depression and throughout the war period, he reported, Americans had grown more and more predisposed to look beyond the privately owned corporate system toward government as the ultimate insurer of their economic survival, particularly their "right to work continuously at reasonably good wages."

Now, as the postwar period commenced, many Americans continued to hold on to this axiomatic belief. For free enterprisers, the implications of this report were formidable:

[D]espite the fact that they look to industry for the bulk of the jobs, a very large majority of the people in the country—and that includes rich people as well as poor people—are committed to the belief that if private industry can't or won't provide jobs for everyone who is willing and able to work, then it is the proper function of government to do it.[24]

Explicit in Roper's review was the degree to which underlying corporate faiths—regarding the sanctity of private enterprise and the primacy of the profit motive—were being widely questioned. Also clear were the ways in which public thinking—particularly regarding governmental activism—threatened to block business' plans for rolling back the incursions of the New Deal.

While a "great majority of Americans" continued to "believe in the capitalistic system," Roper warned, corporations were confronted by a nonnegotiable battery of conditions. A national reordering of priorities—propelled from the bottom up—jeopardized business' long-run objectives. The American people, he enunciated, "have made up their minds to a number of ultimatums."

[O]ne of the ultimatums is that never in the future shall property rights be placed above human rights. Another one is that continued corporation dividends cannot be regarded as being as sacred as continued wages for labor. Rightly or wrongly, the American public wants the guaranteed annual wage. Rightly or wrongly, it believes the guaranteed annual wage can be achieved.

Together, these stipulations testified to a basic weakening of customary corporate prerogatives and capitalist faiths. These provisos, Roper counseled, would have to be addressed by SONJ and other corporations as they set their agendas for postwar America.

At bottom, the prevailing social expectation had become the guaranteed economic security of all people. "The only question in my mind," he concluded, "is whether industry is going to get credit for helping to bring [it] about . . . or credit for opposing it as long as it possibly could."[25] For those present, the implications of this report were both disturbing and clear. The company would have to make the active cultivation of public relations a central component of its business planning.

As the discussion moved along, the sobering gravity of Roper's report gave way to issues of a more particular and actionable nature. How should Standard Oil redefine its public image? What steps could be taken to remold public attitudes toward the New Jersey corporation?

"It is up to us," declared Eugene Holman, one of SONJ's top executives, "to satisfy the general public that our job is being well done." To do so, Holman admonished, the nature and structure of Standard Oil's business had to be reconsidered. Corporate leaders could no longer afford to view themselves simply as oil men.

> ... [I]n the producing field, the refining field, the transportation field, the marketing field, we have very able technicians. But in the past few years we have come to realize that what I might call our human engineering wasn't perhaps being so well done. In order to promote this *human engineering* group, of which you gentlemen are a very large part, we hope to stimulate procedures ... and we hope that we may come to feel that we are doing just as good a job in our human engineering as we are in our other forms of engineering.[26]

Complimenting Roper as SONJ's sociopsychological analyst, Earl Newsom served as the company's primary planner in the field of "human engineering." Brought into Standard Oil at the time of the I. G. Farben debacle, in 1943 Newsom became the corporation's general counsel on public relations.

Newsom's past experience made him ideal for the job. Among other distinctions, he had helped to dig Henry Ford out of a hole after the auto tycoon was exposed as an advance man for the *Protocols of the Learned Elders of Zion,* a counterfeit conspiracy document distributed to inflame anti-Semitic paranoia.

Newsom had carefully cultivated an enigmatic image of himself as a man who was perpetually lost in thought. Though he spent a lifetime working as a servant of power, in his habits he projected a mystique of personal independence and incorruptibility. "[H]e ostentatiously avoided business lunches and had lunch everyday in the same place, eating the same frugal repast and reading his *New York Times.*"

Now, at the 1945 PR conference, Newsom offered general guidelines on how to "develop and maintain in the public mind a favorable image" of SONJ and its affiliates. As was his studied custom, he spoke "in such a low voice that everybody had to lean forward in his chair, so even the most banal utterances took on a portentousness."[27]

Bypassing the kind of bedrock issues raised by Roper, Newsom's strategy gave short shrift to the idea that corporations must reform themselves and their economic practices in response to a new and nonnegotiable set of public "ultimatums." Against Roper's apostate suggestion that a fundamental readjustment of the economic system might be necessary for private industry to survive, Newsom emphasized the necromantic side of public relations, the ways that Standard Oil could employ the contrivances of mass persuasion to trump the stumbling block of a belligerent public.

> If the fundamental problem of a corporation is to disclose to the American people that it is an enterprise with a heart—a good company—a good citizen—an institution to be trusted, then all public relations thinking must be directed toward bringing the American people to recognize that fact. That is the theme. *That* is the motif. *That* is the string on which all the beads must be strung.

The company, Newsom continued, cannot afford to project the public image of a giant and powerful enterprise, insensitive to public indignation, as had been its longtime practice. If we look at Standard Oil "as a kind of mausoleum on a mountain top—a great institution," he warned, "We become awed in the presence of ourselves." Though Standard Oil's power may be a fact of life, Newsom counseled, its public etiquette must be more sympathetic, more accessible. Responding to Link's call for a "new vocabulary" of power, Newsom suggested that SONJ must begin to evolve a commercial vernacular, a way of speaking that meshed with the dynamics of interpersonal relationships.

> What we must remember . . . is that a company can win friends and influence people if it will be quite natural, friendly, easy-

going, frank, colloquial, and unpretentious. It is this friendly, easy-going manner, perhaps more than any other single thing, which, in the long run, will win public confidence.[28]

As the first Public Relations Conference came to an end, a man named Robert Haslam stood up to summarize the conclusions of the gathering. When Standard Oil was attacked by the Truman committee in 1942, the company had summoned Haslam—then the general sales manager—to plug the leaks in the corporate ship. It was Haslam who had founded the public relations department, and it was he who had guided its development from the boardroom ever since. Speaking as a member of the SONJ Board of Directors, Haslam's word bore the imprimatur of corporation policy; his comments on the conference were definitive.

Earlier in the conference, during some informal exchanges, Haslam expressed enthusiasm for Newsom's presentation and its strategic recommendations. Uncomfortable with Roper's more radical systemic approach, Haslam embraced Newsom's emphasis on "the impressionistic, the emotional, as against the factual approach, in order to influence people and provide a good climate for our public relations." Instead of substantively altering company policies— regarding profits, employment, and economic security—Haslam argued that Standard Oil must anthropomorphize its image in the public mind, "present the Jersey Company in the light of being human, being likeable, being generous and honest as against being a large producer, refiner, or marketer of petroleum products . . . "[29]

Now as he brought the meetings to a close, Haslam reiterated this overarching public relations goal with remarkable and instructive frankness. When the company is under attack, he recited, "don't deny something . . . affirm something else. [I]dentify yourself with the things that you want people to think of when they think of you." Implicitly accepting the revised picture of America that had taken hold in the New Deal era and recognizing anticorporate antagonism as a given of postwar American life, Haslam expanded on the lexicon that would be needed to bypass these perilous historical developments.

[W]hen the chairman of our Board gets up on some occasion, he shouldn't say, "I desire in the name of 60,000 stockholders . . ." He says, "I desire in the name of 60,000 American laborers. . . ." Identify yourself not with bond-holders, coupon clippers, Wall Street, but with labor, *with Americans.*

Closing his remarks, Haslam suddenly assumed a tone of dis-quietude. Ideas about a serviceable corporate vocabulary were, once again, overshadowed by the daunting political-economic realities. Despite Haslam's comfort with Newsom's approach, Roper's con-cerns refused to melt away.

Above all else, Haslam warned, the company must not lose sight of the dangerous times it was navigating and of the social democratic ideas that continued to threaten the future of Standard Oil and pri-vate enterprise more generally.

> [T]here is a revolution of ideas right around the corner. . . . We have seen those revolutions and ideas hit us and never knew that they were coming until afterward, and then we would start in figuring out why we never knew. It usually comes out that either we didn't have our ear to the ground, or we weren't looking in that direction . . .
>
> What I am fearful of is that we will not be aware of the thunderstorm that is coming up on the horizon. . . . I am a little fearful that we are a little too smug, and our antenna is not sensitive enough to pick up these wave-lengths.[30]

Thus closed the first in a series of Public Relations Conferences held by Standard Oil. Subsequent conferences would elaborate on issues raised at this inaugural parley, but here, at the Westchester Country Club in November 1945, a new tone was set. A council of elites, meeting to discuss the ways they might conscript the affections of the American public, pondered their future. Some, like Roper, pro-posed the need for corporations to adapt to popular economic expecta-tions that had taken root in the thirties: the need to reevaluate overall economic thinking and to forge an industrial system that would be structurally responsive to social welfare issues. Others, like Newsom, tendered less fundamental approaches, proposing the need to perfect the techniques of mass persuasion and to create a more efficient opinion-management apparatus. As a group, they underscored the unmistakable centrality of public relations as a corporate policy concern and provided a revealing glimpse of discussions and debates that would shape PR practice in the years directly following the Second World War.

■　　■　　■　　■　　■

The uncertainties expressed by the Standard Oil executives and their advisers were hardly unique. Throughout the late forties, the social imperatives of the New Deal and unsettling memories of mass mobilization continued to cast shadows over business thinking. "The most important problem business faces today . . . is the fact that business isn't out of the doghouse yet," recited *Fortune* magazine in May 1949.

> Sixteen turbulent years have rolled by since the New Deal began to rescue the People from the Capitalists, and no one can say that business has retrieved the authority and respect it ought to have if the drift to socialism is to be arrested. Every U.S. businessman, consciously or unconsciously, is on the defensive.[31]

A clear indication of this defensiveness was the rapid growth of corporate public relations. In a review of business' continuing troubles, *Fortune* inventoried this progression:

> Some 4,000 corporations now support whole "public relations" departments and "programs." About 500 independent firms, some of them knocking down more than half a million a year in consulting fees alone, are supported mainly by business.[32]

Richard Tedlow, a business historian, expanded on this development:

> The field was flooded with new practitioners and budgets soared with expenditures for institutional advertising and for experiments with such "educational" devices as comic books and company-sponsored economics courses. More chief executives took a personal hand in public relations, and more counselors were attaining the rank of vice-president or assistant to the president.[33]

Yet beyond the exponential growth of public relations, the assumptions behind corporate public relations were also changing. Enlarging upon approaches initiated by NAM in the late thirties, the tone of PR planning was characterized less and less by narrowly conceived commercial motives and was driven, more and more, by broad political considerations. Amid widespread discussions of the need to build bridges between corporations and ordinary Americans, public relations architects assumed an increasingly evangelical tone.

Vernon Scott, a prominent businessman and leader of a national antitax group, provides a typical example of this shift in thinking. Writing of the need to use public relations as a weapon in defense of "our present economic system" against the "expanding authority of the State," Scott exhorted businessmen to join in "the greatest ideological war of all times," the struggle to depose governmental supervision over economic planning.

> Our public relations effort, to succeed, must always consider the political front. . . .
>
> The opposition is so organized. We are not. . . . Our first line of action . . . is to prove to the American public the superiority of Democratic Capitalism over any other form of social economy. It must be done by example, by comparison, by chapter and verse out of the books of both faiths.
>
> . . . Perhaps it can be done through one of the great national organizations—the U.S. Chamber of Commerce, NAM, CED, or some other. Or perhaps that too will have to be built from the grassroots as the new program begins to unfold. *But coordination we must have, to insure that the whole public gets our message; not just the active practitioners of capitalism.*
>
> Here at home we must constantly preach and prove that a planned economy destroys free markets, shackles free enterprise, reduces the standard of living for all, beats down private initiative and cripples competition, the live [sic] blood of capitalism.[34]

One of the most daunting political obstacles that businessmen faced in the ideological war against government was analyzed by Howard Chase, head of public relations for General Foods and a nationally influential figure in the PR field. Writing in 1945, he observed that the public had become more and more educated in social and economic matters during the depression.

> The American people today . . . are by and large a sophisticated and articulate group. . . . They are full of questions about the economic and social system to which they return and which in large part they will shape themselves.

Inspired by a new sense of confidence in their inalienable rights, ordinary working-class Americans held the conviction that to justify its existence, an economic system must be organized to sustain the greater good. Social standards must be applied to all economic activity. This way of thinking, Chase asserted, required corporate enterprise to "satisfy the individual both in his role as consumer and his role as citizen."[35]

Two years later, Chase continued to issue political admonitions. "Can capitalism survive? . . . [when] three out of four Americans are prepared to say yes to almost any question that reflects discredit on our corporate system?" he asked. Amid "a new human groping for spiritual satisfaction," he responded, the continuation of a free enterprise system requires successful competition "for men's minds and men's loyalties." Unless corporate public relations can gain an advantage in this direction, he concluded, people will continue to expect their government to "keep an eye on business."[36]

Elsewhere in public relations circles similar concerns were being repeatedly aired. In 1946, for example, John W. Hill—cofounder of the public relations behemoth, Hill and Knowlton—argued that a deep divide, isolating corporate management from workers and members of the general public, was the most pressing public relations problem of the day. "[T]he line of communications between management and its workers and neighbors," he maintained, "has broken down and . . . something must be done about it. Industrial management lives in one world, the workers live in another. An iron curtain," he announced, seizing a metaphor ordinarily reserved for a geopolitical context, "stands between them."

The "first step" in bridging this hazardous gulf, Hill instructed, must be efforts designed to gain workers' trust. Reprising an argument made by Theodore Vail during the Progressive era, Hill warned that business can not abandon its social leadership role to the forces of dissension.

> The task of getting facts to workers in acceptable form is not child's play. The mind of many a worker is sealed by his suspicion of the boss. The first step in this job is to win the confidence of workers. . . .
>
> The logical leader of labor is the employer. . . . If the iron curtain is to be torn, it will be up to the employer to do it. The individual employee cannot. And his spokesman, the head of his union, will not, because to most labor union officials the iron curtain is an advantage.[37]

The need to gain the loyalty of workers was an often-repeated theme in this time of transition. The ability of big business to regain control over the direction of American society depended on its capacity to draw adherents to its way of seeing on a mass scale. Evoking Roper's take on the public mind, Claude Robinson—president of Opinion Research, Inc.—reported that many Americans accepted big government as a necessary safeguard against the wiles of reckless corporations. Unless business effectively joined the fray and gained the hearts of its workers, Robinson maintained, the prospects for free enterprise were indeed grim.

> . . . [S]tudies . . . show that the most fertile ground for infiltration of collectivist and authoritarian ideology in this country are the minds of men who work in your factories."

The survival of business, Robinson concluded, would depend on a crusade to convert these workers to a belief in the private enterprise system. "[T]he future of authoritarianism in the United States will be determined by the social understanding of people in the grass roots. It is public opinion in the home precincts that will decide.[38]

A grass roots pro-business movement, however, would not gain converts by speaking in the name of stockholders, bondholders, and coupon clippers. It needed to formulate a commercial vernacular that spoke to everyone. This would be a formidable chore, observed Link of the Psychological Corporation. The prevailing drift of civic instruction, he reported, had thrown the merit of free enterprise into question. "In recent decades," Link contended, "our schools and publications have done a better job in promoting socialism than in promoting the American system of private capitalism . . . a system that combines freedom with plenty." To regain its legitimacy, Link advised, business must do more than simply trumpet its marvelous new products. It must also "promote the principles, the ideas, the freedoms which make plenty possible."

To do so, Link noted, there needed to be a shift from a pubic relations policy that had routinely emphasized the importance of corporate rights to one that spoke in terms of the rights of all people. It was necessary for "a transfer in emphasis from free enterprise to the freedom of all individuals under free enterprise; from capitalism to the much broader concept: Americanism."[39]

Simply put, corporate communications must move away from the vocabulary of the businessman and must appear accessible and familiar to the average American. One writer in *Printers' Ink*, in an attempt to inform this strategy, mimicked the mindset of this American:

> [W]e common men will understand the story better if it comes from someone we know, like the concern down the street where Uncle Will and Neighbor Joe work. We all have greater interest in the things we personally know a little about, and our interest increases in pace with our knowledge.[40]

While Link advised that a conscious manipulation of symbols would harvest the loyalties of working-class Americans, Howard Chase argued that rhetorical devices would not be enough. Unless the private business system substantively delivered on general social expectations that had evolved over the previous decade and a half, Chase argued passionately in 1947, corporate public relations efforts would merely inherit the wind. For capitalism to flourish in these critical times, more fundamental actions needed to be taken.

> I am convinced that this process of identifying business with the great goals of the human race, the great but simple goals,

is all that can maintain today's free corporate system. . . .
[L]et us use every power to identify the owners and managers
with the simple goals—better education for everybody's children, better health and nutrition, better housing, better opportunities based on ability, more security for the aged and infirm,
more respect for the opinion of any man who has opinions.

"Corporate survival," Chase cautioned, "depends on how quickly corporate management catches on."[41]

■   ■   ■   ■   ■

In the wake of the thirties, the argument for drastic action held a
good deal of weight. As *Fortune* magazine summarized the situation
in 1949, social exigencies now challenged the corporation to "make a
policy of its social consciousness."[42]

Chase, who became president of the Public Relations Society of
America (PRSA) in the late forties, added significantly to this way of
thinking. With a rare sense of history, he argued that capitalists must
abandon their knee-jerk conservatism and reconnect to their liberal
roots. They must revive the time when merchants played a leading role
in struggles for democracy, individual freedom, and the general welfare
of society. Business, he maintained, must wrest the mantle of liberalism from government and work to "expand the living standard of the
American people through competitive production and distribution."

"It is time for those of us in industry," Chase sermonized in 1945,
to embrace the "really radical nature of our proposal to increase standards of living." We must abandon "the defensive forever," he
asserted, and "move positively and aggressively into the arenas in
which public opinion is made . . ."

To Chase, public relations must be nothing less than an "operating
philosophy by which our worthy economic institutions can reintegrate
themselves into the basic aspirations of the people of this country."[43] In
brief, a system of *welfare capitalism* must be brought about to arrest
and incapacitate the vexing incursions of a *welfare state*.

Even Edward L. Bernays paid homage to the ideas of welfare
capitalism. To combat "Depression Factors" that had changed the
thinking of most Americans, businesses had to see themselves as
"social, as well as economic" institutions. According to Bernays, busi-

ness must become the advocate of "stabilized employment; pensions; social security; old age insurance; group accident; sickness, hospital and life insurance." They must also take the lead in "the fields of racial relations, housing, and education" and willingly participate in the scrupulous maintenance of "advertising, labelling and packaging" standards. It was essential, he announced, for public relations thinking to reach beyond the use of "slogans" and "incantations."[44]

Others concurred. Writing in the *Harvard Business Review* in 1949, Robert Wood Johnson, head of Johnson & Johnson pharmaceutical company, maintained that business must develop a "permanent and complete social policy." It must assume a position of social "trusteeship," as he put it, to attune its interests to those of the general public.

> Trusteeship would emphasize our points of common interests and responsibility, not merely our differences. Such a spirit would bring new health to the business world. It would overflow into political life, with patriotism and concern for the common good mitigating struggles by pressure groups and special interests.[45]

A year later, writing in the PRSA's *Public Relations Journal*, Johnson endorsed welfare capitalism as the route that business—in the interests of self-preservation—must take. Too many cards were stacked against conventional patterns of corporate behavior. "[U]nless we think and act our best now," he cautioned, "there is a danger that socialism will creep upon us unnoticed."[46]

Contemplating "management's responsibilities in a complex world," Frank Abrams, president of Standard Oil, proposed a similar formula. "If we are to be helpful in advancing our American way of life," he suggested, "we must be willing to show by example that individual objectives can best be served when they are identified with the common good." Corporations, he continued, must evince "a strong sense of responsibility to the community." Emulating doctors and lawyers, businessmen must assume a "professional" sense of "service," Abrams asserted.[47]

This metamorphosis is incomprehensible unless it is evaluated in relation to the New Deal period. During that time, the electorate broadened to include people who had previously been marginal to American political life. Popular conceptions of America and Americans had changed. The thirties had also witnessed an unprecedented governmental focus on the problems of poverty and on the development of programs designed to enhance the social and economic security of all citizens. The voice and the needs of "the people" gained new consideration from political leaders, and the federal government defined itself as the people's champion against the chronic vicissitudes of a "free" capitalist market. Perhaps most important, a large number of formerly disenfranchised Americans came out of the Great Depression with the idea that they were protected by a battery of federally secured social and economic rights. This impression had been confirmed, again and again, as business's opinion experts—Link, Roper, Robinson, and others—studied the anatomy of the public mind.

Against this new and potentially risky terrain, corporate America was forced to reexamine its historic mission. "So long as the major American problem was economic and industrial," wrote Russell Davenport, an editorial consultant for *Fortune,* "we had preceded upon the assumption that private initiative was the way to get things done." In the turmoil of the Great Depression, however, all this had changed.

> . . . [W]hen the New Deal hit the social problem, it boldly reversed this [customary business] assumption. It gave lip service, to be sure, to private initiative so far as economic matters were concerned. But with regard to the social problem it made the curious assumption that the . . . initiative in social matters should lie with government.

The balance of American society had shifted, Davenport observed, "starting a whole new trend in the evolution of America . . . a trend toward giving the government more and more initiative on social matters and then in matters bordering on the social." The rights of private business, he concluded, had been severely compromised by this development, and only the "affirmation of a new principle—the principle of private initiative in social matters"—would overturn this unhealthy tide.[48]

The affirmation of this new principle, however, would require the deployment of two intertwined public relations efforts. First, it would be necessary to incapacitate the legitimacy of New Deal assumptions. The idea that the federal government was the prime vehicle for taking the "initiative on social matters" would have to be contested head-on. Second, as governmental activism was rolled back, it would also be necessary to institute corporate social policies that offered mean-ingful alternatives to the public initiatives of the New Deal. To a sig-nificant degree, far-reaching public relations activities, beginning in the late forties onward, addressed this two-pronged agenda.

In fateful ways, the beginning of the Cold War provided a conve-nient context for the assault on governmental activism. When Winston Churchill described a world divided by an "iron curtain," in Fulton, Missouri, on March 5, 1946, he coined a phrase that would propel American foreign policy for much of the remainder of the century.

A pervasive ether of anticommunism shaped the contours of domestic politics as well. First, the *red scare* helped to sustain an ideo-logical atmosphere of incessant military mobilization as a normal aspect of American life. This atmosphere not only served to safeguard the "traditional property system," but it also justified an uninter-rupted transfer of public wealth to the newly powerful "military-industrial complex."

At the same time that anticommunism rationalized unprece-dented federal expenditures on war materials—reshaping the terrain of America's industrial economy along the way—it also transformed the universe of discourse surrounding federal spending on social pro-grams. While colossal governmental grants to private "defense" con-tractors were typically characterized as unquestionably patriotic—vital to the preservation of American democracy—public spending on fed-erally administered social programs was vilified, more and more, as the subversion of traditional freedoms.

In 1922, Walter Lippmann postulated that to be successful in mobilizing public opinion around a cause, it is necessary to delineate your opposition as villains and conspirators. In defense of private enterprise and against the further implementation of governmental social programs, a vigorous conservative publicity machine took Lipp-mann's axiom to heart. From the late forties onward, it became increasingly common to characterize the New Deal's social Keynesianism as nothing less than a perfidious drift toward communism. A foreign evil menaced the home front, and governmental activism in social and economic affairs was its most tangible expression.

One of the nation's leading publicists in this regard was J. Edgar Hoover. A propagandist more than a cop, Hoover helped inaugurate a merciless publicity environment that again and again depicted the United States as a society under siege. Following this lead, notorious congressional committees (the House Un-American Activities Committee and the Senate Internal Security Subcommittee) launched investigations of Communist infiltration in the United States, and— also marching to Hoover's drumbeat—the commercial media system increasingly presented frightful dramatizations of what would happen if the "Red Menace" was permitted to succeed.

A lurid photo essay in *Look* magazine, "Could the Reds Seize Detroit?" clearly illustrates the ways in which the media provided a venue for anti-Communist fear mongering.[49] Staged photographs portrayed a nightmare vision of America's motor city in the grip of takeover and chaos. One caption described "Red" goons spreading "confusion throughout a terror-gripped city, as this picture shows." Other documentary-style images showed gunmen in the streets, communications centers with operators holding their hands up, jail breaks, seizures of radio stations, and the takeover of police stations. The routinization of such images in American popular culture during this period served primarily to pollute the social environment with paranoia and distrust.

"When a subject appears to be all around him," an influential public relations specialist, Philip Lesly, wrote in 1974, "a person tends to accept it and take it for granted." Offering a profound look at public relations thinking as it evolved in the postwar era, Lesly continued: "It becomes part of the atmosphere in which he lives. He finds himself surrounded by it and absorbs the climate of the idea."[50]

Never was this rendition of the public relations process more fitting than in the late forties and early fifties as anticommunism pushed its way through the American grooves of thought. Not only was the general political climate affected, but in a number of critical areas, the attack on social Keynesianism and on the premise of federally secured rights was both fierce and effective. One such area was health care.

Despite attempts to create a national health care system during the New Deal years, efforts in this direction had not succeeded. Following the war, however, as "public ultimatums" continued to be put forth, the prospect of universal, federally insured health coverage seemed bright. In January 1949, with national health insurance bills pending in Congress, many assumed that passage of this "must" legislation was a foregone conclusion. Among organized national constituencies, only doctors—fearing that their customary prerogatives would be encroached upon—were vocally opposed to national health insurance.

Panicked by the idea that doctors' customary entitlements would be smothered by a national health insurance system, the socially conservative American Medical Association (AMA) resolved to launch a vast and costly public relations campaign to defend the autonomy of private physicians and scuttle the prospect of health insurance legislation being enacted. To manage this effort, the AMA hired Clem Whitaker and Leone Baxter, a California-based husband-wife public relations team.

A decade before, with reform legislation and a number of other factors limiting the ability of customary party structures to function effectively in California, Whitaker and Baxter pioneered mass media campaign techniques—newspaper, radio, and so forth—in support of right-wing candidates.[51] Their methods had been successfully used to malign Upton Sinclair, the Socialist Party candidate for governor of California, and played a role in defeating a referendum that would have placed regulatory controls on chain supermarkets.[52]

When medicine "got militant . . . [and] threw its full weight into the counterattack" against national health insurance, Whitaker and Baxter were brought in to devise the AMA's battle plan. To derail national health insurance, Whitaker explained, public relations conventions had to be pushed aside. Developments that threatened to undermine the traditional power of doctors, he argued, required the use of extraordinary measures.

Most of us have been trained to keep our clients *out of controversy*. Under normal conditions, that is a worthy objective. But these are not normal times—and there are circumstances under which it is both bad public relations and moral cowardice to keep our clients out of controversy.

Postwar America provided one of those circumstances, and the AMA campaign was marked by an aggressive smear attack that linked national health insurance—and government-insured health rights—with communism.

As the campaign was designed, health care needs were downplayed, and the evil of governmental intervention gained the spotlight. The campaign was not based on health care, but was premised, instead, on protecting a way of life. "Our whole economic system is under fire today," Whitaker explained. "[T]he very system we live by is coming under increasing challenge—and we must either stand and defend it, or we must prepare to surrender it."[53]

To defend the AMA's position, as Baxter noted, she and her husband painstakingly exploited the rhetoric of coercion to explain the evil lurking behind the supposed altruism of the health insurance bills. Over an eleven-month period, fortified by the largest public relations war chest ever assembled to that point—$1.4 million—Whitaker and Baxter waged a pervasive and successful public attack on what they christened "Compulsory Health Insurance," adjusting this message to appeal to farmers' organizations; women's clubs; and religious, veterans', business, educational, and civic groups. By November 1949, national health insurance was dead in the water, the victim—in large part—of a calculated public tie-in with an un-American way of life.[54]

The AMA war chest, however, was not simply used to demonize the socialistic complexion of "compulsory health insurance." As Baxter reported, at the tail end of the AMA campaign, while half the funds was used to mount "defense and attack" strategies, the other half was used "for the constructive job of building, extending, and improving the services of the voluntary health insurance system."[55]

"We need the complete confidence and militant support of the American people," Baxter asserted, and tangible alternatives to a federally administered health care system had to be developed. Responding to this necessity—part of *a great compromise* that was forged between big business and organized labor during this period—private health insurance increasingly emerged as an expected part of many workers' "fringe benefits" packages. Though the idea of health insurance as a federally guaranteed right was sacrificed in the process—an occurrence that, in the long run, would prove fateful—it appeared that health care had become a de facto, privately provided entitlement for an unprecedented number of working-class Americans. In the wake of this development, our current health care system—a powerful, privately dominated medical-industrial complex—began to take shape in lieu of a federally stipulated system of care.

Without doubt, the robustness of America's corporate economy—from the late forties well into the sixties—made welfare capitalist programs, like privately run health care, possible. Just as anticommunism served as an ideological springboard for the attack on New Deal principles, America's economic boom of the postwar period buttressed big business' unprecedented ability to provide apparently meaningful alternatives to government-funded programs. Abetted by increasingly pro-business and anti-Communist Congresses and presidential administrations, a shift away from the New Deal's *social Keynesianism* was taking place. More and more, from this period forward, federal policy would be defined by a *commercial Keynesian* approach, one that used federal spending to subsidize private industries.

This shift was particularly evident in the late forties, when private builders and real estate interests mounted a massive public relations campaign against federally sponsored public housing programs. In the years leading to the Great Depression, the private building industry had increasingly focused on the profitable practice of building houses for affluent Americans. As the New Deal addressed a severe housing crisis during the depression, it began to launch federal housing programs aimed at serving the needs of those who had been customarily ignored by private-sector builders and real estate interests. Greenbelt communities and other planned community experiments became an integral part of the New Deal agenda. In support of the "greater good," the promise of decent housing for all Americans emerged as one of the nation's most widely hailed objectives.

Following the war, the promise of new housing for returning veterans and their families picked up again. While some continued to believe that innovative federal housing programs were most capable of securing the needs of the many working- and middle-class Americans who were returning from the war, the private housing industry launched a multilevel PR effort to promote private development and to defeat the spread of "socialistic" pipe dreams.

The assault on government-built housing was closely coordinated with the attack on national health insurance.[56] As with the AMA effort, the campaign for private housing waved a red flag, smearing public housing as part of the treacherous drift toward godless communism.

Sustaining a publicity campaign managed by the PR firm of Bell, Jones and Taylor, private building interests also benefited from opportunistic boosters in Congress who argued that "in city after city, Communists were boisterous in the advocacy of more and more public housing." One of these supporters was Joseph McCarthy, junior Senator from Wisconsin, whose notorious career commenced with a frontal attack on public housing as a Communist plot. "The aim of . . . professional public housers," McCarthy declared, "is to socialize all housing under the guise of providing housing for the underprivileged."[57]

"There are those who maintain that because private enterprise has not solved" the housing crisis, McCarthy observed in a 1947 report, "we should scrap private enterprise and socialize housing." Against such fickle schemes, McCarthy proposed that it "seems only logical that instead of attempting to scrap private enterprise, we should furnish the necessary aids to make it work."[58]

As was the case with the campaign against national health insurance, an anti-Communist assault on federal housing was coupled with a campaign to develop a private low-cost housing program for returning veterans. In support of this campaign, McCarthy's proposal became the guiding U.S. housing policy. The Federal Housing Administration provided guaranteed loans to veterans so they might purchase mass-produced suburban houses built by the private building industry. Ironically, the private alternative to public housing—exemplified by tract developments like Levittown—was subsidized, in large measure, by the so-called scourge of federal spending.

Health care and housing were but two indices of a society that was beginning to withdraw from assumptions that had gained acceptance during the New Deal years. Though many New Deal innovations would remain and federal programs would continue to provide important protections for a period of decades (in areas of social security, unemployment compensation, environmental protection, and occupational health and safety), a surrogate model of

KARL

GROUCHO

Which Marx Gets the Biggest Laugh?

The Marx named Karl, founder of communism, was a dour character who lived in the Nineteenth Century. A deadpan kind of comic of the Buster Keaton-Ned Sparks type, his act was to say funny things as though they weren't funny at all.

The Marx named Groucho, on the other hand, is an out-and-out yak man. He's funny all the way.

You get Groucho's lines right away. Karl's become funny only over the long pull—a few decades or so. Trouble is, sometimes, that a lot of mischief goes on before people get the humor of it. Subtle, Karl's stuff is.

Like where he says capitalism leads to the concentration of wealth in the hands of the few and the impoverishment of the people as a whole. You don't get that one until you try to find a place to park, down-town amid all the impoverished people shopping like mad in the department stores. When you do, it kills you. Nobody is *that* funny.

Or like where Karl says the only answer is for workers to seize the tools of production and hand them over to the government to run. You don't get that until you see newsreels of the new Russian automobiles, and see that they'd be sneered off any used-car lot in America. Then you're doubled up in the aisle, especially when you see that only Generals and Commissars are riding at all. Even Groucho isn't so funny, after all.

Or Karl's line about the miserable hovels in which workers must live, stiff with cold as they huddle about the charcoal brazier. You don't get that until Saturday night when you hear the furnace click on and you notice that the only thing huddled around the charcoal brazier are the hamburgers. That stretches you out holding your sides.

Funny thing is, that only under capitalism is there ever enough money for comedians. So when it comes to comics, we've made our choice. Groucho can stick to romantic roles, where he and his countless admirers will have more fun. We'll stick to Karl. He's the biggest laugh of all times.

E.I. DU PONT DE NEMOURS & CO. (INC.), WILMINGTON DELAWARE

(Advertisement)

BETTER THINGS FOR BETTER LIVING...*THROUGH CHEMISTRY*

July, 1952

social progress was being posed, one that advertised a future of universal well-being, sustained by the benevolence of unencumbered private corporations.

As long as the postwar period of U.S. economic expansion endured, this "welfare capitalist" vision gained adherents. Higher wages, private pension programs, a move from working-class to middle-class lifestyles, and the widespread availability of modern consumer goods provided material validation for a social outlook that, to a great extent, had been promoted by public relations specialists in the years following the war. According to the fable, capitalism had reformed itself. Workers and capitalists had found common ground in a burgeoning consumer culture. There was no more conflict.

As the fifties commenced, a sense of triumph infused business circles. The assault on New Deal principles had gained ground, and through the institution of new social initiatives, business seemed to have moved beyond the reach of historic class antagonisms. In 1951 the editors of *Fortune* magazine crowed about the "permanent revolution" that had taken place in relations between capital and labor. "Never have left-wing ideologies had so little influence on the American labor movement as they have today," they boasted. Because of the general improvement in material living standards and the enactment of tangible programs in response to public ultimatums, social contradictions that had dogged capitalism since the nineteenth century—and had served to motivate the birth of corporate public relations—appeared to have vanished.

"Fifty years ago," *Fortune* editors acknowledged, "American capitalism seemed to be what Marx predicted it would be and what all the muckrakers said it was—the inhuman offspring of greed and irresponsibility. . . . It seemed to provide overwhelming proof of the theory that private ownership could honor no obligation except the obligation to pile up profits."

In the postwar period, however, a "great transformation" had taken place. Common "intellectual stereotypes" of class conflict had suddenly become obsolete. Corporate prosperity, combined with the pressure of public ultimatums, had brought about a total change. People in "moderate income families" the magazine tooted, had radios; electric sewing machines; refrigerators; vacuum cleaners; automobiles; insurance; medical, dental, surgical, and hospital care; and so forth—all achieved through private channels. "It is perfectly evident from the above list, that it is not the capitalists who are using the people, but the people who are using the capitalists."

This world turned upside down, as *Fortune* presented it, was nothing less than the final triumph of public opinion, particularly opinion as represented by "the rising power of [organized] labor, which has forced a revision of capitalist thinking and capitalist practices."[59] In the face of incontestable public ultimatums, according to this narrative, American consumers had become kings and queens and corporations, their humble and ever-faithful servants.

16
Engineering Consensus

F OR THE FIELD OF public relations, like the society around it, the decade following the end of the Second World War was a period of blinding contradictions. On the one hand, "welfare capitalist" PR agendas—underscoring democratic ideals and building on the notion of inherent social and economic rights—announced that the voice of the people had been heard. Corporate America, so went the narrative, was respectfully and deferentially beckoning to its call. According to this majestic promise, the ancient utopian longing for universal well-being was—at last—in the process of being satisfied.

At the same time, however, the crusade against Godless Communism—and the demonization of all but a "private enterprise" point of view—was petitioning people's darkest fears, molding their anxieties into a bleak environment of political silence. Paralleling a determined attempt to respond to the demands of an active public, a reborn Le Bonianism was also emerging, one that sought—once again—to transform the democratic public into a silent and manageable entity.

Nowhere was this curious juxtaposition of democratic ideals and ardent mass manipulation more eloquently found than in Edward L. Bernays's 1947 essay, "The Engineering of Consent."[1] Just as James Madison's Federalist Paper No. 10 provides an incisive glimpse into the thinking that propelled the Founding Fathers to draft a new Constitution for the United States in 1789, Bernays's "Engineering of Consent" offers a revealing look at the ideas that have come to inform the exercise of political and economic power in our own time. The essay remains one of the clearest statements of the assumptions and

This full-page advertisement, placed in the *New York Times* by Edward L. Bernays's PR firm, speaks to the widespread sense of social insecurity that plagued corporations like Standard Oil of New Jersey as the war came to an end.
COURTESY SPECTOR & ASSOCIATES, INC.

strategies that have guided public relations practices in the United States since the war's end.

Preempting the ambience of incorruptibility that surrounds the Constitution, Bernays opened his essay invoking the Bill of Rights. In his reading of these basic constitutional protections, however, he made one curious addition. Conveniently evading the issue of *who controls* or *who has access to* the modern instruments of communication, Bernays declared that "Freedom of speech and its democratic corollary, a free press, have tacitly expanded our Bill of Rights to include the right of persuasion."

Given recent history, the embrace of the Bill of Rights was indispensable. Throughout the Second World War, tales of Nazi propaganda and thought control had given systematized techniques of persuasion an unsavory reputation, one that persisted in the popular culture of the postwar period. It was critical, therefore, for Bernays to couch his argument in terms that were compatible with liberal democratic ideals.

Bernays did not define this expansion of the Bill of Rights as an augmentation of public dialogue, however. Rather, he stated that it was a prerogative permitting those who understood—and had access to—the cognitive highways of the modern media system to guide the views of the population at large. Attempting to dispose of any questions that his interpretation of democracy might provoke, Bernays declared that the breadth and pervasiveness of the mass media in the United States had, by the late forties, made this right of persuasion "inevitable."

> All these media provide open doors to the public mind. Any one of us through these media may influence the attitudes and actions of our fellow citizens.

Bernays then proceeded to outline the implications of this *inevitability* for the public relations specialist.

> The tremendous expansion of communications in the United States has given this Nation the world's most penetrating and effective apparatus for the transmission of ideas. Every resident is constantly exposed to the impact of our vast net-

work of communications which reach every corner of the country, no matter how remote or isolated. Words hammer continually at the eyes and ears of America. The United States has become a small room in which a single whisper is magnified thousands of times.

Given its connectedness to every arena of human interaction—formal and informal, organizational or merely conversational—the contemporary media structure provided publicists with a distribution system that corresponded to social life itself. It had become the surging heart of a modern circulatory system of thought; it pumped blood through the "crisscrossing" vessels and capillaries of human perception; it was the fountainhead from which the most distant extremities might be fed.[2]

Once impenetrably provincial, American society had, in Bernays's view, evolved into a modern highway system. An educated driver, equipped with the proper road maps, he maintained, could reliably transport psychological commerce anywhere that he wished.

Unlike Gabriel Tarde's similar argument—made half a century before—Bernays's remarks were neither speculative nor academic. To Bernays's pragmatic way of thinking, the modern infrastructure of communication disclosed—in its labyrinthine details—the intermediaries through which power would be effectively exercised in contemporary society.

> Knowledge of how to use this enormous amplifying system becomes a matter of primary concern to those who are interested in socially constructive action. . . . [O]nly by mastering the techniques of communication can leadership be exercised fruitfully.

Assisted by experts "who have specialized in utilizing the channels of communication," Bernays wrote, leaders will be able—whenever expedient—to "accomplish purposefully and scientifically what we have termed 'the engineering of consent.'" It can be routinely applied "to the task of getting people to support ideas and programs."[3]

Bernays willingly conceded the "possible evil" inherent in the use of such techniques the ways they might be employed to serve "anti-democratic purposes."[4] To Bernays, however, this caveat in no way invalidated the vital point of his argument. Given the scale of modern democratic society, he believed, the need to "engineer consent" had become a necessary precondition for the exercise of power.

Aware of the manipulative tone of his hypothesis, Bernays offered lip service to the idea of a democratic public as a body of informed citizens. Ideally, he proposed, the "engineering of consent" should be employed only with "the complete understanding of those whom it attempts to win over." "Under no circumstances," he cautioned, "should the engineering of consent supersede or displace the functions of the educational system, either formal or informal, in bringing about understanding by the people as a basis for action."

Venerable principles aside, however, Bernays moved swiftly to the kernel of his argument: the ongoing necessity—in an outwardly democratic society—to manufacture the imprimatur of "popular support" to validate the decision-making activities of elites.

> [The] engineering of consent will always be needed as an adjunct to, or a partner of, the educational process. . . . [I]t is sometimes impossible to reach joint decisions based on an understanding of facts by all the people. The average American adult has only six years of schooling behind him. With pressing crises and decisions to be faced, a leader frequently cannot wait for the people to arrive at even a general understanding.[5]

"Planning for mass persuasion," Bernays advised, "is governed by many factors that call upon all one's powers of training, experience, skill and judgement."[6] He then proceeded to specify the mechanisms through which the "engineering of consent" might be accomplished.

First, the public must be studied and analyzed as one considers the properties of any raw material prior to the manufacturing process.

> What are their present attitudes toward the situation with which the consent engineer is concerned? What ideas are the people ready to absorb? What are they ready to do, given an

effective stimulant. . . . What group leaders or opinion molders effectively influence the thought process of what followers? What is the flow of ideas—from whom to whom? To what extent do authority, factual evidence, precision, reason, tradition, and emotion play a part in the acceptance of these ideas.[7]

To gain a useful profile of the public, Bernays insisted, "painstaking research" must be performed; public temperatures must repeatedly be taken. The mental predilections of the group you wish to influence must be also particularized, to know *how*, or *which*, tactics might be successfully employed. Though Bernays's conception of "research" was not yet conversant with sophisticated demographic survey methods, computerized data analysis, or the use of "focus groups," he reflected an abiding faith in technocratic leadership and in the utility of social science inquiry as essential instruments of modern rule.

As Bernays moved from the problem of research to the question of tactics, it became unmistakably clear that if *leaders* were cognizant individuals, masters of modern science, *the public at large* was intellectually comatose and could be led, for the most part, by calculated appeals to its emotions.

> From the survey of opinion will emerge the major themes of strategy. Those themes contain the ideas to be conveyed; they channel the lines of approach to the public; and they must be expressed through whatever media are used. The themes are ever present but intangible—comparable to what in fiction is called the "story line."
>
> To be successful, the themes must appeal to the motives of the public. Motives are the activation of both conscious and subconscious pressures created by the force of desires. Psychologists have isolated a number of compelling appeals, the validity of which has been repeatedly proved in practical application.

This was a significantly different public from the one reported on by Elmo Roper two years earlier. Despite its battered emotional state,

Roper's public was defined by an insistent presence of mind. It knew that it wanted a guaranteed annual wage, and if private industry failed to bring that about, it would look to the government to do so. Roper's public exercised power; it was inextricably linked to the New Deal and to the mass mobilizations that had altered the political landscape during the thirties. It came to the table with a nonnegotiable set of stipulations: "[N]ever in the future shall property rights be placed above human rights. . . . [C]ontinued corporation dividends cannot be regarded as being as sacred as continued wages for labor."

In "The Engineering of Consent," this headstrong public was conspicuously absent. There was no bargaining table, there was no fractiousness; there were only "open doors to the pubic mind." Sticking to his guns and apparently unfazed by the turmoil of the Great Depression, Bernays painted a portrait of a governable public that was decidedly neo-Le Bonian in its outlook. His public was essentially visceral. It was not a subject, but an object, a thing that could be known and, once known, managed. The capacity to think was not a quality of those who were situated on the receiving end of Bernays's engineered public communications. Thought would only be a hindrance.

This understanding of leadership and of the public underscored the importance of stagecraft. The ability to generate easily digested mental environments would determine what passed for truth. If Jefferson had once maintained that the "diffusion of information" was essential to the livelihood of an informed democratic citizenry, Bernays's essay registered the moment in time when the "diffusion of information" would increasingly serve as a gambit for the manufacture of instrumental truths.

As Bernays explained it, "the engineer of consent *must create news.*" He must orchestrate public occurrences so they will be noticed and will harvest the acquiescence necessary to sustain a desired outcome.

> News is not an inanimate thing. It is the overt act that makes news, and news in turn shapes the attitudes and actions of people. A good criterion . . . is whether the event juts out of the pattern of routine. The developing of events and circumstances that are not routine is one of the basic functions of the engineer of consent. Events so planned can be projected

over the communication systems to infinitely more people than those actually participating, and such events vividly dramatize ideas for those who do not witness the events.

The imaginatively managed event can compete successfully with other events for attention. Newsworthy events, involving people, usually do not happen by accident. They are planned deliberately to accomplish a purpose, to influence our ideas and actions.[8]

Implicit within this argument was a modern rendition of William James's belief that "truth happens to an idea," a total blurring of all distinctions between social fact and theatrical fantasy. To be effective, information must be calculated to stir an audience, to provoke an enduring psychological bond between *the public* and *the corporate*.

At Standard Oil, Earl Newsom epitomized this train of thought. Describing the key factor in a "good public relations program" at the 1946 Public Relations Conference, Newsom cited the need to identify and exploit those symbols to which the public is predisposed to respond.

[A]ll people share some important emotional attitudes . . . it is these very elements which people do have in common that can lead us to the touchstones for which we are looking.

The clear, noteworthy image thrown upon the screen must be one of portraying our company as *wanting the things that people want.* There must be a merging of image and audience if people are to say "That is my kind of company—that is good—let us keep and preserve and extend that institution." The image cannot be one of human exploitation, of ruthlessness, of greed, of selfishness.

The image must be a *human* image. For it must reveal a company as an organization of human beings. For, you see, we are asking people to "join our crowd"—they who want so much to join a crowd.[9]

Behind all this was a recommitment to an idea of a public driven by its emotions, essentially unconscious and incapable of critical reason. It was also a repudiation of the principal of participatory democracy, which had—if for only a brief time—reinvigorated the American political climate during the 1930s. It looked ahead, once again, to a democracy that could be efficiently managed from above. Once condemned as wicked and uncontrollable, the "crowd mind" was now being conceived as a thing to be knowingly incited and instrumentally governed.

■   ■   ■   ■   ■

A tension between the assertion of democratic values and the disdainful manipulation of public sentiments was also reflected in the ways that PR people approached the question of visual imagery in the immediate postwar era. To some extent, this approach may be understood as a predictable reaction to the New Deal's successes in pictorial publicity. The photographs of the Farm Security Administration (FSA) and other examples of New Deal documentation had been extraordinarily effective in galvanizing public attention during the thirties. They had been so successful that, at times, business approaches to visual publicity seemed to borrow directly from New Deal techniques.

A 1941 advertisement for a stock-photography house, for example, punctuates the extent to which New Deal photography had become a visual archetype for truth in the minds of many Americans, one that businesses could not afford to ignore. Beneath a photo of two craggy-faced farmers—jawing with each other at the side of a barn—the text cautioned advertisers that in their choice of advertising photographs, they must be aesthetically wide awake:

THESE FELLOWS RECOGNIZE PHONY FARMERS. . . .
Dirt farmers can spot phony farm pictures in a flash.
Phony farm scenes, too. And you can't blame them if they connect
phony farm pictures in advertising with phony merchandise.
It takes more than whiskers, a red bandana and a
straw in the mouth to make a farmer.
It takes dirt farming.
That is why we suggest—AUTHENTIC farm photographs
in your advertising. Prints sent to agency men
without cost or obligation.[10]

At Standard Oil of New Jersey (SONJ), the desire to commandeer a populist tone, to communicate visual connections between SONJ and the lives of ordinary Americans, led the company, in 1943, to hire Roy Stryker to head a special photographic unit in its public relations division.

When first offered the job, Stryker refused it. After all, he had grown up in a family where each night his father had prayed, *"Please God, damn the bankers of Wall Street, damn the railroads, and double damn the Standard Oil Company!"*[11] *"What would Standard Oil want from me, a New Dealer, the son of a Populist?"* he wondered.[12]

The political climate of the country was changing, however, and by 1942 the government's experiment in social photography had come to an end. Ultimately, Stryker accepted SONJ's offer as an opportunity to continue work he had begun in Washington.

Looking at the photographs taken for SONJ today, one is struck by their kinship to the FSA pictures. Some of the photographers—such as John Vachon and Russell Lee—had worked with Stryker in the thirties; the others were deeply influenced by a New Deal sensibility. While the photographs avoided the extreme poverty and environmental breakdown found in much of the FSA work, the SONJ pictures were steeped in an idea of "the people" that was linked to the New Deal era. Though taken in regions dominated by the oil industry, the pictures were populated by ordinary folks in their ordinary lives. As with the FSA photos, an aura of realism was conjured in the stark eloquence of black and white. There was no explicit promotion of the company or its products.

For SONJ, however, this was exactly the point. Badly in need of an improved corporate image, SONJ embraced Stryker's rudimentary visual populism as something that might transfer an atmosphere of social concern to a company long known for its cold-bloodedness.

The desire to annex the charisma of New Deal aesthetics also drove SONJ's decision, in 1947, to hire Robert Flaherty—the respected filmmaker who made the documentary *Nanook of the North*—to produce *Louisiana Story*. Shot in the bayou country of Louisiana, the film told a poignant story of a friendship between an oil-field worker and a local boy.

As with Stryker's photography project, Flaherty's film did not openly promote the corporation. "The words 'Standard Oil Company

When Roy Stryker headed the FSA photography project, many photographs presented an ironic contrast between the stark realities of ordinary Americans and the faded hyperboles of corporate merchandising. Less than a decade later, in photos taken while Stryker led the Standard Oil (New Jersey) Photography Project, such invidious comparisons vanished, replaced by images in which ordinary folks lived in frictionless proximity to the products and images of commercialism. An example is this 1944 Standard Oil photo by Sol Libsohn, "Soldier Home on Furlough," which places a huge bottle of Royal Crown Cola at the center of a joyful family reunion. Kodak Moments™, "You deserve a break today!" McDonald's commercials, and Friends and Family™ long-distance calling plans were just a few decades away. UNIVERSITY OF LOUISVILLE, PHOTOGRAPHIC ARCHIVES

(New Jersey)' or 'Esso,'" reported company vice president Stewart Schackne to the 1948 Public Relations Conference, "occur nowhere in the film. The only explicit Company connection," he allowed, "is the very slight and tenuous one that Humble [Humble, like Esso, was a principal corporate division of SONJ.] is included in a list of credits at the opening. Many of the picture's sequences," he added, "have nothing whatsoever to do with oil."[13] Here again, the objective was not to sell oil, but to present the company in human terms, to evoke a silent identity of interests between the SONJ and ordinary Americans.

In the case of *Louisiana Story,* the effort bore fruit. Shown at international film festivals, the film earned a number of prestigious awards. As it moved to commercial exhibition, the reviews were enthusiastic, and SONJ's financing of the project gained widespread approval.

"*Louisiana Story,*" raved a writer in the *Saturday Review of Literature,* "is sponsored by one of the most colossal of all industrial empires, Standard Oil of New Jersey. And . . . in the face of all the customary press agentry common to sponsored films, [Flaherty] . . . has produced a poetic vision and lasting human document which will bring pleasure and understanding to audiences for years to come." Regarding SONJ's association with the project, the reviewer continued:

> Many will ask, "What does it do for the sponsor?" Well it doesn't tell you to buy more oil . . . or that oil will win the war or save the peace. . . . It simply says there is a technology involved in getting oil from the earth. . . . It says that the men who do it are hard-working, intelligent, industrial craftsmen, decent and productive.

Even newspapers that were customarily hostile to Standard Oil, found merit in SONJ's involvement. "It so happens," wrote a reviewer in the *New York Star,* "that Standard Oil financed *Louisiana Story,* and if Standard Oil can feel anything, it ought to be delirious with joy. It ought to knock itself out patting itself on the back. For Flaherty, with his knack for making anything he touches endearing . . . has given even his oil well an entrancing human personality. . . . Yes, *Louisiana Story,*" the review closed, "makes a body like Oil."[14]

For Schackne, Flaherty's film and Stryker's photography project went far beyond a credible evocation of the New Deal's democratic ethos. Their achievement, argued a publicity director at the company's 1948 Public Relations Conference, was in their ability to set "an emotional tone" linking the company and the public on a psychological level, one that allowed "the Company and the public" to *"share an experience."*

This psychological communion, Schackne advised, must inform SONJ's public relations thinking overall. One could not expect the public to study and embrace the complexities of a corporate perspective. To guide public opinion it was necessary to speak to those regions of mind and spirit that religion—more than science—had customarily addressed. He continued:

> In this connection I might cite, with entire respect, the Roman Catholic Church, which frames the imposing logic of its theology in a setting designed to stimulate the emotions by color, architectural form, music, and all the beauties of art. . . . [W]e are trying to add to our public relations techniques what might be called some seismographic methods to probe into the depths of feeling as a supplement to the surface instruments of fact.[15]

■　■　■　■　■

Such statements spotlight and exemplify the Janus face of public relations in the years following the war. Accompanying an attempt to respond programmatically to tangible public ultimatums and to speak to democratic expectations that had accelerated in the United States from the early 1930s onward, there was a corresponding effort to erect an emotionally captivating corporate cosmology. Corporations, it was argued, must follow the lead of the Catholic Church and employ images—or other "seismographic" stimulants—to draw public sentiment to the "imposing logic" of the corporate system.

This renewed belief in psychological methods of persuasion was not simply a reiteration of Le Bonian tenets, however. It also reflected current changes taking place in American society. More than any other development of the period, the introduction of television as an American mass medium spoke to and informed these changes.

Years earlier, the poet Paul Valéry had remarked that "[j]ust as water, gas, and electricity are brought into our houses from far off . . . so we shall be supplied with visual or auditory images, which will appear and disappear at a simple movement of the hand, hardly more than a sign."[16] During the twenties, as modern channels of persuasion grew, this vision seemed to be nearing but still stood in the distance. Now, with commercial television's arrival in the late forties, Valéry's prophecy of an audiovisual utility system—a pervasive network of word-and-image faucets—was about to take hold. Unparalleled occasions to mold the public mind were in the offing.

Even during World War II, this buoyant sense of opportunity was evident. Speaking at the Boston Conference on Distribution in 1944, T. F. Joyce—general manager of RCA's Radio-Phonograph-Television Department—chalked out the ways that television would soon change the contours of American life, offering a variety of interests and an unparalleled instrument of persuasion.

> A nationwide television system is the medium which can arouse the spirit and will of the people. Through skillful use of a nationwide television system, American political, business, labor, religious and social leadership can create in the hearts and in the minds of America's 134,000,000 people the desire to bring about the peace, security and plenty that is the dream of every citizen.[17]

It was clear, however, that television would be of profounder service to business than to any other social sector. "No other medium so completely fulfills all the requirements of good advertising," Joyce noted.

> Television appeals at once to both the ear and to the eye. In visual appeal it surpasses printed advertisements. . . . It reproduces lifelike images that move and breathe instead of more static pictures which may have color and form, but show no signs of life. . . . [I]t is possible, therefore, to intensify the effect of a sales message upon the observer. . . . No other medium can do the job so well.

"If we have thirty million television equipped homes by the end of 1955," he exclaimed, "we will have thirty million showrooms where personal, dramatized demonstrations can be made, simultaneously."[18]

Shortly, Joyce's oracle of television's magnetic sway became a truism for those charged with the job of directing the attentions of the public mind. Writing in the *Public Relations Journal* in 1947,

Following the war, to bolster public enthusiasm for the development of nuclear energy, some who had been involved in the Manhattan project sought to impress the population with the safety of atomic technology when properly harnessed. This public relations photograph, taken of a group of Girl Scouts casually hiking past a nuclear reactor, was part of that instructional effort. FROM RACHEL FERMI AND ESTHER SAMRA, *PICTURING THE BOMB* (NEW YORK, 1995). COURTESY NATIONAL ARCHIVES AND RECORDS ADMINISTRATION

C. J. Durban of the U.S. Rubber Company offered his own personal observations of people watching television in the early days following its arrival.

> I have been in many television homes when the witching hour approaches—and this goes for any type of home. There is a bestirring and excitement—the chairs are placed—every-thing is gotten ready—with ash trays, the cigarettes, etc., within reach before it starts. . . . You know how it is. There is no television night in the week in which we mustn't have at

least four extra chairs. When you have something that important to the public . . . [y]ou have a potential public relations tool of tremendous value.[19]

Within this ebullient, if anecdotal, sociology of reception, there was an unmistakable sense that television was an opinion manager's dream come true. Television created the opportunity to guide people's thoughts and behavior in an unprecedented manner, right in their living rooms. In private spaces throughout the nation, the public was now being assembled simultaneously, its eyes and ears all tuned in the same direction, stupefied by the peculiar charisma of a newfangled messenger.

In many quarters, the protean authority of the television medium was being noted with comparable grandiosity. Bishop Fulton J. Sheen—one of the first clerics to test the waters of televangelism— explained that it "is fitting that every new medium be used for diffusion of the Word." Television, he continued, was particularly serviceable to the promulgation of Christian doctrine.

> Radio is like the Old Testament, inasmuch as it is hearing without seeing. Television is the New Testament, for in it the Word is made flesh and dwells in our living room.[20]

Against the memory of mass mobilizations and the immediate thundercloud of public ultimatums, television was not simply inspiring as a technology for communicating ideas. It was also a powerful social metaphor. It accentuated the idea of public life as a spectacle, a thing to watch more than to participate in. In its panoptic architecture—its highly centralized system of distribution, its overwhelmingly privatized mode of reception—it suggested a communicative structure particularly suited to the molding and maintenance of a *virtual public.*

This sensibility is discernible in the thinking of public relations people as they navigated the political quietude and relative prosperity of the fifties. Clearly, corporate public relations was assisted by the climate of the red scare. Those willing to publicly challenge a business point of view were becoming more and more guarded, as the film and broadcast industries—along with educational institutions throughout the country—-were purged of those harboring "impure" thoughts. But the instrument of television was equally intoxicating.

It could wrap "gems of truth and wisdom," as Leone Baxter put it in 1950, "in a scintillating mantle that in one way or another captures the interest of the beholder, makes him stop and listen." It could present "abstract ideas in attractive form to masses of people who are too occupied with their daily lives to think analytically on their own account."[21] As never before, public relations people exuded a sense of unlimited access to people's personal lives and inner psyches. Fortified by television—but mirroring habits of thought that went at least as far back as Gustave Le Bon—the key to their excited sense of power was *the image*.

The notion of *projecting an image* to a public that never assembled as such was becoming the ascendant definition of corporate public relations activity.[22] The capacity to "open closed minds" through "dramatic picture building," as Baxter termed it, seemed more and more feasible.[23]

Such ideas ran through the deliberations of a rapidly expanding opinion-management industry. Across the nation, corporate public relations specialists were becoming increasingly obsessed with the extraordinary authority of images and with television's unparalleled capacity to deliver them.

An example of this new sense of empowerment is found in an unpublished report, "Telephone News on Television," in which Chester Burger—a pioneer in the field of media consultancy—candidly advised American Telephone and Telegraph (AT&T) on the role of television in the company's public relations future. "Telephone News on Television," according to Burger, was one of the first guidebooks ever written on the tactical uses of television as a medium of persuasion.[24]

To some extent, Burger's 1955 report approached television as one might evaluate any potential public relations medium: in terms of the number of people it reached. "People have the television news habit," he began. "[N]etwork news programs reach 15 million homes. ... A medium as important as television, therefore, should receive important consideration in any public relations program."[25]

Yet Burger's report looked far beyond television news' demographic reach. It examined the television medium as a unique tool of communication, one that required a different public relations approach from that used with other media. Already in 1955, one of television's most salient characteristics was its informational brevity, the proclivity among television news producers to process information in the form of "bites." This tendency, Burger recommended, should guide the kinds of materials provided to television news operations: the linguistic conventions that that should be strictly adhered to.

> A written release should be shorter than the average newspaper story. Many newscasters will not use a story that takes longer than 30 seconds to read, and the absolute limit virtually everywhere is one minute.

Given this need for brevity, he continued, the verbal patois of television should be impersonated in its details:

> [S]entence structure should be simplified. Sentences should be conversational. Familiar words should be used. . . . A story should not sound like an official pronouncement. Instead it should sound as if the newscaster were casually telling a story to a friend.[26]

Beyond Burger's attention to the application and framing of words for television, he focused at great length on the *language of the image,* the ways that pictures mutely—yet persuasively—convey meaning. For AT&T, he advised, such considerations should commence with who is selected to represent the company on television. Being telegenic was becoming an essential piece of a corporate executive's job definition.

> The person you choose will represent the telephone company to thousands of viewers. His title or official position with the company will be less important to the Company, the newscaster, and the audience than the impression he makes.[27]

Similar considerations should inform the kind of film footage that is provided to television stations for a news story, he wrote. Inasmuch as "pictures are the language of television," it is necessary to produce materials that are conspicuous in their ability to stir "maximum visual interest." Just as a spokesman's "impression" is more important than his title, the power of film footage must rest, almost exclusively, on "the existing elements of motion and visual interest" in a story.

> Motion picture film has its own language, its own grammar, just as does the language of words. The pictures must be relied upon to tell the story by themselves. *This is so because research psychologists have discovered that the television audience gives most of its attention—some say 75%—to the picture.*
>
> The practical significance of this is that the cameraman must tell your story in pictures. . . . The picture, not the narration has primacy. *The pictures don't illustrate the story; they are the story.* The narration merely helps the pictures.[28]

Public relations was becoming aware of the optic unconscious as never before. If one moved beyond words and relied on images, the message sent out would be irresistible. Charles M. Hackett, of E. I. DuPont's Public Relations Department, emphasized this point, encouraging his peers to embrace the "Forceful and Vivid Vernacular of the Eye" and learn to exploit its uncanny narrative structure.

> [T]he most vigorous employment of pictures—and the one least understood—is the use of the picture itself as the storytelling medium. Here the picture says it all—it speaks in exclamation points, it shouts. It puts across its message in the quickest, most direct way, without need of the written word.
>
> Such a picture has a simplicity—it makes a definite point. It has impact. It is relentless; its conclusion is as inescapable as a black eye.[29]

Professional analysts of public opinion were quick to embrace the drift toward pictorial persuasion. George Gallup, for example, published an article in 1956, betraying with rare candor the extent to which survey researchers were interested in methods of shaping—as much as measuring—opinion. Writing in the *Public Relations*

Journal, Gallup praised the growing number of PR practitioners who were mastering the art of the visual. Radio was still about words, he wrote, but "[n]ow the wheel of technology has turned again and a new band of professionals who think and talk in terms of pictures is emerging. . . . The job of developing a language of pictures will never be finished, but already research is beginning to formulate the principles that make for successful communication through pictures." He went on, citing the ways that producers of television commercials were among the most noteworthy at acquiring these skills.

> Successful picture language uses the video to communicate specific ideas or sales arguments. Effective commercials make sure the "pictures" tell the sales story.[30]

To steer public opinion effectively in the future, Gallup concluded, this skill with television must be cultivated further.

> [W]ords will always be primary vehicles of communication, but now that electronic science has given us new ways to transmit pictures, a great new opportunity is afforded to reach and impress a message on the minds of millions of viewers.[31]

Another prominent pollster, Claude Robinson—president of Opinion Research, Inc., in Princeton, N.J.—shared Gallup's enthusiasm for television, but thought that too few professionals yet understood the new medium. "There is a cultural lag in the use of television as a communication medium," he complained. "Television commercials are still being written for radio, depending mostly on words for the communication of ideas." This anachronistic understanding of how to reach an audience, he proclaimed, must be replaced. "A theory of how to make pictures talk—we might call it 'a language of pictures'—needs to be formulated."[32]

Taking their lead from the example being set by television, a growing number of corporations were recognizing "image" as a crucial piece of capital, one that called for considerable investment. A "corporate visual program is rapidly becoming a complex and indispensable part of corporate public relations," remarked J. Gordon Lippincott, whose company (Lippincott & Margolies) led the way in a profession dedicated to creating a "corporate look." The corporation, Lippincott maintained, must silently broadcast a coherent picture of itself in minute detail.

> Into the corporate look goes a myriad of images—the corporate package, advertisement, trademark, exhibit, logotype, nameplate, stationery, posters, billboards, direct mail, plant or office—and especially the product. These images must transmit a single impression so that the viewer's idea of the company is continually refreshed and enriched—but never contradicted.[33]

To corroborate this vision, Lippincott quoted the *Wall Street Journal*:

> Today's query for corporation presidents [is]: Does your company have a visual identity? Do your buildings, your letterheads, your office decorations, your reports to stockholders, your trademarks, your ads and your products picture you and only you in the public eye? If they don't you may be at a competitive disadvantage.[34]

In 1961, Louis A. Magnani, vice president and executive art director of Marsteller, Inc. (Now Burson, Marsteller), articulately distilled a train of thought that had taken flight at the inception of commercial television and summed up its implications for the job of the PR expert:

> [V]isuals remain in a person's mind long after oratorical appeals to actions have faded away. . . . There's no doubt that the hand is quicker than the eye in the world of magic, so in the equally intangible world of ideas, let's give the eye a hand by dreaming up a good visual to sell the idea.[35]

■　■　■　■　■

Some PR specialists were convinced that televisual strategies would be particularly useful in the political realm, where the ability to assemble publics was an elemental requirement. In 1956—a year when the recognition of the power of images appears to have skyrocketed— James Kelleher, who had done promotional work for Chrysler Corporation and the U.S. Army, proclaimed that from this time forward, political presentations must be deliberately "designed to create an overall impression rather than hammer home specific points."

The politician, he counseled, must be an actor, not a policy expert. "Restrained underplay, the perennial essential of good drama, must be built into every show." To achieve this goal, Kelleher continued, meticulous stage direction is a must. The viewer must be imagined in a home setting, and messages should be crafted to harmonize with this perceptual venue. Visual politics through the medium of television, he explained, "replaces bombastic 'telling' of the usual political speech with the individualized 'showing' which the intimate nature of television and the effectiveness of visual content permits." In short,

> [e]ach political telecast must combine the intimacy of the stage with the planned perfection of a film and confidence inspiring quality of radio.[36]

As Kelleher theorized, at least one man—escorted by a team of experienced handlers—was putting such ideas into practice, apprenticing in a corporate public relations environment that would soon be transposed to the American political stage. His name was Ronald Reagan, and from the beginning, his peculiar metamorphosis from Hollywood actor to president was guided by corporate public relations specialists. Reagan's political biography embodied the evolution of corporate public relations thinking as it had evolved since the 1920s: its gospel of free enterprise aimed at corralling the affections of primarily white, middle-class Americans; its cynical emulation of New Deal politics; its steadfast gravitation toward a rhetoric of images.

Just as corporate PR during the thirties was compelled to respond to FDR's wizardry as a publicist, Reagan's journey toward the public stage was also provoked by Roosevelt's extraordinary public appeal. Some have described the early Reagan simply as an ardent New Dealer, but Howard Chase's reminiscence of him puts this label into clearer focus. In 1991, Chase spoke of a day more than fifty years earlier, when he and his friend Reagan witnessed

President Roosevelt's visit to Iowa City, where both were working in the local media.[37] As FDR's motorcade rolled through town, they watched together from an office window close above the street. Reagan, Chase recalled, was thoroughly mesmerized by Roosevelt, not by the president's policies or his political vision, but by his uncanny magnetism. He found FDR's empathic and strikingly accessible presence electrifying. Years later, even as Reagan moved toward the political Right—first as a corporate spokesman, then as an elected politician—communications lessons learned from FDR were never forsaken.

Reagan's first opportunity to mimic this ideal came in 1954. Paid what was an enormous salary at the time, he left a film career to begin an eight-year stint as an official public spokesman for the General Electric Corporation (GE); his job was to humanize the industrial giant. Not only did he host television's weekly *General Electric Theater,* but he also spent a great deal of time roaming the nation as an affable cheerleader for private enterprise, addressing employees at GE plants across the United States.[38] Traveling from town to town, he would mix with workers and deliver up to fourteen speeches a day. By the end of his tenure, he had visited every company facility and had met with nearly all its 250,000 employees. "We drove him to the utmost limits. We saturated him in Middle America," remembered GE PR man Edward Langley.[39] Expanding his already considerable exposure as a corporate pitchman, Reagan also became a regular speaker for the National Association of Manufacturers (NAM) during these years.[40]

Reagan's appeal was rooted in his remarkable capacity to gain the confidence of ordinary folks. He saw himself as one of them. "Would you laugh," he once asked rhetorically, "if I told you that I think, maybe, they see themselves and that I'm one of them? I've never been able to detach myself or think that I, somehow, am apart from them."[41]

Reagan's telegenic and winsome ordinariness made him a perfect corporate spokesman, an ideal cover for conservative political motives. In his neighborly persona, he allowed white, middle-class everymen to imagine themselves as having actually assumed power. At the same time, he promoted policies that served the interests of a small corporate elite: corporate welfare, tax relief for the rich, high-profit military production, anti-environmentalism, rollbacks aimed at the rights of labor, corporate deregulation, and the dismantling of New Deal–inspired social guarantees.

Managed by a corporate coterie—people conversant with the notion of engineering consent—Reagan's own worldview was credibly prosaic. Neither a technocrat nor a conventional politician, he was, above all, an offspring of Hollywood. Not only had he worked as an actor in Hollywood, but he had also embraced Hollywood's conception of righteousness and heroism. This way of seeing, according to biographer Lou Cannon, was second nature to Reagan, who once described himself as a man with "an abiding belief in the triumph of good over evil," a person who believed in the existence of bona fide "heroes who live . . . by standards of morality and fair play." As Cannon read it, Reagan's bond with the American public was in his and their shared delusions. His mind was occupied by "a world defined by . . . stories, a make-believe world in which heroic deeds had the capacity to transform reality." Inside his head, the "heroic world of make-believe and the real world coalesced. The man who lived in both of them could not always distinguish one from the other, and he came to believe many things that weren't true."[42]

This impressionable character fit GE's conservative political agenda. An unreflective man, Reagan could be tutored, and toward this end—throughout Reagan's years at GE—he was chaperoned by a man named Earl B. Dunckel, who became his right-wing political mentor. As Dunckel and Reagan "travelled in trains and cars and stood about waiting for transportation in the nether hours of the day," noted another biographer, Anne Edwards, Dunckel would "drumbeat conservative politics at him." Soon, Reagan's folksiness was being employed to vilify governmental regulation, to express righteous indignation against "confiscatory" levels of taxation, and to promote other fixtures of the conservative gospel.[43]

Reagan's rise to political prominence drew on the same characteristics that facilitated his work as a corporate booster: his simple vernacular style, his accessibility, and his visceral embrace of Hollywood narrative as a way of seeing and describing reality. At a moment when the engineering of consent had become a given of American political life and pollsters were highlighting the need to master techniques for making "pictures talk," to apply "a language of pictures" to the arts of persuasion, the appearance of Reagan and—more important—of Reaganism, was overdetermined. More than anyone before, he incorporated NAM's approach to public relations as it had developed from the mid-1930s onward; he was the consummate admixture of corporate commercialism, right-wing politics, and homespun, visually oriented fictional entertainment.

Reagan's political career read as if it came directly from Burger's guidebook on PR. His instinctive flair for "staging an event," as Michael Deaver (Reagan's chief PR strategist from 1975 through the late 1980s) described it, was thoroughly attuned to a medium that communicates primarily via pithy visual tidbits.[44] "He came to office," Deaver explained, "at a time when the perception of what was done often mattered as much as what was actually done." Like most public relations thinking from the early fifties onward, Deaver's estimate was predicated on the social fact of television as the glue that both held together and undermined American *public life*.

> These may be harsh thoughts, and not what the scholars and intellectuals and other wizards want to believe. But in the television age, image sometimes is as useful as substance. Not as important, but as useful. . . . This is public-relations chatter, up to a point, and I am not embarrassed by it. Neither is Ronald Reagan.[45]

Reagan's appearance on the political stage was simply emblematic of his time. He was the issue of a society in which public relations had grown into an indispensable, increasingly universal, expedient of power. As the engineering of consent gained legitimacy—and as the demographic study of public attitudes and the packaging of reality grew in sophistication—the long and complicated relationship between publicity and democracy reached a critical juncture.

Democracy and its antithesis—the domination of the public sphere by moneyed elites—were reconciled as one. In 1962, reflecting on his world and questioning the profession he had helped to establish over the preceding twenty-five years, Chase characterized this calamitous unity of opposites both succinctly and eloquently. "The 'engineering of consent,'" he wrote, "implies the use of all the mechanics of persuasion and communication to bend others, either with their will or against their will, to some prearranged conclusion, whether or not their reaching that conclusion is in the public interest."[46] In the years since Chase drafted these words, the predicament for democracy that he so forthrightly described has only deepened.

C O D A

The Public and Its Problems:
Some Notes for the New Millennium

I<small>N</small> M<small>ARCH</small> 1995, as this book neared completion, Edward L. Bernays died in Cambridge, Massachusetts, at the age of 102.[1] Present at the beginning, so to speak, his life (1892–1995) spanned the history that is explored in this book. It is perhaps fitting, then, that just as we opened our quest standing at Bernays's doorstep, so we shall conclude with him.

When I visited with Bernays in the autumn of 1990, I encountered two different people. On the one hand, I met a man who—as witnessed in his nostalgic recollection of Dumb Jack—understood public relations as a necessary response to a society in which expanding democratic expectations were forcefully combating the outmoded assumptions of an old, hierarchical social order. According to this Bernays, the modern belief in universal rights and popular struggles for democracy had confronted elites with a profound question: How could they preserve their social, economic, and political advantages in an age when the idea of a privileged class was coming under mounting attack from below? This first Bernays understood the "public sphere" as contested ground and public relations as a historic response to the vocal demands of a conscious, and increasingly critical, public.

Yet as he described his life and his profession, I glimpsed another Bernays. This one saw the public as a malleable mass of protoplasm, plastic raw material that—in the hands of a skilled manipulator—could be manufactured at will. According to this Bernays, the public mind posed little danger and could be engineered through dexterous appeals to its instinctual and unconscious inner life. This Bernays was the paradigmatic "expert" in a world where "expertise" often refers to a scientifically trained individual's capacity to monitor, forecast, and influence the ideas and/or behavior of others.

This dichotomy characterized Bernays's thinking over a lifetime. In the pivotal years of the late 1940s, for example, Bernays evinced two dramatically dissimilar perspectives on the tasks faced by public relations specialists in a potentially hazardous postwar world.

At one end, in 1947, Bernays maintained that corporate public relations must answer to the ultimatums of a public that had—over the preceding decade and a half—become resolutely aware of its social and economic rights. Toward this goal, Bernays argued, "slogans" and "incantations" would be insufficient. Business must champion and establish policies that would lead to stable employment; adequate old-age pensions; social security; and other forms of insurance, including group accident, sickness, hospital, and life. These concessions, Bernays understood, were necessitated by a public arena that is shaped, at times, by the ideas and actions of ordinary people and by the social expectations they bring to the historical stage. Embedded within this side of Bernays's thinking was an understanding that, willy-nilly, powerful institutions were not always able to govern the dynamics—or the origins—of public expression. The mobilizations of the 1930s had actively punctuated that fact.

At the same time as Bernays was recommending substantive programmatic proposals, however, he was also ordaining the "engineering of consent" as an indispensable instrument of rule. This Bernays was the painter of mental scenery, the fabricator of captivating "pseudo-environments" designed to steer the public mind furtively toward the agendas of vested power. He was a master of stagecraft, shaping "news" and "events" with a hidden hand. Beside the democrat stood the demagogue, a nimble master of illusions, a man who sought to colonize the public sphere on behalf of entrenched managerial interests.

It would be a misconception, however, to see Bernays's contradictions as particular to the man. The ambiguities of his perspective—the murky dissonance separating one who is *responding to* from one who seeks to *manage* the public mind—have marked the history of public relations throughout the twentieth century.

In the period between 1900 and the First World War, for example, the genesis of corporate public relations began as a reply to widespread public indignation at the prevailing practices of big business in the United States. Facing the muckraking publicity of progressivism and terrified by the articulate militancy of America's industrial work-force, large corporations began to employ public relations firms to reconcile the openly declared interests of business with the concerns and goals of a critical—albeit still primarily middle-class—public. In a variety of ways, public relations during this period attempted to provide factual argument and, at times, palpable actions that would answer antibusiness arguments and enunciate a commonality between the private enterprise system and the public interest.

During and after World War I, as progressivism waned and working-class militancy was crushed by a vicious program of repression, the complexion of PR began to change. Inspired by the propaganda successes of the wartime Committee on Public Information and fortified by theories of social psychology, corporate PR moved away from a "public service" ideal and increasingly aspired to stroke and cajole the public psyche. Throughout the twenties, a rapidly expanding legion of public relations experts embraced the conscious manipulation of symbols as the most effective strategy for appealing to the public mind. If, prior to the war, public relations had been fired by the apparition of an aware and discerning population—one that had vigorously influenced the boundaries of public discussion—the public was now being conceived as an unconscious organism, eminently susceptible to the mesmeric power of mass suggestion.

By the late forties, corporate PR had swung the other way. Chastened by a wave of mass mobilizations in the thirties and disciplined by social expectations that had come to the surface during the New Deal period, corporate public relations programs began to mouth New Deal values while advancing a welfare capitalist perspective. Recalling rampant public antagonism toward business throughout the Great Depression and concerned that it might burst forth anew as the war drew to an end, a growing number of corporations initiated pension funds, health plans, and other social security policies that an unprecedented number of Americans now understood to be a constitutionally guaranteed birthright. If the business sector didn't deliver on these promises, PR people reasoned, the public would turn once more toward their government, and the survival of "free enterprise" would be in jeopardy.

As American business flourished during the fifties and prosperity touched the lives of many heretofore "forgotten" Americans, the social emergency of the thirties began to disappear from public relations thinking. Coincidentally, the repressive impact of McCarthyism nursed the assumption that the public was becoming governable once again. In this climate, and emboldened by corporate control of a new and pervasive communications apparatus—television—new ways of thinking began to arise. Though they coincided—at least for a time—with welfare capitalist policies, these new ideas were built on the idea of a fragmentary and spectatorial public that could be swayed by images that were now being pumped, day and night, into each and every American home.

In the years since the 1950s, interactions between public relations and social history have persisted. During the 1960s and 1970s, public ultimatums began to emerge once again. Breaking the hush of the consensus of the fifties, corporate renditions of "the good life" and of the United States as the "land of opportunity" came under mounting scrutiny from within and outside American society. A multiplicity of voices, including those of the civil rights movement, the anti-Vietnam war movement, women's rights activity, and environmentalism, interrogated the values of a commodity culture and testified to the fact that many people were in exile in the "land of opportunity." Irreverent, noncommercial media also began to appear during this period—most notably "underground" newspapers, produced on a shoestring by journalistic fledglings uninstructed in the conventions of a business-dominated press. As these independent media spread throughout the country—reminding a generation that history was in their hands—habitual boundaries separating medium from audience were violated and redrawn.

As countercultural perspectives erupted, and in the face of mounting and diverse opposition, corporate PR thinking became defensive once more. Abandoning the certitude of the fifties, public relations experts now scrambled to address a public arena that seemed to be spinning out of control. "[W]e can preserve our freedom of enterprise only if it fulfills the aspirations of society," remarked Harold Brayman of DuPont in 1964. "We must learn," once again, "to adapt ourselves to the conditions that exist." To rise to the occasion, Brayman counseled, old ways of thinking would be ineffective. "One cannot fight in the jungles of Vietnam," he argued, "with battleships."[2]

David Finn, of the forward-thinking firm of Ruder and Finn, helped to retrain PR thinking during this period. Citing emerging social movements, most of which were questioning the "white bread" homogeneity of corporate life, Finn maintained that the overarching presence of "the corporate image" was not simply ineffective, but represented a fundamental public relations problem. One of a generation of PR men who came forward during the sixties, Finn argued that corporate public relations must shun the "party line" image of the corporation that had been so ardently assembled in the years after World War II. Corporate PR, he advised, must espouse and embrace the principles of diversity and self-determination that were—like it or not—gathering in the streets.

> What is wrong with the "party line" approach . . . is . . . the evils which come in the process of stifling individual initiative. It suggests that it is more important for the corporation to create an impression of monolithic unity than for individuals to express themselves freely.[3]

As had been the case throughout much of the century, this shift in public relations thinking reflected the imprint of popular democracy. If practitioners help to "build respect for variety in public life, for the right of people to hold different opinions and to express them freely," Finn asserted, "I think public relations can thus become an integral part of the democratic process." To be effective, he warned, public relations people must be closely tuned to the political intonations in their work.

> Public relations should . . . be wary of the dangers inherent in conformity, and the fact that its work could create its own brand of "big brotherness" if it is not careful. Public relations should not permit itself to envy the propaganda advantages which totalitarian governments sometimes achieve through their monolithic control of communications. Instead it should learn to respect difference, dissension, conflict, and above all, individuality . . .[4]

For about a decade, beginning in the mid-1960s, much public relations was in synch with Finn's remarks. As had been the case before, there was a need to adapt to changing social conditions. A prime example of this adaptation was the growing number of public relations people who discussed, as never before, the need to acknowledge the demands of the African American population in the United States.

"In the Negro community," wrote D. Parke Gibson, publisher of a newsletter focusing on marketing to African Americans, "the belief still exists, and it will for some time, that there is insincerity on the part of American corporations really to provide equality of opportunity to Negroes." To change this situation, Gibson proposed, companies must "[s]eek the advice of reputable Negro specialists in public relations in order to avoid the possibility of offending Negro Americans through well-meaning but wrong directed action."[5]

James F. Langton, public relations officer of the Bank of America, offered similar counsel. The civil rights struggle, he argued, was an inevitable outcome of America's past. Corporations, he wrote in the *Public Relations Journal,* must sensitize themselves to the history of race relations in the United States.

> After a long and agonizing history of white oppression, white violence and white hate, the Negro today is in a state of revolt. . . . It's time we understood this history and, with understanding, come to realize that Negro hate is the mirror of White hate, and Negro violence a mirror of White violence.[6]

As a start in the direction of redressing African Americans' grievances, he suggested, "There must be some aggressive employment programs designed to seek out and encourage trainable Negro applicants."[7]

To some extent, such ideas were consonant with the history of public relations as an imperative corporate response to popular democratic mobilizations. Here, as had been true in the past, corporations—prodded by the federal government—worked overtime to inaugurate social programs while they flooded the pipelines of persuasion to broadcast a spiritual bond between corporate activities and the interests of diverse American communities.[8]

The corporate recognition of American diversity, however, pointed in other directions as well. To some extent, it provided the core around which future approaches to the engineering of consent would be developed.

■   ■   ■   ■   ■

Whatever else may be said of the social movements of the 1960s, it must be conceded that they were animated by an intensely democratic vision. Young radicals of the period dared to imagine a future world in which social injustices predicated on class, race, gender, and persuasion would be redressed and in which the *wretched of the earth* would be rewarded by a realm of unbounded possibility. At the heart of sixties politics, then, stood the glaring conflict between a democratic ideal of universal rights and tenacious social realities that were still premised on the denial of these rights to significant portions of the population, both at home and abroad. Whether it was African Americans or Chicanos, heterosexual women or gays, U.S. soldiers in the jungles of Vietnam or students on the campuses of American universities, each constituency called America to task, each challenged the nation to implement its democratic pledge. In widespread calls for "participatory democracy," a vision of society, administered collectively by—and according to the needs of—its various constituents, was gaining ground.

As public relations experts approached the tumultuous terrain, however, an ominous shift began to take place. If, at the grassroots level, divergent voices were challenging the society to meet its responsibility to all its people, the opinion-measurement industry began a parallel effort to render this diversity of voices into a set of manageable categories. Beginning in the late sixties and intensifying from the seventies onward, public opinions and behaviors began to be demographically factored into discrete analytical units, an instrumental array of "lifestyles" or "subcultures" to be studied and, once studied, predictably governed. As social or cultural patterns have shifted, of course, specific categories have changed, but the intent of these pigeonholes has remained constant: to provide useful attitudinal road maps that permit compliance professionals—PR experts, political consultants, social psychologists, merchandisers, advertising copywriters, and the like—to target particular groups in an idiom they will perceive to be their own. *Democracy* has given way to *demography* as the prevailing American faith.

•   •   •

In 1940, market research pioneer Paul Cherington argued that opinion polling had provided a scientific instrumentality through which popular democracy could at last be realized. No longer "the ponderous slithering around of an unjelled protoplasm," he wrote, "public opinion has become organic." Modern "principles of statistical sampling," he vowed, had created a reliable mechanism through which "government of the people" could finally be achieved.[9] In the face of this democratic breakthrough, he argued, powerful institutions—public or private—could do no less than obediently submit to the *vox populi*.

To a large extent, this triumphal catechism has only accelerated with the growth of demographic opinion analysis since the late sixties. The customized manufacture of public discourse—serviceable "public opinions" meticulously convened by pollsters, messages or products mindfully calculated to appeal to the affections of particular social groupings—has become epidemic.

As the trend has played itself out, an all-inclusive vision of democracy has been a casualty. While demographically specific approaches to the marketing of ideas is often pointed to as a sign of increased democracy—different groups of people hearing *what they want to hear*—it also enables the public relations establishment to summon opinions and generate messages that exacerbate hostilities between groups, heighten the prejudices of particular sectors of the population, and contribute to an increasingly fragmented—and hence more manageable—society.

Widely publicized *gains* for one demographic group—African Americans, women, gays, or people on welfare, for example—are simultaneously repackaged and advertised as being *losses* for another—whites, men, heterosexuals, or wage earners, for instance. In the process, the New Deal notion of "the people" as a diverse union with common democratic objectives has been demolished. If the New Deal vision of "the people" was convoked around the need to contain the ingrained rapacity of business interests, today popular antagonisms between groups have deepened, while unfettered corporate consolidation is flourishing. Amid carefully orchestrated publicity campaigns against progressive social initiatives, the idea of an inclusive America, along with a general commitment to *the common good*, has become fugitive.

This development was chaperoned by the publicity machine of Reaganism, which reinstalled corporate boosterism, free-enterprise politics, and self-righteous contempt for poor people as the rule of the day. If public institutions were once seen as the province of all people, today the term *public* (as in public education, public housing, public broadcasting, public assistance, and public health) is most often employed to characterize institutions that serve people who are deemed *undeserving* and *undesirable*. Amid a religious celebration of "free" market forces, America has become a society in the process of extinguishing democratic expectations that rose from the bottom up during the 1930s, expectations that informed the allegedly *golden age* of post–World War II prosperity.

Public relations has played a critical role in this change. Since the mid-seventies, corporate PR's defection from the idea of universal rights has been glaring. Citing the pretext of economic exigency, more and more corporations have diminished or dismantled the public policies—welfare capitalist programs—that, three decades earlier, were understood as a necessary response to public ultimatums. Simultaneously, image-management, spin-control, and astro-turf organizing—reinforced by demographics and television—have provided the most visible rendition of public life.

Behind this metamorphosis lie ways of thinking that seek to scale back the gains of a century. Nowhere is this trend more apparent than in Philip Lesly's book, *The People Factor: Managing the Human Climate,* which appeared in 1974. Editor of the influential *Public Relations Handbook,* Lesly aired a social perspective that sheds a distressing light on the dynamics of our current moment. Reflecting on the years since the New Deal, Lesly noted, "Our whole society has grossly overbuilt its expectations of what can be achieved and provided."[10]

> This is a consequence of the *extremism of "democracy"*— never foreseen by the most visionary founders of our democratic society—that seeks to give a voice and power to everyone on every issue and in the running of every institution, regardless of his merit in serving society or ability.[11]

Rejecting the Jeffersonian ideal of an informed citizenry as an indispensable ingredient of democracy, Lesly criticized the wide availability of public higher education as having released unhealthy egalitarian assumptions.

> The multiplication of the number of people who have received advanced education has not only created a vast pool of trained personnel and alert citizens. It has resulted in millions of people who have been educated to think they should have a special place in society.[12]

And elsewhere:

> The expression by every individual of his preferences is the essence of democracy and individual freedom, but one of its effects finds the ignorant demanding control over education—as in ghetto parents' organizations insisting that they make the decisions for "their" schools.[13]

In the face of such developments, Lesly argued, the task of public relations must be to curtail Americans' democratic expectations. Like Gustave Le Bon—who, in the late nineteenth century, bemoaned the unhealthy imprint of democratic revolutions on the expectations of the working class—Lesly looked toward simpler times, when education, among other privileges, was a prerogative of elites and ordinary people knew their place.

Amid the flight from "liberal" values, the ideal of opinion engineering has again seized control of American public life. From the onset of Reaganism, we have witnessed the premeditated undermining of civil rights; the growing economic misery of vast, largely African American populations; and the rollback of opportunity as even a glimmer of a promise in many American communities. The United States is more starkly divided in terms of income than any other industrial nation, and the politics of the National Association of Manufacturers, once widely scorned for placing profit above all other values, is the rule of the day. All this is cavalierly reported as an ineluctable result of shifting public opinion—a euphemism for the triumph of a relatively small right wing that has donned the previously accessible mantle of "the people," while the identity of all others—the numerical majority—has been buried in a sinkhole of demographically reinforced "minority" status.

■　　■　　■　　■　　■

Today, with a powerful machinery of opinion management deeply entrenched—and little coherent opposition heard from below—the meaning and realization of democracy have become more and more elusive. The extent to which power and influence are routinely employed to assemble "phantom publics" on behalf of any purpose challenges us to rethink the structures of social communication and to imagine again the ways by which democratic participation may be accomplished.

Some may argue, looking back on the history recounted in this book, that present circumstances are transient—that, as in the past, the force of democratic expression will undermine and ultimately transgress the engineering of consent. For those who are used to looking at American history as a "pendulum" swinging back and forth between conservatism and liberalism, such an eventuality may seem preordained.

But if one examines other developments chronicled in this book, this interpretation is significantly flawed. Looking at the historical development of public relations as a force in American society, one sees that a consequential change has taken place, one that throws simplistic pendulum theories into question. Coinciding with recurrent swings between public relations as a response to democratic mobilizations and as an attempt to colonize the horizons of public expression, there has been a parallel development. Over the course of this century, while arenas of public interaction and expression have become scarce, the apparatus for molding the public mind and for appealing to the public eye has become increasingly pervasive, more and more sophisticated in its technology and expertise. Economic mergers in the media and information industries, in particular, are only reminders that though many are touched by the messages of these industries, fewer and fewer hands control the pipelines of persuasion.

At the dawn of a new millennium, particularly in the face of this communications imbalance, pivotal questions become more urgent:

- Can there be democracy when the public is a fractionalized audience? When the public has no collective presence?
- Can there be democracy when public life is separated from the ability of a public to act—for itself—as a public?
- Can there be democracy when public agendas are routinely predetermined by "unseen engineers?"

- Can there be democracy when public opinion is reduced to the published results of opinion surveys, statistical applause tracks?
- Can there be democracy when the tools of communication are neither democratically distributed nor democratically controlled?
- Can there be democracy when the content of media is determined, almost universally, by commercial considerations?
- Can there be democracy in a society in which emotional appeals overwhelm reason, where the image is routinely employed to overwhelm thought?
- What developments will emerge to invigorate popular democracy this time around? What will move us beyond prevailing strategies of power that are aimed at managing the human climate?

These are big questions. Their answers, if they are to come, lie beyond the scope of any book. For those who continue to cherish democratic ideals, however, these questions point to an agenda for the future.

■   ■   ■   ■   ■

In thinking about ways to reawaken democracy, we must keep in mind that the relationship between publicity and democracy is not essentially corrupt. The free circulation of ideas and debate is critical to the maintenance of an aware public. The rise of democratic thinking, in fact, cannot be explained apart from the circulation of pamphlets, proclamations, and other literary documents that provided a basis for public discussion and helped to transform once-heretical ideas into common aspirations.

Publicity becomes an impediment to democracy, however, when the circulation of ideas is governed by enormous concentrations of wealth that have, as their underlying purpose, the perpetuation of their own power. When this is the case—as is too often true today— the ideal of civic participation gives way to a continual sideshow, a masquerade of democracy calculated to pique the public's emotions. In regard to a more democratic future, then, ways of enhancing the circulation of ideas—regardless of economic circumstance—need to be developed.

We need to imagine what an active public life might look like in an electronic age. We need to discover ways to move beyond thinking of public relations as a function of compliance experts and learn to think of it as an ongoing and inclusive process of discussion. Ordinary people need to develop independent ways and means of understanding and airing public problems and issues and of acting on them.

In 1927—just as public relations and the modern media system were coming of age—John Dewey remarked that "[o]ptimism about democracy is to-day under a cloud." With its bounteous amusements, he argued, a modern consumer culture was deflecting people from the functional responsibilities of citizenship. While "we have the physical tools of communication as never before," he maintained, the public had minimal access to them and was "so bewildered that it cannot find itself."[14] "There is too much public, a public too diffused and scattered and too intricate in composition."[15]

To move beyond this predicament and to rediscover itself as a social force, Dewey asserted, the public must move beyond its status as an audience of consumers and learn to communicate actively with itself.

> Without such communication, the public will remain shadowy and formless, seeking spasmodically for itself, but seizing and holding its shadow rather than its substance. Till the Great Society [then a common phrase for mass industrial society] is converted into a Great Community, the Public will remain in eclipse. Communication can alone create a great community.[16]

To a disturbing extent, Dewey's speculations on "the public and its problems" continue to resonate. In our commercial culture, the extent to which the public engages in an ongoing and dynamic process of communication—unassisted by the methods and devices of opinion experts—is virtually nil. To move beyond this circumstance, a number of changes need to be made.

Present inequities regarding *who has a say? who gets to be heard?* need to be corrected. The vast power of the commercial communications system today lies in its unimpeded control over the avenues of public discussion. For this situation to change, the public sphere—currently dominated by corporate interests and consciously managed by public relations professionals—must revert to the people.

Though camouflaged by business as usual, the capacity to make such a change happen is within sight. Ironically, the enormous authority of a business-centered worldview is derived from the fact that large corporations have been permitted to occupy and impose upon public properties—such as the broadcast spectrum—without paying any significant rent to the public. For a negligible licensing fee, private corporations harvest an incessant windfall of public influence.

If this practice was to change—if a fund to support public communication, for example, regularly received a fair rent from those who were permitted to exploit public properties commercially—funding for noncommercial venues of expression and for noncommercial arenas of public education would be plentiful. If 15 to 25 percent of all advertising expenditures in the United States were applied this way, the crisis in funding for public arts and education would evaporate. New visions would flourish. Locally based community communications centers—equipped with up-to-date technologies and opening new avenues for distribution—would magnify the variety of voices heard. Schools could more adequately prepare their students for the responsibilities of democratic citizenship.

This issue of education is pivotal, since it has often been a casualty of public relations reasoning. In 1947, Bernays acknowledged this danger when he proclaimed that "[u]nder no circumstances should the engineering of consent supersede or displace the functions of the educational system." Then—contradicting his own admonition—he added that in most situations, an educated public will only interfere with leaders' ability to act. Leaders "cannot wait for the people" to understand issues fully. To harvest public support efficiently, he advised, it is crucial for leaders to arm themselves with the implements of "mass persuasion" and look to the engineering of consent as a strategy of first resort.[17]

Epitomizing public relations doctrine that had been germinating since the First World War, this perspective has had dire consequences for the caliber of public discourse in the United States, particularly in the decades since the end of the Second World War. Inasmuch as public relations is rarely intended to inform the population about the intricacies of an issue and is more often calculated to circumvent critical thinking, it has meant that much of what is put forth for public consumption is intentionally indecipherable on a conscious level. The growing primacy of the image—as the preferred instrument of public address—is predicated on the assumption that images work on people enigmatically, that they affect people without their even realizing that a process of persuasion is going on.

The implications of this predilection, particularly for the ways in which we think about education, are considerable. We live in a world where the modern media of communication are everywhere and inescapable. Instrumental images vie for nearly every moment of human attention. Therefore, it is essential for our schools to move toward the development of critical media and visual literacy programs from the early grades onward.

The systematic examination of media institutions and the forces that influence them will encourage students and teachers to look behind the messages they receive, to uncover what, today, is a predominantly secret world. A better understanding of public relations practices will allow students to see that conventional categories, such as "news" and "entertainment," do not adequately describe the forces at play within them.

In a society where instrumental images are employed to petition our affections at every turn—often without a word—educational curricula must also encourage the development of tools for critically analyzing images. Going back some time, the language of images has been well known to people working in the field of opinion management. For democracy to prevail, image making as a communicative activity must be understood by ordinary citizens as well. The aesthetic realm—and the enigmatic ties linking aesthetic, social, economic, political, and ethical values—must be brought down to earth as a subject of study.

The development of curricula in media and visual literacy will not only sharpen people's ability to decipher their world, but it will also contribute to a broadening of the public sphere. Literacy is never just about reading; it is also about writing. Just as early campaigns for universal print literacy were concerned with democratizing the tools of public expression—the written word—upcoming struggles for media literacy must strive to empower people with contemporary implements of public discourse: video, graphic arts, photography, computer-assisted journalism and layout, and performance. More customary mainstays of public expression—expository writing and public speaking—must be resuscitated as well.

Media literacy cannot simply be seen as a vaccination against PR or other familiar strains of institutionalized guile. It must be understood as an education in techniques that can democratize the realm of public expression and will magnify the possibility of meaningful public interactions. Distinctions between publicist and citizen, author and audience, need to be broken down. Education can facilitate this process. It can enlarge the circle of who is permitted—and who will be able—to interpret and make sense of the world.

One last point. As a precondition for other changes, we need to question demographic categories of identity that, at present, divide the public against itself and separate people who—when viewed from a critical distance—may share common interests. Demographics is a powerful tool of divide and rule. To combat it, we need to rediscover a sense of social connectedness. Beyond looking out for ourselves—as individuals or as members of a particular group—we must also learn to rediscover ourselves in others, to see our concerns and aspirations in theirs.

At present, the champions of vested power insolently claim to be acting in the name of public opinion. Engineers of consent—armed with sophisticated demographic tools—continue to dictate public agendas. For this situation to change, we need to rethink those habits of mind within ourselves that disunite ordinary Americans along lines of class, race, ethnicity, gender, and persuasion, encouraging us to fight it out over increasingly insufficient crumbs. Until a sense of difference is balanced by a sense of commonality, a democratic public will be unattainable. *For the greater good to prevail, we need to imagine ourselves as a greater public.*

NOTES

1: VISITING EDWARD BERNAYS

1. Stuart Ewen, *Captains of Consciousness: Advertising and the Roots of the Consumer Culture* (New York, 1976).

2. Stuart Ewen, *All Consuming Images: The Politics of Style in Contemporary Culture* (New York, 1988).

3. Following this logic and grabbing a factoid, apparently out of thin air, Bernays accounted for Ronald Reagan's popularity in the following terms: "Reagan was interviewed by the *Harvard Crimson* and they came back and recorded that he had an IQ of 105."

4. See Eric F. Goldman, *Two Way Street: The Emergence of the Public Relations Counsel* (Boston, 1948), for a general outline of this perspective.

5. Underlining Bernays's spectacular capacity to create circumstances that transcended the ordinary—his ability to make news—a couple of years after my visit to Bernays, when he was 102 years old, a public brouhaha blew up in the *Boston Globe*, stories reporting a battle for the old man's affections that was then taking place between Bernays's daughters and his fifty-year-old housekeeper with whom he was, reportedly, having a torrid love affair.

2: DEALING IN REALITY: PROTOCOLS OF PERSUASION

1. The term *compliance professionals* is taken from Robert Cialdini, *Influence: The New Psychology of Modern Persuasion* (New York, 1984).

2. Edward L. Bernays, "The Engineering of Consent," *Annals of the American Academy of Political and Social Science* 250 (March 1947), pp. 113–20.

3. Lynn Palazzi, "College Lite," *New York Newsday,* December 1, 1993, Part 2, pp. 54–55.

4. John R. MacArthur, *The Second Front: Censorship and Propaganda in the Gulf War* (New York, 1992), pp. 58–59. MacArthur added that prior to his work for the Kuwaiti royals, Gary Hymel was known "as the apologist for Turkey's habitual torture, killing, and unjust imprisonment of its own citizens, as well as for the persecution of its hapless Kurdish minority" (p. 59).

5. Stephen Engelberg, "A New Breed of Hired Hands Cultivates Grass-Roots Anger," *New York Times,* May 17, 1993, pp. A1, A17.

6. Elyse M. Rogers, *Life Is in the Balance* (Form No. 233–00010–988 BDG)(Midland, Mich.: Dow Chemical Company, 1988).

7. "A Call to Admen: Help Stop Riots," *Advertising Age* 63 (May 4, 1992), pp. 1, 49.

8. Edward L. Bernays, *Crystallizing Public Opinion* (New York, 1923, 1961), p. 35.

9. Edward L. Bernays, *Propaganda* (New York, 1928), p. 19.

10. Bernays, *Crystallizing Public Opinion,* p. 217.

11. Bernays, *Propaganda,* p. 159.

12. *Managing the Human Climate* 142 (September–October 1993), p. 1.

13. *Managing the Human Climate* 145 (March–April 1994), p. 1.

14. *Managing the Human Climate* 142, p. 4.

3: TRUTH HAPPENS: AN AGE OF PUBLICITY BEGINS

1. William James, *Pragmatism: The Meaning of Truth* (Cambridge, Mass., 1978), p. 97. Emphasis added.

2. Ibid., p. 100.

3. Robert Wiebe, *Search for Order 1877–1920* (New York, 1967).

4. Hofstadter described middle-class life up to the middle of the nineteenth century in the following terms: "[T]he United States was a nation with a rather broad diffusion of the wealth, status and power, in which the man of moderate means, especially in the many small communities, could command much deference and exert much influence. The small merchant or manufacturer, the distinguished lawyer, editor or preacher, was a person of local eminence in an age in which local eminence mattered a great deal. In the absence of very many nationwide sources of power and prestige, the pillars of the local communities were men of great importance in their own right." Richard Hofstadter, *The Age of Reform* (New York, 1995), pp. 135–36.

5. Henry Demarest Lloyd, *Lords of Industry* (New York, 1910, 1973), p. 1.

6. Ira Steward, "Poverty," *Statistics of Labor* (Massachusetts) 173 (March 1873), pp. 412–14.

7. Lloyd, *Lords of Industry,* p. 1.

8. John L. Thomas, *Alternative America: Henry George, Edward Bellamy, Henry Demarest Lloyd and the Adversary Tradition* (Cambridge, Mass., 1983), p. 140.

9. The end of Reconstruction and the reconciliation of Northern and Southern economic elites also added to a sense of cultural peril. Alongside the systematic disenfranchisement of recently freed African Americans, from 1877 onward, white middle-class Northerners increasingly saw emancipated blacks as a treacherous element of society, incapable of responsible citizenship, in need of being controlled.

10. Josiah Strong, *Our Country: Its Possible Future and Its Present Crisis* (New York, 1885), reprinted in Henry Nash Smith ed., *Popular Culture and Industrialism, 1865–1890* (Garden City, N.Y., 1967), p. 245.

11. Edward Bellamy, *Looking Backward: 2000–1887* (New York, 1887, 1960), pp. 54, 56, 194.

12. Ibid., p. 54.

13. William Appleman Williams, *The Contours of American History* (Cleveland, 1961), p. 327; and Henry George, *Progress and Poverty: An Inquiry into the Cause of Industrial Depression and of Increase of Want with Increase of Wealth. The Remedy* (New York, 1879, 1929), frontispiece.

14. George, *Progress and Poverty,* p. 3.

15. Ibid., p. 10.

16. Henry Demarest Lloyd, "The Story of a Great Monopoly," *Atlantic Monthly* (March 1881), anthologized in Lloyd, *Lords of Industry,* pp. 1–46.

17. Lloyd, *Lords of Industry*, p. 44. For an extensive and interesting discussion of the influence of Bellamy, George, and Lloyd, see Thomas, *Alternative America.*

18. Hofstadter, *The Age of Reform*, p. 141.

19. Herbert Shapiro, ed., *The Muckrakers and American Society* (Boston, 1968), p. 12.

20. Lincoln Steffens, *The Shame of the Cities* (1904; New York, 1963), pp. 4–5.

21. This issue is addressed at length by Walter Lippmann in *Drift and Mastery: An Attempt to Diagnose the Current Unrest* (New York, 1914).

22. See Jürgen Habermas, *The Structural Transformation of the Public Sphere: An Inquiry into a Category of Bourgeois Society* (1962; Cambridge, Mass., 1991).

23. Eric Goldman, *Two Way Street: The Emergence of the Public Relations Counsel* (Boston, 1948), p. 4.

24. Robert H. Bremner, *From the Depths: The Discovery of Poverty in the United States* (New York, 1967), p. 140.

25. Elizabeth Ewen, *Immigrant Woman in the Land of Dollars* (New York, 1985), p. 81.

26. Hofstadter, *The Age Of Reform*, p. 133.

27. Lillian D. Wald, *The House on Henry Street* (New York, 1915, 1995), p. 2.

28. Florence Hull, "The Home," *Godey's Ladies Book* (February 1894), pp. 173–75.

29. Frank Luther Mott, *American Journalism: A History, 1690–1960* (New York, 1962), p. 546.

30. Frederick Lewis Allen, *The Big Change* (New York, 1952), p. 81.

31. Mark Sullivan, *Our Times: The United States 1900–1925* (New York, 1930), Vol. 3, p. 85. See also Mott, *American Journalism* (New York, 1962), p. 554.

32. Robert Cantwell, "Journalism—The Magazines," p. 22, in Shapiro, *The Muckrakers and American Society.*

33. Sullivan, *Our Times*, p. 85.

34. Jacob Riis, *How the Other Half Lives* (New York, 1891), pp. 164–66, reprinted in Stanley Feldstein and Lawrence Costello, *The Ordeal of Assimilation*, p. 206.

35. Bremner, *From the Depths*, p. 107.

36. Edwin Markham, "The Man with a Hoe," in Oscar Williams, ed., *A Pocket Book of Modern Verse* (New York, 1965), pp. 205–7.

37. Judge Ben B. Lindsay and Harvey J. O'Higgins, *The Beast in the Democracy*, as excerpted in Harvey Swados, *Years of Conscience* (Cleveland, 1962), pp. 41–44.

38. Quote in Sullivan, *Our Times*, p. 84.

4: CONTROLLING CHAOS

1. William E. Leuchtenburg, Introduction to Walter Lippman, *Drift and Mastery* (Madison, 1985; orig. 1914), p. 1.

2. A revolutionary working-class movement was, itself, producing some eloquent publicity. The Industrial Workers of the World (IWW) Manifesto of 1905,

for example, employed a familiar idiom of fact and reason not to argue on behalf of cautious social reform, but to justify the abolition of capitalism.

> The great facts of present industry are the displacement of human skill by machines and the increase of capitalist power through concentration in the possession of the tools with which wealth is produced and distributed. Competition among capitalists is disappearing, class divisions grow ever more fixed and class antagonisms more sharp.

See Joyce L. Kornbluh, *Rebel Voices: An IWW Anthology* (Ann Arbor, 1964), p. 7.

3. Even formerly conservative elements of middle-class America were assuming an anticorporate stance. In articles appearing in *The Congregationalist*, for example, the previously pro-business Congregational ministry denounced a prevailing plague of "moral anemia" in which "great businesses are built up by methods which violate the law of both God and man." Quoted in Louis Galambos, with the assistance of Barbara Barrow Spence, *The Public Image of Big Business in America, 1880–1940* (Baltimore, 1975), pp. 124–25.

4. Walter Lippmann, *Drift and Mastery: An Attempt to Diagnose the Current Unrest* (New York, 1914), pp. 1–3.

5. Herbert Shapiro, ed., *The Muckrakers and American Society* (Boston, 1968), p. 6.

6. Lippmann, *Drift and Mastery,* pp. 155–56.

7. Robert A. Nye, *The Origins of Crowd Psychology: Gustave Le Bon and the Crisis of Mass Democracy in the Third Republic* (London, 1975), p. 3.

8. Gustave Le Bon, *The Crowd: A Study of the Popular Mind* (London, 1896, 1952), pp. 14–20.

9. Gabriel Tarde, "The Public and the Crowd," in *On Communication and Social Influence: Selected Papers* (Chicago, 1969), p. 277.

10. Ibid., p. 312.

11. Ibid., pp. 304, 313.

12. Gabriel Tarde, "Opinion and Conversation" [1898] in *On Communication and Social Influence,* p. 318.

13. Tarde, "The Public and the Crowd," p. 281.

14. Ferdinand Tönnies, *Community and Society* (originally *Gemeinschaft und Gesellschaft*). (East Lansing, Mich., 1957; orig. 1887), p. 221.

15. Edward Alsworth Ross, *Social Psychology* (New York, 1908, 1974), p. 63.

16. Graham Wallas, *Human Nature in Politics* (New York, 1908, 1921).

17. O. W. Firkins, "The Cult of the Passing Hour," *Atlantic Monthly* (May 1914), pp. 663, 667.

18. Ross, *Social Psychology,* p. 64.

19. Pendleton Dudley, "Current Beginnings of PR," *Public Relations Journal* 8 (April 1952), p. 9.

20. Ivy L. Lee, "Publicity," address before American Electric Railway Association, October 10, 1916, Atlantic City. Packet 1, Box 4, Folder 1 of the Ivy L. Lee Collection, Seeley G. Mudd Manuscript Library, Princeton University. This and subsequent items from the Ivy L. Lee Collection, used by permission of the Princeton University Libraries.

21. Gerald Stanley Lee, *Crowds: A Study of the Genius of Democracy and of the Fears, Desires, and Expectations of the People* (London, 1913), pp. 556–57.

22. Alfred McClung Lee, *The Daily Newspaper in America: The Evolution of a Social Instrument* (New York, 1937), p. 440.

23. Ray E. Hiebert, "Ivy Lee and the Development of Press Relations," *Public Relations Journal* 21 (March 1965), pp. 8ff.

24. Alan R. Raucher, *Public Relations and Business 1900–1929* (Baltimore, 1968), pp. 29–30.

25. Samuel Yellen, *American Labor Struggles: 1877–1934* (New York, 1936), p. 238.

26. George Creel, "Poisoners of Public Opinion: Part I," *Harper's Magazine* (November 7, 1914), p. 436.

27. Ibid.

28. *New York Call* (January 28, 1915), reporting on the hearings of the Industrial Commission. From Ivy Lee's personal clippings file, Packet 1, Ivy L. Lee Collection, Seeley G. Mudd Manuscript Library, Princeton University.

29. Lee, "Publicity."

5: "EDUCATE THE PUBLIC!"

1. F. M. Surface, "A Review of Public Opinion Particularly Affecting Standard Oil Company," in Standard Oil (New Jersey) and Affiliated Companies, 1945 Public Relations Conference *Proceedings* (Rye, N.Y., November 19–20, 1945), p. 8.

2. Ray E. Hiebert, "Ivy Lee and the Development of Press Relations," *Public Relations Journal* 21(March 1965), p. 9.

3. Clipping from the *San Francisco Star,* January 9, 1915. Packet 1, Box 4, Folder 1 of the Ivy L. Lee Collection, Seeley G. Mudd Manuscript Library, Princeton University.

4. Clipping from *Toledo Ohio Blade,* May 18, 1915. Ivy L. Lee Collection, Packet 1.

5. Clipping, Carl Sandberg, "Ivy L. Lee, Paid Liar," *New York Call,* March 15. Ivy L. Lee Collection, Packet 1.

6. George Creel, "Poisoners of Public Opinion: Part II," *Harper's Magazine* (November 14, 1914), pp. 465–66.

7. Lee's typewritten testimony before the U.S. Commission on Industrial Relations, City Hall (New York, April 1915). Ivy L. Lee Collection, Packet 1, pp. 31–32.

8. "House of Rockefeller Learns to Talk," *New York Press,* April 11, 1915. Lee's personal clipping file, Ivy L. Lee Collection, Packet 1.

9. Eric F. Goldman, *Two Way Street: The Emergence of the Public Relations Counsel* (Boston, 1948), p. 9.

10. Goldman's *Two Way Street* is a stunning example of such a gloss over. This brief volume was a promotion for the public relations industry and, for the most part, parroted the industry's PR for itself.

11. The company sought to consolidate control of telegraphy, as well. This goal would be accomplished within a decade when AT&T took over Western Union.

12. Alfred McClung Lee, *The Daily Newspaper in America: The Evolution of a Social Instrument* (New York, 1937), p. 442.

13. James Ellsworth, "Introduction to Historical Memoranda on Bell System Publicity," January 17, 1929. AT&T Corporate Archive, Box 1066, p. 4.

14. Ibid., pp. 4–5.

15. Walter S. Allen, letter to Mr. Frederick P. Fish, regarding renewal of contract with the Publicity Bureau, July 22, 1904. AT&T Corporate Archive, Box 1398, Item 14663, pp. 1–2.

16. Ibid., p. 3.

17. James D. Ellsworth, Memos to President Fish regarding news placement, October 3, 1906. AT&T Corporate Archive, Box 1317, Folder, Item No. 16634.

18. Ellsworth, "Introduction to Historical Memoranda on Bell Systems Publicity," p. 6.

19. The emergence of corporate liberalism in the National Civic Federation and Vail's place within it are discussed by James Weinstein, *The Corporate Ideal in the Liberal State, 1900–1918* (Boston, 1968).

20. "Speech to Railroad Commissioners, San Francisco, October, 1915," in Theodore Vail, *Views on Public Questions: A Collection of Papers and Addresses, 1907–1917* (privately printed, 1917), p. 241.

21. Ibid., p. 246.

22. Ibid., p. 248.

23. Ibid., p. 249.

24. "Speech to Annual Conference of Bell Systems, October 1913," in Vail, *Views on Public Questions*, p. 143.

25. Ibid., pp. 143–44.

26. American Telephone and Telegraph, "General Policy" memorandum. AT&T Corporate Archive, Box 56, File on Public Relations-Securities-Competition–1920, p. 2.

27. Morton E. Long, "Public Relations of the Bell Systems," *Public Opinion Quarterly* 1 (October 1937), p. 19.

28. James D. Ellsworth, "Start of General Magazine Advertising," memorandum, January 17, 1929. AT&T Corporate Archive, Box 1066.

29. H. W. Pool, letter to James D. Ellsworth, September 7, 1909. AT&T Corporate Archive, Box 1317, Folder 2, Item 664278.

30. American Telephone and Telegraph, "Confidential" minutes of a "Meeting of Publicity Men of the American Telephone and Telegraph Companies," June 26, 1914. AT&T Corporate Archive, Corporate Box 1310, pp. 16–17, 21.

31. American Telephone and Telegraph, memorandum of September 19, 1912, from Walter S. Allen to Vice President N. C. Kingsbury, establishing a Publicity Bureau for the corporation. AT&T Corporate Archive, Box B–20. A slightly revised version of this memo exists under the following entry: Walter S. Allen, Public Relations, "Plan for Establishing a Public Relations Department, July 23, 1913," Corporate Box 2035.

32. Ibid.

33. The Grange, a national network of farmers' organizations, was of particular interest to At&T because it was seen to "exert a powerful influence throughout the country."

34. American Telephone and Telegraph Company, "Confidential" minutes of a "Meeting of Publicity Men," June 26, 1914.

35. American Telephone and Telegraph Company, Minutes of Advertising Conference Bell Telephone systems, Philadelphia, June 28, 1916. AT&T Corporate Archive, Box 1310, p. 14.

36. "Address at the Opening of the Annual Conference of the Bell Telephone System in New York, October 1913," in Vail, *Views on Public Questions,* p. 155.

37. Other companies dependent on individual consumption also moved to the forefront of corporate public relations thinking. Advertising men were among the first to see the need for PR. See also, David E. Nye, *Image Worlds: Corporate Identities at General Electric, 1890–1930* (Cambridge, 1985), on General Electric's PR-photography activities that commenced as the electric giant moved toward producing and selling home appliances.

6: HOUSE OF TRUTH

1. This is a composite speech combined from actual sources. U.S. Committee on Public Information, "The Income Tax," *Four-Minute Man Bulletin* 26 (March 11, 1918); U.S. Committee on Public Information, "Where Did You Get Your Facts?" *Four-Minute Man Bulletin* 35 (August 26, 1918); and James R. Mock and Cedric Larson, *Words That Won the War: The Story of the Committee on Public Information* (Princeton, 1939), pp. 64, 123–24.

2. Mock and Larson, *Words That Won the War,* p. 51.

3. George Creel, *Rebel At Large: Recollections of Fifty Crowded Years* (New York, 1947), p. 157.

4. George Creel, "Public Opinion in War Time," *Annals of the American Academy of Political and Social Science* 68 (July 1918), p. 188.

5. Mock and Larson, *Words That Won the War,* p. 3.

6. Creel, "Public Opinion in War Time," p. 188.

7. Ralph Chaplin, "The Red Feast," *International Socialist Review* (October 1914), reprinted in Joyce L. Kornbluh, *Rebel Voices: An IWW Anthology* (Ann Arbor, Mich., 1972), p. 328.

8. Creel, *Rebel At Large,* p. 157.

9. William Monroe Trotter, *The Instincts of the Herd in Peace and War* (London, 1916), pp. 147–48, 155.

10. Arthur Bullard, *Mobilising America* (New York, 1917), p. 36.

11. Ibid., pp. 42–43.

12. Ibid., pp. 62–63.

13. Ronald Steel, *Walter Lippmann and the American Century* (New York, 1980), p. 125.

14. Stephen Vaughn, *Holding Fast the Lines: Democracy, Nationalism and the Committee on Public Information* (Chapel Hill, N.C., 1980), pp. 5–6.

15. Creel, "Public Opinion in War Time," p. 185.

16. This theme was developed by William Appleman Williams in his influential historical study, *The Tragedy of American Diplomacy* (New York, 1962).

17. Creel, "Public Opinion in War Time," p. 187. The phrase *House of Truth* was not coined by Creel. A couple of years earlier, when Walter Lippmann came to work for the War Department in Washington, he lived in a house at 1727 Nineteenth Street. Lippmann's home became a watering spot and discussion site for other Progressive intellectuals who had come to work in Washington, and the amount of cerebration that went on within its walls earned for the dwelling the

sobriquet, "House of Truth." See Steel, *Walter Lippman and the American Century*.

18. Vaughn, *Holding Fast the Lines,* p. 24; and George Creel, *How We Advertised America: The First Telling of the Amazing Story of the Committee on Public Information that Carried the Gospel of Americanism to Every Corner of the Globe* (New York, 1920), pp. 9–10.

19. Creel, *How We Advertised America,* p. 162.

20. Vaughn, *Holding Fast the Lines,* p. 199.

21. Mock and Larson, *Words That Won the War,* pp. 93–94.

22. Creel, *Rebel At Large,* pp. 157–58.

23. For a decade preceding U.S. involvement in the war, advertising trade journals had regularly published articles on how advertising could be employed to neutralize conflicts between labor and capital. A 1907 article in *Profitable Advertising,* for example, offered detailed information on how advertising was being adopted to produce an entertaining and instructional newsletter for factory workers in Cleveland. The article suggested that, artfully executed, such publicity was a "medium by which men can be lifted out of the brick-throwing class." Anonymous, "A Daring and Unique Plan to Solve Some of the Problems of the Relations of Labor and Capital by Publicity," *Profitable Advertising* 12 (July 1907), p. 179. See also, Stuart Ewen, *Captains of Consciousness: Advertising and the Roots of the Consumer Culture* (New York, 1976).

24. Creel, "Public Opinion in War Time," p. 188.

25. Creel, *How We Advertised America,* p. 7.

26. Ibid., p. 11.

27. Mock and Larson, *Words That Won the War,* p. 101.

28. Ibid., p. 109.

29. Creel, *How We Advertised America,* p. 133.

30. Albert Hopkins, ed., *The Book of Progress I* (New York, 1915), as quoted in Stuart Ewen and Elizabeth Ewen, *Channels of Desire: Mass Images and the Shaping of American Consciousness* (New York, 1982), pp. 34–35.

31. Creel, *How We Advertised America,* p. 126.

32. Ibid., p. 121.

33. Creel, *Rebel At Large,* p. 169.

34. Creel, *How We Advertised America,* p. 85; and Creel, "Public Opinion in War Time," p. 187.

35. Creel, *How We Advertised America,* p. 85.

36. U.S. Committee on Public Information, "Carrying the Message," *Four-Minute Man Bulletin* 20 (November 26, 1917), p. 5.

37. U.S. Committee on Public Information, *Four-Minute Man Bulletin,* Edition D (June 29, 1918), p. 20.

38. Charles A. Beard and Mary R. Beard, *The Rise of American Civilization* (New York, 1927, 1944), p. 640.

39. Harold D. Lasswell, Ralph D. Casey, and Bruce Lannes Smith, *Propaganda and Promotional Activities: An Annotated Bibliography* (Minneapolis, 1935), p. 9.

40. Creel, "Public Opinion in War Time," p. 191. If any censorship is to be practiced, Creel repeatedly asserted, it must be "voluntary"; newspaper editors should, by their own judgment, refrain from publishing information that might aid or comfort the enemy.

41. Beard and Beard, *The Rise of American Civilization,* p. 640.

42. Ibid., p. 641. Creel denied any direct involvement in these restrictive activities, yet in confidential minutes of the official United States Censorship Board—on which Creel sat—historian Stephen Vaughn uncovered specific instances of the CPI director's complicity in the repression. Vaughn summarized some of his findings:

> Whatever his intentions, whatever hesitancy he may have had about censorship legislation, Creel, the record indicates, was active in the board's discussions and involved in attempts to suppress certain kinds of literature. The minutes of the board from April 3, 1918, indicate a long discussion on the problem of press restrictions and show that Creel received full authority to deal with newspaper censorship. It was also agreed that all magazines in the United States had to submit articles to the Censorship Board several weeks prior to publication. . . . Even if a periodical or newspaper did not fall under the act, there were other ways of bringing it into line. He [Creel] might suggest to the Department of Justice that its editor be prosecuted or that the publication be barred from the mails. Through contact with the War Trade Board, whose representative was on the Censorship Board, he could even stop the publication's supply of newsprint.

From his reading of Censorship Board minutes, Vaughn concluded that "Creel sought to repress material that either presented the United States in an unfavorable light or contained opinions or ideas he felt too dangerous for the American Public." Vaughn, *Holding Fast the Lines,* pp. 222–25.

43. Creel, "Public Opinion in War Time," p. 185.

44. Vaughn, *Holding Fast the Lines,* pp. 156–57.

45. U.S. Committee on Public Information, "Fourth Liberty Loan," *Four-Minute Man Bulletin,* no. 39 (September 12, 1918), p. 3.

46. U.S. Committee on Public Information, "The Junior Four-Minute Men War Savings Contest for the United States of America," *Junior Four-Minute Man Bulletin,* no. 1 (March 11, 1918), p. 20.

47. Harold D. Lasswell, *Propaganda Technique in the World War* (New York, 1927), p. 221.

48. Randolph S. Bourne, *War and the Intellectuals* (New York, 1965), pp. 3–14. Title essay originally published in the *Seven Arts* 2 (June 1917), pp. 133–46.

7: SOCIAL PSYCHOLOGY AND THE QUEST FOR THE PUBLIC MIND

1. Roger Babson, in Howard K. Beale, *Are American Teachers Free?* (New York, 1936), p. 546, quoted in Thomas C. Cochran and William Miller, *The Age of Enterprise: A Social History of Industrial America* (New York, 1942), p. 333.

2. Max Watson, "Careers for a Young Man: Publicity. An Interview with Ivy Lee," *New York Evening Post* (March 11, 1921), Ivy L. Lee Collection. Items listed by name of collection and box number and credited as such: "Ivy L. Lee Collection, Seeley G. Mudd Manuscript Library, Princeton University Libraries." Packet 1, Box 48, Folder 1.

3. Speech of Ivy L. Lee to the Columbia University School of Journalism, November 20, 1921. In ibid., Box 4, Folder 1.

4. "The Meaning of Publicity" (unpublished manuscript, 1924). Ivy L. Lee Collection, Box 1, Folder 2. Emphasis added.

5. For an early overview of social psychology and its influence, see Robert E. Park, "The Crowd and the Public" (1904); see also Robert E. Park, *The Crowd and the Public and Other Essays* (Chicago, 1972).

6. See Chapter 4.

7. Gustave Le Bon, *The Crowd: A Study of the Public Mind* (London, 1896, 1952), p. 10.

8. Ibid., p. 28.

9. Le Bon allowed that the behavior of certain sectors of the world's population continued to be ruled by these hereditary forces. Among them he included women, children, and savages. See ibid., pp. 35–36.

10. Le Bon, *The Crowd*, p. 31.

11. Ibid., p. 207.

12. *Masse and Publikum* (Heidelberg University, 1904). First English translation appears in Park, The Crowd and the Public and Other Essays.

13. Ibid., pp. 5–6, 12, 20.

14. Ibid., p. 57.

15. Ibid., p. 59.

16. Ibid., pp. 56–57.

17. Graham Wallas, *Human Nature in Politics* (New York, 1908, 1921), pp. 45, 52.

18. Ibid., p. 18.

19. Wilfred Monroe Trotter, *The Instincts of the Herd in Peace and War* (London, 1916), p. 244.

20. Ibid., p. 113.

21. Ibid., p. 114.

22. Everett Dean Martin, *The Behavior of Crowds: A Psychological Study* (New York, 1920), pp. 10–11.

23. Sigmund Freud, *Group Psychology and the Analysis of the Ego* (New York, 1922, 1959), pp. 18, 3.

24. Ibid., p. 9.

25. Ibid., pp. 27–58. Freud developed each of his rejoinders to Le Bon in some detail. Citing the ability of a leader to exert hypnotic powers over a crowd of followers, for example, Freud maintained that this circumstance was not terribly different from that encountered in normal love relations. "From being in love to hypnosis," he noted, is a "short step. . . . There is the same humble subjection, the same compliance, the same absence of criticism towards the hypnotist as toward the love object." Similarly, Freud observed, the mystic cords tying individuals to one another within a group were essentially libidinal. The process of projecting personal desire onto others—object cathexis—was, to Freud, a link between the dynamics of the crowd and the sexual lives of individuals.

26. Le Bon, *The Crowd*, p. 19.

27. Ibid., p. 40.

28. Ibid., pp. 35–36.

29. Ibid., p. 41.

30. Ibid., p. 18.

31. Ibid., pp. 61–62.

32. Ibid., p. 68.

33. Ibid., pp. 69–70.

34. Ibid., p. 108.

35. Ibid., p. 71. It may be recalled that Ivy L. Lee disclosed to a group of railroad executives in 1916 that "[i]t is not the facts alone that strike the popular mind, but the way in which they take place and in which they are published that kindle the imagination. The open-and-shut plagiarism from Le Bon indicates that, already by 1916, Lee's thinking had fallen under the influence of the French social psychologist. This pilfered phrasing contradicts Robert Raucher's assertion that Lee had never read Le Bon. See address on "Publicity," before American Electric Railway Association, October 10, 1916, Atlantic City. Ivy L. Lee Collection, Seeley G. Mudd Manuscript Library, Princeton University, Packet 1. Used by permission of the Princeton University Libraries.

36. Richard Sennett, *The Fall of Public Man: On the Social Psychology of Capitalism* (New York, 1974, 1978), p. 127.

37. Trotter, *The Instinct of the Herd in Peace and War,* p. 247.

38. Martin, *The Behavior of Crowds,* p. 7. Emphasis added.

8: UNSEEN ENGINEERS: BIOGRAPHY OF AN IDEA

1. Robert B. Westbrook, *John Dewey and American Democracy* (Ithaca, N.Y., 1991), pp. 281–82.

2. The phrase *manufacture of consent* was coined by Walter Lippmann. See Lippmann, *Public Opinion* (New York, 1922), p. 248.

3. Lippmann's term *Great Society,* shorthand for modern industrial civilization, was borrowed from his mentor Graham Wallas. See Wallas, *The Great Society: A Psychological Analysis.* (Lincoln, Nebr., 1967; orig. 1914).

4. Lippmann, *Public Opinion,* p. 27.

5. Ibid., p. 417.

6. Ibid., p. 59.

7. Walter Lippmann, *The Phantom Public: A Sequel to "Public Opinion"* (New York, 1927), p. 20.

8. Lippmann, *Public Opinion,* p. 81.

9. Ibid., p. 90.

10. Ibid., pp. 89, 95–96.

11. Ibid., pp. 249–61. To Lippmann, people's inability to apprehend their world rationally was also underpinned by his repudiation of Marxism (or at least Marxism as a viable political theory). "Marxians," he wrote, "thought that men's economic position would irresistibly produce a clear conception of their economic interests. Position ought, if their theory were correct, not only divide mankind into classes, but . . . supply each class with a view of its interest and a coherent policy for obtaining it. Yet nothing is more certain than that all classes of men are in constant perplexity as to what their interests are." Ibid., pp. 184–85.

12. Ibid., p. 28.

13. Ronald Steel, *Walter Lippmann and the American Century* (New York, 1980), p. 46. Emphasis added.

14. Ibid., p. 59.

15. Ibid., pp. 196–97, 222.

16. Ibid., p. 32.

17. Ibid., pp. 42–43.

18. Ibid., p. 162.

19. Ibid., pp. 91–92.

20. Ibid., pp. 163, 165–66. Emphasis added.

21. Ibid., p. 166.

22. Ibid., p. 206.

23. Lippmann, *The Phantom Public,* p. 37.

24. Lippmann, *Public Opinion,* p. 234. Emphasis added.

25. Lippmann, *The Phantom Public,* pp. 37–38. Emphasis added.

26. Lippmann, *Public Opinion,* pp. 206–7.

27. Lippmann, *The Phantom Public,* pp. 77–78.

28. Interview with Edward L. Bernays, October 12, 1990. Cambridge, Mass.

29. Edward L. Bernays, *Biography of an Idea: Memoirs of Public Relations Counsel Edward L. Bernays* (New York, 1965), pp. 54–55.

30. Ibid., pp. 57–61.

31. Bernays's CPI activities are discussed in Bernays, *Biography of an Idea,* pp. 155–78.

32. Edward L. Bernays, *Propaganda* (New York, 1928), p. 27.

33. Ibid., p. 9.

34. Interview with Bernays.

35. Edward L. Bernays, *Crystallizing Public Opinion* (New York, 1923, 1961), p. 83.

36. Bernays, *Propaganda,* pp. 53–54. Emphasis added.

37. Ibid., pp. 51–52.

38. Ibid., p. 26.

39. Ibid., pp. 27–34.

40. Ibid., p. 9.

41. Bernays, *Crystallizing Public Opinion,* p. 19.

42. Bernays, *Propaganda,* p. 10.

43. Ibid., p. 25.

44. Bernays, *Crystallizing Public Opinion,* p. 51.

45. Ibid., p. 53.

46. Ibid., p. 137.

47. Bernays, *Propaganda,* p. 150.

48. Edward L. Bernays, "Crystallizing Public Opinion for Good Government," address before the thirty-first Annual Meeting of the National Municipal League and the twenty-first Annual Meeting of the American Civic Association in Joint Session, Pittsburgh (privately printed, 1925), n.p.

49. Bernays, *Propaganda,* p. 49.

50. Ibid.

51. Ibid., p. 65.

52. Ibid., p. 97.

53. Ibid., p. 49.

54. Ibid., pp. 47–48.

55. Bernays, "Crystallizing Public Opinion for Good Government," p. 8.

56. Bernays, *Propaganda,* pp. 9, 94.

57. Bernays, *Crystallizing Public Opinion,* pp. 66–68, 99.

58. Ibid., pp. 162–63. Sometimes Bernays's debt to Lippmann was acknowledged, and sometimes it was not. In other situations, this indebtedness was muddled. Following a footnoted quotation from *Public Opinion* on the use of dramatic conventions to influence the public, which in fact did not come from Lippmann's book, Bernays then followed with his own commentary on the quote, which was plagiarized, nearly word for word, from Lippmann. See *Crystallizing Public Opinion*, pp. 156–57.

59. Bernays, "Crystallizing Public Opinion for Good Government," p. 3.

60. Bernays, *Crystallizing Public Opinion*, p. 170.

61. Ibid., p. 171.

62. The term, *psychological megaphone*, was taken from Leonard W. Doob and Edward S. Robinson, "Psychology and Propaganda," *Annals of the American Academy of Political and Social Science* 179 (May 1935), p. 90.

63. Bernays, *Crystallizing Public Opinion*, p. 162.

64. Bernays, "Crystallizing Public Opinion for Good Government," p. 4.

65. Bernays, *Crystallizing Public Opinion*, p. 173.

66. Harold D. Lasswell, "The Person: Subject and Object of Propaganda," *Annals of the American Academy of Political and Social Science* 179 (May 1935), p. 189.

67. *Imagineering* is a term that was coined in recent years by the Disney Corporation to describe the development of attractions designed to animate the public's imagination. See William Styron, "Slavery's Pain, Disney's Gain," *New York Times* (August 4, 1994), p. A23.

9: MODERN PIPELINES OF PERSUASION

1. See Harold D. Lasswell, Ralph D. Casey, and Bruce Lannes Smith, *Propaganda and Promotional Activities: An Annotated Bibliography* (Minneapolis, 1935). Lasswell's Introduction to this comprehensive bibliographic volume remains one of the most perceptive overviews of American propaganda activities during this critical period. Beyond its specific references, the bibliography as a whole constitutes substantial testimony to the growing importance of propaganda as an aspect of American life.

2. This summary, along with a discussion of the pivotal influence of wartime propaganda, is found in Harold D. Lasswell, *Propaganda Technique in the World War* (New York, 1927).

3. Ibid., pp. 8–9, 220, 4.

4. Ibid., p. 222.

5. John Dewey, *Individualism Old and New* (New York, 1930, pp. 42–43, quoted in Richard S. Tedlow, *Keeping the Corporate Image: Public Relations and Business, 1900–1950* (Greenwich, Conn., 1979), p. 49.

6. John Dewey, *The Public and its Problems* (Athens, Ohio, 1927, 1988), pp. 122–23.

7. Thomas C. Cochran and William Miller, *The Age of Enterprise: A Social History of Industrial America* (New York, 1942), p. 338.

8. Ivy L. Lee, *The Press Today: How the News Reaches the Public* (New York, 1929), p. 37.

9. Ibid., pp. 5–8.

10. Ibid., pp. 36–37.

11. See Erik Barnouw, *A Tower in Babel,* Vol. 1 of *A History of Broadcasting in the United States* (New York, 1966), pp. 64–72. The first commercial station was KDKA in Pittsburgh. Before World War I radio receivers-transmitters had been the province of the U.S. Navy and commercial shipping. Insofar as individual civilians owned and used radios, they were employed for amateur, two-way "ham radio" communications. During the war, amateur radio operations were forbidden, ostensibly for security purposes. While amateur radio commenced again following the war, the war created a stoppage in the civilian radio environment that left the terrain after the war wide open for commercial development. This history is also recounted by Barnouw, pp. 39–64.

12. For an incisive and comprehensive historical discussion of the commercialization of radio and the corporate-governmental war against "radio reform," see Robert W. McChesney, *Telecommunications, Mass Media, and Democracy* (New York, 1993). See also, Barnouw's *History of Broadcasting in the United States* (3 vols.: New York, 1966, 1968, 1970) for a detailed look at these trends.

13. "Politics Discovers the Radio" (editorial), *Philadelphia Public Ledger,* April 30, 1926, p. 550, in W. Brooke Graves, *Readings in Public Opinion, Its Formation and Control* (New York, 1928). Emphasis added.

14. Glen Frank, "Radio as an Educational Force," *Annals of the American Academy of Political and Social Science* 177 (January 1935), pp. 119–22.

15. The Gruenberg piece focuses on the particular impact of radio on children, an ongoing—if, at times, alarmist—theme in mass media criticism. See Sidonie Matsner Gruenberg, "Radio and the Child," *Annals of the American Academy of Political and Social Science* 177 (January 1935), p. 124.

16. William Hard, "Radio and Public Opinion," *Annals of the American Academy of Political and Social Science* 177 (January 1935), p. 105.

17. For a discussion of the progressive roots of social surveys, see Jean M. Converse, *Survey Research in the United States: Roots and Emergence, 1890–1960* (Berkeley, 1987), pp. 22–23.

18. Ibid., p. 89.

19. Henry C. Link, *The New Psychology of Selling and Advertising* (New York, 1932), p. 8.

20. Arthur W. Page, "The Problems of Forecasting Public Opinion in the United States," in *Proceedings of the American Telephone and Telegraph Company, General Publicity Conference, Southern Pines, North Carolina (April 10–16, 1929),* AT&T Corporate Archive, Box 1310, pp. 1–8.

21. Reflecting the trajectory of business-oriented survey research, Link began his work at the Psychological Corporation with a particular emphasis on merchandising. See Link, *The New Psychology.* Shortly, however, Link's vision broadened to encompass a more comprehensive understanding of survey research's social utility.

22. Ibid., p. 81.

23. Ibid., p. 9.

24. Ibid., pp. 79–80.

25. Quoted in ibid., p. 12.

26. Converse, *Survey Research,* p. 108.

27. Link, *The New Psychology,* p. 248.

28. Gallup earned his reputation forecasting a Roosevelt landslide in 1936.

This prediction, which flew in the face of official wisdom, provided a brilliant piece of public relations for the oracular power of polling methods. Archibald M. Crossley, "Straw Polls in 1936," *Public Opinion Quarterly* 1 (January 1937), p. 28.

29. Paul T. Cherington, "Opinion Polls as the Voice of Democracy," *Public Opinion Quarterly* 4 (March 1940), pp. 236–37.

30. Link, "A New Method," quoted in Converse, *Survey Research,* p. 110.

31. Converse, *Survey Research,* p. 124.

32. Robert S. Lynd, "Democracy in Reverse," *Public Opinion Quarterly* 4 (June 1940), p. 220.

33. Ibid., pp. 219–20.

34. Malcolm M. Willey, "Communications Agencies and the Volume of Propaganda," *Annals of the American Academy of Political and Social Science* 179 (May 1935), p. 196. Emphasis added.

35. Marvin N. Olasky, "A Bernays Retrospective," *Public Relations Review* (Fall 1984), quoted in Scott Cutlip, *Public Relations, the Unseen Power: A History* (Hillsdale, N.J., 1994), p. 184. Emphasis added.

10: OPTICAL ILLUSIONS

1. Georges Duhamel, *America the Menace: Scenes from the Life of the Future,* Charles Miner Thompson, trans. (Boston, 1931), pp. xiv, 128.

2. Ibid., pp. 128, 133, 210.

3. Ibid., pp. 27–28.

4. William P. Banning, "Advertising Technique and Copy Appeal," *Bell System Publicity Conference Proceedings* (New York, June 11–15, 1923), pp. 1–16. AT&T Corporate Archive, Box 1310.

5. David E. Nye, *Image Worlds: Corporate Identities at General Electric, 1890–1930* (Cambridge, Mass., 1985), p. 33. For an exhaustive discussion of such activities at General Electric, particularly GE's use of photography, see Nye's entire book.

6. Interview with Edward L. Bernays, October 12, 1990, Cambridge, Mass. See also, *Biography of an Idea: Memoirs of Public Relations Counsel Edward L. Bernays* (New York, 1965), p. 292.

7. H. A. Overstreet, *Influencing Human Behavior* (New York, 1925), p. 29.

8. Ibid., pp. 65, 34.

9. Ibid., p. 50.

10. Ibid., p. 55.

11. Ibid., p. 63.

12. Ibid., p. 65.

13. Ibid., p. 52.

14. The term *agnosia* is employed by neurologists and refers to the brain's ability to receive, yet inability to make sense of, visual or other sensory impulses. See Oliver Sacks, "A Neurologist's Notebook: To See and Not See," *New Yorker* (May 10, 1993), p. 61.

15. Overstreet, *Influencing Human Behavior,* p. 53.

16. Ibid., pp. 55–56.

17. Ibid., pp. 65–70.

18. From the Renaissance onward, of course, Western artists had embraced the challenge of reproducing reality as actually seen by individuals. Use of the camera obscura and the introduction of linear perspective in easel painting had advanced this goal. But realist paintings were, at best, prized as ingenious simulations. With the evolution of photographic cameras and light-sensitive plates, however, all this changed. A technical replication of the human eye—complete with lens, iris, and a silver-coated retina—the camera was able to beget an image that, as never before, was fluent in the language of sight; for millions, it spoke the vernacular of the eye.

19. Walter Benjamin observed that photography released the hand from its customary "artistic functions." Now, as never before, the image was a direct product of an eye "looking into a lens." See Benjamin, "The Work of Art in the Age of Mechanical Reproduction," in *Illuminations: Essay and Reflection* (New York, 1968), p. 219.

20. While photographs rapidly affected the lives and outlooks of millions, they were not, at first, capable of being mass produced. The earliest photographs—daguerreotypes—were one-of-a-kind images. Even with the introduction of photographic negatives—paper, then glass—pictures still had to be printed one by one in a darkroom. With the refinement of halftone printing processes during the 1890s, however, photographs—translated into screened patterns of dots—could be reproduced, like words, on high-speed presses. Now the image could not only duplicate reality, it could broadcast it. With this development, the ability of photography to serve as an instrument of publicity was hastened.

21. The visual documentation of poverty was developed in Great Britain by Henry Mayhew, whose *London Labour and the London Poor* (London, 1861–62), heavily illustrated with engravings, offered an optical catalog of working-class life in mid-nineteenth-century London.

22. Peter B. Hales, *Silver Cities: The Photography of American Urbanization, 1839–1915* (Philadelphia, 1984), p. 197.

23. Lewis Hine, "Social Photography, How the Camera May Help in the Social Uplift." *Proceedings,* National Conference of Charities and Corrections (June 1909), reprinted in Alan Trachtenberg, *Classic Essays on Photography* (New Haven, Conn., 1980), pp. 110–11.

24. Rosalind E. Krauss, *The Optical Unconscious* (Cambridge, Mass., 1993). Krauss evolved this concept from the work of Walter Benjamin, particularly ideas expressed in Benjamin's "The Work of Art in the Age of Mechanical Reproduction," pp. 235–37.

25. Benjamin, *Illuminations,* pp. 236–37.

26. Georg Simmel, "Metropolis and Mental Life," in Eric and Mary Josephson, eds., *Man Alone: Alienation in Modern Society* (New York, 1962), p. 152.

27. Arnold Hauser, *Naturalism, Impressionism, the Film Age,* Vol. 4 of *The Social History of Art* (New York, 1958), p. 230.

28. Earnest Elmo Calkins, "Beauty the New Business Tool," *Atlantic Monthly* 140 (August 1927), pp. 147–48.

29. Advertising psychologist Alfred Poffenberger, as quoted and discussed by Roland Marchand, *Advertising the American Dream* (Berkeley, 1985), pp. 235–36.

30. Designer Harold Van Doren, as quoted and discussed by Stuart Ewen, *All Consuming Images* (New York, 1988), p. 50.

11: SILVER CHAINS AND FRIENDLY GIANTS

1. Edward L. Bernays, *Propaganda* (New York, 1928), p. 75.

2. E. Hofer & Sons "distributed materials to 14,000 daily and weekly newspapers, and was underwritten by a number of large manufacturers and holding companies." See Thomas C. Cochran and William Miller, *The Age of Enterprise: A Social History of Industrial America* (New York, 1942), p. 343.

3. Ibid., p. 340.

4. S. M. Kennedy, *Winning the Public* (New York, 1920), p. 3.

5. Glenn C. Quiett and Ralph D. Casey, "Principle of Publicity" (1926), in W. Brook Graves, *Readings in Public Opinion, Its Formation and Control* (New York, 1928), p. 649.

6. David E. Nye, *Image Worlds: Corporate Identities at General Electric, 1890–1930* (Cambridge, Mass., 1983).

7. Alan R. Raucher, *Public Relations and Business, 1900–1929* (Baltimore, 1968), p. 77.

8. Nye, *Image Worlds,* pp. 18–19, offered the following description of the NELA and its function: "General Electric succeeded in controlling its market not only through the agreement to share all patents with Westinghouse but also through the establishment of a secret holding company. The National Electric Light Association (NELA) was reformed in 1904, ostensibly as a central organization that would assist small independent electrical companies to compete against General Electric . . . and Westinghouse. It purchased these small companies but left their management intact, offering a range of services, including a scientific testing laboratory, a development laboratory, publicity, and technical assistance. In less than a decade NELA absorbed thirty-seven independent manufacturers, which at times joined of their own volition in order to reap the benefits of a larger association. . . . None of these companies knew that General Electric owned 75 percent of the stock in NELA, which became in effect a holding company. . . . As a General Electric Publication stated a half century later, 'Not a soul outside the five organizers of the National, and officials of the General Electric Company, had the slightest intimation that the latter held a controlling interest.' "

9. Edward L. Bernays, *Biography of an Idea: Memoirs of Public Relations Council Edward L. Bernays* (New York, 1965), pp. 444–60.

10. Rexford Guy Tugwell, quoted in Richard S. Tedlow, *Keeping the Corporate Image: Public Relations and Business, 1900–1950* (Greenwich, Conn., 1979), pp. 16–17; 44–46.

11. George E. Mowry and Blaine A Brownell, *The Urban Nation, 1920–1980* (New York, 1981), pp. 4–5.

12. Wesley C. Mitchell, "A Review," *Recent Economic Changes in the United States* (New York, 1929), pp. 874–89, in Stanley Coben, ed., *Reform, War, and Reaction: 1912–1932* (Columbia, S.C., 1972), p. 421.

13. Mowry and Brownwell, *The Urban Nation,* pp. 5–7.

14. Sinclair Lewis, *Babbitt,* quoted in Loren Baritz, ed., *The Culture of the Twenties* (Indianapolis, 1970), pp. 216–17, 220–21.

15. Alvin H. Hansen, "Factories Affecting the Trend of Real Wages," *American Economic Review* 15 (March 1925); and Paul H. Douglas, "The Movement of Real Wages and its Economic Significance," *American Economic Review*

(Suppl.), 16 (March 1926), quoted in Mitchell, "A Review," pp. 427–28, 874–89. See also William Barber, *From New Era to New Deal: Herbert Hoover, the Economist, and American Economic Policy, 1921–1933* (Cambridge, Mass., 1985), pp. 46–47.

16. As quoted in Stuart Ewen, *Captains of Consciousness: Advertising and the Social Roots of the Consumer Culture* (New York, 1976), pp. 22, 28.

17. Irving Bernstein, *The Lean Years: The History of the American Worker, 1920–1933* (Baltimore, 1966), p. 70.

18. Mowry and Brownwell, *The Urban Nation*, p. 8.

19. David F. Hawkins, "The Development of Modern Financial Reporting Practices among American Manufacturing Corporations," *Business History Review* 37 (Autumn 1963), reprinted in Richard S. Tedlow and Richard R. John, Jr., *Managing Big Business: Essays from the Business History Review* (Boston: Harvard Business School, 1986), p. 176.

20. Rexford Guy Tugwell, Thomas Munro, and Roy E. Stryker, *American Economic Life and the Means of Its Improvement* (New York, 1925), pp. 82–83.

21. Though the 10 million stockholders of 1930 were still only 8.1 percent of the population, their weight within the electorate was probably more considerable. In 1928, when the U.S. population was about 120 million and the number of stockholders was nearing 10 million, only about 36 million Americans voted in the presidential election. Of that number, about 21 million voted for the Republican candidate, Herbert Hoover. Given customary voting patterns, one might conclude that stockholders had a disproportionate weight in the election of Republican administrations. See U.S. Department of Commerce, *Historical Statistics of the United States: Colonial Times to 1970,* Part 1, p. 8; Part 2, pp. 1078, 1073.

22. Cochran and Miller, *The Age of Enterprise*, p. 343.

23. George Soule, *Prosperity Decade, From War to Depression: 1917–1929* (New York, 1947, 1962), p. 131.

24. Calvin Coolidge, selection from *The Autobiography of Calvin Coolidge* (New York, 1929), in Coben, *Reform, Wars, and Reaction*, p. 386.

25. Message to Congress, December 4, 1928, quoted in Eric Hobsbawm, *The Age of Extremes: A History of the World, 1914–1991* (New York, 1994), p. 85.

26. Soule, *Prosperity Decade*, p. 141.

27. Cochran and Miller, *The Age of Enterprise*, pp. 343–44.

28. See Andrew Wernick, *Promotional Culture: Advertising, Ideology, and Symbolic Expression* (London, 1991).

29. John Dewey, *The Public and Its Problems* (Athens, Ohio, 1927, 1988), p. 118.

30. John Dewey, *Individualism Old and New* (New York, 1930), p. 9.

31. Calvin Coolidge, quoted in Cochran and Miller, *The Age of Enterprise*, p. 324.

32. William J. Barber, *From New Era to New Deal: Herbert Hoover, the Economists, and American Economic Policy* (Cambridge, Mass., 1985), p. 47.

33. Samuel Yellen, *American Labor Struggles: 1877–1934* (New York, 1936), pp. 292–93.

34. Soule, *Prosperity Decade*, pp. 141–42.

35. Cochran and Miller, *The Age of Enterprise*, pp. 315–16. See also ibid., p. 143.

36. Soule, *Prosperity Decade,* pp. 142–43.
37. Frederick Ackerman, "Forces that Influence the Profession's Future," *American Architect* 141 (May 1932), pp. 30–31. By 1926, the construction industry was already showing signs of trouble.
38. Nathaniel Schneider Keith, *Politics and the Housing Crisis Since 1930* (New York, 1973), p. 17.
39. See John Kenneth Galbraith, *The Great Crash, 1929* (New York, 1955).
40. Keith, *Politics and the Housing Crisis,* p. 17.
41. "Stocks Collapse . . ." *New York Times,* October 30, 1929, p. 1.

12: THE GREATER GOOD

1. Russell D. Buhite and David W. Levy, eds., *FDR's Fireside Chats* (New York, 1993), p. 5.
2. See Nathaniel Schneider Keith, *Politics and the Housing Crisis Since 1930* (New York, 1973), p. 22. See also William E. Leuchtenburg, *Franklin D. Roosevelt and the New Deal* (New York, 1963), pp. 1, 18–20; and Buhite and Levy, *FDR's Fireside Chats,* p. 5.
3. S. H. Walker and Paul Sklar, *Business Finds Its Voice: Management's Efforts to Sell the Business Idea to the Public* (New York, 1938), p. 3.
4. John E. Edgerton, Foreword to *Public Old Age Pensions* (New York, April 1930), pp. 3, 5.
5. *Proceedings of the Thirty-Fifth Annual Meeting of the National Association of Manufacturers, New York City (October 6–9, 1930),* pp. 14–15, quoted in Leuchtenburg, *Franklin D. Roosevelt and the New Deal,* p. 21.
6. Leo C. Rosten, "President Roosevelt and the Washington Correspondents." *Public Opinion Quarterly* 1 (January 1937), pp. 37–38.
7. Richard W. Steele, *Propaganda in an Open Society: The Roosevelt Administration and the Media, 1933–1941* (Westport, Conn., 1985), pp. 4–5.
8. Paul Anderson, quoted in Steele, *Propaganda in an Open Society,* p. 6.
9. "In 1924," wrote historian Irving Bernstein, "Congress had passed the bonus bill for war veterans over the veto of President Coolidge. Each veteran received an adjusted service certificate, based upon the number of days he spent in service, which became payable in twenty years. . . . Massive unemployment after 1929, affecting veterans severely, led to agitation for current payment of the bonus." There was a bill, sponsored by Wright Patman, calling for immediate payment. When that bill failed to pass Congress, the Bonus Army took to the streets. See Bernstein, *The Lean Years: The History of the American Worker* (Baltimore, 1966), pp. 437–38.
10. Leuchtenburg, *Franklin D. Roosevelt and the New Deal,* p. 18.
11. Keith, *Politics and the Housing Crisis Since 1930,* pp. 22–23.
12. John Maynard Keynes, "The End of Laissez-Faire" (1926), in *Essays in Persuasion* (New York, 1931, 1963), p. 321.
13. Ibid., p. 312.
14. Ibid., pp. 317–18.
15. Ibid., p. 317.
16. Ibid., p. 318.
17. Ibid., p. 319.

18. Claude G. Bowers, *Jefferson and Hamilton: The Struggle for Democracy in America* (Boston, 1925). Roosevelt's debt to Bowers is discussed at great length in Graham J. White, *FDR and the Press* (Chicago, 1979), pp. 143–57.

19. Bowers, *Jefferson and Hamilton*, pp. v–vii.

20. White, *FDR and the Press*, pp. 143–44.

21. Ibid., p. 148.

22. Ibid., p. 145.

23. Ibid., p. 148.

24. Ibid., p. 157.

25. Ibid.

26. Ibid., p. 156.

27. Steele, *Propaganda in an Open Society*, pp. 6–8.

28. Betty Houchin Winfield, *FDR and the New Media* (Urbana, Ill., 1990), p. 12.

29. Ibid., p. 13.

30. Eleanor Roosevelt, *The Autobiography* (New York, 1961), p. 141.

31. Winfield, *FDR and the New Media*, pp. 14–15.

32. Hugh Gregory Gallagher, *FDR's Splendid Deception* (New York, 1985), p. 66.

33. James MacGregor Burns, *Roosevelt: The Lion and the Fox* (New York, 1956), p. 152.

34. Gallagher, *FDR's Splendid Deception*, pp. 93–94.

35. Ibid., p. xiii.

36. These efforts included the stabilization of the banking system, the establishment of the Securities Exchange Commission, and the launching of antitrust prosecutions against corporations that artificially rigged prices. They also included components of the National Recovery Administration (NRA) designed to stimulate economic growth and the creation of the Reconstruction Finance Corporation, which supplied loans to businesses that agreed to create new jobs. At another level, the Home Owners' Loan Corporation (HOLC) and the Federal Housing Authority (FHA) refinanced mortgages—on a long-term basis—for small-property owners, helping them to hold on to their homes. "Probably no single measure," argued Arthur Schlesinger, Jr.—referring to the HOLC— "consolidated the middle-class support for the administration." See Keith, *Politics and the Housing Crisis Since 1930*, p. 24.

37. The writing of Adolf Berle, Jr., and Gardiner Means, in *The Modern Corporation and Private Property*, which discussed the ways that monopolies and oligopolies, run by a small number of men, lorded over American economic life through the machinery of a totally "administered market," is clearly evident in this critique of private enterprise. See Leuchtenburg, *Franklin D. Roosevelt and the New Deal*, p. 34.

Programs that pitted governmental regulation against private enterprise included those parts of the NRA that sought to ensure decent wage levels for workers and encouraged them to organize and the National Labor Relations Act (Wagner Act), guaranteeing workers the right to engage in collective bargaining.

Roosevelt was convinced that "certain enterprises could best be carried on under public control," according to Frances Perkins, *The Roosevelt I Knew* (New York, 1946), p. 329. Embodying this viewpoint, a number of federally administered agencies were created to modernize the social infrastructure. The Public

Works Administration, Works Progress Administration, Civilian Conservation Corps, and Tennessee Valley Authority each put people to work on what were considered socially necessary projects: housing; water projects; electrification of the countryside; land reclamation; and the building of roads, bridges, public buildings, and parks. Under the Wagner-Steagall Housing Act, dilapidated slum houses were also cleared, and new community-oriented, federally funded housing developments were built.

13: THE NEW DEAL AND THE PUBLICITY OF SOCIAL ENTERPRISE

1. It should be noted here that in the late thirties, Roosevelt became the first president to employ and rely heavily on scientific opinion polling. See Eleanor Roosevelt, *The Autobiography* (New York, 1961), p. 102.

2. Richard W. Steele, *Propaganda in an Open Society: The Roosevelt Administration and the Media, 1933–1941* (Westport, Conn., 1985), p. 9.

3. Quoted in Leo Rosten, "President Roosevelt and the Washington Correspondents," *Public Opinion Quarterly* 1 (January 1937), pp. 37–38.

4. Interview with Julius C. C. Edelstein, January 23, 1991. Along these lines, Louis Howe also coached the First Lady to hold regular informal conferences with groups of women reporters. "Louis Howe . . . trained me well," Mrs. Roosevelt later reflected. He taught her "to detect the implications of the questions" and, if necessary, "to avoid any direct answer. Roosevelt, *The Autobiography,* p. 172.

5. Betty Houchin Winfield, *FDR and the News Media* (Urbana, Ill., 1990), p. 59.

6. Interview with Edelstein.

7. This specific figure is quibbled with by historian Graham J. White, but even he does not argue with the fact that newspaper publishers were overwhelmingly antagonistic to Roosevelt's presidency. See Graham J. White, *FDR and the Press* (Chicago, 1979), pp. 1–73.

8. Winfield, *FDR and the News Media,* p. 109.

9. Ibid.

10. See Robert W. McChesney, *Telecommunications, Mass Media and Democracy: The Battle for the Control of U.S. Broadcasting, 1928–1935* (New York, 1993). Also see Erik Barnouw, *A Tower in Babel: A History of Broadcasting in the United States to 1933* (New York, 1966), p. 96. Even Herbert Hoover had questioned the wisdom of permitting "the ether" to be exploited as an adverting medium. "It is inconceivable," he ventured, "that we should allow so great a possibility for service to be drowned in advertising chatter."

11. Steele, *Propaganda in an Open Society,* p. 20.

12. Ibid., p. 23.

13. Ibid., p. 21.

14. Ibid., pp. 22–23.

15. Ibid., p. 22.

16. Winfield, *FDR and the News Media,* p. 104.

17. Ibid., p. 106.

18. Frances Perkins, *The Roosevelt I Knew* (New York, 1946), pp. 71–73.

19. Russell D. Buhite and David W. Levy, eds., *FDR's Fireside Chats* (New York, 1963), pp. 12–17.

20. Ibid., p. 69.

21. Ibid., pp. 49–51.

22. Steve Fraser and Gary Gerstle, *The Rise and Fall of the New Deal Order* (Princeton, N.J., 1989), p. 67.

23. James MacGregor Burns, *Roosevelt: The Lion and the Fox* (New York, 1956), p. 274.

24. Buhite and Levy, *FDR's Fireside Chats,* pp. 81–82.

25. Steele, *Propaganda in an Open Society,* p. 27.

26. Maren Stange, " 'The Record Itself:' Farm Security Administration Photography and the Transformation of Rural Life." In Pete Daniel, Merry A. Foresta, Maren Stange, and Sally Stein, *Official Images: New Deal Photography* (Washington, D.C., 1987), p. 1.

27. This attitude reiterated ideas expressed by the Progressive activist Lillian Wald at the turn of the century. Wald had argued that to encourage "a sense of fairness outraged," to communicate "that something is wrong," it was necessary to show the public that behind "each figure" in the statistics stood a "human being." Quoted in Elizabeth Ewen, *Immigrant Women in the Land of Dollars* (New York, 1995), p. 82.

28. F. Jack Hurley, *Portrait of a Decade: Roy Stryker and the Development of the Documentary Photography in the Thirties* (Baton Rouge, La., 1972), p. 10.

29. Ibid., p. 12.

30. Hurley elaborated: "The great documentary photographer and the young teaching assistant became good friends during the weeks and months that *American Economic Life* was in preparation. Hine would come to Columbia with great armloads of pictures drawn from his vast experience in the areas of child labor, poverty, and industrial photography. Did the book need pictures of representative immigrant types? Hine could present examples showing typically Slavic, male and female; typically Nordic male and female, and so on by the dozens. Did the authors need some method of contrasting substandard with standard and high standard housing? Hine had at one time or another taken exactly the photograph needed. So complete were his files that it was never necessary to send him out to take a specific picture. If a search of other sources did not turn up a required illustration, Hine could usually be counted upon to rummage around in his own holdings and come up with what is needed." See Hurley, *Portrait of a Decade,* p. 14.

31. Rexford Guy Tugwell, Thomas Munro, and Roy E. Stryker, *American Economic Life and the Means of its Improvement* (New York, 1925) p. 15.

32. Ibid., p. 27.

33. Ibid., p. 45.

34. Ibid., p. 53.

35. Ibid., pp. 38, 40.

36. Ibid., p. 56.

37. Ibid., p. 87.

38. Ibid., p. 100.

39. Ibid., p. 104.

40. Daniel et al., *Official Images,* p. 32.

41. William Stott, *Documentary Expression and Thirties America* (New York, 1973), p. 76.

42. Hartly E. Howe, "You Have Seen Their Pictures," *Survey Graphic* (April 1940), pp. 236–41.

43. Letter from Stryker to Dorothea Lange, January 1936, as quoted in Lawrence W. Levine, "The Historian and the Icon," in Carl Fleischhaur and Beverly W. Brannan, eds., *Documenting America: 1935–1943* (Berkeley, 1988), p. 38.

44. Letter from Stryker to Sheldon Dick, 1938, as quoted in Alan Trachtenberg, "From Image to Story," in ibid., p. 62.

45. Sally A. Stein, "The Rhetoric of the Colorful and the Colorless: American Photography and Material Culture Between the Wars," Ph.D. diss., Yale University, 1991.

46. Stott, *Documentary Expression and Thirties America,* p. 49.

47. Ibid., p. 29.

48. The marriage of facticity and emotional appeal built on trends that were found in the writings of the muckrakers. The Progressive Era's literary admixture of information and melodrama gained pictorial expression, some twenty years later, in the work of many FSA photographers.

49. Burns, *Roosevelt the Lion and the Fox,* p. 272.

50. Daniel et al., *Official Images,* p. 1.

51. James Curtis, *Mind's Eye, Mind's Truth: FSA Photography Reconsidered* (Philadelphia, 1989), p. 5.

52. Howe, "You Have Seen Their Pictures," p. 238.

53. Maren Strange, *Symbols of the Ideal Life: Social Documentary Photography in America, 1890–1950* (New York, 1989), p. 108. See also, ibid., p. 238.

14: MONEY TALKS: THE PUBLICITY OF PRIVATE ENTERPRISE

1. Eric Hobsbawm, *The Age of Extremes: A History of the World, 1914–1991* (New York, 1994), p. 87.

2. Ibid., p. 96.

3. Ibid., pp. 94, 100. Hobsbawm maintained that the growth of installment selling during the 1920s contributed to the severity of the crash in the U.S. "When the collapse came," he wrote, "it was . . . all the more drastic because in fact a lagging expansion of demand had been beefed up by means of an enormous expansion of consumer credit."

4. E. Pendleton Herring, "Official Publicity Under the New Deal." *Annals of the American Academy of Political and Social Science* 179 (May 1935), pp. 167–68.

5. Ibid., pp. 172, 175.

6. Lubricating this development, noted historian Steven Fraser, the CIO employed public relations techniques to improve its reputation among the general public. See Fraser, *Labor Will Rule: Sidney Hillman and the Rise of American Labor* (New York, 1991), p. 403.

7. A 1938 survey of Muncie, Indiana—the all-American Middletown made famous by Robert and Helen Lynd—revealed that chain stores were widely perceived as "unfair monopolies." Among the chains, the A&P company was singled out as the one that "most people said they'd refuse to patronize because of its policies" (see "Chains, 1938," *TIDE* 12 [January 1, 1938], pp. 21–23).

8. New Deal endorsement of co-ops provoked Harper Sibley, president of the U.S. Chamber of Commerce, to argue in 1936: "It is improper for governmental

agencies to extend preferential treatment, by means of tax exemption, financing or other aid, to consumers' cooperative enterprises, since such enterprises are but another form of competitive force seeking to win the support and patronage of the American consumer." "Co-op Conclave," *TIDE* (November 1, 1936), p. 42.

9. Ibid., p. 20. The New Deal administration, particularly Thurman Arnold, who headed the antitrust division of the Department of Justice, gave support to these critiques of advertising. See "Mr. Arnold on Advertising," *TIDE* (November 15, 1938), p. 25.

10. "Consumer Concern," *TIDE* (July 1935), p. 13.

11. C. B. Larrabee, "Mr. Schlink, Danger Is Not So Much What He Says as in Highbrow Following He Has Created." *Printers' Ink* 166 (January 11, 1934), p. 13.

12. Contributing to business's sense of alarm, cooperatives were also receiving the imprimatur of the government. In 1934, complained an editorial in *Printers' Ink,* business was being threatened by a "vast network of consumer councils," with "some 20,000 committee members" organized "under the banner of the NRA Consumer's Advisory Council." See Editorial, *Printers' Ink* 166 (January 25, 1934), pp. 98–99.

13. "Sore Points," *TIDE* (October 1935), p. 10.

14. See "Chains," *TIDE* (January 1, 1938), p. 22. This sort of appeal to "consumer consciousness" became a trademark of corporate PR and advertising during the twenties. Some corporately sponsored groups even used the term *cooperative* in their titles. See "Era of Good Feeling," *TIDE* (February 1, 1937), p. 22; "Most High," *TIDE* (March 1, 1937), p. 20; and "Puppetry," *TIDE* (November 15, 1937), pp. 17–18.

15. See "Chains," p. 22. To gather public sympathy, business-inspired, third-party front groups often employed the term *consumer* in their titles. In support of the A&P, for example, one of Byoir's organizational contrivances was called the National Consumers' Tax Council. See Irwin Ross, *The Image Merchants: The Fabulous World of Public Relations* (Garden City, N.Y., 1959), p. 118.

16. Nationally, these antichain efforts included the Robinson-Patman bill of 1936. In California, the campaign of the Foundation for Consumer Education—the brainchild of Ted Braun, PR man for the California Chain Store Association, and of Don Francisco of the Lord & Thomas advertising agency—successfully defeated Proposition 22, which would have imposed a tax on chain retailers. See "Tug of War," *TIDE* (October 1, 1936), pp. 22–23. See S. H. Walker and Paul Sklar, *Business Finds Its Voice: Management's Efforts to Sell the Business Idea to the Public* (New York, 1938), pp. 77–78.

17. "Consumer Concern," *TIDE* (July 1935), p. 13.

18. "Co-op Front," *TIDE* (December 1, 1936), p. 42.

19. Samuel S. Stratten, "Public Relations in Steel," *Public Opinion Quarterly* 1 (April 1937), p. 109; and John W. Hill, *The Making of a Public Relations Man* (New York, 1963), pp. 86–87.

20. "Using Advertising to Counteract Unfavorable Propaganda: New York Cotton Commission Merchant Uses Trade Advertisements to Paint Picture of Real Mill Conditions in the South," *Printers' Ink* 151 (April 10, 1930), p. 34.

21. FDR's message on the "Strengthening and Enforcement of Antitrust Law" to the 75th Cong., 3rd sess., April 29, 1938, as quoted in J. D. Glover

(professor of business administration, Harvard University Graduate School of Business Administration), *The Attack on Big Business* (Boston, 1954), p. 12.

22. "Pro Bono Publico," *TIDE* (August 1936), p. 19.

23. T. J. Ross, *The Public Relations Problem of Industry,* American Management Series (New York, 1937), pp. 6–9.

24. Carl Byoir, "The Volcano of Public Opinion," *Public Relations* 1 (First Quarter, 1938), p. 18.

25. Carl W. Ackerman, "How the Government Dominates the Press," *Public Relations* 1 (First Quarter, 1938), p. 11.

26. Colby Dorr Dam, "Business and Life," *Public Relations* 1 (First Quarter, 1938]), p. 5.

27. "Business-and-Government," *Fortune* (August 1938), p. 51.

28. Glenn Griswold, "Public Relations—Some Misconceptions," *Public Opinion Quarterly* 1 (July 1937), p. 129.

29. Glenn Griswold, "The McGraw-Hill Public Relations Forums," *Public Opinion Quarterly* 3 (October 1939), pp. 707–8.

30. Economist Gardiner Means was usually depicted as the center; Rexford Tugwell, the left.

31. James MacGregor Burns, *Roosevelt: The Lion and the Fox* (New York, 1956), p. 153.

32. Raymond Moley, "Social Function of Advertising," *Public Relations* 1 (First Quarter, 1938), p. 23.

33. E. W. Pryor, "Sure as the Rising of the Sun," *Public Relations* 1 (First Quarter, 1938), p. 3.

34. "442 Industrial Leaders Evaluate Public Relations," *Public Relations* 1 (First Quarter, 1938), pp. 24–25. For the growth of opinion research during this period, see relevant sections of Jean M. Converse, *Survey Research in the United States: Roots and Emergence, 1890–1960* (Berkeley, 1987).

35. "Puppetry," p. 17.

36. Glenn Griswold, "Public Relations: First in the Order of Business," *Business Week,* No. 1 in the Reports to Executives series (New York, 1937), pp. 1–2.

37. Walker and Sklar, *Business Finds Its Voice,* p. 39.

38. Ross, *The Image Merchants,* p. 27.

39. Walker and Sklar, *Business Finds Its Voice,* p. 27.

40. Floyd H. Allport, "Toward a Science of Public Opinion," *Public Opinion Quarterly* 1 (January 1937), p. 17.

41. The story of the Brass Hats and the takeover of NAM is found in Richard S. Tedlow, *Keeping the Corporate Image: Public Relations and Business, 1900–1950* (Greenwich, Conn., 1979), p. 61.

42. Robert S. Lund, "Industry's Opportunity and Duty Under the Recovery Plan," National Association of Manufacturers, *Proceedings* (New York, December 7–8, 1933), pp. 75–76.

43. James A. Emery, "The Call of the Sentry," address before NAM's Congress of American Industry (New York, December 4, 1935), pp. 2, 4, 11.

44. "Renovation in NAM," *Fortune* 38 (July 1948), pp. 72ff.

45. Griswold, "Public Relations: First in the Order of Business," p. 3.

46. Budgets, which did not include hefty in-kind contributions from several important communications industries (radio stations, billboard advertising companies, and so forth), were directed to a wide range of public relations activities,

including movies, news-service publications, radio, public speakers, window displays, foreign language services, and slide films. Between 1935 and 1940, the growth in public relations expenditures was dramatic. In 1935, for example, radio expenditures were $65,000; by 1940, radio expenditures were nearly $145,000 dollars. In 1935, the Speakers' Bureau received $15,000 in funding; by 1940, it received nearly $60,000. News-service activity grew from $25,000 in 1935 to about $60,000 in 1940. The variety of public relations activities also expanded over that five-year period. See "Minutes: Meeting of Committee on Public Relations at the Waldorf Astoria, March 18, 1935," NAM Archive, Hagley Museum, Wilmington, Delaware, Acc. 1411, Series 5, Box 1; "Report of the Public Relations Committee," February 1938, NAM Archive, Acc. 1411, Series I, Box 114; and "National Industrial Information Committee: Proposed Budget, January 1 to December 31, 1940," NAM Archive, Acc. 1411, Series I, Box 114.

47. NAM, "N.A.M. at Work in the East-Central Region," Detroit, 1936. NAM Archive, Acc. 1411, Box 114, Series I.

48. "Renovation in N.A.M.," p. 75.

49. "Business Defensive: The National Association of Manufacturers Writes a Campaign to Sell Business to U.S. Citizens," *TIDE* (September 1936), p. 27.

50. NAM, "What Is Your American System All About?" (pamphlet), 1936. NAM Archive, Acc. 1411, Box 114, Series I, pp. 5, 7.

51. George E. Sokolsky, "Crystallizing Public Opinion Nationally," speech to the National Industrial Council (a NAM front group), December 5, 1938, pp. 14–15.

52. NAM Public Relations Advisory Group, Minutes, Monday, October 23, 1939, New York City. NAM Archive, Acc. 1411, Box 112, Series I, pp. 1–2.

53. Ibid., pp. 6–7.

54. James B. Selvage, PR director of NAM, "Memorandum on Community Public Information Programs to Combat Radical Tendencies and Present the Constructive Side of Industry," 1938. NAM Archive, Acc. 1411, Box 111, Series I.

55. Griswold, "Public Relations—Some Misconceptions," p. 129.

56. NAM Advisory Committee on Public Relations, minutes, meeting on March 17, 1939. NAM Archive, Acc. 1411, Box 112, Series I, p. 6.

57. NAM, "N.A.M. at Work in the East-Central Region," Detroit, 1936. NAM Archive, Acc. 1411, Box 114, Series I, p. 3.

58. Walker and Sklar, *Business Finds Its Voice*, p. 22.

59. The minutes of some of these meetings are cited here. They and others may be found in the NAM Archive.

60. NAM, "Outline of Organization and Operation of a Community Program," probably 1938. NAM Archive, Acc. 1411, Box 114, Series I.

61. NAM Advisory Committee on Public Relations, minutes, meeting on March 17, 1939. NAM Archive, Acc. 1411, Box 112, Series I, p. 12.

62. Pamphlet explaining the "Community Program Service of N.A.M.," NAM Archive, Acc. 1411, Box 111, Series I. See also, NAM, *Report of the Public Relations Committee,* February 1938. NAM Archive, Acc. 1411, Box 114, Series I, p. 2.

63. NAM, "Experts All: Who's Who Behind Industry's Public Information Program," 1938. NAM Archive, Acc. 1411, Box 114, Series I.

64. NAM, "Industry Speaks to Millions—with Color-Pictures-Facts." NAM Archive, Acc. 1411, Box 114, Series I.

65. NAM, "Experts All." NAM Archive, Acc. 1411, Box 114, Series I.

66. NAM Advisory Committee on Public Relations, minutes, p. 11.

67. *Young America*, April 19, 1940.

68. By 1941, *Young America* claimed to have the "largest circulation of any general youth magazine." Advertisement for *Young America* in *TIDE* (May 1, 1941), inside front cover.

69. Walker and Sklar, *Business Finds Its Voice*. p. 22.

70. NAM brochure, *The National Industrial Council presents "America Marching On" and "Frontiers of the Future," Two One-Reel Sound Motion Pictures Featuring Lowell Thomas. Available Without Cost for Schools and Private Showings.*"

71. Into the 1950s, it should be inserted, films like these provided civics lessons for schoolchildren throughout much of the United States. Interview with Ros Petchesky.

72. William Bird, "Enterprise and Meaning: Sponsored Film, 1939–1949." *History Today* 39 (December 1989), pp. 24–30.

73. Gustave Le Bon, *The Crowd: A Study of the Popular Mind* (London, 1896, 1952), p. 68.

74. Walter Lippmann, *Public Opinion* (New York, 1922), pp. 163, 165–66.

75. Hartley E. Howe, "You Have Seen Their Pictures," *Survey Graphic* (April 1940), p. 237.

76. NAM, Minutes of Meeting of Committee on Public Relations, Waldorf Astoria Hotel, New York City, March 18, 1935. NAM Archive, Acc. 1411, Box 1, Series V, p. 1.

77. National Association of Broadcasters, "The American Family Robinson," *NAB Reports* 7 (August 11, 1939). See also "Industry's Own Radio Program" and undated advertisement for the program. Luke Robinson was played by Bill Adams, whose voice was familiar to millions as the narrator of Henry Luce's staunchly pro-business newsfilm series, *The March of Time*.

78. Typescript synopsis. NAM Archive, Acc. 1411, Box 113, Series I.

79. Pamphlet promoting *Your Town*. NAM Archive, Acc. 1411, Box 113, Series I.

80. To ensure the distribution of its slide-sound programs—which combined film strips and 33 1/3 rpm records—NAM provided schools with the necessary equipment for showings. This deal—offering equipment in exchange for a school showing NAM propaganda to students—prefigured Whittle Communications' current *Channel One* television program, in which the company offers free audiovisual equipment to economically needy school systems that agree to show Whittle's commercially sponsored "news" programs in homeroom classes.

81. NAM, script for *Flood Tide*. A brochure on sound-slide films, *Ideal for Club Programs!* probably 1939, contains complete transcripts of sound tracks. NAM Archive, Acc. 1411, Box 113, Series I.

82. Robert L. Lund, *Report of Public Relations Committee* of NAM, 1937, p. 2; and NAM, *Report of the Public Relations Committee,* February 1938. NAM Archive, Acc. 1411, Box 114, Series I, p. 1.

83. NAM Advisory Committee on Public Relations, minutes of meeting on March 17, 1939, p. 14.

84. Mikhail Bakhtin, Introduction, to *Rabelais and His World* (Cambridge, Mass., 1968), pp. 6–19.

85. Warren I. Susman, "The People's Fair: Cultural Contradictions of a Consumer Society." In *Culture As History: The Transformation of American Society in the Twentieth Century* (New York, 1984), pp. 211–29.

86. Ibid., p. 214.

87. Larry Zim, Mel Lerner, and Herbert Rolfes, *The World of Tomorrow: The 1939 World's Fair* (New York, 1988), p. 9.

88. Sussman, "The People's Fair," p. 223.

89. John Deventer (editor, *The Iron Age*), "Jobs in the World of Tomorrow And . . . A Job for the 'World of Tomorrow.'" *The Iron Age* (February 9, 1939), unpaginated reprint.

90. Bernard Lichtenberg, "Business Backs New York World Fair to Meet the New Deal Propaganda," *Public Opinion Quarterly* 2 (April 1938), p. 314.

91. Ibid., p. 315.

92. The surname Middleton was—most certainly—a play on "Middletown," the name that Robert and Helen Lynd gave to Muncie, Indiana, in their classic study of a quintessential American town, *Middletown*.

93. Like Margolies in *The American Family Robinson* and consistent with the prevalent bias, Makaroff is typecast as a Jewish revolutionary.

94. Bird's discussion of this film was particularly useful here. See Bird, "Enterprise and Meaning," pp. 24–30.

95. Susman, *Culture as History,* p. 225.

96. Walter Dorwin Teague, "Proposal for Exhibition of the National Association of Manufacturers, New York World's Fair" (April 25, 1940), NAM Archive, Acc. 1411, Box 115, Series I.

97. "New York Fair: For Industry, An Answer and a Promise," *TIDE* (May 1, 1939), pp. 20–21.

98. See "Resignation," *TIDE* (March 15, 1939), pp. 26–27.

15: PUBLIC ULTIMATUMS

1. Walter Benjamin, "The Work Of Art in the Age Of Mechanical Reproduction," (1936), in Benjamin, *Illuminations: Essay and Reflection* (New York, 1968), p. 241.

2. Rex Harlow, *Public Relations in War and Peace* (New York, 1942), p. 157.

3. NAM, Philadelphia Executives Conference: Public Relations, *Proceedings* (Philadelphia, October 19, 1943), p. 2.

4. *TIDE* (April 15, 1944), 17.

5. During the First World War, George Creel's experience as a Progressive journalist meant that he was able to bring state-of-the-art publicity techniques to the dissemination of war propaganda. Similarly Elmer Davis, who was appointed to head the Office of War Information (OWI), also represented the cutting edge of media know-how. At CBS in the thirties, he had been the architect of the highly condensed five-minute newscasts. See "Elmer Davis, OWI: The President Finally Appoints a Propaganda Minister," *TIDE* (July 1, 1942), pp. 11–12.

For further information on the OWI, see Elmer Davis "OWI Has a Job," *Public Opinion Quarterly* 7 (Spring 1943), pp. 5–14. See also, Lester G. Hawkins, Jr., and George Pettee, "OWI—Organization and Problems," *Public*

Opinion Quarterly 7 (Spring 1943), pp. 15–33; and Alan M. Winkler, *The Politics of Propaganda: The Office of War Information, 1942–1945* (New Haven, Conn., 1978). Discussions of the OWI are also found in Erik Barnouw, *The Golden Web: A History of Broadcasting in the United States, 1933–1953* (New York, 1968); John Morton Blum, *"V" Was for Victory: Politics and American Culture During World War II* (New York, 1976); Charles J. Rolo, *Radio Goes to War: The "Fourth Front"* (New York, 1942); Holly Cowan Shulman, *The Voice of America: Propaganda and Democracy, 1941–1945* (Madison, 1990); Thomas C. Sorensen, *The Word War: The Story of American Propaganda* (New York, 1968); Richard W. Steele, "Preparing the Public for War: Efforts to Establish a National Propaganda Agency, 1940–1941," *American Historical Review* (October 1970), pp. 1640–53; Sidney Stahl Weinberg, "Wartime Propaganda in a Democracy: America's Twentieth Century Information Agencies," Ph.D. diss., Columbia University, 1969.

6. W. J. Weir, "Opportunity!" *Printers' Ink* 199 (October 1942), p. 13.

7. "Free Enterprise," *TIDE* (December 1, 1943), p. 42.

8. NAM, Philadelphia Executives Conference, *Proceedings* (Philadelphia, October 19, 1943), p. 2.

9. To record these efforts, Glenn Griswold, a former editor and publisher of *Business Week*, also launched a newsletter for industry, *Planning for Postwar*, in October 1943. After the war the newsletter was renamed *Public Relations News*. *Public Relations News* continues to be published by Griswold's widow and longtime publishing partner, Denny Griswald. See "Postwar News, *TIDE* (October 15, 1943), pp. 96, 98.

10. "Postwar Program," *TIDE* (January 1, 1943), pp. 57–58.

11. NAM, Philadelphia Executives Conference, *Proceedings*, p. 20.

12. Austin P. Fisher, "Assign Your 'Labor Relations' to a Sales Minded Executive," *Printers' Ink* 202 (March 26, 1943), p. 15.

13. "Psychological Corp.," *TIDE* (January 1, 1943), p. 32.

14. W. W. Suitt, "Business Must Continue to Tell Public It Is Trying to Do the Right Thing," *Printers' Ink* 219 (August 31, 1945), pp. 19–20.

15. War Advertising Council, *From War to Peace: The New Challenge to Business and Advertising* (New York, 1945).

16. Interview with Leo Bogart, March 14, 1991.

17. Matthew Josephson, *The Robber Barons* (New York, 1934, 1962), pp. 114–20, 277–78.

18. F. M. Surface, "A Review of Public Opinion Particularly Affecting Standard Oil Company," in Standard Oil Company (New Jersey) and Affiliated Companies, 1945 Public Relations Conference, *Proceedings* (Rye, N.Y., November 19–20, 1945), p. 8.

19. Gilbert Burck, "The Jersey Company, Part 1," *Fortune* (October 1951), p. 182.

20. Surface, "A Review of Public Opinion Particularly Affecting Standard Oil Company," pp. 8–9.

21. Burck, "The Jersey Company, Part I," p. 182.

22. Interview with Bogart.

23. Elmo Roper, "An Analysis of Current Public Opinion," Standard Oil Company (New Jersey) and Affiliated Companies, 1945 Public Relations Conference, *Proceedings* (Rye, N.Y., November 19–20, 1945), p. 2.

24. Ibid.

25. Ibid., pp. 2–3.

26. Eugene Holman, "The Importance to the Jersey Organization of an Informed Public Opinion," Standard Oil Company (New Jersey) and Affiliated Companies, 1945 Public Relations Conference, *Proceedings* (Rye, N.Y., November 19–20, 1945), p. 27. Emphasis added.

27. Interview with Bogart.

28. Earl Newsom, "Approaches to the Public Relations Function," Standard Oil Company (New Jersey) and Affiliated Companies, 1945 Public Relations Conference, *Proceedings* (Rye, N.Y., November 19–20, 1945), pp. 36–37.

29. Comments by Robert Haslam, Standard Oil Company (New Jersey) and Affiliated Companies, 1945 Public Relations Conference, *Proceedings* (Rye, N.Y., November 19–20, 1945), p. 37.

30. Robert T. Haslam, "Scope of the Jersey Enterprise," Standard Oil Company (New Jersey) and Affiliated Companies, 1945 Public Relations Conference, *Proceedings* (Rye, N.Y., November 19–20, 1945), p. 108. Emphasis added.

31. "Business Is Still in Trouble," *Fortune* (May 1949), pp. 67–71, 196–200.

32. Ibid., pp. 68–69.

33. Richard Tedlow, *Keeping the Corporate Image: Public Relations and Business, 1900–1950* (Greenwich, Conn., 1979), pp. 150–51.

34. Vernon Scott, "The Conflict of the Two Faiths," *Public Relations Journal* 2 (November 1946), pp. 10–14, 33, 12–14, 10. Emphasis added. [This article is extracted from an address made by Scott before the Board of Directors of the Indiana State Chamber of Commerce on October 5, 1946.] "Mr. Scott is a Kentuckian, born in 1903. Eighteen of his business years were spent as an officer of the California State Chambers of Commerce. Since then he has been retained by other civic organizations in a consulting capacity on matters of organization and finance. He is the president of the firm of Vernon Scott and Loring Schuler, Organization and Industry Counselors with offices in Chicago and San Francisco. He is vice president of the National Tax Equity Association." Scott, "The Conflict of Two Faiths," p. 10.

35. Howard Chase, "Treat the Individual as Consumer and Citizen," *Public Relations Journal* 1 (November 1945) pp. 25–26.

36. Howard Chase, "Human Relations: The Key to Corporate Survival," *Public Relations Journal* 3 (July 1947), p. 12.

37. John W. Hill, "Industry's Iron Curtain," *Public Relations Journal* 3 (July 1947), pp. 4–5.

38. Claude Robinson, "The Human Mind and Industry's Future," *Public Relations Journal* 3 (April 1947), p. 4.

39. Henry C. Link, "Is Freedom the Issue?" *Public Relations Journal* 4 (February 1948), p. 14.

40. George C. McNutt, "20 Topics for Your Public Relations Advertising," *Printers' Ink* 212 (July 6, 1945), p. 19.

41. Chase, "Human Relations," p. 25.

42. "Business Is Still in Trouble," *Fortune,* p. 69.

43. Chase, "Treat the Individual as Consumer and Citizen," p. 26.

44. "Bernays on Fear," *TIDE* (March 7, 1947), p. 56.

45. Robert Wood Johnson, "Human Relations in Modern Business," *Harvard Business Review* 27 (September 1949), p. 527.

46. Robert Wood Johnson, "We Believe . . . ," *Public Relations Journal* 6 (January 1950), p. 6.

47. Frank W. Abrams, "Management's Responsibilities in a Complex World," *Harvard Business Review* 29 (May 1951), pp. 29, 34.

48. Russell W. Davenport, "A New Field for Private Initiative," *Public Relations Journal* 7 (July–August 1951), pp. 4–5. Emphasis added.

49. James Metcalfe, "Could the Reds Seize Detroit," *Look* (August 3, 1948), pp. 21–27.

50. Philip Lesly, *The People Factor: Managing the Human Climate* (Homewood, Ill., 1947), p. 223.

51. "Whitaker & Baxter: Political Pitchmen," in Irwin Ross, *The Image Merchants: The Fabulous World of Public Relations* (Garden City, N.Y., 1959), pp. 65–83. Regarding Whitaker & Baxter's beginnings, Alexander Heard offered the following explanation: "The lush, chaotic politics of California afforded enormous opportunities for anyone who could provide a sensible and economical way to run a political campaign. The presence of large numbers of referenda created contests in which ad hoc alignments shifted from one election to the next. New campaign organizations had to be constructed to wage each fight. The cross-filing system in the primaries confused whatever tendencies existed toward stable factional lines within the parties. And there was not much by the way of party organizations in the first place, a condition partly attributed to California's nonpartisan municipal elections. Whitaker and Baxter . . . responded to a market opportunity created by the frequent referenda and the technical demands of the communications media. The inability of party and factional structures to prosecute political campaigns even for their own candidates created a vacuum. Public relations firms stepped in to fill the vacuum." See Heard, *The Cost of Democracy* (Chapel Hill, N.C., 1960), p. 420.

52. The campaign to defeat Upton Sinclair's bid for governor of California in 1934, along with Whitaker & Baxter's pivotal role in that campaign, is penetratingly discussed by Greg Mitchell in *The Campaign of the Century: Upton Sinclair's Race for Governor of California and the Birth of Media Politics* (New York, 1992).

53. Clem Whitaker, "Professional Political Campaign Management," *Public Relations Journal* 6 (January 1950), pp. 19, 21.

54. Irwin Ross, *The Image Merchants: The Fabulous World of Public Relations* (Garden City, N.Y.), pp. 222–23.

55. Leone Baxter, "Public Relation's Precocious Baby," *Public Relations Journal* 6 (January 1950), p. 23. Emphasis added.

56. My thinking about the public housing question during the post–World War II era has been profoundly influenced by Roslyn Baxandall and Elizabeth Ewen. Their forthcoming book, *Gimme Shelter: The Rise and Fall of the Suburban Dream*, will provide readers with a more substantial exploration of this issue and its long-term implications. Otto Schrifigresser, *The Art and Business of Influencing Lawmakers* (Boston, 1951), p. 219.

57. U.S. Congress, *Congressional Record*, 80th Cong., 2nd sess., 1948, pt 2, pp. 1230, 2823. As quoted in David Oshinsky, *Senator Joseph McCarthy and the American Labor Movement* (Columbia, Mo., 1976).

58. Joseph McCarthy, "Housing Study and Investigation," U.S. Senate, Joint Committee Study and Investigation of Housing, Hearings, 80th Cong., 1947, p. 5.

59. Editors of *Fortune* magazine, in collaboration with Russell W. Davenport, *U.S.A.: The Permanent Revolution* (New York, 1951), pp. 66–67.

16: ENGINEERING CONSENSUS

1. Edward L. Bernays, "The Engineering of Consent," *Annals of the American Academy of Political and Social Science* 250 (March 1947), pp. 113–20.

2. Ibid., p. 113.

3. Ibid., pp. 113–14.

4. Bernays was aware of this danger from personal experience. According to Bernays's 1965 autobiography, Joseph Goebbels—the Nazi propaganda minister—was an avid fan of Bernays's writings. Bernays's source was Karl von Wiegand, foreign correspondent for the Hearst Newspapers.

"During the summer of 1933," Bernays reported,

> Karl von Wiegand . . . was telling us about Goebbels and his propaganda plans to consolidate Nazi power. Goebbels had shown Wiegand his propaganda library, the best Wiegand had ever seen. Goebbels, said Wiegand, was using my book *Crystallizing Public Opinion* as a basis for his destructive campaign against the Jews of Germany.
>
> This shocked me, but I knew any human activity can be used for social purposes or misused for antisocial ones. Obviously the attack on the Jews of Germany was no emotional outburst of the Nazis, but a deliberate, planned campaign.

See Edward L. Bernays, *Biography of an Idea: Memoirs of Public Relations Counsel Edward L. Bernays* (New York, 1965), p. 652.

5. Bernays, "The Engineering of Consent," pp. 114–15.

6. Ibid., pp. 118–19.

7. Ibid., p. 117.

8. Ibid., p. 119.

9. Earl Newsom, "Elements of a Good Public Relations Program," Standard Oil Company (New Jersey) and Affiliated Companies, 1946 Public Relations Conference, *Proceedings* (Rye N.Y., December 2–3, 1946), pp. 75–76.

10. *TIDE* (April 1, 1941), p. 66.

11. Steven W. Plattner, *Roy Stryker: U.S.A., 1943–1950, The Standard Oil (New Jersey) Photography Project* (Austin, Tex., 1983), p. 15.

12. "A Portrait of Oil—Unretouched," *Fortune* (September 1948), p. 102.

13. Stewart Schackne, "Some Considerations Underlying Jersey's Public Relations Activities," Standard Oil Company (New Jersey) and Affiliated Companies, 1948 Public Relations Conference, *Proceedings* (New York, October 21–22, 1948), p. 79.

14. Ibid.

15. Ibid., p. 82.

16. Walter Benjamin, "The Work of Art in the Age of Mechanical Reproduction," in Benjamin, *Illuminations: Essays and Reflection* (New York, 1968), p. 219.

17. "Enter: Aesthetics," *TIDE* (December 1, 1943), p. 2.

18. Ibid., pp. 7–8.

19. C. J. Durban, "Television as a Public Relations Tool," *Public Relations Journal* 3 (May 1947), p. 11.

20. T. J. McInerney, "Television Gets Religion" (extension of remarks of Hon. Thomas J. Lane of Massachusetts in the House of Representatives, Thursday,

June 12, 1952), *Congressional Record,* Appendix, p. A3834.

21. Leone Baxter, "Public Relation's Precocious Baby," *Public Relations Journal* 6 (January 1950), p. 23.

22. Irwin Ross, *The Image Merchants: The Fabulous World of Public Relations* (Garden City, N.Y., 1959), pp. 17–18.

23. Baxter, "Public Relations Precocious Baby," p. 23. As the proponent of "dramatic picture building," Baxter theorized that for PR to be effective, ideas must be presented in an "attractive form." "Your gems of truth and wisdom have to be wrapped in a scintillating mantle that in one way or another captures the interest of the beholder, makes him stop and listen." Baxter defined public relations as "presenting abstract ideas, in attractive form to masses of people who are too occupied with their daily lives to think analytically on their own account." Compare with the idea of people as thinking-critical.

24. Interview with Chester Burger, May 20, 1991.

25. Chester Burger, "Telephone News on Television," Unpublished report prepared for the American Telephone and Telegraph Company, September 1955, p. 2.

26. Ibid., p. 10.

27. Ibid., p. 11.

28. Ibid., p. 18. Emphasis added.

29. Charles M. Hackett, "The Forceful and Vivid Vernacular of the Eye," *Public Relations Journal* 12 (November 1956), pp. 15, 18.

30. George H. Gallup, with Leyton E. Carter, "TV's Sorriest Commercials," *Public Relations Journal* 12 (August 1956), p. 9.

31. Ibid., p. 28.

32. Claude Robinson, "The Gentle Art of Persuasion," *Public Relations Journal* 12 (June 1956), p. 4.

33. J. Gordon Lippincott and Walter P. Marguelies, "The Corporate Look—A Problem in Design," *Public Relations Journal* 13 (December 1957), p. 4.

34. Ibid., p. 27.

35. Louis A. Magnani, "Think Visually," *Public Relations Journal* 17 (December 1961), p. 23.

36. James F. Kelleher, "TV's Perennial Star: The Political Candidate," *Public Relations Journal* 12 (April 1956), p. 18.

37. Interview with Howard Chase, July 8, 1991.

38. Ronnie Dugger, *On Reagan: The Man and His Presidency* (New York, 1983), pp. 12–13. He received $125,000 and then $150,000 for hosting the television program and took in additional income from his itinerant activities.

39. Lou Cannon, *Reagan* (New York, 1982), p. 93.

40. Ibid., p. 96.

41. Ibid., p. 306.

42. Ibid., p. 19.

43. Anne Edwards, *Early Reagan: The Rise to Power* (New York, 1987), pp. 452–57.

44. Michael K. Deaver with Mickey Herskowitz, *Behind the Scenes: In Which the Author Talks about Ronald Reagan and Nancy Reagan . . . and Himself* (New York, 1987), p. 74.

45. Ibid., pp. 73–74.

46. W. Howard Chase, "Nothing Just Happens, Somebody Makes It Happen," *Public Relations Journal* 8 (November 1962), p. 5.

CODA: THE PUBLIC AND ITS PROBLEMS: SOME NOTES FOR THE
NEW MILLENNIUM

1. Bernays and I corresponded with each other for some time after our autumn 1990 meeting. I sent him a copy of Chapter 1, "Visiting Edward Bernays," when it was completed in late 1994. Unhappily, he passed away before he was able to respond to my narrative of our encounter.

2. Harold Brayman, "Public Opinion: A New Sovereign Power," *Public Relations Journal* 20 (January 1964), p. 14.

3. David Finn, "Should Communications Be Monolithic?" *Public Relations Journal* 18 (June 1962), p. 22.

4. Ibid., p. 23.

5. D. Parke Gibson, "Image Building Necessary in the Negro National Community," *Public Relations Journal* 21 (October 1965), pp. 47, 49.

6. James F. Langton, "What Should the Business Response Be to the Negro Revolution?" *Public Relations Journal* 21 (June 1965), pp. 12ff.

7. Ibid., p. 17.

8. Paul T. Cherington, "Opinion Polls as the Voice of Democracy," *Public Opinion Quarterly* 4 (March 1940), pp. 236–38.

9. Philip Lesly, *The People Factor: Managing the Human Climate* (Homewood, Ill., 1974), p. 26.

10. Ibid., p. 8.

11. Ibid., p. 86.

12. Ibid., pp. 104–5.

13. John Dewey, *The Public and Its Problems* (Athens, Ohio, 1927), pp. 122–23.

14. Ibid., p. 137.

15. Ibid., p. 142.

16. Edward Bernays, "The Engineering of Consent," *Annals of the American Academy of Political and Social Science* 250 (March 1947), pp. 114–15.

BIBLIOGRAPHY

Abrams, Frank W. (president, Standard Oil of New Jersey). "Management's Responsibilities in a Complex World." *Harvard Business Review* 29 (May 1951): 29–34.

Ackerman, Carl W. "How the Government Dominates the Press." *Public Relations* 1, (First Quarter 1938): 10–11.

"Advertising May Take the Place of Strikes." *Printers' Ink* 115 (April 21, 1921): 25–26.

"Advertising Overcomes Neighborhood Opposition to Building Factory." *Printers' Ink* 108 (June 24, 1919): 68, 72.

"Advertising Tempest in the OWI." *TIDE* 17 (May 1, 1943): 15–16.

"Advertising to Help Industrial Relations." *Printers' Ink* 108 (September 25, 1919): 8, 10.

"Agents vs. Co-ops." *TIDE* 14 (January 15, 1940): 22–23.

Ainsworth, Gardiner. "The New York Fair: Adventure in Promotion." *Public Opinion Quarterly* 3 (October 1939): 694–704.

Allen, Frederick Lewis. *The Big Change: 1900–1950.* New York: Bantam, 1952, 1965.

Allen, Walter S. Letter to Mr. Frederick P. Fish regarding renewal of contract with the Publicity Bureau, July 22, 1904. AT&T Corporate Archive, Box 1380, Item 14893.

———. Memo to Mr. Frederick P. Fish (president of AT&T) regarding articles placed in magazines by the Publicity Bureau (Boston), January 22, 1906. AT&T Corporate Archive, Box B1201, Item 559249.

———. "Policy of this company in regard to criticism." Memorandum to Frederick P. Fish, President, AT&T, January 31, 1906. AT&T Corporate Archive, Box 1326, Item 16096.

Allport, Floyd H. "Toward a Science of Public Opinion." *Public Opinion Quarterly* 1 (January 1937): 7–23.

Allport, Floyd H. and Milton Lepkin. "Building War Morale With News Headlines." *Public Opinion Quarterly* 7 (Summer 1943): 211–21.

Amberson, Rosanne. "Tell Your Story to Tomorrow's Customers: Educational Materials Increasingly Important in the Public Relations Program." *Public Relations Journal* 6 (May 1950): 2, 20–21.

American Newspaper Publishers Association. *Free Publicity* (Bulletin No. 2058). New York: American Newspaper Publishers Association, September 15, 1909. AT&T Corporate Archive, Box 1317, Folder 2, Item 665069.

American Social History Project. *Who Built America? Working People and the Nation's Economy, Politics, Culture and Society* (Vol. 2). New York: Pantheon, 1992.

American Telephone and Telegraph Company. *1907 Annual Report of the Directors of American Telephone & Telegraph Company to the Stockholders for the*

Year Ending December 31, 1907. Boston: Alfred Mudge & Son, 1908.

————. *1908 Annual Report of the Directors of American Telephone & Telegraph Company to the Stockholders for the Year Ending December 31, 1908.* Boston, AT&T: 1909.

————. *1909 Annual Report of the Directors of American Telephone & Telegraph Company to the Stockholders for the Year Ending December 31, 1909.* Boston, AT&T: 1910.

————. *1911 Annual Report of the Directors of American Telephone & Telegraph Company to the Stockholders for the Year Ending December 31, 1911.* New York, AT&T: 1912.

————. *1914 Annual Report of the Directors of American Telephone & Telegraph Company to the Stockholders for the Year Ending December 31, 1914.* New York, AT&T: 1915.

————. *1915 Annual Report of the Directors of American Telephone & Telegraph Company to the Stockholders for the Year Ending December 31, 1915.* New York, AT&T: 1916.

————. *1916 Annual Report of the Directors of American Telephone & Telegraph Company to the Stockholders for the Year Ending December 31, 1916.* New York, AT&T: 1917.

————. Corporate memo of September 19, 1912, from Walter S. Allen to Vice President N. C. Kingsbury, establishing a Publicity Bureau for the corporation. AT&T Corporate Archive, Corporate Box B–20. A slightly revised version of this memo exists under the following entry: Walter S. Allen, Public Relations. *Plan for Establishing a Public Relations Department,* July 23, 1913. AT&T Corporate Archive, Box 2035.

————. "General Policy" memorandum. AT&T Corporate Archive, Box 56, File on Public Relations—Securities—Competition—1920.

————. "Confidential" minutes of a "Meeting of Publicity Men of the American Telephone and Telegraph Company, and Associated Companies" (J. D. Ellsworth, elected chairman; Clifford Arrick, elected secretary), June 26, 1914. AT&T Corporate Archive, Corporate Box 1310.

————. "Minutes of Advertising Conference Bell Telephone System," Philadelphia, June 28, 1916. AT&T Corporate Archive, Box 1310.

————. "Work in Hand" memorandum of December 10, 1907. AT&T Corporate Archive, Box 1317, Folder 1.

"American Way." *TIDE* 13 (April 1, 1939): 9–11.

Angell, Norman. *The Public Mind: Its Disorders: Its Exploitation.* New York: Dutton, 1927.

————. "The Teacher and the Public Mind." In W. Brooke Graves, ed., *Readings in Public Opinion, Its Formation and Control,* 242–44. New York, 1928.

"Anti-Chain Laws." *TIDE* 10 (July 1936): 26–27.

Antilla, Susan. "The Nicest Investor Research That Money Can Buy." *New York Times,* Sunday Business section, May 23, 1993, 5.

Applebome, Peter. "How Atlanta's Adman Pushes the City to Sell Itself." *New York Times,* February 9, 1993, A16.

"Are Company Athletic Teams Worth While?" *Printers' Ink* 152 (September 25, 1930): 89–90.

"Ave, Atque Vale." *TIDE* 12(August 1, 1938): 19–20.

Baird, Jane B. "New From the Computer: 'Cartoons' for the Courtroom." *New*

York Times, Sunday Business section, September 6, 1992, 5.

Baker, Stephen (vice president in charge of special projects, Cunningham & Walsh). "The Art of Building a Corporate Identity." *Public Relations Journal* 18 (January 1962): 16–20. (Originally published in Baker, *Visual Persuasion,* New York, 1961.)

Ballard, Helen. "Meat Sales Increased Via the Culinary Instruction Route." *Printers' Ink* 8 (August 21, 1919): 33–36.

Banning, William P. (Information Department, AT&T). "Advertising Technique and Copy Appeal." Bell System Publicity Conference *Proceedings,* June 11–15, 1923, New York. AT&T Archives, Corporate Box 1310.

———. "The Service of Publicity." *Proceedings* of the American Telephone and Telegraph Company, Bell System Publicity Conference, Southern Pines, North Carolina, April 1928. AT&T Corporate Archives, Box 1310.

Barber, William J. *From New Era to New Deal: Herbert Hoover, the Economists, and American Economic Policy, 1921–1933.* Cambridge, Mass., 1985.

Barclay, Hartley W. (editor of *Mill & Factory*). "The American Way," address to the Rotary Club of New York, September 2, 1937. Self-published, 1937.

Bard, F. N. (vice chairman). *Report of the Public Relations Committee of NAM,* June 1936. NAM Archive, Hagley Museum, Wilmington, Delaware. Acc. 1411, Series I.

Baritz, Loren, ed. *The Culture of the Twenties.* Indianapolis, 1970.

Barnard, Anne. "How Do Advertising Agencies Treat Public Relations?" *Printers' Ink* 224 (July 30, 1948): 32–33, 54, 56.

Barnouw, Erik. *The Golden Web: A History of Broadcasting in the United States to 1933.* New York, 1968.

———. *A Tower in Babel: A History of Broadcasting in the United States to 1933.* New York, 1966.

Bartlett, John T. "Colorado County Levies an Advertising Tax." *Printers' Ink* 108 (September 11, 1919): 145–46.

Barton, Bruce. *The Man Nobody Knows.* New York, 1925.

———. "Four Main Accomplishments of Modern Advertising." *Printers' Ink* 149 (October 3, 1929): 3–6, 179.

Baxter, Leone. "Public Relations Precocious Baby." *Public Relations Journal* 6 (January 1950): 18, 22–23.

Beard, Charles A. and Mary R. Beard. *The Rise of American Civilization.* New York, 1927, 1944.

"Beer Census in Philadelphia." *Printers' Ink* 166 (January 11, 1934): 36.

"Beer Is Four." *TIDE* 11 (May 1, 1937): 22–23.

Bellamy, Edward. *Looking Backward: 2000–1887.* New York, 1887, 1960.

Bennett, Wallace F. *The Very Human History of "NAM."* New York, 1949.

Bernays, Edward L. *Biography of an Idea: Memoirs of Public Relations Counsel Edward L. Bernays.* New York, 1965.

———. *Crystallizing Public Opinion.* New York, 1923, 1961.

———. "Crystallizing Public Opinion for Good Government." Published address before the thirty-first Annual Meeting of the National Municipal League and the twenty-first Annual Meeting of the American Civic Association in Joint Session, Pittsburgh. Privately printed, 1925.

———. "Engineering of Consent." *Annals of the American Academy of Political and Social Science* 250 (March 1947): 113–20.

————. "Molding Public Opinion." *Annals of the American Academy of Political and Social Science* 179 (May 1935): 82–87.

————. *Propaganda.* New York, 1928.

————. "A Telephone Interview with. . . . " *Public Relations Journal* 19 (September 1963]: 11ff.

————. "Testimony before the Subcommittee on Overseas Information Programs of the Senate Committee on Foreign Affairs, March 31, 1953." *Congressional Record,* Appendix, A1949–A1950.

"Bernays?" *TIDE* 9 (June 1935): 15–16.

"Bernays in Boston." *TIDE* 10 (October 15, 1936): 20–22.

"Bernays on Fear." *TIDE* 21 (March 7, 1947): 54–56.

Bernstein, Irving. *The Lean Years: The History of the American Worker, 1920–1933.* Baltimore: Penguin, 1966.

Bingham, J. R., and A. L. Frederick. (director and associate director, respectively, WMCA Motion Picture Bureau). "Wartime Use of Films Spurs Interest of Industry." *Printers' Ink* 212 (July 27, 1945): 27–28.

Bird, William. "Enterprise and Meaning: Sponsored Film, 1939–1949." *History Today* 39 (December 1989): 24–30.

Blake, Casey. "Below the Battle." *The Nation* 252 (February 25, 1991): 239–41.

Bogart, Leo. *Commercial Culture: The Media System and the Public Interest.* New York, 1995.

Bourne, Randolph S. *War and the Intellectuals.* New York, 1965. Title essay originally published in *The Seven Arts* 2 (June 1917): 133–46.

Bowers, Claude G. *Jefferson and Hamilton: The Struggle for Democracy in America.* Boston, 1925.

Brayman, Harold (director of Public Relations, E. I. DuPont de Nemours & Co. from 1942). "The Challenge of Today." *Public Relations Journal* 14 (May 1958): 13ff.

————. "Public opinion: A New Sovereign Power." *Public Relations Journal* 20 (January 1964): 14ff.

————. "The Real Basis of Our American Way." *Public Relations Journal* 8(January 1952): 3–4, 16.

Bremner, Robert H. *From the Depths: The Discovery of Poverty in the United States.* New York, 1967.

Briggs, Thomas H. (professor emeritus, Teachers College, Columbia University, and director, Consumer Education Study, National Secondary-School Principals). "PR and Economic Education." *Public Relations Journal* 9 (May 1953): 9ff.

"Bright Side." *TIDE* 9 (July 1935): 16.

Browne, Malcolm W. "City Lights and Space Ads May Blind Stargazers." *New York Times,* May 4, 1993, C1, C8.

————. "DNA From the Age of Dinosaurs Is Found." *New York Times,* June 10, 1993, A1, B10.

Buhite, Russell D. and David W. Levy, eds., *FDR's Fireside Chats.* New York, 1993.

Bullard, Arthur. *Mobilising America.* New York, 1917.

"Buna Rubber." *TIDE* 14 (February 15, 1940): 21.

Burck, Gilbert. "The Jersey Company, Part I." *Fortune,* October 1951, 181–84.

————. "The Jersey Company, Part III: Public Relations for the Long Pull." *Fortune,* October 1951, 108ff.

Burger, Chester. "Telephone News on Television." Unpublished report prepared
  for the American Telephone and Telegraph Company, September 1955.
Burnett, Verne (PR counselor, New York City). "Who Are Our Publics?" *Public
  Relations Journal* 3 (January 1947): 3–8, 35.
Burns, James MacGregor. *Roosevelt: The Lion and the Fox.* New York, 1956.
Burson, Harold (chairman, Burson-Marsteller). "Beyond 'PR': Redefining the
  Role of Public Relations." Paper delivered at the Institute for PR Research
  and Education, twenty-ninth Annual Distinguished Lecture, Union League
  Club, New York, October 2, 1990.
Bush, Gregory W. *Lord of Attention: Gerald Stanley and the Crowd Metaphor in
  Industrializing America.* Amherst, Mass., 1991.
"Business-and-Government." *Fortune,* August 1938, 49–51.
"Business Defensive: The National Association of Manufacturers Writes a Cam-
  paign to Sell Business to U.S. Citizens." *TIDE* 10 (September 1936):
  27–28.
"Business Is Still in Trouble." *Fortune,* May 1949, 67–71, 196–200.
Byoir, Carl. "The Volcano of Public Opinion." *Public Relations* 1 (First Quarter
  1938): 18–19.
Calkins, Earnest Elmo. "Consumptionism: Get the Consumer to Use Up the
  Goods He Now Merely Uses." *Printers' Ink* 151 (May 22, 1930): 49–52.
"A Call to Admen: Help Stop Riots." Editorial, *Advertising Age* 63 (May 4,
  1992): 1, 49.
Calver, Homer N. "Just About Ten Years Later." *Public Relations Journal* 14
  (January 1958): 10ff.
Cannon, Lou. *Reagan.* New York, 1982.
"Chains, 1938." *TIDE* 12 (January 1, 1938): 21–23.
"Chains and the Public's Good-Will." *Printers' Ink* 150 (February 27, 1930): 183.
"Chains Will Now Court Public Opinion in Earnest: National Association Faces
  Propaganda Issue Squarely and Organizes Educational Program." *Printers'
  Ink* 149 (October 3, 1920): 33–41, 168–72.
Chandler, Alfred D., Jr. "The Beginnings of 'Big Business' in American
  Industry." *Business History Review* 33 (Spring 1959): 2–32.
———. *The Visible Hand: The Managerial Revolution in American Business.*
  Cambridge, Mass., 1977.
Chase, Howard. "Human Relations: The Key to Corporate Survival." *Public
  Relations Journal* 3 (July 1947): 11–15, 25–26.
Chase, W. Howard. *Issue Management: Origins of the Future.* Stamford, Calif.,
  1984.
———. "Nothing Just Happens, Somebody Makes It Happen." *Public Relations
  Journal* 18 (November 1962): 5ff.
——— (then president of the Public Relations Association of America). "Public
  Relations in Perspective." *Public Relations Journal* 12 (January 1956):
  6–7, 22.
——— (then director of PR for General Foods). "Treat the Individual as Con-
  sumer and Citizen." *Public Relations Journal* 1 (November 1945): 25–26.
Cherington, Paul T. "Opinion Polls as the Voice of Democracy." *Public Opinion
  Quarterly* 4 (March 1940): 236–38.
Cialdini, Robert B. *Influence: The New Psychology of Modern Persuasion.* New
  York, 1984.

"Circus of Science." *TIDE* 10 (February 1936): 19–20.

Clark, Fred G. (general chairman, American Economic Foundation). "Exploding the Profit Myth." *Public Relations Journal* 3 (June 1947):13–17.

Cmiel, Kenneth, *Democratic Eloquence: The Fight over Popular Speech in Nineteenth-Century America*. New York, 1990.

Coben, Stanley, ed. *Reform, War, and Reaction: 1912–1932*. Columbia, S.C., 1972.

Cochran, Thomas C. and William Miller. *The Age of Enterprise: A Social History of Industrial America*. New York, 1942.

Cole, Roland. "Creating Good Will for the Local Branch." *Printers' Ink* 149 (November 21, 1929): 65–72.

"Consumer Concern." *TIDE* 9 (July 1935): 13, 16.

Converse, Jean M. *Survey Research in the United States: Roots and Emergence, 1890–1960*. Berkeley, 1987.

"Co-op Baiting." *TIDE* 12 (October 1, 1938): 40, 42.

"Co-op Conclave." *TIDE* 10 (November 1, 1936): 18–20.

"Co-op Front." *TIDE* 10 (December 1, 1936): 38, 42.

"Co-op Inquiry." *TIDE* 11 (April 1, 1936): 21–22.

"Co-ops." *TIDE* 10 (August 1936): 24.

"CO-OPS." *TIDE* 17 (September 15, 1943): 90, 92–93.

"Copy that Causes Trouble." *Printers' Ink* 108 (June 17, 1919): 172.

Cordasco, Francesco, ed. *Jacob Riis Revisited: Poverty and the Slum in Another Era*. Garden City, N.Y., 1968.

Cortez, John P. "Ads Head for Bathroom." *Advertising Age*, May 18, 1992, 24.

Creel, George. *How We Advertised America: The First Telling of the Amazing Story of the Committee on Public Information that Carried the Gospel of Americanism to Every Corner of the Globe*. New York, 1920.

———. "Poisoners of Public Opinion: Part I." *Harper's Magazine*, November 7, 1914, 436–38.

———. "Poisoners of Public Opinion: Part II." *Harper's Magazine*, November 14, 1914, 465–66.

———. "Public Opinion in War Time." *Annals of the American Academy of Political and Social Science* 68 (July 1918): 185–93.

———. *Rebel At Large: Recollections of Fifty Crowded Years*. New York, 1947.

Crossley, Archibald M. "Straw Polls in 1936." *Public Opinion Quarterly* 1 (January 1937): 24–35.

Cunningham, E. A. "The Employer and the Returning Service Man." *Public Relations Journal* 1 (October 1945): 2–7.

Curti, Merle. "Public Opinion and The Study of History." *Public Opinion Quarterly* 1 (April 1937): 84–87.

Curtis, James. *Mind's Eye, Mind's Truth: FSA Photography Reconsidered*. Philadelphia, 1989.

Cutlip, Scott M. *Public Relations, The Unseen Power: A History*. Hillsdale, N.J., 1994.

Dam, Colby Dorr. "Business and Life." *Public Relations* 1 (First Quarter 1938): 5–7.

Daniel, Pete, Merry A. Foresta, Maren Stange, and Sally Stein. *Official Images: New Deal Photography*. Washington, D.C., 1987.

"A Daring and Unique Plan to Solve Some of the Problems of the Relations of Labor and Capital by Publicity." *Profitable Advertising* 17 (July 1907): 179.

Davenport, Russell W. (editorial consultant, *Fortune* Magazine, employed by *Time*, Inc., since 1923). "A New Field for Private Initiative." *Public Relations Journal* 7 (July–August 1951): 3–5, 16, 18.

Davis, Elmer (director, Office of War Information). "OWI Has a Job." *Public Opinion Quarterly* 7 (Spring 1943): 5–14.

Deaver, Michael K. with Mickey Herskowitz. *Behind the Scenes: In Which the Author Talks About Ronald and Nancy Reagan . . . and Himself.* New York, 1987.

DeParle, Jason. "Keeping the News in Step: Are the Pentagon's Gulf War Rules Here to Stay?" *New York Times*, May 6, 1991, A9.

———. "Report, Delayed Months, Says Lowest Income Group Grew." *New York Times*, May 12, 1992, A15.

Deutsch, Claudia H. "Gay Rights, Issue of the 90's." *New York Times*, Sunday Business Section, April 28, 1991, 23.

DeWeese, Truman A. "The Editor with the 'White Spats.' " *Profitable Advertising* 17 (August 1907): 262–63.

———. *The Principles of Practical Publicity: Being a Treatise on "The Art of Advertising."* Philadelphia: George W. Jacobs, 1908.

———. "Shredded Wheat Gets Its Message before Teachers and Pupils." *Printers' Ink* 139 (April 21, 1927): 186–88.

Dewey, John. *Individualism: Old and New.* New York, 1930.

———. *The Public and Its Problems.* Athens, Ohio, 1927, 1988.

Dickinson, Roy. "Advertising Methods to Be Used to Speed Recovery." *Printers' Ink* 164 (July 27, 1933): 29–31.

———. "Advertising's Opportunity." *Printers' Ink* 108 (June 24, 1919): 45–52.

———. "National Advertiser and NRA: As the Campaign Progresses Under the Sign of the Blue Eagle, Basic Social Changes Loom." *Printers' Ink* 164 (August 3, 1933): 47–49.

Dodge, Martin. "Public Relations and the Labor–Management Melee." *Public Relations Journal* 1 (November 1945): 10–14.

Doob, Leonard W. "An 'Experimental' Study of the Psychological Corporation." *Psychological Bulletin* 35 (1938): 220–22.

Doob, Leonard W., and Edward S. Robinson. "Psychology and Propaganda." *Annals of the American Academy of Political and Social Science* 179 (May 1935): 88–95.

Dudley, Pendleton (PR pioneer with specific early experience working for meat packers). "Current Beginnings of PR." *Public Relations Journal* 8 (April 1952): 8–10, 14.

Dugger, Ronnie. *On Reagan: The Man and His Presidency.* New York. 1983.

Duhamel, Georges. *America the Menace: Scenes from the Life of the Future*, Charles Miner Thompson, trans. Boston, 1931.

Durban, C. J. (director of advertising, U.S. Rubber Company). "Television as a Public Relations Tool." *Public Relations Journal* 3 (May 1947): 1–4.

Edholm, C. L. "Pictorial Advertising that Appeals to the Different Races." *Printers' Ink* 108 (June 17, 1919): 112, 116.

Editors of *Business Week*. "Public Relations: First in the Order of Business." Number 1 in the Reports to Executives series. New York, January 23, 1937.

Editors of *Fortune* Magazine, in collaboration with Russell W. Davenport. *U.S.A.: The Permanent Revolution.* New York, 1951.

Edwards, Alice. "Consumer Interest Groups." *Public Opinion Quarterly* 1 (July 1937): 104–11.

Edwards, Anne. *Early Reagan: The Rise to Power.* New York, 1987.

"Eighty-Five Percent Wrong." *TIDE* (November 15, 1936): 48–50.

Eisenhower, General Dwight D. (induction speech as president of Columbia University). "None of Us Dare Stand Alone." *Public Relations Journal* 4 (November 1948): 7–10.

Elliott, Stuart. "The Media Business." *New York Times,* October 28, 1991, D10.

Ellis, Aytoun. *The Penny Universities: A History of the Coffee-Houses.* London, 1956.

Ellsworth, James D. "Introduction to Historical Memoranda on Bell System Publicity." Memo "for reference and not for publication," January 17, 1929. AT&T Corporate Archive, Box 1066.

——— (of Michaelis & Ellsworth, Industrial Statistics, 126 State Street, Boston). Memos to President Fish regarding news placement, October 3, 1906. AT&T Corporate Archive, Box 1317, Folder 1, Item 16634.

———. Memorandum to Theodore Vail, Boston, September 24, 1909. AT&T Corporate Archive, Box 1317, Folder 2, Item 665069.

———. "Start of General Magazine Advertising." Memo "for reference and not for publication," January 17, 1929. AT&T Corporate Archive, Box 1066.

"Elmer Davis, OWI: The President Finally Appoints a Propaganda Minister." *TIDE* 16 (July 1, 1942): 11–12.

"Emergency Council." *TIDE* 11 (April 15, 1937): 24–26.

Emery, James A. "The Call of the Sentry," address before NAM's Congress of American Industry, December 4, 1935. New York, National Association of Manufacturers, 1935.

"Employees' Advertising and Mawkish Sentimentality." *Printers' Ink* 108 (June 10, 1919): 151–52.

Engelberg, Stephen. "A New Breed of Hired Hands Cultivates Grass-Roots Anger." *New York Times,* May 17, 1993, A1, A17.

Enrico, Dottie. "Reporter Feels Like a Fish Hooked by Publicity Stunts." *New York Newsday,* October 7, 1991, 35.

"Enter: Aesthetics." *TIDE* 17 (December 1, 1943): 88, 90.

"Enter Durstine." *TIDE* 13 (August 1, 1939): 22–23.

"Era of Good Feeling," *TIDE* 11 (February 1, 1937): 23–25.

Ewen, Elizabeth. *Immigrant Women in the Land of Dollars.* New York, 1985.

Ewen, Stuart. *All Consuming Images: The Politics of Style in Contemporary Culture.* New York, 1988.

———. *Captains of Consciousness: Advertising and the Social Roots of the Consumer Culture.* New York, 1976.

"Fair Films." *TIDE* 13 (November 1, 1939): 56–57.

"Fair Findings." *TIDE* 13 (November 1, 1939): 28–30.

Fairman, Milton. "The Practice of Public Relations." *Public Relations Journal* 8 (December 1952): 5–7, 17.

Fawcett, Brian. *Public Eye: An Investigation Into the Disappearing of the World.* New York, 1990.

"Financing for a Bush Speech Is Attacked." *New York Times,* October 4, 1991, A16.

Finn, David (president and cofounder of Ruder and Finn, Inc., New York). "Should Communications Be Monolithic?" *Public Relations Journal* 18 (June 1962): 20ff.

Firkins, O. W. "The Cult of the Passing Hour." *Atlantic Monthly* 53 (May 1914): 661–68.

Fisher, Austin P. "Assign Your 'Labor Relations' to a Sales-minded Executive." *Printers' Ink* 202 (March 26, 1943): 15–17.

Fleischhauer, Carl, and Beverly W. Brannan. *Documenting America: 1935–1943.* Berkeley, 1988.

"Food Future." *TIDE* 9 (September 1935): 24–26.

"Ford and C.I.O." *TIDE* 15 (January 15, 1941): 42.

"Ford Motor's New Campaign." *TIDE* 18 (March 15, 1944): 19–20.

"442 Industrial Leaders Evaluate Public Relations." *Public Relations* 1 (First Quarter 1938): 24–25.

"Forward America." *TIDE* 9 (February 1935): 13–14.

Foster, James H. "The Printed Page as a Means of Establishing Corporate Character." *Printers' Ink* 108 (June 31, 1919): 3–6, 153–63.

Frank, Glenn. "Radio as an Educational Force." *Annals of the American Academy of Political and Social Science* 177 (January 1935): 119–22.

Fraser, Steven. *Labor Will Rule: Sidney Hillman and the Rise of American Labor.* New York, 1991.

Fraser, Steve and Gary Gerstle. *The Rise and Fall of the New Deal Order.* Princeton, N.J., 1989.

"Free Enterprise." *TIDE* 17 (October 1, 1943): 42.

Freud, Sigmund. *Group Psychology and the Analysis of the Ego.* New York, 1922, 1959.

Gabler, Neal. "Now Playing: Real Life, the Movie." *New York Times,* Section 2, October 20, 1991, 1, 32–33.

Galambos, Louis, with the assistance of Barbara Barrow Spence. *The Public Image of Big Business in America, 1880–1940.* Baltimore, 1975.

Galambos, Louis, and Joseph Pratt. *The Rise of The Corporate Commonwealth: United States Business and Public Policy in the 20th Century.* New York, 1988.

Gallagher, Hugh Gregory. *FDR's Splendid Deception.* New York, 1985.

Gallup, George H., with Leyton E. Carter. "TV's Sorriest Commercials." *Public Relations Journal* 12 (August 1956): 7–9, 26ff.

Gelb, Leslie H. "Untruths . . . ," *New York Times,* News of the Week in Review, October 27, 1991, 15.

George, Henry. *Progress and Poverty: An Inquiry into the Cause of Industrial Depressions and of Increase of Want with Increase of Wealth. The Remedy.* New York, 1879, 1929.

Gibson, D. Parke (publisher of *Race Relations and Industry,* a newsletter on the Negro market). "Image Building Necessary in the Negro National Community." *Public Relations Journal* 21 (October 1965): 47ff.

Gilman, Don E. (executive vice president, Western Oil and Gas Association). "The New-found Spirit of Business." *Public Relations Journal* 2 (February 1946): 14–17.

Glover, J. D. *The Attack on Big Business.* Boston, 1954.

"GM Advertises Consumer Survey." *Printers' Ink* 166 (January 4, 1934): 72.

Goldman, Eric F. *Two Way Street: The Emergence of the Public Relations Counsel.* Boston, 1948.

"Good House V." *TIDE* 13 (December 15, 1939): 14–15.

Goodman, David S. (in charge of public relations for General Electric, X-Ray Division). "Community Synchronization." *Public Relations Journal* 15 (February 1959): 18ff.

Graves, W. Brooke. *Readings in Public Opinion, Its Formation and Control.* New York, 1928.

Griswold, Glenn. "The McGraw-Hill Public Relations Forums." *Public Opinion Quarterly* 3 (October 1939): 704–9.

Griswold, Glenn. "Public Relations—Some Misconceptions." *Public Opinion Quarterly* 1 (July 1937): 126–31.

Gruenberg, Sidonie Matsner. "Radio and the Child." *Annals of the American Academy of Political and Social Science* 177 (January 1935): 123–28.

Habermas, Jürgen. *The Structural Transformation of the Public Sphere: An Inquiry into a Category of Bourgeois Society.* Cambridge, Mass., 1991; orig. 1962.

Hackett, Charles M. (Public Relations Department, E. I. DuPont de Nemours). "The Forceful and Vivid Vernacular of the Eye." *Public Relations Journal* 12 (November 1956): 15–16, 28ff.

Hales, Peter B. *Silver Cities: The Photography of American Urbanization, 1839–1915.* Philadelphia, 1984.

"A Happy New Year." *TIDE* 9 (January 1935): 11–12.

Hard, William. "Radio and Public Opinion." *Annals of the American Academy of Political and Social Science* 177 (January 1935): 105–13.

Harlow, Rex F. "Persuasion and Public Relations." *Public Relations Journal* 13 (October 1957): 14–18.

———. *Public Relations in War and Peace.* New York, 1942.

Harold F. Strong Corporation. *Roads to Public Favor: Some Comments on Five Confusing Terms: Publicity, Press Agentry, Promotional Organization, Public Relations,* New York, privately printed pamphlet, 1935.

Harris, Evelyn. "Relationship Between The Bell Telephone Companies and the Press, and Responsibilities of the Companies in That Respect." *Proceedings of the American Telephone and Telegraph Company, General Publicity Conference, Southern Pines, North Carolina, April 10–16, 1929.* AT&T Corporate Archives, Box 1310.

Harris, Huntington, and Paul M. Lewis. "The Press, Public Behavior and Public Opinion." *Public Opinion Quarterly* 12 (Summer 1948): 220–26.

Hawkins, David F. "The Development of Modern Financial Reporting Practices Among American Manufacturing Corporations." *Business History Review* 37 (Autumn 1963): 135-68.

Hawkins, Lester G., Jr., and George Pettee. "OWI—Organization and Problems." *Public Opinion Quarterly* 7 (Spring 1943): 15–33.

Heins, W. R., "Can Advertising Measure Up to This Job?" *Printers' Ink* 202 (February 5, 1943): 160.

"Henderson's Merchants' Minute Men Challenge the Chains." *Printers' Ink* 150 (February 20, 1930): 3–8.

Herring, E. Pendleton. "Official Publicity Under the New Deal." *Annals of the American Academy of Political and Social Science* 179 (May 1935): 167–75.

Hiebert, Ray E. *Courtier to the Crowd: The Story of Ivy Lee and the Development of Public Relations.* Ames, Ia., 1966.

———. "Ivy Lee and the Development of Press Relations." *Public Relations Journal* 21 (March 1965): 8ff.

Hill, John W. (senior partner, Hill and Knowlton). "Industry's Iron Curtain."
   Public Relations Journal 2 (November 1946): 3–9.
———. *The Making of a Public Relations Man.* New York, 1963.
Hine, Lewis. *America and Lewis Hine, Photographs 1904–1940.* New York, 1977.
———. "Social Photography, How the Camera May Help in the Social Uplift."
   Proceedings, National Conference of Charities and Corrections (June 1909).
   Reprinted in Alan Trachtenberg, *Classic Essays on Photography,* 109–13.
   New Haven, Conn.: Leetes Island Books, 1980.
Hobsbawm, Eric. *The Age of Extremes: A History of the World, 1914–1991.* New
   York, 1994.
Hofstadter, Richard. *The Age of Reform.* New York, 1955.
Hollingsworth, Sydney Pierce. "Pioneers—Blair, Barnum and Lee." *Public
   Relations Journal* 1 (November 1945): 15–18.
Holmes, Steven A. "Corporations Are Deserting Group Battling Rights Bill."
   New York Times, May 25, 1991, 9.
Holzman, Franklyn D. "How C.I.A. Invented Soviet Military Monster." *New York
   Times,* October 3, 1991, A24.
House, Stanley G. "Put the Advertising Approach into Communications with
   Employees." *Printers' Ink* 224 (September 10, 1948): 44, 46, 48.
Howe, Hartley E. "You Have Seen Their Pictures." *Survey Graphic,* April 1940,
   236–41.
Hoynes, William. *Public Television for Sale: Media, the Market, and the Public
   Sphere.* Boulder, Colo., 1994.
Hurley, F. Jack. *Portrait of a Decade: Roy Stryker and the Development of Docu-
   mentary Photography in the Thirties.* Baton Rouge, La., 1972.
"Informing the Public," Part 2, "Report to Members," NAM News, May 6,
   1950, 15–28.
"Is Anybody Listening?" *Fortune* 42 (September 1950): 77ff.
"Is This the Way to Sell the Story of Business?" *Printers' Ink* 202 (February 26,
   1943): 76.
Ivy L. Lee Collection. Items listed by name of collection and box number and
   credited as such: Ivy L. Lee Collection, Seeley G. Mudd Manuscript Library,
   Princeton University, Packets 1 and 2.
"Ivy Lee and John D." *Public Relations* 1 (First Quarter 1938): 14.
Jackson, Merrick. "How Employee Publications Aid the Battle of Production."
   Printers' Ink 202 (February 26, 1943): 20–24, 70.
James, William. *Pragmatism/The Meaning of Truth.* Cambridge, Mass., 1978.
   Combined edition of two books, originally published in 1907 and 1909,
   respectively.
Jefferson, Thomas. "Inaugural Address," March 4, 1801, reprinted in Adrienne
   Koch and William Peden, eds., *The Life and Selected Writings of Thomas Jef-
   ferson.* New York, 1944.
Johnson, Robert Wood. "Human Relations in Modern Business." *Harvard Busi-
   ness Review* 27 (September 1949): 521–41.
———. "We Believe. . . ." *Public Relations Journal* 6 (January 1950): 6.
Jones, Edward D. "Publicity as a Policy." *Annals of the American Academy of
   Political and Social Science* 85 (September 1919): 314–20.
Jones, John Price. *Public Relations—Public Policy and Commercial Publicity.*
   New York, 1933.

Jordan, Virgil. "The Basis of Recovery." Address to the Annual Convention of NAM, December 5, 1934, Waldorf-Astoria. NAM Archive, public documents, Hagley Museum, Wilmington, Delaware.

Josephson, Matthew. *The Politicos*. New York, 1938, 1966.

———. *The Robber Barons*. New York, 1934, 1962.

Joyce, T. F. "Television and Post-War Distribution." Presentation to Boston Conference on Distribution, October 17, 1944. (Typescript distributed by RCA.)

Kalser, Konstantin (president, Marathon TV Newsreel, Inc.). "Newsfilm for Industry." *Public Relations Journal* 15 (June 1959): 7ff.

Katz, Daniel. "Do Interviewers Bias Poll Results?" *Public Opinion Quarterly* 6 (Summer 1942): 248–68.

Keith, Nathaniel Schneider. *Politics and the Housing Crisis Since 1930*. New York, 1973.

Kelleher, James F. "TV's Perennial Star: The Political Candidate." *Public Relations Journal* 12 (April 1956): 6–7, 18–19.

Kelly, Michael. "Identity Crisis." *New York Times,* The Week in Review, August 23, 1992, 1.

———. "The Making of a First Family: A Blueprint." *New York Times,* November 14, 1992, 1, 9.

Kennedy, Bill (of J. Walter Thompson Co., New York). Letter to the Editor. *TIDE* 15 (September 1, 1941): 66–67.

Kennedy, S. M. *Winning the Public*. New York, 1921.

Keynes, John Maynard. *Essays in Persuasion*. New York: W. W. Norton, 1931, 1963.

Knauth, Oliver. "America's Stake in Foreign Information." *Public Relations Journal* 3 (December 1947): 3–7, 40.

Kornbluh, Joyce L. *Rebel Voices: An I.W.W. Anthology.* Ann Arbor, Mich., 1972.

"Kresge Has New Department for Service." *Printers' Ink* 108 (August 14, 1919): 185.

Kuttner, Robert. *The End of Laissez-Faire: National Purpose and the Global Economy After the Cold War.* New York, 1991.

Lane, James B. *Jacob A. Riis and the American City.* Port Washington, N.Y., 1974.

Langton, James F. "What Should the Business Response Be to the Negro Revolution?" *Public Relations Journal* 21 (June 1965): 12ff.

Larned, W. Livingston. "Advertising That Is Helping to Adjust the Labor Situation." *Printers' Ink* 108 (June 17, 1919): 122–32.

Larrabee, C. B. "Mr. Schlink, Danger Is Not So Much What He Says as in Highbrow Following He Has Created." *Printers' Ink* 166 (January 11, 1934): 10–13.

———. "The Publisher Speaks: The Idea Is Not New." *Printers' Ink* 224 (July 30, 1948): 5.

Larson, Cedric and James R. Mock. "The Lost Files of the Creel Committee of 1917–1919." *Public Opinion Quarterly* 3 (January 1939): 5–29.

Lasswell, Harold D. "The Person: Subject and Object of Propaganda." *Annals of the American Academy of Political and Social Science* 179 (May 1935): 187–93.

———. *Propaganda Technique in the World War.* New York: Knopf, 1927.

Lasswell, Harold D., Ralph D. Casey, and Bruce Lannes Smith. *Propaganda and*

Promotional Activities: An Annotated Bibliography (prepared under the direction of the Advisory Committee on Pressure Groups and Propaganda of the Social Science Research Council). Minneapolis, 1935.

"Latin America: A Progress Report on U.S. International Radio." *TIDE* 15 (April 1, 1941): 70–72.

Le Bon, Gustave. *The Crowd: A Study of the Popular Mind.* London, 1896, 1952.

Lee, Alfred McClung. *The Daily Newspaper in America: The Evolution of a Social Instrument.* New York, 1937.

Lee, Gerald Stanley. *Crowds: A Study of the Genius of Democracy and of the Fears, Desires, and Expectations of the People.* London, 1913.

———. *Inspired Millionaires: A Forecast.* New York, 1908.

Lee, Ivy L. *The Press Today: How the News Reaches the Public.* New York, 1929.

Lesly, Philip. *The People Factor: Managing the Human Climate.* Homewood, Ill., 1974.

———, ed. *Public Relations in Action.* Chicago, 1947.

Leuchtenburg, William E. *Franklin D. Roosevelt and the New Deal.* New York, 1963.

Levine, Lawrence W. *Highbrow Lowbrow: The Emergence of Cultural Hierarchy in America.* Cambridge, Mass., 1988.

Levy, Donald N. "The Mass Market for Publicity Features." *Public Relations Journal* 14 (February 1958): 18ff.

Lewis, Tom. *Game of Honor.* New York, 1982.

"The Liaison Officer in Advertising." *Printers' Ink* 108 (August 14, 1919):145–53.

Lichtenberg, Bernard. "Business Backs New York World's Fair to Meet the New Deal Propaganda." *Public Opinion Quarterly* 2 (April 1938): 314–20.

Lilienthal, David E. (head of the TVA and chairman of the Atomic Energy Commission). *Big Business: A New Era.* New York, 1952, 1953.

Link, Henry C. "How to Prepare Questions for Consumer Research." *Printers' Ink* 166 (January 11, 1934): 37–41.

——— (vice-president, The Psychological Corporation). "How to Sell America to Americans." *Public Relations Journal* 3 (July 1947): 3–7, 36–38.

———. "Is Freedom the Issue?" *Public Relations Journal* 4 (February 1948): 1–2, 14.

———. *The New Psychology of Selling and Advertising.* New York, 1932.

Link, Henry C., and A. D. Freiberg. "The Problem of Validity vs. Reliability in Public Opinion Polls." *Public Opinion Quarterly* 6 (Spring 1942): 87–98.

Lippincott, J. Gordon, and Walter P. Marguelies. "The Corporate Look—A Problem in Design." *Public Relations Journal* 13 (December 1957): 4–6, 27.

Lippmann, Walter. *Drift and Mastery: An Attempt to Diagnose the Current Unrest.* Madison, 1985; orig. 1914.

———. *The Phantom Public: A Sequel to "Public Opinion."* New York, 1927.

———. *Public Opinion.* New York, 1922.

Lloyd, Henry Demarest. *Lords of Industry.* New York, 1910; reprinted 1973.

Long, Morton E., "Public Relations of the Bell System." *Public Opinion Quarterly* 1 (October 1937): 5–22.

"The Loss of Personal Touch." *Printers' Ink* 108 (August 21, 1919): 168.

Lovejoy, J. M. (president, Seaboard Oil, New York). "Public Goodwill and the Oil Producer." *Public Relations Journal* 3 (June 1947): 32–37.

Lund, Robert L. (president of NAM). "Industry's Opportunity and Duty Under the Recovery Plan." National Association of Manufacturers, *Proceedings*, pp. 69–76. New York, December 7–8, 1933.

———. *Report of Public Relations Committee* of NAM, 1937. NAM Archive, Hagley Museum, Wilmington, Delaware. Acc. 1411, Box 112, Series I.

Lynd, Robert S. "Democracy in Reverse." *Public Opinion Quarterly* 4 (June 1940): 218–20.

MacArthur, John R. "Remember Nayirah, Witness for Kuwait?" *New York Times*, January 6, 1992, A17.

"Magazines Go to War." *TIDE* 17 (January 1, 1943): 40–42.

Magnani, Louis A. "Think Visually." *Public Relations Journal* 17 (December 1961): 22ff.

Marchand, Roland. *Advertising the American Dream: Making Way for Modernity, 1920–1940*. Berkeley, 1985.

Markel, Lester. "Advertise the News!" *Printers' Ink* 115 (June 16, 1921): 73–76.

Maurer, Herrymon. *Great Enterprise: Growth and Behavior of the Big Corporation*. New York: Macmillan, 1955. (Portions of this book appeared, in different form, in *Fortune*. Copyright is held by Time, Inc.)

Mayo, Elton. "The Irrational Factor in Human Behavior: The 'Night-Mind' in Industry." *Annals of the American Academy of Political and Social Science* 110 (November 1923): 117–26.

McCarthy, Joseph. "Housing Study and Investigation," U.S. Senate, Joint Committee Study and Investigation of Housing, Hearings, 80th Cong., p. 5. Washington, D.C., 1947.

McChesney, Robert W. *Telecommunications, Mass Media and Democracy: The Battle for the Control of U. S. Broadcasting, 1928–1935*. New York, 1993.

McInerney, T. J. "Television Gets Religion" (extension of Remarks of Hon. Thomas J. Lane of Massachusetts in the House of Representatives, Thursday, June 12, 1952). *Congressional Record*, Appendix, A3833–5.

McLaren, Robert. "How Blue Jeans Were Restyled Into a Status Symbol." *Public Relations Journal* 19 (November 1963): 26–28.

McLuhan, Marshall. *The Mechanical Bride: Folklore of Industrial Man*. Boston, 1951.

McNutt, George C. "20 Topics for Your Public Relations Advertising." *Printers' Ink* 212 (July 6, 1945): 19–20, 88–93.

Meier, Barry. "Dubious Theory: Chocolate a Cavity Fighter." *New York Times*, April 15, 1992, A1, D23.

Michaelis, G. V. S. Letter to Mr. Frederick P. Fish, April 4, 1904. AT&T Corporate Archive, Box 1398, Item 14663.

———. Memo to Mr. W. S. Allen, public relations liaison at AT&T, July, 21, 1904. AT&T Corporate Archive, Box 1368.

Miles, H. E. "Selling Both Dealer and Consumer by Educational Advertising." *Printers' Ink* 108 (September 4,1919): 125–26, 128.

Miller, Raymond W. "Keepers of the Corporate Conscience." *Public Relations Journal* 1 (October 1945): 8–14.

Mitchell, Broadus. *Depression Decade: From the New Era Through New Deal: 1929–1941*. New York, 1947, 1961.

Mitchell, Wesley C. (head of the National Bureau of Economic Research). "A Review." *Recent Economic Changes in the United States*, pp. 874–89. New

York, 1929. In Stanley Coben, ed., *Reform, War, and Reaction: 1912–1932.* Columbia, S.C., 1972.

Mock, James R., and Cedric Larson. *Words That Won the War: The Story of the Committee on Public Information.* Princeton, N.J., 1939.

Modley, Rudolf. "Talking Business in Pictures." *Public Relations* 1 (First Quarter 1938): 12.

Moley, Raymond. "Social Function of Advertising." *Public Relations* 1 (First Quarter 1938): 23.

"Most High." *TIDE* 11 (March 1, 1937): 20–21.

Mowry, George E., and Blaine A. Brownell. *The Urban Nation, 1920–1980.* New York, 1981.

"Mr. Arnold on Advertising." *TIDE* 12 (November 15, 1938): 25–30.

Murray, Philip (president of the CIO). "Labor's Political Aims." *American Magazine,* February 1944, 28–29, 98.

NAM. "Declaration of Principles Relating to the Conduct of American Industry Adopted by the Congress of American Industry" (December 8, 1939). NAM Press Service. NAM Archive, Acc. 1411, Box 112, Series I.

———. "Experts All: Who's Who Behind Industry's Public Information Program," 1938. NAM Archive, Hagley Museum, Wilmington, Delaware.

———. "Ideal for Club Programs!" 1939? Contains complete transcripts of sound tracks. NAM Archive, Hagley Museum, Wilmington, Delaware.

———. *Minutes of Meeting of Committee on Public Relations,* Waldorf Astoria, New York, March 18, 1935. NAM Archive, Acc. 1411, Box 1, Series V.

——— "N.A.M. at Work in the East-Central Region," Detroit, approximately 1936. NAM Archive, Acc. 1411, Box 114, Series I.

———. *The National Industrial Council presents "America Marching On" and "Frontiers of the Future," Two One-Reel Sound Motion Pictures featuring Lowell Thomas. Available without Cost for School and Private Showings.* NAM Archive, Acc. 1411, Box 112, Series I.

———. "Outline of Organization and Operation of a Community Program," probably 1938. NAM Archive, Acc. 1411, Box 112, Series I.

———. *Report of the Public Relations Committee,* February 1938. NAM Archive, Acc. 1411, Box 114, Series I.

———. "The Role of the N.A.M. Public Information Program Today," 1939. NAM Archive, Acc. 1411, Box 112, Series I.

———. "Vigilance Today for a Free Enterprise Tomorrow" (early 1940s). NAM Archive, Acc. 1411, Box 112, Series I. Includes names of corporate connections.

——— *What Is Your American System All About?* (pamphlet), 1936. NAM Archive, Acc. 1411, Box 114, Series I.

NAM Advisory Committee on Public Relations. Minutes, meeting on March 17, 1939. NAM Archive, Acc. 1411, Box 112, Series I.

"NAM Crusade." *TIDE,* 17 (December 15, 1943) pp. 21, 23.

Namorato, Michael Vincent, ed. *The Diary of Rexford G. Tugwell: The New Deal, 1932–1935.* New York, 1992.

National Association of Broadcasters. "The American Family Robinson." *NAB Reports* 7 (August 11, 1939).

National Association of Manufacturers, Congress of American Industry. "Declaration of Principles Relating to the Conduct of American Industry," *Proceedings,* 1939.

National Association of Manufacturers, Congress of American Industry. "Platform and Resolutions." *Proceedings.* December 5–6, 1934.

National Association of Manufacturers, Philadelphia Executives Conference: Public Relations. *Proceedings.* Philadelphia, October 19, 1943.

National Association of Manufacturers. Thirty-fifth Annual Meeting, *Proceedings.* New York, October 6–9, 1930.

"National Conference: NAM's Fourth Session for Public Relations Executives Achieves a Record Attendance." *TIDE* 21 (February 14, 1947): 56–58.

Nelson, Hale. "The Corporation Looks at Its Social Environment." *Public Relations Journal* 23 (September 1967): 23ff.

"A New Technique in Journalism." *Fortune,* July 1935, 65–66.

"New York Fair: For Industry, An Answer and a Promise." *TIDE* 13 (May 1, 1939): 20–21.

"Newspaper Headlines." *TIDE* 17 (August 15, 1943): 82, 84.

"N.R.A." *Printers' Ink* 164 (August 10, 1933): 82.

Nye, David E. *Image Worlds: Corporate Identities at General Electric, 1890–1930.* Cambridge, Mass., 1985.

Nye, Robert A. *The Origins of Crowd Psychology: Gustave Le Bon and the Crisis of Mass Democracy in the Third Republic.* London, 1975.

Nye, Vernon. "Will It Happen in America?" *Public Relations Journal* 3 (July 1947): 8–10.

Oil Industry Information Committee of the American Petroleum Institute. "How To Take the Sin Out of Size." *Public Relations Journal* 12 (November 1956): 6–10, 18ff.

"Only Advertising Makes Discoveries Valuable." *Printers' Ink* 115 (June 30, 1921): 138.

"Opinion Engineers." *TIDE* 21 (January 10, 1947): 53.

Oregon Executives Conference on Public Relations. *Proceedings.* Portland, October 12, 1944. Sponsored by the National Industrial Information Committee of the NAM.

Orwell, George. *Nineteen Eighty-Four.* New York: Harcourt, Brace, 1949.

Overstreet, H. A. *Influencing Human Behavior.* New York: W. W. Norton, 1925.

Owen, James K. "Saturday Morning in Dayton." *Public Relations Journal* 8 (September 1952): 10–12.

Page, Arthur W. "The Problem of Forecasting Public Opinion in the United States." *Proceedings* of the American Telephone and Telegraph Company, General Publicity Conference, Southern Pines, North Carolina, April 10–16, 1929. AT&T Corporate Archives, Box 1310.

Park, Robert E. *The Crowd and the Public and Other Essays.* (Chicago: University of Chicago Press, 1972.

"Patman's Price Bill. *TIDE* 10 (July 1936): 30–32.

Pells, Richard H. *Radical Visions and American Dreams: Culture and Social Thought in the Depression Years.* New York, 1973.

Perkins, Frances. *The Roosevelt I Knew.* New York, 1946.

Perry, Roland. *Hidden Power: The Programming of the President.* New York, 1984.

Peterson, Eldridge. "Every Company Has a Public Relations Problem." *Printers' Ink* 224 (July 30, 1948): 25.

"Plain Talk: General Motors Directs Some at Car Owners and Employes [sic]." *TIDE* 13 (May 15, 1939): 25–26.

Plattner, Steven W. *Roy Stryker: USA, 1943–1950, The Standard Oil (New Jersey) Photography Project.* Austin: University of Texas Press, 1983.

Pollack, Andrew. "Two Remedies That Save Lives: Doctors Prescribe the Costly One." *New York Times,* June 30, 1991, 1, 19.

Pool, H. W. (advertising manager, *Moody's* magazine). Letter to James D. Ellsworth (still in Boston at the Publicity Bureau), September 7, 1909. AT&T Corporate Archives, Box 1317, Folder 2, Item 664278.

"A Portrait of Oil–Unretouched." *Fortune,* September 1948, 102ff.

"Postwar Advertising." *TIDE* 17 (December 15, 1943): 76.

"Postwar News." *TIDE* 17 (October 15, 1943): 96, 98.

"Post-War Problems." *TIDE* 17 (July 1, 1943): 24–26.

"Post-War Program." *TIDE* 17 (January 1, 1943): 57–58.

"Potential Headache." *TIDE* 9 (January 1935): 14.

"Prescription." *TIDE* 11 (May 15, 1937): 30.

"President Coolidge Attacks Propaganda." *Printers' Ink* 130 (January 22, 1925): 25–26.

"Price Bill." *TIDE* 10 (August 1936): 22–23.

Printers' Ink Jury of Marketing Opinion. "Advertisers Accept P.R. as Top Management Job." *Printers' Ink* 224 (July 30, 1948): 26–29.

"Pro Bono Publico." *TIDE* 10 (August 1936): 19–20.

"Propaganda." *TIDE* 15 (August 15, 1941): 13.

Pryor, E. W. "Sure as the Rising of the Sun." *Public Relations* 1 (First Quarter 1938): 3.

Psychological Corporation. "A Study of Public Relations and Social Attitudes." *Journal of Applied Psychology* 21 (December 1937): 589–601.

"Psychological Corp." *TIDE* 15 (December 25, 1941): 46–48.

"Psychological Corp." *TIDE* 17 (January 1, 1943): 32–33.

"Public Relations." *TIDE* 11 (May 15, 1937): 62.

"Public Relations." *TIDE* 12 (August 15, 1938): 27.

"Public Relations." *TIDE* 19 (June 15, 1945): 19–21.

"Puppetry." *TIDE* 11 (November 15, 1937): 17–19.

"Put the Churches on Your Prospect List." *Printers' Ink* 108 (August 14, 1919): 93–95.

"Qualifications for Membership in the American Association of Advertising Agencies." *Printers' Ink* 115 (April 14, 1921): 177–85.

Quiett, Glenn C., and Ralph D. Casey. "Principles of Publicity" (1926). In W. Brooke Graves, ed., *Readings in Public Opinion, Its Formation and Control,* pp. 649–66. New York, 1928.

Quigley, Martin. "Public Opinion and the Motion Picture." *Public Opinion Quarterly* 1 (April, 1937): 129–33.

Rabinovitz, Jonathan. "Influencing Shoppers During the Moment of Decision." *New York Times,* Sunday Business Section, August 18, 1991, 4.

Rankin, Virgil. "The Weathervane." *Public Relations Journal* 1 (October 1945): 18–19.

Raucher, Alan R. *Public Relations and Business, 1900–1929.* Baltimore, 1968.

Regier, C. C. *The Era of the Muckrakers.* Chapel Hill, N.C., 1932.

"Reject the Application." *Printers' Ink* 139 (April 7, 1927): 232.

"Renovation in N.A.M." *Fortune,* July 1948, 72–75, 165–69.

"Resignation." *TIDE* 13 (March 15, 1939): 26–27.

Rice, Samuel O. "Bootleggers of the Advertising Business." *Printers' Ink* 121 (September 5, 1922): 145–50.

Riegel, O. W. "Propaganda and the Press." *Annals of the American Academy of Political and Social Science* 179 (May 1935): 201–10.

"The Rising Communist Tide, USA," Editorial. *Public Relations Journal* 7 (March 1950): 2.

Roat, Evelyn C. "Current Trends in Public Relations." *Public Opinion Quarterly* 3 (July 1939): 507–15.

Robertson, A. W. "Big Business Is Good Business." *American Magazine*, April 1947, 26–27, 117–22.

Robinson, Claude. "The Gentle Art of Persuasion." *Public Relations Journal* 12 (June 1956): 3–5, 24.

———. "The Human Mind and Industry's Future." *Public Relations Journal* 3 (April 1947): 2–9.

Robinson, Claude, and Walter Barlow. "Corporate Image–Fad, Or the Real McCoy?" *Public Relations Journal* 15 (September 1959): 10–13.

Robinson, Edward J. "A Psychologist Looks at Public Relations." *Public Relations Journal* 11 (November 1955): 3–5.

"Rockefeller Group." *TIDE* 15 (April 15, 1941): 13–14.

Roden, J. Kenneth. "Teen-agers Accept Challenge of Free Enterprise." *Public Relations Journal* 20 (July 1964): 10ff.

Rogers, Elyse M. *Life Is in the Balance* (Form No. 233–00010–988BDG). Midland, Mich., 1988.

Roosevelt, Eleanor. *The Autobiography.* New York, 1961.

Roper, Elmo. "Classifying Respondents by Economic Status." *Public Opinion Quarterly* 4 (June 1940): 270–72.

———. "The Public Looks at Business." *Harvard Business Review* 27 (March 1949): 165–74.

"Rorty Roars." *TIDE* 17 (December 15, 1943): 24.

Ross, Edward Alsworth. *Social Psychology.* New York, 1908, 1974.

Ross, Irwin. *The Image Merchants: The Fabulous World of Public Relations.* Garden City, N.Y., 1959.

Ross, Robert D., and Edward C. Portman (PR men). "Not Just Free Enterprise." *Public Relations Journal* 6 (January 1950): 7, 24.

Ross, T. J. *The Public Relations Problem of Industry.* New York, 1937.

Rosten, Leo C. "President Roosevelt and the Washington Correspondents." *Public Opinion Quarterly* 1 (January 1937): 36–52.

Rothenberg, Randall. "P.R. Images Spread, Via Satellite." *New York Times,* September 9, 1991, D1, D8.

Sacks, Oliver. "To See and Not See." *New Yorker,* May 10, 1993, 59–73.

Schlesinger, Stephen, and Stephen Kinzer. *Bitter Fruit: The Untold Story of the American Coup in Guatemala.* Garden City, N.Y., 1982.

"School Teachers Advertise for More Pay." *Printers' Ink* 108 (August 28, 1919): 179.

Schiffer, R. Michael, and Michael F. Rinzler. "No News Is No News." *New York Times,* Op-Ed page, January 23, 1991.

Schneider, Keith. "A Longtime Pillar of the Government Now Aids Those Hurt by Its Bombs." *New York Times,* June 9, 1993, A18.

Schrifigresser, Otto. *The Art and Business of Influencing Lawmakers.* Boston, 1951.

Scott, Vernon (president, Vernon Scott and Loring Schuler; vice president, National Tax Equality Association, Chicago). "The Conflict of Two Faiths." *Public Relations Journal* 2 (November 1946): 10–14, 33.

Selvage, James B., PR director of NAM. *Memorandum on Community Public Information Programs to Combat Radical Tendencies and Present the Constructive Side of Industry,* 1938. NAM Archive, Acc. 1411, Box 111, Series I.

Sennett, Richard. *The Fall of Public Man: On the Social Psychology of Capitalism.* New York, 1974.

Shapiro, Eben. "TV Commercials Chase Supermarket Shoppers." *New York Times,* May 25, 1992, 35.

Shapiro, Herbert, ed. *The Muckrakers and American Society.* Boston, 1968.

Shulman, Holly Cowan. *The Voice of America: Propaganda and Democracy, 1941–1945.* Madison, 1990.

Silverberg, Louis. "Citizens' Committees: Their Role in Industrial Conflict." *Public Opinion Quarterly* 5 (March 1941): 17–35.

Simpson, Christopher. *Science of Coercion: Communication Research and Psychological Warfare, 1945–1960.* New York, 1994.

Sinclair, Upton. *The Brass Check: A Study of American Journalism.* Pasadena, Calif., 1931.

Skidelsky, Robert. *John Maynard Keynes: The Economist As Savior, 1920–1937.* New York, 1992.

Sloan, Alfred P., Jr. "Proving Ground of Public Opinion." *Printers' Ink* 164 (September 21, 1933): 92–93.

Smith, Willard K. "The Mystery in Style Creation." *Printers' Ink* 121 (October 26, 1922): 21, 25.

"Social Responsibilities." *TIDE* 19 (March 15, 1945): 19–21.

Sokolsky, George E. "Crystallizing Public Opinion Nationally." Speech to the National Industrial Council, December 5, 1938.

Solomon, Leo M. "Let's Look at Pictures." *Public Relations Journal* 5 (October 1949): 17–21.

"Some Thoughts About Public Relations Counsel." *Printers' Ink* 224 (July 30, 1948): 30–31.

"Sore Points." *TIDE* 9 (October 1935): 10–11.

Soule, George. *Prosperity Decade, From War to Depression: 1917–1929.* New York, 1947, 1962.

Southern California Executives Conference on Public Relations (sponsored by the National Industrial Information Committee of NAM). *Proceedings.* Los Angeles, October 3, 1944.

"Standard's Gift." *TIDE* 17 (May 1, 1943): 17–18.

Standard Oil Company (New Jersey) and Affiliated Companies. 1945 Public Relations Conference *Proceedings.* Rye, N.Y., November 19–20, 1945.

―――. 1946 Public Relations Conference *Proceedings.* Rye, N.Y., December 2–3, 1946.

―――. Public Relations Conference *Proceedings.* Rye, N.Y., December 15–16, 1947.

―――. 1948 Public Relations Conference *Proceedings.* New York, October 21–22, 1948.

Stange, Maren. *Symbols of the Ideal Life: Social Documentary Photography in America, 1890–1950.* New York, 1989.

Steel, Ronald. *Walter Lippmann and the American Century.* New York, 1980.

"Steel vs. CIO." *TIDE* 10 (September 1936): 15, 18.

Steele, Richard W. *Propaganda in an Open Society: The Roosevelt Administration and the Media, 1933–1941.* Westport, Conn., 1985.

Steffens, Lincoln. *The Autobiography of Lincoln Steffens.* New York, 1931.

Stein, Sally A. "The Rhetoric of the Colorful and the Colorless: American Photography and Material Culture Between the Wars." Ph.D. diss., Yale University, 1991.

Steward, Ira. "Poverty." *Statistics of Labor* (Massachusetts) no. 173 (March 1873).

Stott, William. *Documentary Expression and Thirties America.* New York, 1973.

Stratten, Samuel S. "Public Relations in Steel." *Public Opinion Quarterly* 1 (April 1937): 107–11.

Suitt, W. W. "Business Must Continue to Tell Public It Is Trying to Do Right Thing." *Printers' Ink* 212 (August 31, 1945): 19–20.

Sullivan, Mark. *Our Times: The United States, 1900–1925.* Vol. 2: *America Finding Itself.* New York, 1927.

Susman, Warren I. *Culture As History: The Transformation of American Society in the Twentieth Century.* New York, 1984.

Sussmann, Leila A. (staff member, Bureau of Applied Social Research, Columbia University). "The Personnel and Ideology of Public Relations." *Public Opinion Quarterly* 12 (Winter 1948–49): 697ff.

Swados, Harvey, ed. *Years of Conscience: The Muckrakers.* Cleveland, 1962.

Tarde, Gabriel. *The Laws of Imitation.* New York, 1903.

———. *On Communication and Social Influence: Selected Papers.* Chicago, 1969.

Tedlow, Richard S. *Keeping the Corporate Image: Public Relations and Business, 1900–1950.* Greenwich, 1979.

Tedlow, Richard S., and Richard R. John, Jr. *Managing Big Business: Essays from the Business History Review.* Boston, 1986.

Thomas, John L. *Alternative America: Henry George, Edward Bellamy, Henry Demarest Lloyd and the Adversary Tradition.* Cambridge, Mass., 1983.

Thompson, John A. *Reformers and the War: American Progressive Publicists and the First World War.* Cambridge, Mass., 1987.

"Thunder on the Left." *TIDE* 9 (September 1935): 22–23.

"Time to Talk Back." *Printers' Ink* 166 (January 11, 1934): 90–91.

Tipper, Harry. *The New Business.* New York, 1914.

"To the Ladies." *TIDE* 12 (September 1, 1938): 16–18.

"Trend of Electric Railways Is Toward More Advertising." *Printers' Ink* 121 (October 12, 1922): 105–6.

Trickett, J. M. "What Is Wrong—With Management's Public Relations?" *Public Relations Journal* 3 (September 1947): 10–13.

Trotter, Wilfred. *The Instincts of the Herd in Peace and War.* London, 1916.

True, James. "Trickery, Fraud, Hoax and Bunk–The Press Agent's Tools." *Printers' Ink* 130 (March 19, 1925): 101–7.

"Tug of War." *TIDE* 10 (October 1, 1936): 21–22.

Tugwell, Rexford Guy, Thomas Munro, and Roy E. Stryker. *American Economic Life and the Means of Its Improvement.* New York, 1925.

Turner, Ralph. "Culture Change and Confusion." *Public Opinion Quarterly* 4 (December 1940): 579–600.

"Uneasy Food." *TIDE* 9 (August 1935): 28–30.

U.S. Committee on Public Information. "Carrying the Message." *Four-Minute Man Bulletin,* no. 20 (November 26, 1917).

———. *Four-Minute Man News,* Edition A (October 17, 1917).

———. *Four-Minute Man News,* Edition D (June 29, 1918).

———. "Fourth Liberty Loan." *Four-Minute Man Bulletin,* no. 39. Washington, DC: U.S. Government Printing Office, September 12, 1918.

———. "The Income Tax." *Four-Minute Man Bulletin,* no. 26 (March 11, 1918).

———. "The Junior Four-Minute Men War Savings Contest for the United States of America." *School Bulletin,* no. 1 (March 11, 1918). Washington, D.C.: U.S. Government Printing Office, 1918.

———. "Where Did You Get Your Facts?" *Four-Minute Man Bulletin,* no. 35 (August 26, 1918).

"The U.S. and Advertising Abroad." *TIDE* 17 (November 15, 1943): 19–20.

"U.S. Asks 200,000 How to Better Railroad Service." *Printers' Ink* 166 (January 11, 1934): 28–29.

"U.S. Chamber." *TIDE* 17 (January 15, 1943): 25–26.

"Using Advertising to Counteract Unfavorable Propaganda: New York Cotton Commission Merchant Uses Trade Advertisements to Paint Picture of Real Mill Conditions in the South." *Printers' Ink* 151 (April 10, 1930): 33–34.

Vail, Theodore Newton. *Views on Public Questions: A Collection of Papers and Addresses, 1907–1917.* Privately printed, 1917.

Van Deventer, John H. "Jobs in the World of Tomorrow and . . . a Job for the 'World of Tomorrow.'" *The Iron Age* (February 9, 1939). Unpaginated reprint.

Vaughn, Stephen. *Holding Fast the Lines: Democracy, Nationalism and the Committee on Public Information.* Chapel Hill, N.C., 1980.

Walker, S. H., and Paul Sklar. *Business Finds Its Voice: Management's Effort to Sell the Business Idea to the Public.* New York, 1938.

Wallas, Graham. *The Great Society: A Psychological Analysis.* Lincoln, Nebr., 1914, 1967.

———. *Human Nature in Politics.* New York, 1908, 1921.

———. *Our Social Heritage.* New Haven, 1921.

"War Advertising." *TIDE* 17 (July 15, 1943): 74.

War Advertising Council. *From War to Peace: The New Challenge to Business and Advertising.* New York, 1945.

Warner, William B. "The Manufacturer and Private Enterprise." Speech presented at the Pacific Coast Manufacturers Conference, San Francisco, June 7, 1938. NAM Archive, Hagley Museum, Wilmington, Delaware. NAM Archive Acc. 1411, Box 112, Series I.

Watkins, Charles Alan. "The Blurred Image: Documentary Photography and the Depression South." Ph.D. diss., University of Delaware, June 1982.

Watson, John B. "What Is Behaviorism?" (1926). In W. Brooke Graves, ed., *Public Opinion, Its Formation and Control,* 39–47. New York, 1928.

Weinstein, James. *The Corporate Ideal in the Liberal State, 1900–1918.* Boston, 1968.

Weir, W. J. "Opportunity!" *Printers' Ink* 199 (April 10, 1942): 13–14.

West, Paul B. "Needed Vitally: More Favorable Public Opinion of Corporations." *Printers' Ink* 212 (September 14, 1945): 11, 106ff.

Westbrook, Robert B. *John Dewey and American Democracy.* Ithaca, N.Y., 1991.

Whitaker, Clem. "Professional Political Campaign Management." *Public Relations Journal* 6 (January 1950): 19–21.

White, Graham J. *FDR and the Press.* Chicago, 1979.

"White House Tries New Way to Press's Heart: Barbecue." *New York Times,* June 9, 1993, A17.

Whitman, E. S. (director of public relations, United Fruit Company). "Effective Public Relations Helps Extend the American Way." *Public Relations Journal* 11 (August 1955): 8–9.

"Who Thinks What." *TIDE* 12 (May 15, 1938): 35.

Wicker, Tom. "An Unknown Casualty." *New York Times,* March 20, 1991, A29.

Widener, Alice, ed. *Gustave Le Bon, the Man and His Works.* Indianapolis, 1979.

Wiebe, G. D. "Merchandising Commodities and Citizenship on Television." *Public Opinion Quarterly* (Winter 1951–52): 679–91.

Willey, Malcolm M. "Communication Agencies and the Volume of Propaganda." *Annals of the American Academy of Political and Social Science* 179 (May 1935): 194–200.

Williams, William Appleman. *The Contours of American History.* Cleveland, 1961.

Wines, Michael. "Bush's Responses Come From Script." *New York Times,* November 27, 1991, B9.

Wines, Michael. "In Scripts for Bush, Questions on Image." *New York Times,* November 28, 1991, A16.

Winfield, Betty Houchin. *FDR and the News Media.* Urbana, Ill., 1990.

Wood, Gordon S. *The Radicalism of the American Revolution.* New York, 1992.

"World and Steel." *TIDE* 10 (December 15, 1936): 13.

Yellen, Samuel. *American Labor Struggles: 1877–1934.* New York, 1936.

Young, John Orr. "Adventures in Advertising: Free Enterprise—Talking to Itself." *Printers' Ink* 224 (August 6, 1948): 37, 68, 70, 72.

Zellerbach, J. D. "What Does Labor Really Want?" *American Magazine,* May, 1947, 38–39, 146–48.

Zim, Larry, Mel Lerner, and Herbert Rolfes. *The World of Tomorrow: The 1939 World's Fair.* New York, 1988.

INDEX

DATE DUE
